1 MONTH OF FREE READING

at

www.ForgottenBooks.com

By purchasing this book you are eligible for one month membership to ForgottenBooks.com, giving you unlimited access to our entire collection of over 1,000,000 titles via our web site and mobile apps.

To claim your free month visit:
www.forgottenbooks.com/free564452

* Offer is valid for 45 days from date of purchase. Terms and conditions apply.

ISBN 978-0-483-99648-9
PIBN 10564452

This book is a reproduction of an important historical work. Forgotten Books uses state-of-the-art technology to digitally reconstruct the work, preserving the original format whilst repairing imperfections present in the aged copy. In rare cases, an imperfection in the original, such as a blemish or missing page, may be replicated in our edition. We do, however, repair the vast majority of imperfections successfully; any imperfections that remain are intentionally left to preserve the state of such historical works.

Forgotten Books is a registered trademark of FB &c Ltd.
Copyright © 2018 FB &c Ltd.
FB &c Ltd, Dalton House, 60 Windsor Avenue, London, SW19 2RR.
Company number 08720141. Registered in England and Wales.

For support please visit www.forgottenbooks.com

THE SCOURGE;

OR,

MONTHLY EXPOSITOR

OF

IMPOSTURE AND FOLLY.

VOL. III.

What! arm'd for virtue when I point the pen,
Brand the bold front of shameless guilty men,
Lash the proud gamester in his gilded car,
Bare the mean heart that lurks beneath a star;
Can there be wanting to defend her cause,
Lights of the church, or guardians of the laws?
Could pension'd Boileau lash in honest strain,
Follies and vices, e'en in Lewis' reign,
Could Laureat Dryden pimp and friar engage,
And neither Charles nor James be in a rage,
And *I* not strip the gilding of a knave,
Unplac'd, unpension'd, no man's tool or slave!
I will, or perish in the generous cause,
HEAR THIS, AND TREMBLE, YE WHO 'SCAPE THE LAWS.

POPE.

LONDON:
PRINTED AND PUBLISHED BY W. N. JONES,
THE PROPRIETOR,
NO. 5, NEWGATE-STREET;
And sold by all the Booksellers in the United Kingdom.

1811.

PREFACE.

To express at stated intervals his gratitude for past indulgence, and to renew his promises of future excellence, is a duty which custom has imposed on every periodical writer, and which the editor of the Scourge is unwilling to consult his own inclination by neglecting. Yet it is not easy on such occasions to avoid the language of the boaster, or the suppliant: to speak with confidence without provoking the charge of egotism, or to express the emotions of honest diffidence, without assuming the tone and manner, of a writer who trusts to the kindness of the public for that approbation which should be granted only to his merits.

If the editor of the Scourge were permitted to express the feelings of the moment in language prompted by the occasion, he would say that he *has accomplished* much, though much remains to be accomplished. Obstacles, of every kind and in every shape, oppose the successful progress of the periodical satirist. The prejudice excited against productions similar to the Scourge, by the misconduct and imbecility of a host of rivals and predecessors; the claims on the editor's forbearance that are indirectly advanced in the usual intercourse of life; the dread of lacerating, beneath a fictitious name, and beneath the garb of temporary folly, the feelings of individuals whose general character he admires, the difficulty (arising from the construction of libel) in obtaining avowed and confidential correspondence, and the impossibility of reposing confidence in anonymous communications, all conspire to render his duty as arduous as it is unpleasant, and to excite an occasional wish that the publication of which he has undertaken the superintendence, were modified into one of those mild and inoffensive productions, in which the virgin seeks for " a pattern of needlework," and the old woman details *his* sepulchral progress. By those who have any personal interest in the failure of satirical works, or who wish to obtain at an easy expence the reputation of sensibility, it is insinuated that personal satire ought not to be encouraged, that to invade the recesses of domestic privacy is unmanly and ungenerous, and that to assume the office of a censor implies at once unpardonable vanity and inveterate malignity. To the charge of invading the recesses of domestic privacy, unless there be included in the appellation the retreats of the harlot and the gambler, we can only reply by a positive assertion of its falsehood; but to the accusation of vanity we may oppose the authority of almost every name that has been distinguished in modern literature. It will not be asserted that literary excellence alone, gives to the man of genius a jurisdiction over the conduct of his fellow creatures ; and if moral rectitude be the required qualification, a modern satirist may without any disparagement to his modesty, lay claim to an equal right of censure with Juvenal or Churchill. Personal satire is objected to, it is said, because it lacerates the feelings of private individuals: if, then, we confine its application to public men, where are we to draw the line between the individual, and the minister, or the servant of the public? And if such a distinction could be drawn, the attempt to prove that it had even been observed by the ancient or modern satirists, would (as we shall prove at an early opportunity) be worse than abortive. We are content to labour beneath the disapprobation of those who discover in the personal satires of Dryden the effusions of envy and malignity.

Even compared with productions avowedly devoted to the pursuit of learning and philosophy, we are not sure that our pages are peculiarly deserving of censure for undue severity. There is nothing in the pages of the SCOURGE to be compared with the attack on the late Mr. Ritson by the Edinburgh Reviewers: the charge of scurrility will apply with greater justice to several prominent articles in the British Critic, than to any thing we have written ; and the very newspapers that abound with paragraphs on the licentiousness of the press, insinuate in a manner not to be mistaken, that Sir Francis Burdett corresponds with Talleyrand, and that Cobbett is rewarded for his political labours by the Emperor of France. The journalists, whether weekly, or monthly, or quarterly, forget that stupidity is more pardonable than wickedness; all their sympathies are excited at the first alarm in favor of a harlot, a swindler, or a drunkard; but for either difference of political opinion, or a non-observance of the canons of Aristotle, or the composition of a hasty and imperfect essay, they have no mercy. They reserve all their indulgence for vice, and all their indignation for fatuity or negligence.

THE SCOURGE.

JANUARY 1, 1812.

CONTENTS.

TO CORRESPONDENTS, see back.
THE BARON AND THE ELEPHANT, or, ÆTNA IN AN UPROAR............1
The Baron's escape from drowning..2
Kitchen melody....................3
Assault on Sophia's chastity.......4
The Baron in Hindostan...........5
Combat on Mount Etna...........6
Strange catastrophe...............7
Vienna Court Gazette..............8
Observations on the Baron's advertisement....................9
His conduct reviewed............10
THE WHIPS. Sketch I...........11
Capt. ——'s financial schemes....12
His marriage....................13
THE PULPIT, No. VI............14
Sermon preached at the church of St. Bride's, Fleet-street, on Sunday, Dec. 1, 1811, by the Rev. Mr. Jones, curate and evening lecturer ....ib.
On prophecy 15
Distinction between prophecy and foresight......................16
Object of prophecy...............17
The Roman augurs................18
The Persian expedition...........19
Ambiguities of the Delphic oracle 20
Character of Mr. Jones...........21
THE DANCING COLONEL....22
A fashionable oracle..............23
His transmission from Ireland.....23
His money negociations............24
THE HYPERCRITIC, No. V.
The New Quarterly Review, and Colonial Register..............ib.
Bigotry of Mr. Gifford............26
Excellencies of the Edinburgh Review..........................27
Lord Sidmouth and his friends....28
Mr. Canning and his party........29
Lord Sidmouth and his coterie....30
Mr. Wilberforce and his partizans 31
Lord Grenville at Oxford.........32
Their mathematical acquirements 33
GRAPHIC AND MEDICAL NUISANCES......................33
Exhibition of certain prints......ib.
Licentious pamphlets and placards 35
TO THE DIRECTORS OF THE EAST INDIA COMPANY......ib.

Military establishments at Croydon 36
Liberal scale of education........37
An accomplished matron........38
THE LOVERS, AN ODE.......39
Princely passion..................40
A drawing-room scene............41
Address to Hymen...............42
AN OFFICIAL DELINQUENT..ib.
Lottery tricks....................43
A ticket stole from the wheel.....44
Mr. ——'s official career........45
THE LITERATURE OF THE WHIPS....................46
Their secretary's circular.........47
Captain A——'s speech........48
Eloquence of a bold dragoon.....49
TO CHARLES BRANDLING, Esq. M. P. 50
Corporate abuses.................51
Provincial peculation............52
Sir M. W. Ridley...............53
Exertions at Newcastle...........54
Curious mode of keeping accounts 55
THE ADULTRESS; or, Reflections on a late Instance of Fashionable Infidelity....................56
The matrimonial *Tempest*........ib.
Native habits of the female sex...57
Domestic intercourse of the higher classes.......................58
Adultery excusable in a woman of rank 59
System of adulterous reciprocity explained......................60
Peculiarities of Sir ——'s situation 61
The footman's conduct examined...62
State of national morals..........63
JOHN BULL and the REHEARSAL 64
Mr. Sheridan's activity...........65
The critics and Mr. Kemble......66
THE ART OF RISING IN THE WORLD, A Fragment.
Miseries of virtue................67
The prudence necessary to literary success 68
Felicities of profligate authorships..69
A vision........................70
DEFENCE OF Lt. Armstrong....71
Mrs. Clarke's real character......72
THEATRICAL REVIEW........73

TO CORRESPONDENTS.

For an explanation of the Caricature, see page 64.

We beg leave to return our best acknowledgments to Veritas, he would add considerably to the obligation could he favor the Editor with a confidential interview.

The statement of a friend of Joanna Southcott shall be properly employed in the course of the present month ; and if we be satisfied that any part of our informant's communication was incorrect, it shall meet with an early contradiction.

J. S. a Friend; a Brighton visitor ; Piscator, &c. &c. on the subject of the *Worthing fracas*, are inadmissible.

We are obliged to Peace and Equality; it is a pity that his language is not as decorous as his remarks are entertaining.

Dr. Puzzle Pate has sent us a paradox, which we leave to the admiration, or if they please, to the solution of our readers:

" What is blacker than a white swan,
Or more insignificant than a lean ALDERMAN."

Of a " Eulogy on Devon's Duke," we shall insert the first stanza for the edification of the public:

" Illustrious duke, as chaste as snow,
  Pure as thy spotless mother :
Diana owns thee for her son,
Adonis for his brother."

The anecdotes of Lady M. The account of two unfortunate affairs, or the D——ss of M——— versus Mrs. H. must be authenticated.

The Political Observer and the Reviewer are unavoidably postponed.

To Clarissa we shall transmit our private remarks on the documents with which she has favoured us.

In our last number the first rhyme of the third stanza of the Address to Mr. Perceval should be *showing* instead of *knowing*.

THE SCOURGE.

JANUARY 1, 1812.

THE BARON AND THE ELEPHANT;
or, Etna in an Uproar.

Sir,

The Baron De Geramb having just announced that his crop of whiskers for the year 1812, is nearly arrived at its full growth; and Mr. Polito having declared that the Elephant will be able in a week or two to tread the stage with the requisite majesty and grace, without endangering the toes of the biped performers; I beg leave most respectfully to submit to your consideration, an outline of the grand melo-drama, in which these two *great* and celebrated actors are intended to make their first appearance. Excited to amicable rivalry by the far-famed feats of his friend Mr. Coates, the Baron burns with ungovernable ardor to contend with him for the palm of histrionic excellence; and to personate the smock-faced Romeo or the unbearded Frederic, would not only be unworthy of so noble a personage, but extremely difficult, without the obliteration of his labial ornaments; a measure from which, if his exalted mind could entertain it for a moment, he is precluded by his contract with your correspondent Mr. Project. The part of the hero in Artaxerxes, was at first selected for his *debut* : but the Baron had scarcely proceeded in its examination so far as the first scene, before he exclaimed, " Vat de devil, am I to be one *cocu*, une very bonne joke, ma foi; I vill not it!"

cutions of the law, is seen wandering along the shore of the Elbe, at the moment when a British frigate arrives before the mouth of that celebrated river, in order to put in execution the decrees of blockade. The Baron paces to and fro in agitation and despair, pronounces the name of Sophia! and rushes into the waves. The crew of the English frigate witness the act; but unacquainted with the race of Whiskerandi, they are lost in doubt, whether the floating animal be a sea-horse or a bear; till the appearance of his hessians above the surface of the wave, as he struggles for existence, induce them to suspect that the object of their curiosity may possibly be a human native of some remote region of the globe! The boat is therefore sent out to his assistance, and the next scene introduces him to the cabin of the frigate; the sea-boys eye him with amazement, while the officers interrogate him respecting his history. He answers nothing, but produces, from his pocket, a bundle of letters from Sophia, a passport through the French dominions, a book of cheques on the Parisian treasury, and a copy of instructions.

The scene now changes to Cadiz, where the disconsolate Sophia is discovered scouring the kitchen utensils of her cruel and haughty master, Don Scipio Grindero. Her eyes are poetically declared to be brighter than her pans, and blacker than her stove. As she scrubs the kettle, she unconsciously fills it with her tears, and then carelessly places it on the hod.

THE COOK MAID'S SONG, (*Sophia.*)

Oh! straight as a poker, but not so slim,
   Is my true love the Baron bold;
As brown as a toast are his whiskers grim,
Not a pan in my kitchen looks brighter than him,
   And compared to his passion my oven is cold.

Tho' Sancho the footman so straight and tall,
   A fine looking fellow may be,
Side by side with the Baron he's not handsome at all;
And when once he would kiss me, I cried with a squall,
   I'm *meat* for your master, so don't be so free!

Don Whiskerandos to his Sophy is true,
   And faithful still will he prove;
For once in the arms of our English Sue,
I caught him and beat him from brown to blue,
   Crying, there is some *sauce* for your *mutton*, my love!

My master Grindero may fret and fume,
   His passion may *boil*, while I *roast* the old boy,
He's the gout, and the phthisic, and head-ache and rheum-
Atics; and were I to yield, I presume,
   A very fine kettle of fish I should fry.

We'll *dish* our foes, and *smoke* the don*,
   And the people put in a dreadful *stew;*
Like a bright pair of tongs, still joined in one,
Tho' asunder: the mob we'll look down upon,
   And a *match* so well managed will never look *blue.*

* *Don Grindero.*

>   I think of my true love, so fine and so *great*,
>   If I at the kitchen *grate* but look,
>   I'll not *mince* the matter; with the Baron so sweet,
>   I'm as full of love as an egg's full of meat,
>   And I'll be a gay lady by hook or crook.

Enter her master Don Scipio; he attempts her chastity, but armed with virtue and the tongs, she repulses him; again he proceeds to the assault, but the sight of a red hot poker induces him to desist; the poker cools, and by a *ruse de guerre* he gains possession of the fire-place. He now assails the unhappy maiden for the third time, but just as he is about to accomplish his object, the kettle of *tears* boils over, and scalds his foot; and while he is bellowing in all the agony of pain and anger, the lovely Sophia effects her escape. But her joy is of short duration: she is seized upon by the police, accused of attempting her master's life, and condemned to be cast into the sea. Scene changes to the shore. The maiden is brought forward, and thrown from the summit of a rock: she is seen struggling with the waves, but just as the spectators have lost all hope of her preservation, and she sinks, apparently to rise no more, the Baron Whiskerandos, who had made his peace with the ministry of England, dashes from the rock, and buffeting the waves with a majestic grace, snatches his beloved mistress from an aqueous grave. The shores resound with acclamations, and the people await with impatience a nearer view of her deliverer; but the Baron with a promptitude and spirit of enterprize peculiar to himself, fastens the fair one's dishevelled locks in a true lover's knot to his own whiskers, and thus supporting his precious burden proceeds to England.

Scene first, Act second, therefore, discovers him and his mistress over a comfortable steak at the Saracen's Head, whither they had come in the stage-coach; and where the Baron expresses his determination to remain till he receives the necessary remittances. An interesting dialogue ensues, in which Sophia relates the outrage of Don Scipio Grindero. The Baron swears by his mustachios that he will revenge her wrongs ; but he has no wish for another watery excursion ; his late enterprize having more than sufficiently damaged his insignia. While he is deliberating on the best mode of accomplishing his object, the newspaper is brought in; Mr. Sadler's air-balloon strikes his eye ; he immediately resolves on an aerial voyage, and orders a post-chaise for Hackney. Scene changes to the scite of the balloon; and as these machines are perfectly new to the stage, it is not to be doubted that this part of the melo-drame will be received with universal approbation. The ascent will be conducted under the superintendence of Mr. Sadler; the elevation of the machine will display the front face of the Baron to the utmost advantage, and the representative of the lovely Sophia will perform many surprising evolutions on the slack rope attached to the machine.

Act the third. View of the palace of the Great Mogul. The Mogul and his courtiers on their knees in the front of the palace, worshipping a distant object that appears hovering in the air, and is perceived as it descends to be the Baron and Sophia in their aerial vehicle. They descend to the earth, and alight with the assistance of the guards, through whose ranks the Baron proceeds with great dignity, sweeping away with the see-saw motion of his whiskers whole regiments of opposing troops. The Great Mogul testifies the most profound reverence ; entreats him, but in vain, to partake of a cold collation ; and finding that he will not honour his court by a prolonged residence, orders a variety of magnificent presents to be presented to the exalted pair. Sophia contents herself with a necklace of diamonds, and the baron with an elephant. The animal is fastened to the parachute, like a hog on a sign-post, and after a due observance of etiquette, they accomplish their re-ascension amidst the hymns of the multitude. Scene changes to Cadiz—Don Scipio's chamber—a letter is brought to him, which he reads aloud.

To Don Scipio Grindero.

Most obnoxious reptile,

Inasmuch as thou hast attempted to violate the marble chastity of that master-piece of heaven, the lovely Sophia, mistress of me, the knight of the hairy countenance, come forth! vile caitiff, and, upon that flaming mountain whose bowels rage with heat as vehement as that which scorches the bosom of a devoted lover, expiate thy crimes. So shall the flames of dishonourable love be punished by the devouring bowels of the terrene volcano, and bravery and worth be the instruments of the wrath of Venus. Thy mortal enemy,

From my aerial mansion.   WHISKERANDOS.

The scene changes to Mount Etna; solemn music. At length the mountain vomits forth a shower of burning lava, by the light of which the Baron and Sophia are discovered hovering over the crater of the volcano. While they are singing a duet, Don Grindero is discovered slowly ascending the mountain on an Andalusian donkey. The elephant is unloosed from the car, and standing on one edge of the crater, throws its proboscis to the opposite brink, so as to form a bridge across the burning abyss. Sophia, the Baron, and the Spaniard now alight, and the two warriors take their stations, one at the root and the other at the tail of the proboscis, while the fair spectator stands aside to witness the combat. The report of their pistols startles the elephant, he rushes down the declivity into the yawning furnace, bearing away with him the unfortunate Baron, while Don Grindero, seizing the ropes of the balloon, which still hovers over the scene of action, ascends into the air, from whence having arranged his machinery, he pounces on the amazed Sophia, and bears her off in triumph.

The next scene represents the interior of the Devil's A—a-Peak in Derbyshire: the Baron is discovered seated in a bucket, which slowly ascends towards the mouth of the cavern; as he rises he deplores in adagio, the singeing of his whiskers, by the fires of the volcano.—View of an interior apartment at the New Hummums. Sophia and Grindero are discovered at the breakfast table. They sing a duet, in which she repeats her vows of constancy to the Baron, and the Spaniard expresses his amazement at her coldness, and his conviction of the destruction of her lover in the fires of Mount Etna. At this juncture the newspaper is brought in; and Don Grindero reads the following paragraph:

" We hear that the renowned Baron Whiskerandos is about to lead to the hymeneal altar the lovely and accomplished Miss T. L. the heiress of immense property, and possessed of every virtue that can contribute to the happiness of the matrimonial state." Sophia faints away: at this moment the Baron enters and falls at her feet; his scorched whiskers supply the place of burnt feathers: their odour restores her to her senses; but she no longer regards him with her former sentiments. She gives her hand to Don Grindero, who favours the audience with a polacca; the Baron hangs himself in his whiskers, and the piece concludes with the funeral procession, in which the ghost of the elephant appears as chief mourner!

As the merit of the preceding sketch seems chiefly to depend on its conformity to historical truth, we gladly embrace the opportunity of verifying and illustrating its most important scenes, by the subjoined advertisement; written, as we are assured, by the *chère amie* of the Baron, and paid for by himself.

" Many of our countrymen having noticed with astonishment the peculiar taste that the Baron Geramb has ever displayed in this country for every thing that tends to celebrity or popular distinction, we have collected the following details of him, which being strictly authentic, will serve as a proof of his having possessed that taste before he visited England, where every thing original or

Court Gazette.—Presburg, Aug. 26, 1806.

" On the 21st of this month, at eleven o'clock in the evening, a workman belonging to this place inadvertently fell into the Danube. On seeing him fall, and hearing his screams, an immense crowd of persons soon assembled, but no one among them attempted to rescue him. Not one boat being in readiness, which was absolutely necessary to send to his assistance, every other means threatening inevitable death to those who would have bravery enough to undertake it; as the Danube, in consequence of the very heavy rains overflowed, which likewise added to the rapidity of its course, particularly in this part: at this critical juncture the Baron Ferdinand Geramb, arch-chamberlain of service to his majesty the Emperor of Austria, who is so renowned for his many noble and exalted actions, and who in the last war raised the regiment of her majesty the empress, which he conducted before the enemy, now appeared. At the sight of the unhappy sufferer to fly to his relief, by plunging himself in the waves without even undressing, was for him the affair of a moment; and after a short interval he was plainly perceived, with the unfortunate he had saved, evidently struggling with the strength of the torrent. At length, aided by an inimitable courage and dexterity he brought him safe on shore. In addition to this exemplary action, not content with having saved his life, he likewise made him a handsome present."

In *The Ambigu* of the 20th of September, 1807, (taken from the French Journals.)

" The intrepid *Ferdinand Baron Geramb,* famous for his travels, his writings, and more particularly for his conduct during the last war, when he commanded as colonel to an Austrian regiment, has recently had an affair at Palermo which characterizes him. Having disputed with an officer of distinction, he was challenged by him, which he accepted, but upon conditions that the combat should take place on the summit of Mount Etna, and that if either of the two should fall, the centre of the volcano should become his tomb. The officer avoided the burial, having only had his arm fractured by the Baron's second shot. The latter received a ball in the crown of his hat." *Times, &c. December* 10*th,* 1811.

Were an Englishman to decline the challenge of a rival, unless he consented to take a journey to Etna or Vesuvius, he would be branded as a coward, or derided as a madman. If the " *muzzle to muzzle*" bravadoes of General Clavering were regarded with mingled feelings of pity and derision, it may be easily predicted, that the exploits of Baron Ferdinand Geramb will be contemplated with other emotions than admiration and reverence. We beg leave to hint to this ostentatious personage, that true dignity never supposes itself to be the object of distrust, nor descends to those vulgar and desperate artifices, by which the *pretenders* to rank, and birth, and personal importance, obtain a transient and delusive notoriety. When an individual is reduced to the evident necessity of attracting the public notice by his personal eccentricities; when he has repeated recourse to the meanest arts of newspaper puffing; when he obtrudes himself on the notice of the daily journalists, yet listens to their sarcasms with the most sensitive alarm, and to their doubts of his pretensions with an irritation, that can only be appeased by the expectation of legal vengeance: it is not ungenerous to conclude that he entertains a secret consciousness of his own unworthiness; that he has no substantial and satisfactory grounds of self-estimation: and that there is some circumstance of his history, or some defect in his pretensions, of which he shrinks from the discovery. Still less will the justice, or the liberality of these conclusions be disputed, if the obnoxious individual has passed that period of life, in which the impetuosity of youth is received as an apology for extravagance of conduct; if his career of notoriety be pursued, at a distance from the scenes of his youthful exploits, and from those who are best able to judge of his pretensions; if his present pursuits be of a more profligate description than those which he asserts to have marked his entrance into life; and if according to his own confession, he has forsaken the society of princes and statesmen in his own country to become, among a foreign people, the patron of their buffoons, and the associate of their fourth-rate pretenders to fashionable notoriety. The real friends to the Baron Geramb, would frankly inform him, that every individual in his peculiar situation, and pursuing his career is regarded by the English nation, (whether justly or unjustly, we shall not venture to decide,) as an ideot, a madman or a ———; as the tool of his companions, the victim of insanity, or the artful agent of secret purposes, under the disguise of thoughtless eccentricity.

We shall leave him therefore to muse in expressive silence, his gratitude for our frankness, assured at least that the impression of our admonitory pages, on his susceptible feelings, will not be less forcible, or less pleasing, than that of his own mustachios on the sensibility of the Wanstead heiress.

London, Dec. 12th, 1811.

THE WHIPS.

Sketch I.

It is extraordinary, that these associations are composed of the lowest (to speak delicately) of what are called, men of fashion.—We shall present our readers with biographical sketches of the whole fraternity; but an eminent member of "*the Buxton club,*" having lately entered into the holy state of matrimony, we give him the precedence. "*The Captain*" is the supposed son of a man who was first heard of as a slave-driver in the West Indies. He married a daughter of his master by one of his slaves, and it is said, contributed to his premature death. Be that as it may, he succeeded to his property; and hastily disposing of it, hurried to England with a large sum in money and produce—unfortunately he forgot to take with him the mulatto founder of his fortunes; who, poor woman! was left in her native island, destitute and forlorn. His villany soon broke a heart, which his previous cruelties had already deeply wounded. On Mr. ———'s method of life in this country it is useless to dilate. It is sufficient to say that he had two sons by a female servant, who to the hour of his death continued in the most menial capacity of his household; the youngest of these sons is our present subject. His father, or reputed father, did not consider him worthy even the common education of a natural child. He was allowed to fight his way in the kitchen, and was the constant companion of the lowest servants of the house. As, however, his age encreased, he was perpetually a subject of complaint, as being an incumbrance in the way of the servants; and this notwithstanding his size was diminutive, infinitely below the usual order of lads of his age. On this account, although hardly able to write his reputed name, a very inferior situation was procured for him in one of the public offices in Somerset-house. From this, he was soon dismissed for absolute incapacity. Mr.———, having him thus returned upon his hands, and not knowing what to do with him, or how to get rid of him, was induced to procure him a commission in the army, and out came our hero, an officer of his majesty's———. In the mean time his brother proving to be a perfect ideot, was placed on the parochial charity-school, where he remained until the death of the supposed father, when "*the captain*" found himself possessed of a moiety of the whole plunder of the poor West Indian, that second Yarico, that miserable example of misplaced confidence. The other moiety of Mr. ———'s wealth, being the property of the wretched ideot, " *the captain*" at once removed him from his miserable abode, and placed him in one of those private receptacles, where objects of his unhappy description are cheaply received and provided for. There he at present remains; and our hero of course possesses the whole property of his supposed father. In order to have this possession most safely to himself, he shewed consummate art and ingenuity. The property was chiefly in the public funds, in plate, and in a collection of pictures of considerable value. His first step was to alter the position of the whole: he exchanged the funded property into other securities, invested a considerable sum in annuities, at the most exorbitant interest he could obtain; and sold the pictures to a celebrated nobleman for a large sum. By these means he secured to himself possession of the whole property, and his poor brother was allowed to remain in the ample wretchedness of a private madhouse!

But his honors had not yet attained their full growth. Conscious that he had *no native name*, he was desirous of obtaining one: to effect this, he purchased a seat in parliament, and although he has never yet presumed to open his mouth but upon one occasion, yet his " *parliamentary duties*" are the constant theme of his discourse. His personal vanity is extreme: although scarcely of the lowest size of man, yet his presumption is hardly to be described. He is the most contemptible of the human race. Ignorance, ostentation, and avarice, are the leading features of his character. In order to increase his funds he had recourse to the most detestable practices of usury. His principal source of income proceeds from annuities, arising from small sums advanced to distressed men, who were obliged to give exorbitant interest to obtain money as a temporary relief. In this pursuit he was, and still is an apostle of the celebrated Jew King; and under his auspices advertised for customers in the money-lending line. Many are the necessitous men, who will sigh deeply at this recitation: the Marquis of H—— will here at once recognize his old acquaintance. The following anecdote we give, in the certainty that its notoriety places it beyond contradiction. The Hon. B——y C——n was induced to answer an advertisement signed A. B. offering to lend money to men of family, and giving a reference to a coffee-house in the city. Thither Mr. C. repaired, and to his astonishment our hero was the A. B. who was thus increasing his own revenue, by taking advantage of the necessities of the distressed. Mr. C. could not restrain his indignation. He expressed himself in the strongest terms of abhorrence.— " Well may you, Captain———," said he, " revel in luxury; well may be your establishment the most sumptuous in town, when you have recourse to means infamous as these of supporting them:" and after having seen the little man shrink into his native nothingness, he left him to digest the lesson he had so opportunely received.

He has lately entered into the sacred bonds of matrimony, and has led his blushing bride into the house occupied before by his several successive mistresses, who were always the lowest refuse of prostitution. In the very carriage in which these women appeared, this *delicate creature* (who had been hawked and offered to every old and young man in town, and whose union with the captain was a trick on both sides which turns out a mutual disappointment,) now shines conspicuously eminent.

This article has already extended to too great a length: it will be continued in our next, in which will be submitted to the public eye, the adventures of the lady mother, with notes critical and explanatory, as connected with her, of "*the Fiddler*" and of her arts to entrap his son into a matrimonial alliance with her other daughter; not forgetting the fiddler's own history, or the means he adopted to enter the whole family with which he he is allied, to its eternal disgrace, and to the misery of his wretched wife, the unfortunate Lady ——.

THE PULPIT, No. VI.

Sermon preached at the Church of St. Bride's, Fleet-street, on Sunday, Dec. 8, 1811, by the Rev. Mr. Jones, Curate and evening lecturer.

TEXT.

Exodus, Chap. XIX. verse 18.—And mount Sinai was altogether on a smoke, because the Lord descended upon it in fire; and the smoke thereof ascended as the smoke of a furnace, and the whole mount quaked greatly.

The Jewish history, it has been said, presents us with a phenomenon to which that of other nations affords no parallel, and holds no resemblance. A nation led on by a train of contrivances from obscurity to grandeur in performance of a long-past promise to a remote ancestor; its progress advanced by none of the usual steps of rising nations: led on through a long trial of calamities, which were constructed to invigorate and purify the national character; sometimes subdued and oppressed by the hands of those who had been previously announced to them as their punishers; sometimes raised and led up from captivity by an interposition which contradicted all the forms of human agency and human experience; exhibiting from the commencement to the close of their singular career, a feature which was never exhibited by any other people in a light so strong, so plain, so undeniable—the incessant, avowed, and actual agency of Providence conducting an immense series of complicated concerns to an end of the most signal import to the world. The constituent characters of this history are as singular as its general aspect. The whole exhibits a broad and grand impression of a superior hand, a system of provisions and precautions full of wisdom and mystery: offering like the frame of universal nature, much to confound and astonish our feebler faculties; but like it evincing by the evident display of beneficence: by the obvious design, the mighty purpose, and by the undeviating performance, that " the hand which made them was divine."

The argument from the coincidence of prophecy with fact in the annals of this extraordinary people, cannot be resisted by any mind that is qualified to estimate the value of testimony. That prophecy must have proceeded from God, which sustains the general principles of his moral laws, and is strictly performed under circumstances which leave no room to suspect a shadow of collusion between the deliverer of the prediction and the agent by whom it is visibly brought to pass. All the tests which rational doubt, or even querulous and carping scepticism have conceived for the examination of truth, have been applied to the investigation of the Jewish predictions, and applied only with the effect of making their *general* authenticity more clear, decided, and unquestionable.

Prophecy is the most singular and most striking of all the evidences which have been given in support of revelation. Miracles do not come down to us with such immediate evidence, or command such willing yet irresistible conviction. The miracles of our Saviour cannot be resisted by unprejudiced understandings: their plainness, their useful object, their extent, their total distinctness, from all that we have ever conceived of human power, give an irresistible attestation to a mind calmly weighing the true against the false. But there is a spirit of cold incredulity in the general heart, which peculiarly sets itself against this species of evidence. With prejudices of this complexion it is not enough to shew the total improbability of human artifice in the wonderful works of a Being who had no connection with the resources of earthly power, or the extreme difficulty of evading the scrutiny of a whole people, excited to the discovery, by every motive of national pride and popular interest. It is not enough to urge the perfect abstraction from those motives which usually excite mankind to laborious efforts. Wealth was not the object, because in any country the simple gift of healing disease would have showered down riches on its possessor. Power was not the object, because though our Saviour declared himself a monarch of more than human authority, he drew back from popular admiration. Fame must have been an idle expectation in a country, bounded and closed up from the general intercourse of nations; of which the people were themselves despised by the Gentile world, while they scorned connection with the heathens as an inferior generation. Fame might have been found in Greece and Italy. He "who spake as never man spake," might have found auditors and admirers, as his apostles did in countries where fame was immortality; but he had other views strongly distinct from power, or wealth, or fame. He came to do his Father's business, and that business was to die.

The argument from miracles is powerful, and it appeals with peculiar force to the ruder minds of men. But the argument from prophecy is still more powerful, and it appeals to philosophers. If prophecy be proved by the event, and proved to the satisfaction of the enquirer, there can be no doubt that it was the work of a being superior to man. There is nothing in human prescience that does not admit of a clear distinction between its extent, and that of inspired foresight. The regular succession of certain consequences to certain causes, may establish a connexion between them, sufficient for the usual direction of reason. But conjecture is the extreme extent to which the faculty reaches; and the most sagacious calculator can frequently only guess the result of the most common causes. Rational foresight never presumes beyond a few years, but in prophecy we have a power looking into ages, speaking in a language not understood, nor intended to be understood by the generation in being; but addressed to generations that are to rise in other lands, and other countries; and resting a large share of its credibility on the want of connection between the events of the time at which the prophecy was delivered, and those of the distant period at which it was to be brought to pass. If events of this obscure, singular, and surprising order, are declared by men who could have no possible influence on their performance, and who had slept in their graves for many generations before the actors in the completion of the prophecy were born, there is a sufficient ground for the belief of an interposition superior to that of man. If the object of the prediction should be obviously the cause of human purity, the honor of God, and the happiness of his creatures, the power must come from heaven. Satan cannot be divided against himself. Admitting that the most specious delusions were permitted for a while, it could not be continued without betraying itself by its effects; and it is perfectly inconsistent with the idea which God has given us of himself, either in his revealed word, or in the creation which surrounds us, to suppose that he could permit a delusion which would overpower our reason, when exerted sincerely for the attainment of religious truth, or transfer the native and simple worship of the human heart to the adversary alike of God and man. Religion is the great concern of human beings: national grandeur is without it insecure, and individual existence, a fretful, weary, unsubstantial dream.

The great events on whose fulfilment the credit of the prophetic inspiration rests, were of an order which could not have come within the sphere of human speculation. Some of them depended on miraculous interference;

some of them related to circumstances, which were then so far without the reach of human foresight, that modern ages are compelled to remain in ignorance of their nature, though they acknowledge their occurrence. They were foretold many centuries before they were realized; and the prophet and the historian were ultimately found to have detailed the same facts, in nearly the same order, and the same expressions. There is nothing parallel to the character of the Jewish prophet in the religious establishments of the ancient world. In Rome, the soothsayer was a mere creature of office; whose predictions, so long as the barbarism of the people allowed him to predict, were drawn from sources, evidently unfitted for the discovery of truth, and only used by the designing to impose on the superstitious. The satire of Cicero on the college of augurs, would not have been hazarded by a man of his habitual deference to public decency, unless it were merely a repetition of the public opinion. In Greece, some loftier superstitions gave a more imposing influence to the art of the diviner. The northern provinces, in which the oracles of Delphi and Dodona were situated, are to this day distinguished by those features of stern and gloomy grandeur, which dispose the mind to superstition. An immense tract of loneliness, broken by chains of mountains, and rapid streams, and ancient woods; the thousand sounds and shapes that came upon the senses of the enthusiast; the shadowy and fantastic lights that broke upon him through the sacred groves; the rustling of the unseen cataract, the voices of the rising storm, the perpetual rolling of the thunders along the brow of Olympus and Octa; the sudden and abrupt magnificence of the precipices that seemed to touch the heaven; the dark terrors of the mountain pass; the melancholy and unbroken solitude of that immense forest, which once overshadowed the land from Phocis to the shores of the Illyrian Sea; all formed a crowd of influences from which neither vigor, nor insensibility, nor preparation of mind could turn away unawed or unsubdued

When the Persian troops were sent to plunder Delphi, they were repulsed in their first attack, and believed that they were repulsed by the deity himself. Those barbarians hot with the lust of plunder, despising the superstitions of the Greeks, and looking on Delphi as the repository of the richest treasure in the world, were awe-struck by the scene in which the temple stood; and after an attempt defeated by a few priests and peasants, fled back through Greece, declaring that the oracle was defended by more than mortal powers, and that they had heard the trumpet and the thunder of the deity. The Greek, whose superstition, at once graceful and sublime, had peopled all nature with fine forms and living energies, shapes of surpassing loveliness, and forms of god-like power; the subtil and sensitive Greek, whose fancy had worshipped a nymph in every spring, and a genius in every grove, must have given himself up with full submission to the magic of a solemn rite, that led him through shades and solitudes, the majesty of forests, as old as the creation, and mountains never climbed by human foot, up to the gates of the temple, into the midst of monuments of all that was glorious in the history of his country, and from them before the sacred shrine. It is not in the power of a modern imagination to conceive the enthusiasm, the reverential awe, the fervent adoration of this creature of sensibility, when after passing the perils of his long journey, he found himself within the portals of the temple dazzled by the sudden blaze of wealth and splendor, to which the most remote kings of Asia had contributed; surrounded by the memorials of his ancestors, the tripods, the inscriptions, the statues of ivory and gold, the monuments of Grecian heroes and legislators; the trophies, the Persian spoils, the works of Grecian art, the magnificent presents of foreign princes, the gifts of Crœsus; and the sculpture of Praxiteles.

The solemnity of the rite that was still to prepare him for the oracle: the rigorous fast, the sacrifice, the darkness, the nocturnal sounds, the wild and fitful music, the sleep on the skins of the slaughtered victims, at length brought him into the presence of the Pythia, to gaze upon a form that seemed scarcely human, uttering the oracle in the bold language and fierce gestures of insanity. The whole system shews, even in its adaptation to human weakness, a sense of defect which was incompatible with a consciousness of superior agency. The responses were, as might be expected, generally incoherent and inexplicable; in those few which have been preserved to us as models of oracular wisdom, there is nothing beyond a studied and ingenious ambiguity of language; which providing for the credit of the oracle, whatever the event might be, gave sufficient evidence at once of artful impotence, and necessary caution.

The Jewish prophet was frequently a man engaged in the usual occupations of humble life, a shepherd or a husbandman, until the moment when he was summoned to unfold before the monarch and the people, the decrees of the Almighty Spirit who had called him to be the minister of his word. He then came forward, without pomp, without attendants, without preparation; and in the face of danger and authority, he denounced the visitation which was to come upon the land. There appears to have been in the character of the genuine prophet, no tampering with the powers which were eminently interested to purchase the silence of this high asserter of unwelcome truths. He came unattended into the palace of the king; before his courtiers and his guards charged him with his crimes, declared the sentence by which he was to be driven from the throne, and then calmly retired beyond the reach of his revenge.

To those who evade the force of prophecy, by asserting that the supposed predictions were written after the occurrence of the events to which they relate, the peculiarities of the prophetic portraiture must be an insurmountable stumbling-block. The forgers of fictitious writings for a particular purpose, would have naturally aggrandized the persons from whom they pretended their oracles to be derived: they would have endeavoured to enforce them by splendid tales of official dignity; by introducing the prophet to an exalted station in the palace of his sovereign, by cloathing him in gold and purple: his forms of incantation would have been decribed as supernaturally solemn and mysterious: his communications with the Almighty would have been detailed with all the eloquence that language could display, and attended with all the brilliance that the imagination of the ambitious forger could conceive. These are objections most usually urged by the advocates of infidelity against the only prophetic book (the Revelations) of which the authenticity is disputed, even by orthodox christians: and if we allow the force of such remarks, when they militate against the authority of the church, it is only fair that their manifest tendency should be admitted, when they serve to confirm the wavering, or satisfy the rational believer.

To him who admits the force of these remarks, it will scarcely be necessary to point out the evident application of many parts of the prophetic writings to the most important events that have occurred in the history of the world; and it is, therefore, with considerable regret, that we observe the prevalent disposition in our orthodox preachers, towards bringing forward every fact recorded in scripture as typical of the future state of the christian church. There are innumerable prophecies so distinct and so important, as to be dwelt upon with pleasure and edification, without adducing the passage of the Jordan as typical of our Saviour's passage through the gates of hell.——Mr. Jones, like many of his brethren, permitted his enthusiasm to run away with his discretion; and adduced the history of the journey through the wilderness, as *typical* of the journey of christians through the world of sin. As an illustration of our progress through life, we have no objection to the subject; but it is worse than presumption, to suppose that the Almighty suffered a nation of four millions of people to waste away by fa-mine and the sword, merely that future generations might admire the beauty of the parallel.

The discourse of Mr. Jones was incoherent, unconnected, and ungrammatical. He is never content to be rational and impressive—he must constantly endeavour to astonish. Inelegant bombast is the peculiar characteristic of his style, and awkward violence of his manner: he is just as well qualified to expound the words of life and death, as Mr. Diestrichsen to deliver lectures on the laws of honor. To

> " Rend with tremendous sound our ears asunder,
> With gun, drum, trumpet, blunderbuss, and thunder,"

was once regarded as peculiarly characteristic of a Blackmore; but the unfortunate auditor whom vicinity of residence may seduce to an occasional visit at St. Bride's, will be too certainly convinced, that on some occasions the description may be as applicable to the parson as the poet.

THE DANCING COLONEL.

In our account of the *soi-disant* Colonel, in a former number, we were unfortunately in an error, which, as is our custom, we are anxious to correct. " Dennis," was the uncle, not the father of the hero; but they followed similar professions, and were eminently celebrated as the best chairmen of their day. Dennis's history is well known: as knife-boy at a club-house in St. James's-street, he opened his career. There he passed his noviciate: at eighteen he was introduced into the honorable fraternity of the knights of the pole, by Mr. Thady Marra, a famous chairman of that day. His subsequent intercourse with the well known Charlotte Hayes; his successive occupations in her seraglio as chairman, pimp, bully, and paramour, are still well remembered. Eventually, through her means, he became enabled to send an offer to his brother in Dublin, to join his fortunes in London. This man was too poor to undertake the journey, and too strongly inpressed with the conviction of the native unworthiness of his family, to believe the golden story of Dennis; yet not wishing to break entirely with a brother, who had annually sent him a few pounds, he decided, after a long consultation with Katty his faithful companion, (who added to their little store, by most industrious exertions in manifold capacities at the Castle Guard-room in Dublin,) upon sending the first fruits of their loves to his uncle. At this particular crisis, a regiment of the Dublin Garrison happened to embark for England. One of the grenadier serjeants had a *peculiar friendship* for Katty; to his care, then, was our hero confided from his native cellar in Barrack-street; and under his auspices was he landed at Liverpool, where he first inhaled British air. He was received by his uncle with kindness; and Charlotte treated him as an adopted son. His early youth was passed in her haram: here his glorious talent for the mutual accommodation of the sexes was first formed, and here was that embryo first created, which has since ripened into such happy maturity. His adventures in camp, garrison, and quarters, are fresh in the memory of many of our fashionable readers; nor is it necessary to repeat the history of the court martial, by which he was broke, and deprived of his favorite title, (which he still is weak enough to retain,) for peculation and fraud. On the death of his uncle, he succeeded by will to the estate at C——: unhappily for him it turned out an Irish legacy in every sense of the word, being mortgaged for more than its value; and it is a well known and absolute fact, that our hero's vanity is such, that to possess the titular honor of being proprietor of C——, he absolutely paid the interest of the mortgage, which was 130l. per annum beyond the rental. Sir W—— well knows this fact; for he purchased the estate under a foreclosure by the mortgagee, and the colonel had not one shilling to receive!!!

The profits of his various occupations are now materially on the wane; his talents for sexual accommodation having failed him in his old age: for now that he has passed his sixtieth year, his appearance is getting too disgusting, even to exhibit as a pander. On this account and on the success of his rival, Madam D'Erville, who is a cheaper and more certain agent, his sources of income are gradually exhausting. He has lately had recourse to two new methods of life; they are both amiable and interesting: the one is to negociate the sale of the Opera beauties, among the men of the third rate circle, where yet he can gain admittance. In this pursuit, he last year realized several hundred pounds, by negociating with two noblemen, a baronet, and an honorable, for the little affairs of Mad. C., Mad. M. Mad. N., and Mad. S. He boasts of his having anticipated his friends in the happiness to which he introduces them. The ladies say no; and his really forbidding appearance is a strong corroboration of their truth. His other, and equally lucrative employment is, the being jackall in chief to a certain class of desperate gamesters of this town, who prey upon the inexperience of youth, and who by themselves and their trusty agents, are always on the look out for the devoted victims of their arts. We shall lay before the public a list of the most honorable fraternity. Our duty is to SCOURGE the infamous; and we will fulfil it: tremble therefore ye who prey on the credulity or weakness of your fellow creatures: your arts shall be exposed, in the anxious hope, that your villanies by publicity may cease to have effect!

London,
December 23d, 1811.

THE HYPERCRITIC.—No. V.

The New Quarterly Review, and Colonial Register.

The talents of Mr. John Gifford have long since found their proper level in the estimation of the public. Fluent without eloquence, intelligent without any unusual portion of acuteness, and well informed without much variety or profundity of knowledge, he is adapted for that species of composition, which " all who run may read;" which amuses rather than delights, and which does not disappoint expectation, only because it does not provoke it. His political habits and opinions conveniently accord with his powers and attainments: a servile Pittite, and a bigotted intolerant, he finds a suitable exercise of his literary talents in that peculiar species of specious and fluent declamation, which entertains without disturbing the literary idler, and lulls the compunctions visitings of that numerous body of individuals, to whom enquiries are *inconvenient*. To such phrases as " social order, and our holy religion," "all that is great, and generous, and virtuous;"—" the sacred code delivered by our forefathers,"—"reverential feelings of awe and veneration," we have no other objection, than that however applicable in themselves, they supply the place of reasoning and of truth; but the fluency with which he applies the words and expressions, revolutionary miscreants, base faction, vile wretches, civic traitors, modern Robespierres, and the scum of jacobinism, is worthy of more decided reprobation; not only because they display the imbecility of the writer who employs them in a very striking point of view, but because they are at once malignant and unjust; subversive of every principle on which legitimate discussion has been conducted by the teachers and benefactors of mankind, and possessing an evident tendency to render literary warfare synonymous with personal hostility, and restore that era of persecution, in which error of opinion was visited with the punishment of moral criminality.

We are happy to observe, that the language of the Colonial Register is more subdued in its tone, and more decorous in its selection, than might have been expected from our knowledge of his former writings. But he still continues to substitute bold and common-place assertion for argument; and by the due admixture of positive epithets, to assume every question, before he condescends to examine the statements, that bear on its solution.

"Every one knows, (he says,) who knows any-thing of public characters, and political events, that Mr. Pitt not only did attempt to refute, but did actually refute to the perfect satisfaction of the largest majority in parliament which ever sanctioned with their support any minister in this country, every accusation which the members of opposition brought against him, on the subject of war and peace." Those who admire, in the preceding instance, the felicity and brevity with which Mr. Gifford dismisses many disputed questions, and establishes many important propositions, and who are satisfied with the concise mode of argument, by which it is proved that the majority in the house of commons always vote in subservience to the dictates of conscience; that their conviction must always be infallible: that the greater a majority, the more reasonable must be the conclusion that its decision is right; and *therefore* that our system of warfare for the last twenty years, under the guidance of Pitt, was invulnerable to objection, or attack, will find in the pages of the New Quarterly Review many other examples of philosophical discussion, not less adapted to their taste.

But violence and bigotry will sometimes be excused, in consideration of the talent by which they are supported. " Materials for thinking" may be drawn from the ingenious suggestions of the writer with whose principles we do not coincide, or of whose general prejudices we are compelled to disapprove; and profound or accurate information may be supplied by those who pervert it to a disingenuous purpose, or whose powers are inadequate to luminous or philosophical deduction. But it is the misfortune of Mr. Gifford and his coadjutors, that they never delight by the brilliance of their serious speculations, or the felicity of their playful efforts; that they communicate little which was not known before, and seldom erect an ingenious or solid superstructure on the materials collected by their neighbours. The distinctness of perception, and minuteness of analysis, displayed by the Edinburgh Reviewers in their criticism on Southey's Curse of Kehama; the keen and sarcastic irony of their answer to Styles, and their reply to Copplestone; the forcible conciseness of their summary respecting the Walcheren expedition; the extensive research that distinguishes the review of *Dutens* on Arches, the philosophical ingenuity of their literary contest with Dugald Stewart; and the powers of reasoning that peculiarly characterise their political articles, are all wanting in the publication before us. Its authors place nothing that is old in a new light, and seldom elicit a fact that is unknown, or an idea that the most superficial reader can pronounce to be original. To express obvious conceptions, in a respectable manner, to connect the detached portions of a popular argument in a comprehensive form, and convey the deductions of good sense, from views occasionally correct, but frequently imperfect, in a style at once voluble and perspicuous, are the only excellencies to which they can justly pretend. Their chief error is diffuseness: they dwell on detached parts of a subject with scrupulous prolixity, yet overlook many important points of discussion, and weary you with proofs of a trifling corollary, while the chain of regular investigation is broken or entangled. They are good manufacturers of tolerable writing, but will never be mistaken for statesmen, or wits, or scholars, or philosophers.

The first article—a review of Courtenay's State of the

Nation, is rather judicious than profound, and more elegant than instructive. Its observations on the state of parties may save us the labour of future explanation, and convey to our readers no unfavourable impression of the work.

"Lord Sidmouth's coterie consists possibly of half a dozen peers, and half that number of commoners. These gentlemen are remarkable for soundness of religious principle, for goodness of intention, and for mediocrity of talent. Mr. Canning's little senate comprizes, we believe, that gentleman himself, Lord Leveson Gower, Mr. Huskisson, Mr. Sturges Bourn and Mr. Dent, with an occasional straggler or two. Here is indeed *multum in parvo,* a paucity of numbers, but great respectability of political and financial skill and talent. A third division, at the head of which Mr. Wilberforce is placed, is much more numerous. It comprehends occasionally as many as thirty members; the Thorntons, Mr. Babington, and all those gentlemen who are reputed to have a peculiar cast in their religious principles belong to this division. Mr. Bankes too sometimes votes with it, as did Mr. Stephen before he was made a master in chancery. It will not be incurious to take a very cursory view of these different collections of individuals in the house of commons, who keep aloof as it were from all parties and from each other, and preserve a kind of surly independence. There is another description of members, amounting to about half a dozen, with Sir Francis Burdett as their chief; whose principles and whose object are too well known to enquire any elucidation from us.

" First, be it observed, Mr. Canning's slender band of senators have for their principal object the acquisition of power for their chief, and consequently for themselves. Mr. Canning, it is known, was educated by the friends of Mr. Fox, with a view to enlist him in the ranks of opposition. Circumstances which it is needless to recal, gave to his pursuits a different direction; and to his mind a different bias. He came into parliament first, and afterwards into office, under the auspices of Mr. Pitt. With wit, information and talents to recommend him; with the example of such a master to improve him, and with the interest of such a patron to promote him, it was not likely that the youthful candidate should remain long stationary. He accordingly rose from a subordinate situation in the foreign department to the head of it. While there, his official correspondence did not belie the opinion which the public had formed of his abilities. On the disgraceful separation of Mr. Pitt's friends; disgraceful we mean to those who formed a junction with his political enemies in opposition to him, Mr. Canning preserved his honour unsullied, and remained faithful to his patron. On the death of Mr. Pitt; whose loss is every day more and more deeply deplored; whose services are every day more and more justly estimated, and whose merits are every day more and more justly acknowledged, Mr. Canning adhered to that portion of Mr. Pitt's friends who adhered most closely to his policy: acting with them in the first instance when out of power, and subsequently returning to office with them when they nobly vindicated the rights of their sovereign, maintained his independence, and rescued him from the most formidable league which an overbearing aristocracy ever formed for the humiliation of their king. Up to this period of his public career, Mr. Canning's respectability kept pace with his principles. As secretary of state for the foreign department, he upheld the honour of his country, and maintained a dignity of tone and character becoming his station; while as a parliamentary speaker he improved by habit, and displayed at one time a brilliancy of imagination which fascinated, and at another a strength of reasoning which convinced his hearers," &c.* * * * After expressing their opinion that his conduct towards Lord Castlereagh was reprehensible, and his statement unsatisfactory, they proceed.—" The truth, it is understood, was, that on the death of the Duke of

Portland, Mr. Canning wished Mr. Perceval to resign the premiership to the Marquis Wellesley, to retain his own situation, and to make Mr. Huskisson chancellor of the Exchequer. In fact, he greatly overrated his own powers and influence, while he as much underrated the power and influence of Mr. Perceval, who it is true has far exceeded the expectations of his most sanguine partizans.

"It was his desertion which influenced the decision to make conciliating advances to the leaders of opposition; the result of which served to fix Mr. Perceval in a seat, which it is but common justice to observe, he consented to fill, from patriotism and not from ambition; and most worthily, indeed, under circumstances of peculiar difficulty, has he filled it. Three of the gentlemen who constitute the majority of Mr. Canning's parliamentary friends, accompanied him in his retirement from office, and very naturally look forward to the period when they may accompany him in his return.

"Of Lord Sidmouth's coterie little is to be said. They form one of the links in the chain of the Grenville party; but they differ essentially both from the Grenvillites and the Foxites on certain leading questions of public policy. Lord Sidmouth himself has not been inaptly termed a political puritan. * * * * It is impossible not to pity the feelings of this benevolent peer (on the seizure of the Danish fleet,) but alas! they are not the feelings of a statesman, nor are his opinions such as should actuate the councils of a great empire. The truth is, that accidental circumstances once placed Lord Sidmouth in a situation greatly above the level of his intellects. He is a plain, good sort of man, with sound religious and moral principles, with excellent intentions, but with no energy of character, and no strength of mind. There was a certain solemn and sober seriousness in his deportment and delivery, while he filled the chair of the house of commons, which imposed not merely on the multitude but on the majority of the house itself; at a time too, when it possessed a much greater proportion of talent than it can boast of at present. It must not be forgotten that this honest gentleman was recommended both by Mr. Pitt and by Lord Grenville as a fit successor to the former; it should be remembered also that they both promised him their support, so long as he should persevere in the line of policy that had marked their own administration, and that they actually did support him until they ceased to approve his conduct. * * *

"The few members of either house attached to Lord Sidmouth, have much the same casts of character with himself. They are all good moral men; and some of them have a solidity of talent, and an extent of information which render them useful adjuncts to any administration: and if we may be allowed to judge from their past conduct they will have no objection to become the adjuncts of any administration."

"Mr. Wilberforce's division of parliamentary combatants, from a congeniality of opinion, from an uniformity of object, and from the extent of ts numbers, approaches much nearer to what is called a *party*, than either of the two preceding bands. And they are entitled, probably, to more respect, because they are as a body more independent; though there are individuals among them, who act neither independently nor consistently. In another respect, too, they have more of the appearance, and of the consequence of a party. For they are sufficiently numerous to turn the scale which ever way they wish it to preponderate, in every case on which the opinions of the house are pretty nearly divided. This is an advantage which no other body of men in the house possess. It would be folly to suppose that the members of the party are not fully aware of the importance attached to this circumstance. And as among them are some who made no scruple, during Mr. Pitt's administration, to convert their parliamentary influence into a source of private emolument, and as since that period, in a notable instance, the same individuals sacrificed their public duty to considerations of personal interest, it is not uncharitable to suppose, that the same disposition may still prevail. The party, however, as a party, and especially their two leaders, Mr. Wilberforce and Mr. Bankes, are wholly exempt from any imputation of the kind. The peculiar nature of Mr. Wilberforce's religious principles has given a complexion to his public conduct, of which his enemies seldom fail to avail themselves; it has also affixed to his name a kind of stigma, which ought by no means to attach to it. For Mr. Wilberforce, as a man of knowledge, and a man of business, is a most useful member of parliament. On all public questions too his vote, during the whole of his political career, has been manifestly the result of the deliberate conviction of his mind. However mistaken he may have been on particular points, it is impossible to withhold from him, without the greatest injustice, the praise of having acted conscientiously. Mr. Bankes too, is an independent man; but his rage for œconomical reform, which has miserably degenerated into public parsimony, ever productive of mischievous consequences to a state, exhibits a striking contrast to his personal establishment."

The subjoined statement will not be entirely without interest to our Oxford readers.

"After Mr. Canning's retirement from office, when a vacancy occurred by the death of that virtuous and lamented nobleman, the Duke of Portland, in the high office of chancellor to the university of Oxford, Mr. Canning interested himself for the success of the Duke of Beaufort. On this occasion two things were obvious to every one who thought at all on the subject; 1. that they who supported Lord Eldon and they who supported the Duke of Beaufort, had so far one common object, that they all wished to prevent the success of Lord Grenville; and, 2. that by dividing the opponents of Lord Grenville, they materially strengthened his lordship's interest. Indeed this appeared so certain to *some friends* of the Duke of Beaufort, and to *some friends* of Lord Eldon, that a proposal was actually submitted to the former to compare lists for the purpose of ascertaining which of the two candidates had the fairest prospect of success, in order that he who should be found to have the least chance should make over his interest to the other for the purpose of securing the exclusion of their common opponent. The proposal itself was so rational and so obviously conducive to the end which both parties had avowedly in view, that it was conceived no objection could possibly be made to it. Mr. Canning however did object to it: he insisted that the Duke of Beaufort should abide the issue; and to this strange decision alone is Lord Grenville indebted for the dignity which he now enjoys in the university of Oxford."

The admission that neither the Duke of Beaufort nor Lord Eldon had any other object in view than to prevent the election of Lord Grenville, is an involuntary sacrifice of interest to truth.

The deficiency of the New Quarterly Reviewers in scientific information, is strikingly exemplified in their criticism on Hutton's Course of Mathematics. It is a mere index to the work: displaying neither laborious accuracy nor ingenious investigation: and bears the same comparison with the Edinburgh reviews of De Lambre and La Place as Bonnycastle's Algebra to the Principia of Newton. It would be more prudent to avoid mathematical subjects altogether, than to astonish and fatigue their readers with any further extracts from common-place dissertations on projectiles and waterfalls.

On the whole, we would advise Mr. *John* Gifford to return to his usual avocations, and to be content with the emoluments of his monthly journal, and the honors of his official situation. The Antijacobin Review is more likely to flourish under his immediate auspices, than under the superintendence of Mrs. West: it commands a respectable circulation, and may be rendered a still more effective vehicle of his political sentiment. But from the present undertaking, he can derive no emoluments, but what are dependent on the caprice of ministers; and the dignity of editor to a New Quarterly Review, will not, we conceive, afford any adequate compensation for thankless and unprofitable labour. To Mr. Redhead Yorke, who appears from internal evidence to be a principal contributor, the same advice will equally apply: as a weekly writer under a variety of disguises he may be useful and entertaining; but nature did not intend him for a statesman or philosopher.

GRAPHIC AND MEDICAL NUISANCES.

Sir,

The superiority of the present enlightened generation, over their timid and ignorant forefathers, can scarcely be doubted by any of your civic and pedestrian readers. Many years have not elapsed, since obscenity was regarded as disgraceful: and a premature knowledge of physical causes and effects, was supposed to corrupt the heart, in proportion as it extended the sphere of curiosity. But the philosophers of our own time are of opinion, that vice becomes less dangerous the better it is known; and that a perfect acquaintance with its deformity is the best security of youth against its insidious approaches. That this is the persuasion at least of our worthy magistrates, is evident from the impunity with which the most indecorous prints and indelicate advertisements are daily exhibited to the notice of the public; productions which a few years ago, would have subjected their exhibitors to a dungeon or the pillory, and which might almost vie with the monstrosities of Morland.

From George-street, Mary-le-bone, to Chancery-lane, the windows of the petty book shops have been for some time decorated with a print of Dick *v.* Dick, on a delicate question of sexual potency, illustrated with interesting and explanatory dialogues. The Strand has been long annoyed by a fellow with a placard, on which is inscribed "Misfortunes the Bane of Pleasure," and accompanied with auxiliary observations more fully illustrating the subject, who delivers hand-bills of a nature the most improper to every age and sex. An emissary from Poppin's-court, Fleet-street, initiates young gentlemen from school into all the mysteries of vice; and communicates the materials of prurient meditation to veteran profligates. That the magistrates have the power of abating these nuisances is evident; that they have not done so, in some measure elucidates the danger of conventional censorship, and the miseries of which all puritanical associations are productive. For some time they officiously assume the powers of the magistracy, who gladly relinquish an invidious and unpleasant duty to auxiliaries so enthusiastic and so able; but in time their zeal subsides: they render themselves obnoxious to every class of the community, and are reduced themselves to the same degree of inefficiency with the legal officers of police. The suppression of licentious pamphlets and indecent placards, is a voluntary but superfluous duty on the part of the Society for the Suppression of Vice, and is the required duty of the magistrate; but what has been at one time the duty of both is now the business of neither: and the town has been corrupted, that the worthy and literary suppressioners might have an annual opportunity of writing doggrel, talking nonsense, and eating a good dinner.

Yours, respectfully,

F. S.

TO THE DIRECTORS OF THE EAST INDIA COMPANY.

Gentlemen,

In the exercise of your official functions, your utility to the body, of which you are the representatives, and to the nation over whose commercial prosperity you have obtained so paramount an influence, must be unavoidably circumscribed by the peculiarity of your situation. Possessing an extensive patronage it is the interest of a large proportion of the people of England to applaud your conduct on every possible occasion; and to coincide in whatever views you may find it pleasant, or convenient, to entertain. The ministry are occasionally reminded of their errors, by the zeal of opposition; and are taught, by the united exertions of their political enemies, to suspect that their plans may occasionally be conceived in error, or rendered abortive, by the guilt or incapacity of their dependents. But the lords of India are seldom doomed, in affairs relating only to their domestic policy, to hear the language of complaint or remonstrance. The discipline prevalent in their public schools is beneath the notice of a politician, and only falls within the notice of parents, who dare not complain, or of dependents, whose retention of their offices depends on their silent subservience.

That you will regard the statement of facts, therefore, that I am about to lay before you, with equal surprise at their existence, and regret that they should not have become the subjects of more early investigation, I am willing to believe. The late disturbances at Hertford may possibly have awakened you to a slight suspicion, that your scholastic establishments are not perfectly faultless in their original design, or their practical execution. You appear, indeed, with a true spirit of mercantile prejudice, to have devoted all your attention, and displayed all your liberality to your *civil* students, while your military cadets are left to the discretion and generosity of their tutors.

The military institution at Croydon was originally established at Woolwich under the superintendence of Dr. Andrews: who kindly accommodated forty cadets in a house, that had not long before been found just equal to the comfortable residence of a dozen pupils. Seven or eight young gentlemen, therefore, of whom the majority had arrived at their seventeenth year, were obliged to herd together in one apartment; and every other part of the scholastic discipline was conducted on a similar scale of liberality and prudence. Many privations however were endured by the students, in the expectation that on their removal to a mere eligible residence their grievances would be redressed. After due enquiry the servants of the company selected Croydon as the most eligible place of education: but on the removal of the students they found no change in their treatment or accommodation. The positive regulations of the school were indeed preventative of personal comfort or enjoyment, and have seldom been equalled in the annals of absurdity. For young gentlemen, almost arrived at manhood, educated for the artillery and engineer department of the company's service, expected to possess the feelings and acquire the habits of gentlemen, and about to be exposed to all the luxurious temptations of the east, a system of diet was established that of all others was best adapted to stimulate every sensual appetite, and to make them look forward with impatience to the period of emancipation and enjoyment. Four pieces of bread and butter, and a bason of cold tea for breakfast; one piece of bread to a dinner without vegetables; two pieces of bread and butter, and a basin of sky blue, or tea washings, coloured with milk, at six o'clock, and one piece of bread for supper, was the luxurious fare of these "gentlemen cadets." Every article of furniture, and all the eating and cooking apparatus were dirty beyond description. Eighty *gentlemen* were liberally allowed to have among them three drinking mugs, and one man servant. Though eighty pounds are paid by the company for each cadet, exclusive of cloathing; and the articles of dress are supplied under your immediate superintendence; yet by some mismanagement on your own parts, or that of your servants, one half of the whole number *were usually obliged to absent themselves from church, for want of decent cloathing.*

Nor were these the only mortifications, great as they were, and disgraceful as they would be considered to the poorest charity-school in the kingdom, of which they had occasion to complain. The esprit de corps, the feelings of self-respect, of decorum, and manly generosity, that it ought to be the first object of military education to cherish and develope, were either destroyed or repressed by the interference of a lady of the family, who whatever may be the merits of her husband, has no claim to respect for her accomplishments. Like the wife of some daily pedagogue, whose scholars pay him sixpence a week for his scholastic labours, she took upon her to *scold* the young gentlemen, to treat them like so many black-guard little urchins, to pry into all their secrets, and rummage all their depositaries of bread or apparel. As a proof of her politeness, and of the gentlemanly decorum so creditable to the " lords of Asia," with which the establishment is conducted, it will be sufficient to relate, that being told by the cadets that they were in want of wash-basons, she elegantly replied " *Go and wash in the horse-pond!*"

Even that part of the œconomy of the establishment, on which the health, or even the existence of the cadets may depend, is deplorably neglected. The airing of sheets is not particularly attended to, and the medical department is not conducted with any unusual degree of attention and assiduity.

Such is only a superficial recapitulation of the manner in which this " military seminary" has been and is yet conducted. If all the future generals of Indostan, and the military heroes who are hereafter destined to defend the possessions of the company, be sentenced to pass the same ordeal, an Indian officer will scarcely be distinguished by habits or reputation above the *soi-disant* colonels of America.

I remain,
Gentlemen,
Your obedient humble servant,
An Observer.

London,
Dec. 24th, 1811.

THE LOVERS—an Ode.

While T——y, wealthy maid, was ruing,
Time mispent in fruitless wooing,
Suitors five with ardor swelling;
Made their constant home her dwelling;
Praying, fighting, swearing, drinking,
From vice or folly seldom shrinking:
Till once, 'tis said, worn out with waiting,
They swore they'd know sans more debating,
Each playing his appropriate part,
Who best deserved her virgin heart.

First W—— rushed, his nose on fire,
  And prostrate on the carpet laid;
No amorous sounds his lungs suspire,
  His snorings only reach the maid.

Next D——'s duke his luck to try,
  Salutes the fair in accents sweet;
But stammering, blushing, trembling, shy,
  He stumbles o'er the coxcomb at her feet.

Recovered from his prostrate state,
  In sighs alone his grief he tells:
And his full bosom, hapless fate!
  At once with port and speechless passion swells.

But thou! oh P——e, with legs so nimble,
  French or German was the figure,
  That sooth'd the heavenly virgin's rigor,
And made thee dearer than her topaz thimble?
Amidst the mazes of the sprightly dance,
  He trips and turns as merry as a grig:
And as the Self resounds, or Drops of Nantz,
  More beauteous wave the locks of T——y's wig,
While to the hollow drum, and squeeking fiddle,
They hand in hand curvet it down the middle.

And longer had they danced, but with a frown
- C—— gracefully aro:e;
Flush'd with a purple grace
He shows his honest face,
- Then threw his princely 'kerchief down;
And with an amorous look,
From out his fob his diamond snuff-box took;
And ever and anon with gentle beat,
He pats its ivory lid so neat,
And tho' sometimes, each gentle pause between,
Dejected Jordan by his side,
Her soul-subduing voice applied;
Yet still the prince, with simp'ring mien,
Unable to conceal his pain,
Gaz'd on the fair
Who caus'd his care,
And sigh'd, and look'd, sigh'd and look'd, sigh'd and
look'd and sigh'd again.
Oh! happy prince! each raptured minion cries,
Oh! happy prince, obsequious John replies.
With ravished ears
Great Cl——e hears;
Affects to nod;
Assumes the god,
And seems to shake the spheres:
At length with love and joy at once opprest,
The sopha yields his royal ——— rest.

With moistened eyes just fresh from weeping,
His pockets empty, spoiled his sleeping,
From hazard see the stripling dupe appear,
One hand contains a pistol, one a song:
One meant for W——y, t'other for Miss L———.
So Mars with Cupid ran his joint career.
Scarce had he heard the distant voice of Pole,
Before he pocketed the scroll,—
From his weak grasp the empty pistol fled—
That pistol! emblem of its owner's head,

Down the steep stairs on terror's pinions born,
He seeks the well-known inn, and journies back
  forlorn.

But oh! how heightened was the festive scene,
  When the bold B—— trod the spacious floor,
They would have thought who saw his ghastly stare
And lofty strut, a monkey to a bear.
  In some far distant land, this (worthy) bore.
Furr'd was his neck, death from his bosom grinn'd,
  And on his cap two cross-bones struck their
    view;
  In shape like his, the crafty devil knew,
Had he appeared, not lovely Eve had sinn'd.
With his bold arm, so oft he'd stemm'd the flood,
  The wave had washed all modesty away;
Through fire v——— and through goose's blood,
  He'd rak'd and eat of life his devious way;
His w————s serv'd to veil the smile malign,
To hide 'neath folly's mask the dark design,
  And from his arts to turn the public gaze away.

Vain were the prince's trickling tears,
The blubbering D———'s bashful fears,
    Sir G———'s thundering snore,
  The Baron's labial sprouts so long,
  Or stripling Kilworth's namby-pamby song,
The wondrous offspring of his riper years:
    A wealthier youth the cap of victory wore.
To happy P—— her hand advancing
  He led her to the grand piano,
And now on him, now on the music glancing,
  She strum'd the lively Morgiana.
They would have thought who heard the strain,
  Cramer himself aerial notes was playing.
Except when gazing to relieve her pain,
Her eyes on Pole, lingering too long remain,
  Her sympathizing digits much delaying;

While W———y nodding, with his head keeps
 time,
Like Bacchus on the Victory's prop sublime!
 Rising and sinking with the boisterous main!

Oh! Hymen, to thy sacred fane
Why looks the virtuous youth in vain;
Why share thy once propitious sway,
With him whom none but wretched fools obey;
And close thy gates against the virtuous few,
Whose wealth is scanty, as their hearts are true?
Resume, propitious deity, thy sway:
On virtue shed thy mild benignant ray;
The salutary influence impart,
To sooth the passions, and to mend the heart;
Appear in form as radiant and sublime,
As, in our fathers' elder time:
Another race of worshippers create,
And justify the tales thy aged sons relate!

AN OFFICIAL DELINQUENT.

To investigate the private characters of every individual, whom they may select to fill the subordinate departments of office, is a task which the leaders of the state will shrink from as equally invidious and unnecessary. The representation of respectable friends, is all that circumspection can usually require, and all that in common cases it is able to obtain; but that an individual labouring under the most obnoxious imputations, and regarded by a large majority of the commercial world with equal distrust and abhorrence, should have been selected as the object of ministerial patronage, not only in spite of the prejudices so generally entertained, but apparently on account of the villanies, for which he has been the most notorious, is a circumstance not less afflict-

Lottery tricks. 43

ing to the lover of his country, than delightful to the pretended patriots, who regard the corruptions of the state with malignant pleasure as the forerunners of universal disaffection.

But the person, whose exploits we are about to record, was not only elected to his present office under circumstances resembling those we have described, but has been retained in his situation, notwithstanding the most frequent and minute representations of his character to the persons under whose immediate superintendence he is placed. To him, therefore, or to his patrons, all future delicacy would be superfluous: and having already performed our duty to the ministers, it only remains to justify our conduct to the public.

About the year 1774, there was resident on St. Dunstan's hill, Tower-street, a person named Lowndes, a boxmaker, whose son, a pupil at the Blue-coat school, was one of those appointed to draw the lottery; which at that time consisted of sixty thousand tickets, and occupied forty days in drawing. The person in office to whom we allude, in conjunction with the father of the boy, devoted some weeks to instruct him in the art of concealing tickets beneath his sleeve. Having thus succeeded in obtaining a particular number from the wheel, the stitches with which it was sewed, were cut open, the number seen, and the ticket sewed up again, and retained in the possession of the two confederates. They effected insurances at all the lottery offices, which at that time were innumerable, paying a trifling premium to receive a large and disproportionate sum, provided the ticket specified should be drawn on a given and distant day. Wagers also were made to a considerable amount, and every other mode adopted that was likely to render their villany productive. The day appointed came, the hour arrived at which the blue-coat-boy relieved his companion, and the identical ticket (concealed in the sleeve of his coat) was drawn, and proclaimed. At night Messrs. L. and ―― went round to collect their wagers and insurances; but the lottery office keepers had taken the alarm: they saw too plainly that what had occurred could not be the effect of chance; and Mr. Golightly went to Whitehall, where the government lottery office was then kept, and examined the ticket, which appeared to have in it double the usual number of needle holes, a circumstance occasioned by its being restitched, after they had ascertained its number. As soon as the discovery was published, the cornfactor with whom Mr. ------ was clerk, dismissed him, the box-maker fled, and the boy was turned out of the Blue-coat school: but as insurance was then, as it is now, illegal, no prosecution took place. Mr. ------ now became informer, and for some time subsisted by the exercise of that honourable profession. About the year 1784, the celebrated Molesworth, a lottery calculator, possessed of much commercial ingenuity, and transacting business under the fictitious cognomen of Shergold, invented various plans for selling lottery chances, and Mr. ------ was bribed with hush-money to a considerable amount. The success of Molesworth induced a Jew named Pope, calling himself *Margray*, to try his success in similar projects; and by exceeding his rival in pecuniary donations, he secured the silence of our hero, and obtained his services. By information, and a convenient pliability, with regard to the form and nature of an oath, he effected the ruin of Shergold,* who was committed to Bridewell. In this extremity he had again recourse to his quondam friend, and the immediate cause of his distress: by paying one guinea for every ten shillings paid by Pope, he regained his services, and applied them to so effectual a purpose, that a month had scarcely expired before Pope was reduced to the same situation with himself. His election to the office he now retains, shortly after the committal of Shergold, can only be accounted for, by supposing that government conceived him to be peculiarly versed in all the rogueries of insurance. For many years he obtained a considerable livelihood by mak-

---

* Alias Molesworth.

ing all those who did illegal business take a licence from himself as well as from the Stamp office. To avoid the accusation of bribery, however, at the time of receiving the expected *douceurs*, he gave in return a note of hand, well knowing that those who had advanced the money durst not sue him, so long as they continued their illegal practices. But there was no end to his rapacity: habits of the most profligate extravagance, the necessities of a numerous family, and the claims both for amorous and commercial purposes of the females whom he employed to give evidence in cases of illegal insurance, &c. all contributed to render his demands as frequent as they were exorbitant. At length his career was partly checked by the procedure of his former employer and his subsequent victim, Mr. Pope, who commenced an action against him on one of his notes of hand, which —— was too prudent to defend. His forbearance, however, was nearly fatal to his depredatory schemes, as they shewed that his future demands might be resisted with impunity. Since that period his attention has been directed to the acquisition of hush-money from the proprietors of little goes; but he is not less adventurous than at any former period of his official career; and by various artifices, some of which we shall detail as soon as is consistent with prudence, he is enabled to obtain a handsome income, independent of his regulated salary, from the fears of all who deal in stamps, or who have any illegal connection with the lotteries. He was employed to marshal the evidence against Thelwall, Horne Tooke, &c. and has on many occasions been a useful instrument of ministerial vengeance. He is by birth a Portuguese, and bears in his countenance the perfect expression of his soul.

"Green, dark, and rotten is the mouldering *bark*,
The kindred offspring of its parent *Wood*."

It is surely possible to obtain the services of informers without elevating one of their fraternity to a situation of official responsibility, and subjecting every subordinate

missal from the ———ship. It remains therefore, to be determined whether this public exposition of his character will be regarded as more worthy of ministerial attention, than the private representations of the most respectable merchants of the city. They cannot mistake his personal identity, and if he continues in his present situation, he must be indebted for his good fortune to the fears of his patrons.

THE LITERATURE OF THE WHIPS.

Sir,

I am commissioned by this honourable society to make an appeal about their virtue, honor, and so forth; moreover relating to some aspersions against them, besides all the unpleasant things that are talked over about us, and particularly about our characters, as every one knows that reputation's reputation, character being valuable in this world, and a good name is what ca'nt be got back, when once lost, any more than a ———, or a man's own hair after he has begun to sport a wig; so I'm sure that you will see the propriety, &c. of due satisfaction in a public way, as we are all great men and are well known about Portman-square, and don't like to be laughed at; and you may perhaps get a good fat milling, if you do not

cruel to flesh them, any more than you have a right to wound my feelings, or my friend Martin's, or any of our honourable body. But brevity is the thing, after all; and as I am d——d savage when people wont stick to the point, I will tell you my meaning in two words, which is more than is ever done by your rigmarole preachers who talk about virtue, and all those kind of things as long as one might drive at a clean cream-coloured pace down to Newmarket and back again. Why, Lord! people don't like long, boring palavers; I know it can't be—why didn't old B—— when he was of our regiment, prose away at mess, till we all wished him at the devil; and isn't there G——when he gets hold of you, does'nt he tell one long stories as long as my arm? why to be sure he does: and isn't it all downright convexity? why every body knows it; so I'll say no more about the matter.

Well, Sir, our worthy B——, not knowing much of composition and all that, desired me to write circulars to all our sporting friends, about the scandalous, lying, and so-forth things that you have given out to public gaze: so I sat down, and wrote this enclosed epistle, without looking, as I will swear before any magistrate in London, at any dictionary or grammar; except indeed, a slight peep or two at Mr. Lowth, and one Johnson, a great huge Bible-looking affair.

Gentlemen,

This honourable society being resolved to take into their profound meditation several letters of this honorable society in a work called the SCOURGE, which were never written by this honourable society, and determined on defending their characters with their last drops of blood, I was requested by you know who just to scribble a line or two for him.

I remain, gentlemen,
With the highest respect,
Your esteemed friend.

I am sure that I shall never forget our meeting. We

were all quite up, as glad as my off-horse to see one another. So the president after drinking our healths with three times three, was twice encored in a very good speech which opened our transactions, and when he had finished, up starts that great man Lord ---; and said exactly as follows, for he kindly lent me the lining of his hat to copy it from. "So, gentlemen, we are come to a glorious *rencontre*, in being thus *guarded* by a pitiful satyre, who has no comprehensible idea of *ves* or of any other intellectible properties. We have no deficiency, gentlemen, in spirit, or really I should begin to precipitate that our inertness proceeded from temerity. But the minimy of loquaciousness is best; so I will, gentlemen, with your permission, redeem my seat."*

Little ------, my particular friend, next distinguished himself by speaking something like what follows.

"I protest, Mr. President, I would rather have mortgaged my whole estate, than that any thing so excessively unpleasant should have occurred. It is really warm, Mr. President---I am sure that you will permit me to throw aside my superior covering. Thank you, my Lord! Gentlemen, I shall not detain you long, as the stove is so oppressive. It is my firm opinion that the person who betrays our little affairs, whether it be, (a dip in your Maccabau, Mr. President, if you please,) whether it be, I say, one of ourselves, or some unknown by-stander, he should, I think, be treated with the utmost energy by the members, individual and collective. For my own part I shall, I am sure, with great pleasure subscribe my guinea towards the engagement of any menial individual capable of exercising his whip effectually without sub-

---

* *Qu.* Is this the same gentleman, who on being asked by the moderators at Cambridge, for a definition of the word *motive*, replied, A man may be said to be *acted* (actuated) by a motive, who acknowledges the invention (intervention) of a superior palsy (impulse) One of his sporting brethren informed them, on being asked a few questions in astronomy, that Ory-on (Orion) was in *Boots* (Bootes.)

jecting us to legal proceedings, of which I have the most sensitive detestation. I am seriously inclined to believe that the most energetic measures should be pursued. Pray, my lord, how is your sweet little cherub, and how does her ladyship approve of the little token! This is a most important question, gentlemen! Mr. H.'s new collar is very interesting I declare. Pray be seated. Mr. President. Having so fully and I hope so explicitly avowed my sentiments, permit me to return my best thanks for the attention with which you have honoured me, and to give place to a more able and more worthy speaker.

Sir G—— ———— was the next. Gentlemen, he exclaimed; Gentlemen, you will perhaps suppose me to be in a hell of a passion, at what that d—— person of a Scourge has said about my education, and my virtue, and my dissipation, and my tits; but don't suppose that I care any thing about satires and Scourges, and litera-ture! d—— me if I do—No! no! gentlemen! curse me if I a'nt as cool as a cucumber; and bl--- me if any body dares say otherwise; devil take me if I don't thrash him as long as I can stand over him. Why, gentlemen, a'nt I a gentleman every inch of me; and ha'nt I beheaded the enemies of my country; and did'nt I learn at Cambridge philosophy, and mathematics, and declamations, and every thing else; and did'nt I buy them of *Maps*, and a'nt they my own, and don't I know how to chop logic, and all that? Why I can write a love-letter with the best of them; and if I ben't quite so ready at Greek, and all that, why I can talk ———— and mind my tits, and drink my wine, and be a jolly fellow, and that is more than they can do, let me tell you. Why wasn't Bacchus a great man, and wasn't he a god, and didn't those great men the Romans worship him, and han't our friend told us about a Phæton, and Ovid, and Jerry Behum and the sun, and an't we much better than they were, considering that we are all christians, which every one knows is much better than being a papist, or a trinity, or any of those things.

———— Sir G——'s face now began to look red, so we advised him to sit down and leave us to finish the affair.

Mr. Tag, the poet, now came forward, and offered us his services, to draw up the resolutions—which we all admired, and think that for style, and every thing of that sort they can't be beat.*

Yours,
A WHIP.

TO CHARLES BRANDLING, Esq. M. P.

Sir,

Placed, as you are in a situation, peculiarly favourable to the correction of those abuses that I am about to develope, and implying, in a considerable degree, the performance of those duties, which have ultimately devolved on those public spirited and independent individuals, whose labours I am about to commemorate, I shall make no apology for selecting you as the object of the present address. Quiescent on every subject of importance to your constituents, concurring in every measure pursued by that corporation of which you are a member, however unjust or oppressive it might prove to those numerous individuals of whom you are the nominal representative; inattentive to the parliamentary interests of your constituents, and regardless of their local causes of complaint; it would ill become me to weaken the force of my observations by any sentiment of affected delicacy towards your private or public character. Your birth, your education, and your influence, all conspire to render you the most important member of the honourable fraternity whose proceedings it is my present duty to detail; and to recal you to the sense of what is due to yourself and your constituents, would be to effect an important change in the morals and situations of your friends and parasites. But it must not be concealed, that in thus selecting you as the object of my present address, I have an object in view more immediate, at least, if not more important than

---

* The resolutions, &c. in our next number.

the correction of our corporate abuses and the obtention of effectual justice to the freemen and inhabitants of this wealthy town. I am not without hope, that your constituents may be enabled, by the subsequent exposition, to determine how far you are worthy of their present confidence or their future approbation: remembering your silence respecting circumstances so important, so singular, and so evidently within the sphere of personal inspection, they may probably resolve, when an opportunity shall again occur, of expressing their feelings and opinions, to select as their representatives, men who either have already proved that they are not unmindful of their interests, or who have not testified, by the uniform tenor of their conduct, a decided hostility to reasonable and respectful complaint. A wealthy and numerous body of electors are surely above the pecuniary influence of a Brandling or a Ridley; and the independence of the rich will be some ground of confidence to the resentment of the poor.

The corporation of Newcastle had been so frequently exposed to attack, respecting the validity of their charter, that it would not have been absurd to anticipate some degree of propriety and prudence in the exercise of the privileges it conveyed, and the employment of the sums of which it secured the possession; but when the independent freemen proceeded to demand a statement of their revenues, and an account of their expenditure, they at first regarded all such appeals with obstinate contempt: when the language of the burgesses became too strong to remain unnoticed, they treated the advocates of justice with repulsive and arbitrary violence; and now that the facts which these gentlemen endeavoured to substantiate, have been proved, beyond the possibility of evasion, they have seized with eagerness on the first and the only opportunity of gratifying their revenge, on the individual whose property and influence have chiefly contributed to their detection. It is too notorious to be disputed that whatever cause of just complaint Mr. Clayton may have possessed, his prosecution of Major Anderson was promoted for party purposes, and urged and supported by the united influence of the corporation: fortunately for Mr. J. Clarke, his discretion has been equal to his activity, and he has hitherto refrained from any act, that under the pretence of individual injury, could be converted into a pretext of collective persecution.

To the ministers themselves, and to all who are interested in the state of our representation, or in the general welfare of the country, the following statement will possess more than usual interest. It is to be feared that there are many Newcastles throughout the empire; and I have the most cogent reasons for believing that the present exposition will be the forerunner of similar discoveries in many other corporate towns. But to enter more immediately on the subject. The revenues of the free burgesses of Newcastle upon Tyne, arising from royal grants, conferred on our ancestors for gallantly defending the boundaries of the kingdom against the incursions of the Scots, have been, for the last three years, viz.

1809.—36,501l. 6s. 2d.
1810.—39,846l. 7s. 3¼d.!!!
1811.—36,445l. 8s. 3d.

And taking the average of these three years, the annual revenue will amount to 37,264l. 9s. 6¼d. We will take that average therefore for the last twenty years, though it should not be forgotten that in 1804 the corporation lost, by an ill-conducted lawsuit with Sir William Leighton, one of the aldermen of London, about 6000l. per annum, a sum which I do not include in the preceding estimate. The whole amount therefore of monies received for the last twenty years is no less than 745,288l. 11s. 3d.; added to which the corporation were indebted by their own acknowledgment (in 1810) 96,318l. 9s. making a *total* of 841,607l. 0s. 3d. Now admitting that the corporation have made not only the most liberal but the most extravagant allowance to their chief magistrate and his subordinate officers, it might surely be expected that out of this immense revenue either a considerable sum should be devoted to continued accumulation, or expended according to the obligations of the charter and the demands of justice, in contributing to the comfort, the pleasure, and the accommodation of the inhabitants of Newcastle.

To this application of their revenues however they have the most invincible and the most natural objection. Many members of the corporation have wives and families: a few hundreds obtained from the public chest "*can injure no one*," and it is of no use to be better than one's neighbours. In addition therefore to the sums diverted in former years to the private purposes of certain individuals, after their arrival at the treasury of the corporation, enormous emoluments have been obtained by several of its members from the connivance of their brethren. The most valuable property has been retained in their possession for many years at only a nominal rent, and even the arrears of such accommodating bargains have been suffered to accumulate. The premises of Mr. C——n, at the *Ballast hills*, valued by a moderate estimate at 300l. per annum, were let to that gentleman for 3l. 10s. per annum, and even this rent had remained unpaid for the last twenty years. One person lets back to the corporation a part of his ground for four times the sum that he pays them for the whole premises; and your worthy coadjutor Sir Matthew White Ridley has been left so long in the possession of his leaseholds, without any demand for their renewal, that the boundaries between his property and that of the corporation cannot be determined: so that in addition to the pecuniary advantages he must have derived from obtaining them at inadequate rents, from the non-payment of arrears, &c. he has in all probability added to the extent of his estates, by encroachments (whether voluntary or not I have no right to enquire) on the property of the public.

After suffering in this manner, several thousands annually to fill the pockets of favored individuals instead of benefiting the community, it might have been expected that the officers of the corporation would be careful at least to expend the sums that they actually received in contributing to the beauty of the town, and the convenience of its inhabitants. But of the 844,000l. that have been committed to their management, no traces can be discovered. Newcastle has been for many years the dirtiest town in the kingdom: all the nuisances that formerly rendered Edinburgh the object of disgust, and the theme of reprobation, are practiced in the chief town of Northumberland at all hours and with the most perfect impunity: every modern structure that adorns its streets, or contributes to its comfort and to the extension of its trade, has been erected by the enterprizing spirit of individuals, or by the collective exertions of persons independent of the corporation. Two thirds of the bridge have been paid for by a very heavy toll, and the rest by the bishop of Durham; the assembly rooms were built by the county: two hundred pounds only being drawn from the town chest, though no erection could be of more service to Newcastle, as by becoming the focus of intercourse to the county families, they were the occasion of a large expenditure.

The church of All Saints, which though better adapted for a theatre than a church, is certainly an elegant building, was erected at the expense of the parish. As for the new Court-house, they have not only refrained from any pecuniary contribution towards its completion, but the county has been obliged to gain access to its scite by a narrow and dirty avenue, lest they should trespass on the property of the town.

The public charities are deplorably neglected: a public-spirited individual, to whom the chief merit of bringing the corporation to account must be principally ascribed, asserts that on his visits to the Freeman's hospital, he found its inmates dying of cold and hunger; the Free-school is only a sad memento of former times; the Library is neglected, and every other institution is in a state of ruin or decay. Even the projected canal from Newcastle to the Irish sea, has been denied the support of the corporation; and the literary society, established not only for the diffusion of general literature, but for cultivating a knowledge of the mines, manufactures, and natural productions of the county, is studiously discouraged, partly because it is in some measure independent of their power, and partly because its secretary is not a member of the church of England.

The mode of keeping the corporate accounts, or the form in which they are published, is disgraceful to the individuals, to whose inspection they are submitted, and to the public whose just curiosity they are intended to satisfy. For 'building committees disbursements,' we are charged in the accounts of last year, 5,852l. 5s. 8d. but in what these disbursements consist, they have not chosen to inform us. Under the head of sundry contingent disbursements, and tradesmen's bills, we are presented with a charge of 6,215l. 2s. 5d. without any means pointed out by which we can ascertain either the actual payment of such a sum, or for what purposes it was expended. Such a statement is, in fact, a most impudent mockery of justice; and can only be paralleled in that period of our history, when his majesty's item of five millions, was received as a satisfactory account of our expenditure: It is impossible to refrain from the indulgence of risible emotions on observing that out of 36,450l., 447l. are announced with great pomposity to have been expended on the hospitals; and that until the discoveries of Major Anderson, several items were placed opposite the names of annuitants, who had long since left this sublunary scene.

Much of the inveteracy with which Major Anderson has been pursued, was owing to the suspicion, that his endeavours to bring the corporation to account, were made with no other view than to obtain a popularity, which on a dissolution of parliament, might enable him more effectually to contend with you and your colleague for the representation of your native town. Whether this design was seriously entertained by Major Anderson, or not, I am not enabled to determine; but it would have done no discredit to his understanding or his principles: to have given the most substantial proofs of independence and intrepidity, is a just claim on the approbation of the burgesses, and a rational ground of self-congratulation to himself. If in the prosecution of his object, he has been occasionally hurried to warmth of expression, or of action, it ought to be remembered, that indiscretion is more pardonable than servility to the meanest of mankind, and connivance in the most dishonorable practices; and that the major could not have rendered himself popular by the *correction of abuses,* had there been no *abuses to correct*!

I remain, Sir,
Your very obedient servant,
QUONDAM.

THE ADULTRESS; OR REFLECTIONS ON A LATE INSTANCE OF FASHIONABLE INFIDELITY.

THE late discovery in high life is well calculated to excite a train of mournful reflections in every individual of rank or refinement, whose perceptions have not been vitiated by the continual contact of corruption, or who has not yet so deliberately forgotten what is due to his Creator and himself as to sacrifice every nobler feeling of his nature to the pursuit of notoriety. With a countenance that glowed with the bloom of health, and sparkled with the mingled expression of virtue and intelli-

ness than modesty; a heart susceptible of the most exquisite emotions, and an understanding originally fertile, cultivated with unusual care, and developed under the most propitious auspices; who could have conceived the degradation of a woman like Lady ———, without dismissing with indignation the momentary anticipation from his thoughts, or express his conviction of her infidelity, without abjuring his faith in existence of female virtue, and his confidence in the fidelity of a female's attachment, by whatever barriers the approaches to her chastity may be secured, or under whatever form of loveliness she may enslave the soul, and captivate the eye?

Yet the indiscretion of Lady ——— may be accounted for on principles that preclude every emotion of rational surprize, and deprive the great world of the right to censure, as they withhold from her husband any power of complaint. To the laxity of fashionable morals, occasioned by the facilities of introduction to females of abandoned character and profligate manners, the misfortunes of Sir H——— may be ascribed, without any inclination to palliate the conduct of the unfortunate female at the expence of her superiors. Where prostitutes are the idols of every society, and the objects of universal adulation; when the matron is eclipsed and outrivalled by the mistress; what are the rewards of conjugal fidelity?

The conduct of women is not influenced by abstract principles, and by the remembrance of legal and conventional distinctions, but by the continually operating example of the society in which they move, and by those habits which education has rendered almost instinctive, and which were originally formed without any immediate reference to positive precept. The position that adultery is more infamous in the wife than the husband, because by a dereliction of her conjugal fidelity she may become the mother of a spurious offspring, may be very convenient to the lawyer, and very satisfactory to the abstract moralist; but such an argument in favour of matrimonial chastity obtains no influence over the female mind. If no habitual feelings of self-respect will preserve the matron from the approaches of adulterous love, it will be vain to call to her remembrance the guilt of producing an illegitimate issue. Should she be restrained by such a consideration from the commission of actual crime, what would be the value of her fidelity? Though her body might remain unviolated, what mode of discipline would restore her to her original purity, or cleanse the pollution of her mind? It is better to be the object of public sarcasm, and to know the extent of his domestic calamity, than that the unfortunate individual should remain for years the dupe of pretended affection, and the slave of hypocritical allurement.

That among the middle classes, therefore, the violation of the marriage vow on the part of the female should be visited with merited disgrace, while the frailty of the husband is regarded with comparative indulgence, must not be ascribed to the impression that infidelity of the wife is more dangerous to personal property, and more likely to vitiate the laws of inheritance, but to the persuasion that an adultress must have surmounted many obstacles, and sacrificed many of the best feelings of her nature, to the gratification of her libidinous desires. In the male sex continence is scarcely considered as a virtue; even after marriage they are exposed to the strongest and most repeated temptations; and to fortify their resistance, there remain only the restraints of duty and affection. But the adultress must have surmounted these restraints and many more: she must have thrown aside the native habits of the female character; all the delicacy of her sex, and all the feelings that education has cherished or instilled. She must have sinned in defiance of shame and in the society of virtue: reminded by the presence of every female companion who surrounded her of the enormity of her crime; fortified against the delusions of licentious passion by the silent admonition of daily intercourse.

In the middle classes, therefore, the husband, whatever may be his own frailties, has a right to complain of the infidelity of his wife; and her former associates may, without any imputation on their benevolence or consistency, withdraw their countenance, and revolt from her society. But in the higher ranks, if the injured individual be guilty of incontinence, or unable to contribute to the happiness of the marriage state, to resent the infidelity of his wife would be unjust and cruel in himself, as to discountenance her would be mean and hypocritical in her former associates. A fashionable husband has no other security for the fidelity of his wife, nor any other ground of confidence in her virtue, than personal preference. She must be faithful to him, not because she is afraid of man, nor is ashamed of adulterous intercourse, but because she loves him better than any other individual. She is educated in no principles of religion; she sees the adultress caressed in every circle that she honours with her presence; she cannot but observe that the offspring of an acknowledged prostitute is received with the most courteous welcome, by the great, the wealthy, and the eminent; and who but a driveller or a hypocrite would expect that she should retain her fidelity any longer than is perfectly accordant with her wishes and convenience?

It is evident, therefore, that in the fashionable world the wife and the husband are precisely in the same situation. They are educated with the same notions of sexual purity; they are taught to place an equal value on chastity of temperament and decency of manners; and they both enter into the nuptial contract with the same feelings, and from the same motives. If, therefore, the lady forms an attachment to the footman, she has precisely the same right to pursue her inclinations, as if the husband were to be captivated by the charms of the nursery-maid: considered with reference to the customs of exalted society, the cases are precisely parallel, and Sir H. was no better justified in lacerating the unfortunate knight of the shoulder-knot, than lady —— would have been, had she chosen after every discovery of her husband's weakness to flay the object of his nursery amours.

We find accordingly that in the families of our most eminent nobility, the principle of reciprocity is openly acknowledged. Lord A. condescends to witness the amours of his wife, and her ladyship becomes in return the sponsor of his illegitimate children. The deceased " worthy" of opposition, cohabited alternately, and under the same roof, with the late duchess and the present dowager. The legitimate and the spurious issue were educated in the same nursery, and the duchess was rewarded for her indulgence, by full permission to sleep with the man of the people as often as might be convenient or desirable. Mr. and Mrs. A. their footman and cook-maid, perform every morning a quartetto—Col. and Mrs. M. drive to Chandos-street in their own carriage; solace themselves for a few hours with their respective partners, and sympathize on their return homewards, in the disclosures of each other; and a register office in full business, till lately, at the west end of the town, was established under the superintendence of a female of rank, for the sole purpose of providing her beloved lord with convenient attendants on her person.

It is not impossible that a young girl of rank may be taught by her nurse, or possibly by her mama, some of the common-place maxims of conduct; but as soon as she is ushered into life, every scene that she is doomed to witness contributes to the corruption of her principles, and the depravation of her habits. Suppose that her mother or her governess, alarmed by some indications of *vitality*, pours forth a lecture on decency and virtue: the lecture is finished, and she hastens to the drawing-room. Among the favourite companions of her mama, and the most conspicuous ornaments of the circle, are the duchess of D. Lady F. Miss Fitz C——, and the ladies T——. It now occurs to her observation, that for many years the first of these females was at once the procuress and the p———e of a deceased nobleman, that the second has long been notorious for profligate intrigue, that the third is the issue of an illegitimate connection, and that the fourth have continued for the last two years to glory in the remembrance of their incestuous intercourse. Yet she cannot be unconscious that the dowager is one of the most brilliant stars in the hemisphere of fashion; that Lady ——— has easy and welcome access to every circle, however select, and every mansion however circumspect its owner; that Miss F——— is received with homage as sincere though not so profound as the heiress apparent to the crown; and that the sisters are the intimate confidents of the wives and sisters of our ministers of state. She trusts to the evidence of her senses, and forgets the lessons of her nurse and the exhortations of her governess.

If adultery in general, therefore, be among the higher classes so venial and so natural a crime, still less ought its commission by the present delinquent to be visited by her equals with any severity of censure. Worn out in the pursuit of licentious pleasures; a victim to the infirmities of age, before he had attained the maturity of manhood; her husband could not seal the nuptial contract under any other impression than that of immediate disappointment and protracted unhappiness. His body exhausted by disease, and his feelings blunted by the continual attrition of vicious excitement, he could not have the folly to believe that a young and lovely woman would resign herself to the arms of native deformity and personal impotence, with any other determination than to exercise the privileges that usually attach to fashionable wedlock. Her selection of a menial to become the partner of her bed was probably occasioned by her experience, in the person of her husband, how little the external demeanour of a gentleman accorded in certain cases with the qualifications of a lover.

But it is asserted that if the lady be forgiven, the infidelity of the servant cannot be excused. But even he might appeal for apology to the example of his master, and to the habits of polished society.—He may ask, in his own defence, whether to yield under every possible circumstance of temptation to the allurements of his mistress, be more reprehensible, than under the sacred name of friend, to tempt the virtue of a wife, without any inclination to gratify any other passion than the love of notoriety; whether to seduce the daughters of his tenants be more virtuous or meritorious, in the master, than to yield to the blandishments of a profligate but captivating female, in the servant. Yet exploits like these are not only the topics of table conversation, but the themes of facetious remark, and the necessary preliminaries to the reputation of a man of spirit. Every circumstance conspired to palliate the misconduct of the menial paramour: that he should be flattered by the attentions of his mistress was natural: seduction in the form of beauty and beneath the garb of rank, would excite his passions with tenfold power: he must have been an ideot not to perceive the advantages to be derived from her patronage, and more virtuous than the majority of his fellow creatures to prefer his duty to his interest. Profligate as the English people are become, they surely have not learnt to estimate the criminality of an individual by the amount of his rent-roll, or the gradation of his title: it is to be hoped that vice continues to be vice, whether it be committed by the master or the servant; and that frailty in a porter is not regarded as more infamous than deliberate and desperate villainy in a baronet.

When Sir —— became a party to the flagellation of his servant, is it possible that he had no compunctious visitings of conscience? can it be believed that he punished the delinquency of an unfortunate menial, without remembering how often he had violated the confidence of friendship; without recalling to his mind the judicial evidence by which he was convicted of a calm, deliberate, and persevering system of seduction; without being paralyzed by the remembrance of the pathetic and animated charge in which the presiding judge expressed, on that memorable occasion, his abhorrence of his character, his pity for the deluded victim of his adulterous artifices, and his compassion for the unsuspecting husband, whose hospitality he had rewarded by the destruction of his domestic peace? Or, when he committed his lady to the guidance of fortune, and invited a professional friend to become the witness of her frailty, could he forbear to enumerate the unhappy beings to whom he has been the occasion of similar disgrace; whose prospects of future happiness were blighted by his approach, and whom he seduced from the paths of peace and virtue, to walk in the ways of infamy: condemned to sustain the privation of every comfort, abandoned by society because to their female frailties was superadded the crime of poverty, and left by their seducer to linger out the remnants of existence in unpitied and hopeless destitution?

When prostitutes shall be excluded from the mansions of the great, and from association with the wives and daughters of the noble and the eminent; when the illegitimate offspring of a prince shall be placed on a level with the bastards of other exalted characters; when sexual purity shall be considered as a virtue, and innocence be regarded with the admiration that is at present the usual tribute to profligate effrontery—then, and not till then, it will be consistent and becoming for Sir—— and those who compassionate him, to complain of the infidelity of their wives, and inflict corporal or legal punishment on the detected adulterer. But the ravings of delirious wickedness, the exclamations of anguish that are wrung from the profligate, when he becomes a sacrifice to his own maxims, and the object of deserved retribution, excite no sympathy. From the libidinous and profligate hypocrites, who exist only in the presence of the great; from all who shrink from the name, while they indulge in the practice of vice; who condemn adultery, yet court the adulterous, they may obtain a momentary pause of formal attention; but by the virtuous and the rational; by all those who own the existence of a superior

JOHN BULL AND THE REHEARSAL.

Sir,

Curiosity is the mania of the English people: they must see and hear, and feel every thing that can be seen, or heard, or felt, without the most imminent danger to their fortunes or their persons. To understand them indeed is a matter of greater difficulty and less immediate moment. John Bull will gape with wonder when he ought to investigate; and is more enchanted by the sight of a phantasmagoria than addicted to the study of optics.—A true Englishman myself, I shall not so far forget my native character as to give you any explanation of the scene that I have just witnessed; to gaze on the enclosed sketch, and to make a Christmas puzzle of the subjoined description, will be an appropriate exercise for the majority of your readers; and if any individuals more inquisitive or more idle than the rest, be inclined to ask me what is the *meaning of these things*, or whether they have any ostensible purpose, I must refer them to the Covent-Garden treasury, or to the monarch of Great Russel-street.

The most conspicuous performer at the rehearsal of this morning was a tame elephant adorned with the trappings of the east, extremely docile, and bearing on his proboscis a kind of kindred monster, a sort of wild man in the woods; with mustachios as brown as his boots, and more luxuriant than the imagination of a modern poet.

Upon his back was mounted a portly gentleman, who not content with his natural elevation, was striving to render himself still more conspicuous by striding over the cross-bars of a kind of throne, composed of *aitches*. A representation of Folly seemed to enjoy with unusual glee the scene before him, while he poured from out of his bag several thousands of those uncommon articles called guineas. The person holding the tambourine was nearly undressed, and had just thrown his mantle and his sock to a care-worn gentleman, who did not seem to be a *young* pretender to reputation as a tragedian. Involved in the proboscis of the elephant the expiring figure of Comedy, who had been gazing with rapture on the page of Congreve, presented an afflicting spectacle. On the right a *cockscomb* in the character of Lothario, was mangling the body (for he had always been a stranger to the spirit) of a literary worthy, whose features I should not have remembered, had not a punning performer in the robes of King Arthur, exclaimed, half in jest and half in earnest, and with less attention to spelling than pronunciation, " Lord what a Rowe!" Arrayed in the most gaudy plumage, the fellow seemed to be too pleasantly occupied in murdering the ancient favorite of the public, to attend the long train and bushy Petti-Coates of Mrs. Siddons, who moved majestically away though laden with two heavy bags, the produce of her concluding season. Astride a butt, on which was inscribed " Whitbread's *stale*," was seated the Bacchus of modern times, the red-nosed luminary of Drury-lane and St. Stephen's, the immortal author of the School for Scandal. He was busily employed in bartering large quantities of froth in exchange for guineas and bank notes; which were conveyed to him by John Bull with one hand, while with the other he held up a paper on which was inscribed " A guinea a week for native talent." A perch, on the left, was occupied by a tomtit, which seemed to be quite elated with its situation, notwithstanding the screaming of the stupid and noisy bird that had obtained a place by its side. In the back ground of the prince's side, a sculpture representing Indecency unveiling Nature, held a conspicuous and appropriate place. On casting my eyes towards the foot of the stage, I was much amused by the tricks of a thorough-bred spaniel, who fawned upon the Baron with the most docile assiduity, and whose supplicatory looks towards Mr. K. himself bore a mingled expression of gratitude and expectation. It was evident, however, from the mode of action, that this was a very clever dog. In one corner of the stage, the insignia of tragedy were thrown aside, ready to be swept away at the conclusion of the rehearsal. The bust of Shakespeare, and the volumes of our ancient dramatists, were trampled under the feet of the elephant; and every object that met my observation, seemed to announce the triumph of *spectacle* over truth, and nature, and refinement.

I remain, Sir,

Your obedient servant,

OBSERVATOR.

THE ART OF RISING IN THE WORLD:

A FRAGMENT.

From L——'s dark shores where drowsy Dulness sleeps,
And palsied Science o'er her offspring weeps,
Where the black tribe of wealthy meanness flocks,
And broods o'er sugars, candles, coals, and stocks;
Where statesmen herd with thieves, and priests with w——s,
The mingled refuse of the Scottish shores;
And heroes drunk, in wild confusion tost,
Stare 'midst the fumes of smoke and brandy lost;
At length relieved, no more obscure I sing,
What dire effects from amorous causes spring;
A nobler theme the lofty strain inspires,
And fills my bosom with a poet's fires!

Miseries of virtue.

Divine inspirer of the artful song,
Satire! to thee, the poet's prayers belong;
Assist my verse! and may no cant'ring prose,
Or crippled verse, that hobbles as it goes,
Disgrace my page; let learned Matthias speak
In half-formed numbers graced by grabbled Greek.
Peace to his shade! I tune no feeble strain,
But teach the young life's towering heights to gain.

Far hence ye few whom gainless virtue charms,
Ye clasp a phantom in your empty arms;
For you nor power nor wealth its glow displays,
No servile crowds exulting sing your praise;
No courtier bows to ask your vote severe;
No beauty deigns your silent suit to hear:
Shunn'd by the great, and hated by the fair,
Your hours glide on in solitary care;
In want's low vale, your humble lives are led,
Unknown you sink amidst the village dead!

But ye whose breasts the nobler passions prove
Of proud ambition, avarice, or love,
Attend my strain, no painful truths I tell,
No canting nonsense quote from smooth Durell:
For you I sing what potent charm will raise
A virgin's love, or gain a critic's praise,
What soothing strains a prude delights to hear,
What whispered flattery charms a statesman's ear.

Fool that I was, when life and love were young,
No strains but those of artless truth I sung;
As o'er my head the pine's dark shadows wav'd,
And round my feet the murmuring waters lav'd,
Through my warm breast love's sick'ning ardors ran,
And thus the wild and guiltless lay began:
Sweet maid! whose charms inspired the trembling song,
When first I wandered ———'s sweet banks along;
Whose tuneful voice, and beauteous form might move,
A syren's envy and an angel's love;
Ah! why these soft rebukes? Thy jealous fear,
Lest envious time should shew me insincere.

The joys of virtue and of love deride,
With fickle falsehoods, treacherous arts deceive,
While each false vow the simple maids believe;
By heaven I swear, nor time nor space shall part
Thy lov'd remembrance from my faithful heart;
Whether I roam by poverty opprest,
A weary wanderer thro' the world's wide waste,
Or blest by wealth beyond misfortune's power,
Unknown I sink in life's declining hour,
Still shall thy influence guide my devious way,
When wealth or beauty tempts my steps to stray.

Such were the sighs, the whispering zephyr bore,
With playful wing, along the echoing shore;
All nature laughed to hear the simple tale,
And magpies hooted from the neighbouring vale.
———— silvery tide lav'd gently on the strand,
And washed Eliza's praises from the sand.
Vain is the anxious, virtuous lover's care,
No bashful student wins the fickle fair,
No sound so sweet even listening angels hear,
As flattery's music to a virgin's ear.
* * * *
But if ambitious of a noble name,
Thy feet attempt the slippery heights of fame,
Waste not thy hours the paths of truth to tread,
No canting scribbler by a duke is read,
While nervous ———— pines in want away,
The restless night and solitary day:
Be thine the task, religion to oppose,

Nor genius now nor learning dares to claim,
The glorious wreath of fashionable fame.
While whining Moore reveals his lecherous pains,
And Bowles attempts to rival Pindar's strains,
—— loads the grasping oilman's shelf,
Read and admired by Bensley and himself;
A silent sacrifice to virtue's cause,
He leaves to Moore a wondering world's applause.

See with its Gorgon pointing to the skies,
Obscured by smoke, Minerva's Temple rise,
There many a feeble song and amorous tale,
Well fill'd by slander finds a ready sale,
There bound in red, a " Brighton Story" lies,
And hot-press'd " Kisses" strike the wond'ring eyes,
On yonder shelf " a Tale suppressed" is seen,
On this repose " the Libertines" obscene;
Here lisping Busbys grace the groaning shelves,
And Holstein boasts his twice twelve thousand twelves.
While pois'd in wavering scales poor Weston lies,
The ruthless Birch, or greedy Newman's prize,
And strew'd in heaps upon the dusty floor,
Neglected Foster falls to rise no more.
Alas! no friend to learning enters here,
For there no critic sheds the silent tear,
No well-drest blood deplores their hapless fate,
No Todd redeems them from their prostrate state.
In dark oblivion's gloomy realms they glide.
And leave the world to Morton deified.

Who now believes that Johnson's nervous page
That yield delight in every distant age?
Tho' blest with thought sublime in language strong,
He pours the tide of eloquence along,
Alas! no court to powerful vice he pays,
Nor wealth directs his pen, nor passion sways,
No pointless puns disgrace his manly sense,
No jests licentious give the good offence:
In virtue's cause alone his strength he tries,
Lamented only by the good he dies!

* * * *

The strain is past: no more entranced, I hear
The muse's whispers strike my listening ear:

By pensive cares, and anxious fears opprest,
A deepening gloom o'erpowers my labouring breast;
Sleep's soothing influence on my temples steals,
And night's dark shades the silent world conceals;
In peaceful rest my weary eyelids close,
In grateful ease my languid limbs repose,
In the still silence of the gloomy night
A beauteous maid appeared before my sight;
Her auburn hair in artless ringlets flow'd,
Her radiant cheeks with heavenly lustre glow'd;
Her eyes whose fire with mingled pity strove,
Beam'd the mild splendor of celestial love:
Around her form a thousand graces play'd,
A thousand charms her ivory neck displayed;
O'er her fair limbs a snow-white vest she wore,
A silver zone enclasped her waist before,
——" Hear me!" she said, " or virtue's voice no more
Shall point thy steps from pleasure's dangerous shore.
Too soon, alas! no guardian power to guide,
Thy strength shall sink beneath life's stormy tide;
In fruitless grief thy youthful years shall fade,
And sorrow lead thee to the silent shade.
Ah! now no more amidst my guiltless train
Thy verse the suffrage of the good shall gain,
No more by truth inspir'd thy spotless page,
Shall lash the vices of a guilty age,
With Cleveland's prose thy kindred verse shall shine,
And aged harlots hail thy wit divine!"

* * * *

Silent I heard to penitence reclaimed,
And curst the fools who virtue's cause defam'd.
What! tho' no titled rabble croud the door
Of him who bravely ventures to be poor,
Tho' pride and wealth may squint with scornful eye;
On him who truth prefers to flattery;
Yet still for him has heaven rewards in store,
That pride might envy, avarice deplore:
The conscience clear, the calm unclouded day,
The peaceful night, the mild yet steady ray
Of piety, that cheers life's darkest gloom,
And lights the prospects of a world to come:

Blest by the Almighty power with gifts like these,
Let H―― strive the giddy great to please;
Calm I'll look on, while villains rise to fame,
And Grenville's honor'd with a patriot's name!

LAST WORDS: OR, ARMSTRONG *versus* CLARKE.

SIR,

As a friend of Mr. Armstrong permit me to inform you that the gentleman alluded to in the paragraph of the Morning Herald was not Mr. Best the brewer, a young man of high honor and unimpeachable connections, but little Mr. Best, the antagonist of Lord Camelford, and the husband of the daughter of Lord Aldborough. This contradiction is more necessary, as to the one such a report would do infinite harm, while it could not contribute to the mortification of the other. As for the assertion that this friend of Mary Ann Clarke has thought proper to make, that Mr. Armstrong participated in the profits of a marker at the billiard-table, it is too incredible for belief. If she knew such a circumstance, how happens it that he continued to reside along with them without intimating her discoveries? As for Mrs. Clarke's regularity, virtue, &c. they are pretty well known to a large proportion of the community: her daughters may be educated in decent principles, but how are they to evade the influence of example?

The truth is, that this notorious woman fleeces every body she can, and then holds them up to the ridicule of the public. In this manner she has treated her protectors and friends, all who possessed a claim on her gratitude, or had disclosed their secrets to her in the confidence of love or friendship. First the duke became the object of her treacherous machinations, then Col. Wardle, next to him Major Dodd, and so on for a long progression downwards, till we arrive at Mr. Armstrong. If she had any just cause of public complaint against that gentleman, why did she not manfully avow it, instead of coming before the world with a charge of which the sole criminality attached to herself? If she thought it improper that any modest woman should visit her, or be seen in her company, she has a very correct idea of her character and situation. But what must we think of a female, who first obtains the sanction of a married couple, and as soon as they have served her purpose, basely proclaims to the world the sacrifices they have made? As for the pretty story about the Pandeans, &c. which is most probable?— that Mrs. C——— should tell a lie, or that a married and respectable woman should be guilty of the conduct ascribed to Mrs. Armstrong?

I remain, very respectfully,
Your humble servant,
E. E.

We have received many letters from the same quarter as the preceding, and on the same subject. We have selected that of E. E. as the best written, and most rational; but cannot conscientiously assert, that it has impressed us with more favorable sentiments towards Mr. Armstrong than we formerly entertained. We now dismiss the subject; we hope for ever; and trust that no further trials on our patience shall be made.

THEATRICAL REVIEW.

The notorious Mr. Coates, the Romeo of Bath and Richmond, the proprietor of the cock equipage; famous at the expence of reputation, and distinguished for every thing that does *not* characterise the gentleman and the man of sense, made his metropolitan *debut* at the Haymarket theatre, in the character of the gallant and the gay Lothario. We have already attempted to characterise this gentleman's mode of acting; but we were not prepared for an exhibition at once so painful and so ludicrous as that which, on this occasion, it became our duty to witness. The most outrageous madman in St. Luke's never displayed greater wildness of countenance, or greater extravagance of action, than this would-be Garrick. With a face expressive only of the meaner passions, a form by no means remarkable for its symmetry, and an address the very reverse of elegant or insinuating, his occasional appeals to the audience in *propria persona* only tended to exasperate our displeasure, and to aggravate our astonishment. Yet there was such a perfect and original expression of self-complacency in the curvature of his eye-lids, and the protrusion of his lips, that every other emotion was overpowered in the unrestrained and irresistible indulgence of the risible faculties. At first he was received with good-humoured plaudits, but the laughter soon became incessant; the imitations of chanticleer from the gallery entirely drowned the accents of the gay and gallant hero, and at length overcame his fortitude. He advanced to the front of the stage, but the effect of his countenance was irresistible; a universal *cachinnus* convulsed the pit and the galleries; even the visitors of the dress-boxes lost their accustomed self-command, and one overpowering peal shook the theatre to its base.

When he had in some degree recovered from his indignation at this unexpected reception, and the more friendly spectators had obtained a cessation of the uproar, he graciously informed them that he was a man of rank and fashion, that for a broad horse-laugh "to come between the wind and his nobility," was most horrible; that he had assumed the character of Lothario for the benefit of a buxom widow, who entertained a high opinion of his parts; and that if the vulgar people who presumed to consider him as a bad actor, would leave the house, he "putting his hand on the place where his purse should have been," would pay for them. What a lucky thing it is for some people, that they have the amazing fortune of fifteen hundred a year; it gives them a right to insult the poverty of those whose good opinion they would stoop to the meanest artifices to obtain, and secures them from the necessity of self-examination. Had the very poorest porter in the gallery exclaimed in apparent earnest, "What a fine looking man he is!" the bosom of Lothario would have overflowed with gratitude. So inconsistent is purse-proud ignorance with itself!

The other speeches were shorter, more humble, and more ineffectual: the hero's choler was now changed to indignant firmness; the curtain fell in the middle of the fifth act, and Lothario, the gallant and the gay, proceeded with a puff to the office of the Herald.

During the performance, he was occupied in playing to the Baron Geramb. He nodded to him when he should have bowed to his mistress: when the Baron cast an encouraging glance in return, his countenance beamed with the expression of joy; but when the whiskered nobleman was sullen and inattentive, the hero was moping and melancholy. While he was uttering, therefore, the words of Rowe, his countenance spoke the language of despair; and when he told us that his misery was insupportable, his appearance testified that his happiness was complete.

His acting, however, was productive of temporary benefit. The house was crowded; and with reference to her acceptance of his services, the widow Fairbur has had no occasion to become, in her own person, a *fair penitent*.

In reply to the observations of the critics, Mr. Coates has addressed a letter to the Morning Herald, so replete with nonsense and bad grammar, that the observer is puzzled to determine whether his histrionic or literary efforts be the least-worthy of endurance. He justly observes, that his person was not of his own creation, and that if it be not remarkable for symmetry, or elegance, he cannot help it; but he forgot that if he could not remove his deformities, he possessed the ability to refrain from their exposure. Ugliness and awkwardness are not reprehensible in themselves; but when they expose themselves to public observation, and claim the honors of grace and beauty, they become the just objects of sarcastic ridicule, or indignant reprobation. As a coxcomb, Mr. Coates is quite at home: let him drive his appropriate vehicle, or mount the Bristol stage, instead of the Haymarket, and we shall be silent with regard to his fu-

month in the character of Sir Pertinax Macsycophant. As he has not yet appeared for the second time, we have had no opportunity ourselves of deciding on his pretensions. But to obtain the approbation of the public, notwithstanding the impressions left upon its mind by the excellence of Cooke, is, in itself, a proof of commanding talent.

It is asserted, in defence of the introduction of equestrian exhibitions, and the repetition of splendid spectacles at the Covent Garden theatre, that while such representations as these are necessary to attract the multitude, the lovers of Shakespeare and Congreve are equally gratified; that the expression of human feeling, and the delineation of human character, are not superseded by the introduction of quadrupeds, but relieved; that he who does not admire Timour the Tartar, may become a spectator of Macbeth, and that he who takes no interest in the gambols of an elephant, may weep over the sorrows of Ophelia. But the sophistry of this mode of defence will evidently appear from a statement of the truth. The majority of play-going characters would attend and applaud a tragedy of Shakespeare, would be delighted by a farce, and would retire to their homes with a full remembrance of all the emotions they had felt, and all the sentiments they had heard. By repeated visits, they would acquire a relish for the delineation of actual manners, and for all the excellencies of our legitimate dramatists; and even were they condemned to a final absence from the theatre, all their theatrical associations would be connected with the name of Shakespeare, and all their prepossessions be in favor of a regular drama. But at present, after witnessing Hamlet, we are favored with Blue Beard: whatever addresses itself to the eye is longer and more vividly remembered than that which appeals to the understanding: the elephants and the mountains, and the castle, become the subjects of family conversation, while the prince of Denmark is forgotten; when the junior branches attend the theatre for the first time, they remember what fine things they had heard of Blue Beard, and regard the play only as a dull preliminary to a delightful treat; one visit for the sake of spectacle, gives occasion to another; the taste of the rising generation, and ultimately of the public, is placed at the mercy of a scene-painter, and monsters become the *dramatis personæ*.

But it is asserted that a full attendance cannot be drawn

without these and similar excitements. On this observation we shall observe that we admit it to be true; yet in the days of Garrick no such excitements were necessary; a full attendance is not required to afford the managers a handsome profit; and the remark therefore proves nothing more than that it is natural for the managers to make the concern as profitable as they can. But from this view of the subject arises the very natural and very decisive question, why are the taste and morals of the nation to be dependent on the discretion or self-denial of the managers? The chamberlain has in all probability the power of preventing the appearance of those motley exhibitions that now disgrace the national theatre, and if he has not it should be granted to him. That he may, if he pleases, prevent the appearance of a quadruped on the stage of the theatre royal, we have no hesitation in asserting, and even this advancement to reform would have a beneficial influence.

In the management of its plot the "Golden Fish" is neither better nor worse than its predecessors. The scenery is splendid beyond all former parallel, the tricks amusing, and the acting excellent. The contortions and vibrations of Miss Worgman in the fish, must delight the connoisseurs in the minutiæ of Christmas exhibitions; and the view of the comet, and the unclouded heaven, may possibly be admired by that large majority of the people who pass their lives in London, without dreaming that there is a firmament above them, or that the beauties of nature are superior to those of Parliament-street, or Hoxton-square. The elephant is of a size unusually small; has not been drilled into the performance of any entertaining evolutions, and is upon the whole a very dull and very useless performer. The artificial animal has a much more striking effect, and the real one can be seen at Exeter Change.

For bustle and business, however, Harlequin and Padmanaba must yield precedence to the Lyceum pantomime. It is called the White Cat, but the White Lion would have been equally appropriate. Prince Polidore finds himself in a wood, the shades of which are pervaded by a glancing and interrupted light, which at length is modified into a distinct and settled brilliance. The trees are transformed into the letters F. A. I. R. Y. though of what alphabet, whether Saxon, English, or Blackletter, it would puzzle Mr. Pinkerton himself to determine. The unseen fairy tells him to follow a floating ball of fire which leads him to an enchanted hall, where he finds about a dozen distressed damsels with their faces covered, and is informed by an inscription that they are all metamorphosed into cats. Perhaps it is meant to insinuate that they are all tabbies; but in that case why were the apes, the poetical companions of old maids, forgotten? At any rate, a view of their phizzes would have been productive of amusement; but they condescend not to unveil, and it would have answered the purpose just as well to have metamorphosed them into *b*——*s*. In return for disenchanting the fair creatures he is presented with a magic sword, and runs the usual course of pantomimic heroes. Some of the tricks are particularly excellent. The transmutation of Millbank and preparations for the erection of Vauxhall Bridge, into the complete structure in a different point of view was peculiarly excellent. The first of these views was finished with as much effect as if it had not been adapted for metamorphosis. The transmutation of a new reading of Shakespeare into an Elephant, was a *fair hit*, though not logically or rhetorically correct. The real Elephant is not the offspring of these new readings, but is substituted for Shakspeare himself, and would have been so had no new readings ever perplexed us. The scenery was far superior to what could have been expected, considering the extent of the stage: the last scene surpasses in effect any similar effort that we have witnessed.

The dramatic representations of the Christmas week are seldom the proper subjects of criticism; but having had no previous occasion to mention the name of Mr. Putnam, we cannot resist the opportunity of expressing our surprize at his return to the London stage. Industry, the first great requisite to the success of genius, has only aggravated his defects. He is destitute of dignity, yet wants the easy negligence by which he who does not possess it appears to disclaim it: he solicits attention to his attitudes by all the arts of studied display, yet at last disgusts you by his awkwardness. Forgetting that Kemble has become the object of critical admiration, in spite and not by virtue of his natural defects, he imitates his guttural pronunciation, and copies those peculiarities of manner which in menial actors are the most unpardonable defects. There is a peculiarity too, in the movement of Mr. Putman's body, that would give a ludicrous effect to exertions more respectable than his. He never addresses one of the dramatis personæ in a direct and manly attitude, but twists his body into such a position, that while his knees project towards the orchestra, his chest is opposite the stage box. He has a strange trick likewise of standing as if the instep of his left shoe were moving on a pivot, while the right is pushing with might and main against the boards. Let him have recourse to a dancing-master.

The return of Miss Smith, who is announced this evening to perform the part of Elwina; in Mrs. More's tragedy of Percy, will be hailed by the dramatic public with a satisfaction proportionate to the mortification they experienced from her protracted absence. That she will supply the place of Mrs. Siddons, we dare not hope: the combination of so many natural requisites, with so many acquired perfections, is scarcely to be expected, till after a long interval of dramatic mediocrity. Miss Smith is an able substitute; but we hope that the present declarations of Mrs. Siddons are like those that have preceded them, and that her occasional appearance in future years may serve to stimulate the industry and repress any prematurity of self-confidence, that may be displayed by her adopted successor.

Saturday, December 28th, 1811.

SCOURGE.

FEBRUARY 1, 1812.

CONTENTS.

TO CORRESPONDENTS, see back.	
DRURY-LANE THEATRE, AND MR. SHERIDAN........... 87	
Influence of Mr. Sheridan on the press...................... 88	
State of the Drury-lane concern.. 89	
Mr. Whitbread's exertions...... 90	
Their want of funds........... 91	
Conduct of Mr. S.'s friends...... 92	
On a third theatre.............. 93	
THE MAGISTRATES........... 94	
Poets transformed into magistrates 95	
Mr. Gifford's services.......... 96	
THE —— HOUSE SPY..... ib.	
Satirical writings defended....... 97	
Scandal most easily obtained in high life.................. 98	
Its conspicuous characters described..................... 99	
M——'s debut as hair-dresser.. 100	
Adventures at Paris........... 101	
Appearance at the —— house .. 102	
AMERICAN POETRY....... 103	
Raleigh and Penn 104	
The American character........ 105	
The great and glorious struggle.. 106	
American style................ 107	
Influence of climate on genius.. 108	
Elegies of Gray and Mason..... 109	
Champions of philanthropy.... 110	
THE DUKE OF CUMBERLAND AND MAJOR SEYMOUR DAVIES................. 111	
The duke at an election...... 112	
Obtains the treasury papers.... 113	
The major's reward........... 114	
Attends at St. James's......... 115	
The ministers discourage his economical plans............ 116	
Cumberland v. Cumberland.... 117	
Affidavit v. Correspondence ... 118	
Contradictions between the duke and the major............. 119	
On the princely character...... 120	
THE REVIEWER, No. VIII... 121	
The life of Richard Cumberland Esq., &c. By William Mudford ib.	
Mr Pinkerton's rhymes....... 122	
Burlesque criticism............ 123	
Intellectual character of Cumberland................... 124	
His dramatic excellence........ 125	
His attainments as a scholar.... 126	
Sir James Bland Burgess...... 127	
Cumberland's colloquial character..................... 128	
His social virtues............. 129	
The ardor of his friendships.... 130	
STOCK-JOBBING CLERKS... 131	
BENEVOLENT INSTITUTIONS. 132	
Romantic schemes alone to be encouraged................. 133	
New roads to clerical ambition.. 134	
Nature of Bible societies....... 135	
Principles on which they are conducted, censured........ 136	
Specious arguments for, refuted. 137	
COUNTERPART to the WARM CHILD.................. 138	
Nottinghamshire piety........ ib.	
THE APHRODISIAN SOCIETY, COUNCIL-ROOM......... 139	
Speech of the prioress of —— .. ib.	
Triumphs of adultery.......... 140	
An important debate.......... 141	
The Countess's defence of adultery..................... 142	
Semiramis and Ninon D'Enclos.. 143	
Conjugal accommodation...... 144	
HISTORY OF THE ASPLAND HEIRESS. Chap. I........ 145	
History of its founder.......... 146	
Its connections and alliances.... 147	
The Chaplain's visit........... 148	
His discoveries................ 149	
Adventures in the barge ...,... 150	
DOGGREL ATTACKS ON THE REGENT.................. ib.	
Poetical libels................. 151	
The Royal sprain............. 152	
On doggrel and dullness........ 153	
The Royal Bloods............ 154	
The duke of Y.'s bed-chamber . 155	
Scenes at Oatlands............. 156	
Report of Royal Stripes........ 157	
Col. Mac, and princely relaxations 158	
An amorous scene............. 159	
Libellous ballads.............. 160	
THE WIDOW FAIRBUR, OR, DISCOVERY UPON DISCOVERY................. ib.	
The widow Fairbur............ 161	
Her pursuits.................. 162	
MR. GILLET and MR. STOCKDALE.................... 163	
Mr. REDHEAD YORKE...... 164	
THEATRICALS 165	

NOTICE TO CORRESPONDENTS.

So large a portion of this number has been devoted to subjects of general and immediate interest, as to render unavoidable the postponement of several amusing jeux de esprit; among which Poll Raffle's Lottery, or the Wellesley exhibition, shall obtain the first place.

Lind-amira is received.

The *ci-devant* Posture Mistress, and Sicilian Courtezan, with several interesting anecdotes of a naval hero, are in preparation.

The Whips, No. II., in our next.

We are obliged to the gentlemen at the Cocoa Tree; but are sure that on reflection they will acknowledge the propriety of abstaining from remark on the intrigues of the Life-guards till the decision of the expected court-martial shall be made known.

The assertion respecting Lieut. Kelly is incorrect.

In the explanation of the article on the funds of Drury-lane, it should be observed that under the provisions of the act only ten per cent. on the amount of the subscriptions can be drawn, till all the claimants be satisfied.

A Constant Reader is referred to the successor of Braham at Covent Garden.

The Mentorian Puffs; P. L.; A Peeper at Carlton House; a Voyage from Antrim; and the History of a most destructive Tempest, are under consideration.

The Review of Milner on Architecture; Paddy Ponsonby's speech; an Essay on Constitutional Retrospection; and Memoirs of a Ministerial Mansion, are inadmissible.

THE SCOURGE.

FEBRUARY 1, 1812.

DRURY-LANE THEATRE, and Mr. SHERIDAN.

Sir,

The liberty of the press is sometimes more deeply injured, by the dishonorable compact of its retainers, than by all the restraints and oppressions to which it may be subjected by the hand of an impolitic and arbitrary government. While the minds of the public journalists remain unfettered, or while interest operates in counteracting the tyranny of power, some freedom of discussion on every topic unconnected with politics will remain; and occasional efforts to reestablish the independence of the press, will testify the presence of a spirit, which whenever it surmounts the immediate obstacles by which it is obstructed, diffuses its light with tenfold lustre, and burns with a splendor proportionate to the efforts employed for its extinction. But when the persons connected with the press submit themselves in voluntary subservience to a man, whose genius only serves to embellish meanness, palliate extravagance, and ennoble selfishness; when they become the willing instrument of his most profligate schemes, and sacrifice the interest of the public to his private convenience, there is no hope of remedy, but in the death of the individual. The influence of such a man is gradually and imperceptibly obtained: its progress excites no jealousy; its operation is not resisted, because it binds the will in voluntary chains: injustice to the cause of truth and liberty, assumes the form of homage to exalted genius; and he who would frown defiance on a Gibbs, or resist with indignation the proposals of a Yorke, permits no compunctious visitings of conscience to dissuade him from blandishing the vices, and concurring in the wildest and most injurious speculations of a Sheridan.

It is a fact more lamentable than singular, that with the exception of the Examiner and the Morning Post, scarcely a single journal at present exists, which is not in some degree devoted to the personal service of the modern Alcibiades. It is a sufficient ground for the rejection of an advertisement or a paragraph at many of the newspaper offices, that it may be unpleasant to the feelings, or injurious to the interests of Mr. Sheridan. If any article in opposition to Drury-lane was sent for admission, the answer usually received was " it will displease the Sheridans ;" if the insertion of a statement, substantiated by the necessary documents, respecting the claims of the old renters was requested as an act of public justice, it was replied thàt nothing could be consistent with public justice that injured the Sheridans: the Sheridans were boldly avowed to be of more importance than the majority of our nobles; and their interests openly preferred to those of the great body of the people. Whether any publication yet remains beside the journals above referred to, in which truth and justice are paramount to the influence of the Sheridans, the fate of this letter will determine. You have boasted of independence, it remains to be seen whether that imposing name have any other meaning in the vocabulary of a modern writer, than hostility to the servants of the crown.

To the *public* virtues of Mr. Whitbread no man has had more frequent opportunities of contributing his testimony, than the writer who now addresses you. With the habits and the temper of a Bonaparte in his domestic connections, he no sooner steps forth to the execution of his senatorial duty than he throws aside his monkish garb, and assumes the robe and the presence of a patriot. On every great occasion his conduct has been that of a man deeply anxious for the salvation of his country, and sacrificing every private and petty interest to the faithful performance of his duties as a servant and representative of the people. But even Mr. Whitbread has become the tool of Sheridan: he contentedly sacrifices the honest fame that he had obtained by a long series of important services, and becomes the willing instrument of designs, from which if he perceives their tendency, he ought to withdraw his support: and in which it is to be hoped that nothing but a total unacquaintance with dramatic speculations could have permitted him to engage.

That Mr. Whitbread should devote his personal influence to the service of his friend, does credit to the virtues of his heart: the extent, the success of his exertions bear honorable testimony to the warmth of his attachment, and to the estimation in which he is held by the most respectable classes of society. No man could have benefited the Drury Lane partnership in an equal degree: and few individuals would have employed their power of being useful to an equal extent. But having done what he could, by fair and candid representations of the state of the concern, he should have left the less honorable part of the business to men who had no character to lose, and whose statements would only have weighed with the public in proportion to their correctness. There was no reason why he should come forward and declare that only two claimants remained whose demands were uncompromised; that the whole of the claims might be commuted for £150,000, and that there was even no doubt of the final completion of the building: he must have known that these statements were erroneous, or he must have paid but a slight attention to the subject. Permit me, Mr. Editor, to ask by what vouchers he has ascertained the number of the outstanding claimants, or the value of their claims; from whence the cash for the erection of the theatre is to proceed, and on what grounds he rests his hope that the building will be completed?

In the first place I can assure you that notwithstanding the formidable list of names appended to the report, not one hundred thousand pounds have yet been even nominally subscribed. Many of the shares purchased by the " noblemen and gentlemen," who extend the catalogue are only single shares of one hundred pounds. ' They have begun the erection of the building with no other capital than the amount of the insurance, and the value of the ruins, with only 100,000l. more in expectancy; with the certainty, that even with that sum in possession, only half the theatre can be completed, and without the ability to satisfy a single claimant, supposing all the claimants to have consented to a compromise. But,

2. There is every reason to believe, that of claims actually outstanding, for which Mr. Whitbread has obtained no vouchers, and of which no compromise will be made, no less than 120,000l. remain to be liquidated. Supposing it *possible* that these should be commuted for 30,000l. in what way is Mr. Whitbread enabled to provide for so enormous an addition to the estimate? But if it be in the power of any claimants to keep in the back ground, and come forward with the full amount of their claims, whenever they suppose the funds of the theatre to be in a prosperous condition, what security have the new subscribers for the regular administration of their property? Is it not evident, that from the source pointed out, obstructions, not only to the building of the house, but to the productiveness of the property, and to the division of the revenue, will continually occur; that litigation will exhaust the receipts, and continual discord distract the managers of the concern?

3. Mr. Whitbread has exhausted all his powers of argument and persuasion; every mode of literary insinuation has been employed: wit has combined with wit to sing the praises of Sheridan, and the glories of Drurylane; pathos has been called in to the aid of logic: at one time the servants of Whitbread appeal to the avarice of the public, and at another to its patriotism: we

are reminded of the father's genius, the son's indisposition, and the daughter's possible viduity: the senate is invaded by dramatic amateurs; the parliamentary reporters intersperse their *hears!* and their notes of admiration at the end of every speech of the managers of old Drury; the belles at the west'end of the town, are adorned with Drury medals, exhibiting a phœnix rising from its ashes; yet with the combination of all these efforts, and of all the industry that these circumstances exhibit, allowing Mr. Whitbread's most favorable statement to be correct, and admitting Mr. Sheridan to be the very paragon of all that is disinterested, economical, and virtuous, what are the prospects held out to the subscribers? 100,000l. have been, according to the *exparte* statement, actually subscribed: the cost of the building will be 150,000l., and the whole expence must amount to 300,000l. Having done all, therefore, that could be done, they are compelled to acknowledge a deficit of more than 200,000l. Having failed in obtaining that sum by their late extraordinary efforts, they have nothing to hope from futurity. Supposing, therefore, that the building is completed, it must open with an actual debt of 200,000l., without any variety of dresses or scenery, with incumbrances for the benefit of the Sheridans, and with one or two obstinate claimants whose ability to injure bears no proportion to the amount of their demands.

But the fact is, that the progress of the building must be speedily stopped; the persons interested will then come forward with doleful lamentations that so fine a structure should be left to " the peltings of the pitiless storm," like the modesty of Sheridan to the assaults of a Covent-garden mob. If the artifice excites compassion, a few subscriptions will be obtained, and another foot added to the walls. But if the public remain inexorable, Mr. Sheridan will come forward, and after many preliminary professions of generosity, modesty, and honor, will remind the public, that he freely and fairly surrendered his claims for a compensation inadequate to their worth, rather than impede the progress of the building, or disturb the cordiality of the subscribers; that trusting to the fulfilment of their engagements, he had exerted himself for the benefit of the original renters and proprietors; that to his interest alone, it has been owing that the new structure reared its head above the surrounding palings; and that while the other persons interested in the concern stood looking on, he was fighting their battles in the senate, and exciting the friendly exertions of Mr. Whitbread; that to deny him, therefore, some renumeration for disappointed hopes, and unrepaid exertions, would partake at once of injustice and ingratitude; that he throws himself on the generosity of those whom he has the honor to address, and leaves it to them to consider the extent and the urgency of his claims. A friend will now come forward, and propose, in due form, that instead of contingent remuneration from the receipts of the intended theatre, an absolute investment on the existing property of stones and wood be granted to him and his heirs for ever. The motion will excite no astonishment, for it is favorable to Mr. Sheridan; a man who must be provided for whoever is sacrificed to his interest, and who has so long exercised the privilege of doing as he pleases, that to deny him its continuance in old age, would be the climax of all that is indecorous and illiberal.

Having thus shewn that Drury-lane cannot be rebuilt at present, and that every future effort to rebuild it must necessarily be more unpropitious than the present, the conclusion necessarily arises, that either its patent should be sold to the subscribers to a third theatre, or, which is better, that a third patent should be granted for the performance of the English legitimate drama. So long as there was any prospect of the re-establishment of Drury-lane, the proprietors of a third theatre evidently abstained from opposing its interests, or employing any argument in their own favor that might either injure their property or provoke their hostility. They endeavoured to prove that a third theatre was necessary, even supposing Drury-lane to be risen from its ashes. They were soon convinced, however, that the only serious opposition with which they had to contend, originated with the friends of Mr. Sheridan, who exerted themselves in the House of Commons with so much effect, as to prevent all hope of success to the petitioners, so long as the same prejudices should continue. But now that all has been done for New Drury that can be done; when the exertions of the committee of the third theatre can in no way obstruct the progress of Mr. Whitbread and his friends; and that it is proved beyond the possibility of doubt that the patent in the hands of its present proprietors can never be employed to an efficient purpose; it is surely reasonable to expect that even those who deny the necessity of a third theatre, will admit the want of a second, and contribute to the erection of a substitute for Drury-lane. All patents are granted for the benefit of the public: it could not be in the contemplation of the crown, when it granted the Drury-lane patent that the public should be deprived of stage exhibitions at the pleasure of the persons in whose favor it was granted; that it should exclude other adventurers in theatrical property, while it itself laid dormant; and injure the public, without enriching its proprietors.

It is distressing to witness the acts to which a genius like that of Sheridan has been doomed to stoop, in the pursuit of trivial gains and petty advantages; and it must be afflicting to his friends, that the viduity of his daughter-in-law should be made the subject of appeal to the merciful consideration of the privy-council, in the presence of Mr. Sheridan himself. That if he were rendered independent, he would be a better man, let us charitably hope; that he would not then be an obstruction to any plan of advantage to the public is highly probable; and that he would no longer be an object of insulting but mistaken pity, is not less certain, than that he who now addresses you can forgive his errors in consideration of his poverty.

A THEATRICAL AMATEUR.

THE MAGISTRATES.

The deficiency of our present system of police, has at length been acknowledged by the ministers themselves, and may, therefore, be descanted upon without any fear of legal visitation. The administration of the system, however, is more deserving of reprehension than the system itself, and all attempts either by the auxiliary introduction of military bodies, by augmenting the number of subordinate officers, or restoring the efficiency of the midnight watch, must terminate in disappointment, unless the majority of the present magistrates be superseded by men of unembarrassed minds and of bodily activity: who can make it their business to fulfil the duties of their situation; whose attention is not necessarily diverted from the subject before them, by the allurements of books, or good eating, or dramatic exhibitions; who understand the world as it is, much better than they remember what it was, or can imagine what it ought to be. As the members of a convivial and literary club, where the luxuries of a plentiful repast and copious libations should be the precursors of critical or philosophical disquisition; where those who could not shine might be permitted to repose, and the sluggish or the apoplectic should remain as the tools of the dabblers in metre and the collectors of dramatic anecdotes, it would be difficult to point out a set of more appropriate persons than the bench of magistrates. But as forming the directors of our police, as men in whom it is natural to require some portion of acquaintance with the world, and no inconsiderable share of personal and undivided activity, it would be vain to seek after any apology for their selection. That the penult in crevere is short in Horace and long in Juvenal, that *Lelontai* is a plural noun; that there remains a balance in the hands of the Drury-lane treasurer of £447 16s. $8\frac{1}{2}d.$ and that an easterly wind hastens the crisis of a haunch of venison, are discoveries of some importance in themselves, and would be received with all appropriate reverence, were not the lives or fortunes of the people sacrificed to their investigation. A poet whose days have been passed in the cultivation of literary excellence, and who is never so happy as when measuring couplets in his study, is a respectable and interesting personage; a bustling, meddling, intriguing appendage to the theatres, may be useful and convenient in his peculiar province; and an old man worn down with infirmity, of a feeble person and decayed faculties, deserves at once our pity and indulgence; but why should the impotence of age be exposed on the bench to the derision of the vulgar, and the exultation of the criminal? what reason can be given for drawing the poet from his study, or the manager and arbitrator from the only pursuits to which he devotes his steady, unremitting and enthusiastic exertions? A canting parasite of the ministers, who rings his monthly change on jacobinism and infidelity, may be deserving of encouragement; but why is he to be dragged from his Review to shew the world how little attention he can spare to the duties of his new situation, and how very possible it is that a man may write with fluency on " social order" without possessing any resources by which he may contribute to its practical support?

But it will be replied by the friends of these magistrates, that they are a set of meritorious men, who have contributed by their writings to the glory and the advantage of their country, or rendered themselves by an active and beneficial interference in the management of public institutions, the objects of a just and liberal patronage. To expect that such men should relinquish their favorite pursuits, and forget the confirmed habits of their lives, is not less cruel than absurd: that they should be rewarded for their virtues or their services, no one possessed of the feelings and principles of a gentleman will dispute; and that they should be the mere servants of the public, drudges without relief, and dependants without consolation, is revolting to every feeling of humanity.

That the merits of the gentlemen alluded to are of a description so uncommon or so various as to demand of the nation a liberal reward, it is not our present business to deny; but if they have really deserved well of their country, they have a right to ask not only for a remuneration, but for a remuneration imposing no laborious duties, and depreciated by no unpleasant obligations. Let the poet be rewarded as a poet, and let such a pension be granted to the victim of infirmity as may alleviate his sufferings, and dissipate the fears of superannuated indigence; but do not commit the safety of the public for the value of a pension: let Mr. Nares receive a handsome allowance for his former services, and let him be superseded by a gentleman of middle age, in the full possession of his personal and bodily faculties; reward Mr. Gifford for his exertions in the Antijacobin review, and exalt to his situation some individual who will not sacrifice the cause of justice to the cadence of a paragraph, or indite eulogies on Pitt, when he ought to be employed in the prevention of crime and the detection of guilt.

THE —— HOUSE SPY.

To obstruct the path to returning virtue, by denying forgiveness to repentance, or to urge the criminal to a desperate perseverance in iniquity, by visiting his former indiscretions with unrelenting severity, is one of the inevitable effects of satire indiscriminately applied or injudiciously conducted. It is the duty therefore of a public writer before he depreciates the present character of an individual, by recording his early progress in the ways of vice, to enquire how far his youthful errors may have been expiated by the tenor of his later conduct, and to determine whether under all the circumstances of his life, to draw his frailties from their drear abode, may not be to gratify the curiosity of the public, at the expence of the general welfare, and of justice towards the obnoxious individual. It is to be feared that if the lives of all men even from the cradle to the grave were subjected to rigid scrutiny, but few would be found, who had not, at some period of existence, indulged in the contemplation of vices, from the commission of which they were only restrained by *circumstance*. The majority have been at some moment of their lives incipient traitors, robbers, and adulterers. Where the corruptions of human nature therefore have been excited into temporary action, it is both just and reasonable that subsequent return to virtue, of which the sincerity is attested by a long and steady perseverance, should be received as a proof that the triumph of vice was only momentary, and that the feelings and the principles of virtue have obtained a fixed and decided predominance.

That these considerations have been fully impressed on our minds during the repeated exercise of our satirical duty, we hope that no one who has honored our pages with a candid examination will deny. We have not selected any individual as the object of reprobation, unless his influence on the morals of the public were present and immediate. The security of ourselves and contemporaries from the contagion of vicious example, and from the rapacity of depredators who would have preyed on the incautious and unexperienced under the mask of fashion, or beneath the garb of virtue, has always been the chief object of our exertions. Wickedness that had long slumbered in inertion, or that had been in some degree expiated by subsequent reversion to the paths of virtue, we have permitted to retire from the gaze of public curiosity; but towards the hardened sinner, who after repeated exposure still perseveres in his course of iniquity, and is too stupid to obey the dictates of prudence, or too insensible to feel the miseries of guilt, neither duty nor inclination will permit us to entertain the same forbearance.

Some of our readers indeed may be inclined to regard our exertions in the exposure of villainy with contempt, because some of the heroes of our narratives have derived their origin from, or have practised their early depredations among, the lower or middle classes of society. It naturally suggests itself to those who are unacquainted with the routine of periodical publications or who have observed the manners and constitution of society with a superficial and unenquiring eye, that a knowledge of the intrigues of such persons necessarily implies either a suspicious acquaintance with their haunts and habits, or a degrading indulgence in the collection of mean and petty scandal. But the task of ferreting out the history of a man's life for the purpose of satirical exposure, is a task that we gladly leave to the pursuit of those to whose temper and habits it may be congenial. What we have hitherto communicated to the world of the conduct and character of notorious persons, has either been the current conversation of the day, substantiated by evidence and embodied in our pages, or the legal and authenticated information of the victims of vice and profligacy, divested of the colouring that truth may have received from resentment and revenge. As the great, the wealthy, and the polished, are usually selected as the dupes of successful villainy, and are necessarily the most able to investigate the origin of their wrongs, and the best qualified to trace their authors through all their transformations and vicissitudes, we have seldom found it necessary to step beyond our usual circle of intercourse for the gratification of our enquiries, and for the materials of public exposition. What individual is better acquainted with the history of Sedley than Lord Headfort; or who is better qualified to elucidate the character of Dubost than Mr. Thomas Hope?

When the reader of a work like ours is startled by an occasional recurrence to vulgar life, he forgets how many of our fashionable characters, and how large a proportion of the most active managers of our public institutions, and the most renowned of our public benefactors and instructors, have derived their origin from lanes and alleys eastward of Temple Bar, and how closely they imitate all the habits of the inhabitants of Broad-street. The sons of prostitutes, who sport the *ci-devant* pupils of their mothers, barbers who have forsaken the razor for the whip, and discarded serving-men, who lend their quondam masters their own property at an interest of cent. per cent. are the most conspicuous *automata* who tread the *pavé*, and the most delightful animals who skim the road, and monopolize the park. To describe the fashionable world as it is, would be to begin with Dyot-street, and finish with Manchester-square. Let the L——, the Gr——, the M——s, and the L——s, express their indignation as they will: to swear, and drink, and talk bad grammar, and indulge in licentious conversation, would become the night-cellar or the apple-stall; to cheat a tradesman of a guinea, yet spend it on a harlot; to sacrifice integrity, and honor, and the principles of a gentleman, to the ambition of equivocal notoriety, is characteristic only of a poltroon; to rise by dirty and infamous arts from the shop-board to the drawing-room, deserves the gallows or the pillory: yet the gaze and the envy of the young, the patronage of the wealthy, and the plaudits of the great, are the rewards of him whose conduct is restrained by no observation of decorum, whose actions are regulated by convenience, and whose origin is as 'obscure as his principles are wicked, and his manners repulsive and contaminating.

The subject of our present strictures, has no other claims to the notice of the fashionable world, than the anthority which his connection with the ——— house enables him to exercise over their amusements. The persons to whom the management of that concern is entrusted, unacquainted we believe with his past history or his genuine character, repose in his integrity the most unbounded confidence: the profits of his speculations as a coal merchant, enable him to gratify whatever caprice he may entertain, and to support the friends of Mr. Taylor in every mode of encroachment on the rights of others, and of annoyance to those obnoxious subscribers, who have stood forward as the champions of the public interest. By what fatality it happens that the majority of the courtiers who surround the monarch of the King's Theatre are the outcasts of society, and the opprobria of human nature, it would require the sagacity of a Stewart to explain; but it is not less certain than extraordinary, that Mr. —— is scarcely more worthy of public abhorrence than his brethren, though about fifteen years ago he was convicted under the name of Jones of burglary, and sentenced to seven years transportation.

His original profession was that of a hair-dresser. The ancient inhabitants of Mary-le-bone still remember his dexterity in the use of the razor, and his expertness in the noble art of manufacturing perriwigs. Like Lord Castlereagh and many other magnanimous gentlemen, whom nature intended for the bulk or the stable, he was inspired by the workings of an ambitious fancy; and resigned the humble scene of his tonsoric operations to some honest and but less enterprizing drudge, who preferred indigence to dishonesty, and thought a steady hand and a fine-edged razor, the noblest possessions to which human ambition could aspire. Love is always the attendant on great and enterprizing spirits. As bully therefore to a house of infamous notoriety, where he had formerly exercised his paternal profession, he obtained the most well-earned applause, and acquired the external recommendations of a stern countenance, a stately gait, and a boisterous elocution. One of the young ladies of the mansion was about to take a trip to France, and selected Mr. —— as her protector. On their arrival at Paris, she obtained a noble and wealthy dupe, and liberally rewarded the services of her companion, who assumed a fictitious name, became a constant frequenter of the gambling houses and the theatres, and by the liberal display of his money, and the repeated mention of distinguished names among the nobility of England, obtained some degree of credit and of welcome among individuals whose proneness to conviviality exceeded their discriminative powers. One of these gentlemen he had drawn into an extensive speculation, of which he had nearly obtained the profits, when the unfortunate arrival at Paris of a gentleman to whom we are indebted for the materials of his history, gave an unexpected termination to his schemes. Our hero and his host were sitting at dinner, when the name of one of his oldest friends was announced. He made no difficulty in receiving him *en famille;* the first congratulations had scarcely subsided, before the host observed our adventurer and Mr. —— to look on each other with some peculiarity of expression. After dinner his friend requested him to retire for a few moments on private business. "Who," he asked, " is the gentleman who dines with you?"—" A gentleman of fortune from England; his name is Smith, and he is the intimate friend of Lord Moira, Mr. Fox, and General Fitzpatrick—one of the family of Sir Sidney, and one of the Prince's coterie!!"—"My dear friend," replied the other; " you are deceived—the fellow is a barber—I knew him under the name of ——, he has frequently shaved me, and I always found him to be an impudent, idle, lying vagabond—give me leave to treat him as he deserves!"—So saying, he proceeded to the dining room with the intention of inflicting upon his person a summary punishment; but the *ci-devant* barber conscious of his frauds, and suspecting the purport of their consultation, had already effected his retreat. His departure from Paris was as precipitate as the emergency required; but a great city is necessary to the perpetration of extensive and successful villainy, and London became once more his hiding and his resting-place.

By what arts he supported life, or in what iniquities he indulged till his appearance at the Old Bailey, it would be worse than useless to enquire. That he did remain at Botany Bay for the prescribed period of transportation we believe: nor should our pages have been devoted to the commemoration of his infamy, had misfortune taught him humility, or correction virtue.

For the last two years he has been chiefly distinguished as the factotum of a certain manager, and a busy and treacherous attendant at every meeting called by the creditors or proprietors. At a public meeting called by several individuals interested in the affairs of the establishment, he distinguished himself as one of the most conspicuous and most active members, and was about to ascend the chair, when he was confounded by the entrance of the same individual who had contributed to his detection at Paris. He immediately disappeared; the surprize of the gentleman was extreme—as far as his personal influence extended, he cautioned the subscribers against confiding their property to his care, and warned his friends of the infamous association into which they had been betrayed; but in all public establishments dupe succeeds to dupe: wealth will cover a multitude of sins; and they who detest an individual as a rogue, will serve him as a master.

His riches have been obtained by practices of the most mean and fraudulent description. The sacks in which his coals are sent to the houses of the purchasers must be marked with the name of the owner at a certain distance from the top. Unfortunately the distance from the bottom is not mentioned in the act; and if as is usually the case the quantity delivered is not subjected to measurement, the shortness of the sacks, (for they are about six inches less at the bottom than they ought to be,) is not observed. His purchasers are defrauded of thirty per cent. on the value of the commodity, and the sums thus obtained are squandered on parasites and King-street prostitutes.

AMERICAN POETRY.

The character of a rising community like that of the United States is always a more pleasing object of prospective than of immediate contemplation. To embellish it therefore with adventitious attractions, and transmute the indications of future excellence into actual perfection, will always be a favorite amusement of the few speculative men whose leisure exceeds their talents, and whose patriotism overpowers their sense of honesty. Of these delusions, as far as relates to their religious and political institutions, we have before endeavoured to expose the fallacy; and we feel it our present duty, not only to demonstrate that their present claims to poetical excellence are unjust, but that any expectation of its attainment till after the lapse of many ages must be more than problematical.

How much the poetry of Europe has been indebted for its most pleasing ornaments, and its most interesting subjects to the fables of classical mythology, and the legends of popish superstition, it would be useless to explain. The delusions of ignorance and idolatry, however they may be regretted by the philanthropist, or despised by the philosopher, have always been a fertile source of materials to the poet. Nor have the local superstitions of our own country been less frequently adapted to the purposes of poetical amplification. The dramas of Macbeth, and of the Midsummer Night's Dream, are in themselves sufficient to demonstrate how much assistance the real poet can derive from the grossest absurdities of vulgar superstition. It is better for every purpose of the poet, that our groves should have been consecrated to Woden, and our rivers to Sabrina, than that they should be remembered as the haunts of cannibalism, or designated by barbarous and disgusting epithets.

There is no duty more congenial to the feelings, or

more worthy the genius of a poet, than to describe the manners and to celebrate the virtues of the early inhabitants of our native country. We love to trace, in the untutored wildness of the aboriginal Britons, the leading features of that manly and independent character, which is at once the pride and the security of their civilized descendants. The prowess of Boadicea, and the fortitude of Caractacus, will always excite emotions of retrospective enthusiasm in our people, of which bravery and intrepidity are the characteristic virtues. But to what period in the history of his country can the American look back with other feelings than humiliation and disgust? Those favored spots, which are now the seats of legislation and the emporia of commerce, were once the refuge of barbarians, cruel in prosperity, and servile in misfortune; allied by colour and disposition to the domestic slaves of their European conquerors, the objects of popular alarm and legislative jealousy. It is obvious that every sentiment of personal pride and patriotic attachment, will lead the successors of such a race to draw a veil over the early history of their country, and to turn aside from the scenery that has witnessed their warlike exploits, and their religious ceremonies, with feelings of indifference to its natural beauties, and of aversion for the people by whose crimes and abominations it has been polluted.

Deriving their origin from a country, which political events have taught them to regard with feelings of habitual hostility, the Americans have no ancestorial atchievements to record, no founder whom their patriotism will permit them to commemorate. To retrace the wanderings and celebrate the virtues of a Raleigh or a Penn, would be to emblazon the biographical annals of a nation, to which they are indebted not only for their political existence, but for all the refinements of civilized society. Their knowledge of science and of letters, and even that spirit of liberty which excited them to the establishment of independence, are borrowed from a people whose proficiency in the arts of government, and the *literæ humaniores*, they no longer regard but with envious rivalry. The most transient allusion to the past is calculated to repress that fervor of patriotism, uninspired by which the productions of every writer, however gifted by nature, or improved by study, must be vapid and inanimate. An American poet can take no pleasure in the recollection of a period, when his native soil was dependent for its existence on the mother country, and if he confine the excursions of his fancy within the limits of the circle of events that has rolled its course since the establishment of American independence, what is there to be found that can ennoble his efforts, or animate his enthusiasm? His native scenery we have already shown to be unadapted to the purposes of poetry; and the artificial institutions which form the bulwarks of American society, have neither the beauty of youth, the stability of manhood, nor the dignity of age. Nothing that surrounds him, or that can present itself to his imagination, displays a single feature of the awful or the venerable. There are no national reliques of antiquity, over which the pensive may lament the uncertainty of life, and the instability of sublunary grandeur; no productions of the chissel or the pencil, which may recal to the lovers of virtue, and the admirers of genius, the remembrance of departed excellence; no princely institutions for the furtherance of piety and learning, and the relief of disease and indigence. There are no hospitals to commemorate the liberality of her merchants; no cathedrals to attest the rank of her clergy, or the piety of her people; nor any university to celebrate the munificence of her statesmen. The numerous sources of poetical association, that arise from the contemplation of the inanimate memorials of genius, piety, and valour, must for many ages remain unopened to our American descendants.

Such therefore are the local disadvantages to which a transatlantic poet is subjected, that he neither possesses any national subject of poetical celebration, nor if he were able to select from the history of mankind a theme worthy of his genius, would he be able to elevate and adorn it, by that association of sentiment and imagery which peculiarly distinguishes the poet from the rhymster. But should it not be forgotten that from all the *foreign* sources to which a European poet can refer for a theme of epic celebration, when the events of his own country are apparently exhausted, he is equally excluded. With what pleasure could a republican record the exploits of princes, or celebrate the virtues of a hereditary episcopacy? The pomp of courts, and the " pride and circumstance of war" must be contemplated by an American poet through the spectacles of books, and he therefore views them without distinctness or enthusiasm. There still remains so much of kingly splendor, and knightly courtesy, among the different nations of Europe, that the magnificence of the feudal and chivalrous ages is neither uncongenial to the feelings nor beyond the powers of an attentive observer of modern manners, or a poet conversant with the monuments of former ages. But the pride of a noble aristocracy, and the ostentation of romantic valour, are equally abhorrent from the prepossessions, and uncongenial to the imagination of a republican merchant and agriculturist; and should it happen by some strange caprice of fortune that an American endowed with the qualifications of a poet, is a secret admirer of monarchical government, his necessary unacquaintance with all the accompaniments of kingly grandeur and the splendid scenery of courts, must subject him to the necessity of substituting laboured declamation for the natural and appropriate expression of his feelings.

That " great and glorious struggle" which terminated in the independence of America is totally unsusceptible of poetical embellishment. There was nothing generous in the motives of the people, or romantic in the character of their chief. We are afraid that however well the moral virtues and the constitutional intrepidity of

Washington may be adapted to a regular eulogy, he would bear but an unfavorable comparison as the hero of an epic poem, with the bullies and barbarians of ancient Greece. It may be as praiseworthy for a people to resist the payment of a stamp duty as to fight in defence of their altars and their homes, but it is not, equally poetical: a nation of warriors struggling against the overbearing power of cruelty and lust, will always be a more interesting spectacle than a commercial populace, whose first emotions of political enthusiasm terminate in the seizure of a cargo of tea and the demolition of a custom-house. It was not the hope of saving five per cent. on the value of their morning beverage that fired the breasts of the heroes of Thermopylæ.

Nor will the American poet be able to atone for his inevitable deficiency in the higher qualities of poetry, by his superiority in the humble requisites of style and versification. It would be trifling with the patience of our readers to prove that the further a colony recedes from its mother country, in policy and manners, the more will the purity of its original diction be violated, and the delicacies of its idiom be forgotten. Whatever be his ambition or assiduity, a writer will not long be able to preserve his language and phraseology uncontaminated by the barbarisms and impurities of colloquial intercourse. His style will display all the stiffness and embarrassment that characterize the compositions of the modern Latinist, without his purity of diction or correctness of construction: in his most successful efforts the lighter shades of synonomic difference will glide into indistinctness, and all flexibility of expression be therefore unattainable.

To causes such as these rather than to the influence of climate may be ascribed the apparent sterility of American genius. It is not the existence of poetical power in the inhabitants of the new continent that we are disposed to deny, but the possibility of its developement; and there is too much reason to conclude that the same obstacles will produce the same effects, for a period that would exhaust even the patience of Mr. Jefferson. Though the positions of Montesquieu be more ingenious than correct, and the statue of the Abbe Raynal less remarkable for justice than asperity, the hopes of the American president do more credit to his patriotism than his philosophy.

As we are not of opinion that the progress of genius is bounded by the accidental peculiarities of geographical situation, that one country shall excel in the arts of life, and in every liberal pursuit, because it has been favoured by the hand of nature with every charm of native scenery; or that another shall be condemned to intellectual sterility, because its soil is barren, and its sky inclement: as we cannot persuade ourselves to believe that wit and imagination are influenced by every change of climate and every variation of the needle, or that the mental faculties partake so much of the grossness of material things, as to be sublimed to volatility by the heats of Barca, and frozen to inertness amidst the snows of Lapland, we shall not so far imitate the writers we have mentioned, as to deny the Americans the praise of literary capability, because their view is limited on one side by a vast and boundless ocean, and their inquiries exhausted on the other by interminable forests. But it is obvious that many of the causes we have enumerated, as having hitherto retarded the expansion of American genius, will retain their force amidst all the storms of political convulsion; and that the greater number of them will produce their usual effect, as long as their present form of worship and government shall continue. A nation that possesses no established system and belief, and of which the religious ceremonies are as discordant and capricious as its provincial customs, will never be able to derive any accession of poetical imagery and allusion from the duration of its political existence. In a country so distracted by schism, the poet must either espouse the sentiments of his own sect, and thus degrade his production by the quibbles of controversial divinity, or he must wave the introduction of every christian doctrine, and thus confine himself to those general principles of natural theology, which being simple in themselves, and obvious to the feeblest imagination, neither require nor admit the aid of poetical amplification. The effusions of pure theism, which human genius has been able to produce, are few in number, and depend for their excellence not on sublimity of thought; for the attributes of the Almighty rather oppress than invigorate the flight of a poetical fancy, but on that felicity of expression and purity of language, which we have already demonstrated to be without the reach of American emulation. When we consider how much the poets of modern Europe have been indebted to the union of church and state, and to the influence which that alliance produces on the manners of the people; and when we contemplate the feelings of prescriptive veneration, with which the monuments of ancient piety are regarded, by the multitude, and how much the expression of sympathy in those feelings embellishes and animates the compositions of our national poets, we shall be easily convinced that an established religion is one of the most important sources of political delight. Let those who estimate its influence at a trifling value, refer once more to the elegies of Gray and Mason, to the night-piece of Parnell, and to almost every other production that melts us by its pathos, or delights us by its beauty.

The spirit of transatlantic liberty has an irresistible tendency to evaporate in petty jealousies and local quarrels; and the patriotism of the poet, instead of extending its views to the general interests of the empire, is circumscribed by the narrow boundaries of his native province. In England the prosperity of counties and corporations, is gladly sacrificed to the welfare of the community: in America, on the contrary, the great object of contention is not whether peace or war will conduce to the collective interests of the empire, but whether Pensylvania shall suffer more from a rupture with Europe than Connecticut, or Virginia derive greater advantages from a commercial treaty than New York: the laureat of a republic thus torn by intestine rivalry, will never have a subject more worthy of celebration than the procession of an electioneering rabble, nor any emotion of patriotism more pure and exalted than that of a London alderman at a turtle feast.

To these observations it will be triumphantly replied that the American poet is content to resign the crimes of princes and the miseries of war, to the congenial temper of his European predecessors; that the pride of hereditary rank, and the bigotry of an intolerant religion are equally the objects of his derision and abhorrence; and that he will gladly yield to the slaves of greatness, and the advocates of murder, all the pretensions of a poet, if he can be distinguished by the noble but less envied title of a CHAMPION OF PHILANTHROPY.

The boast of independence and philanthropy is always in the mouth of an American; but on what foundation does he rest his claims to a possession so valuable, and a virtue so exalted? The squabbles of an American senate would disgrace a meeting of turnpike commissioners; and we may therefore conclude that the principles and interest of the people are sacrificed to the private animosities of their representatives: the retention of twelve hundred thousand slaves in hopeless bondage is congenial to the habits of the nation, and sanctioned by the edicts of the legislature; and we may therefore suppose, without injustice, that they are acquainted only with the name of liberty, and that their philanthropy evaporates in flowery declamation, or rhapsodical enthusiasm.

THE DUKE OF CUMBERLAND AND MAJOR SEYMOUR DAVIES.

Excited by a very natural expectation of degrading his exalted oppressor in the estimation of the people, and impelled by the prospect of pecuniary relief from the embarrassments to which he had been subjected by his subservience, Major Davies has committed to the public a narrative of his transactions with the Duke of Cumberland, from the date of the Hampshire election in 1806, to the termination of their correspondence, in August, 1810. His statement, however, while it fully exemplifies the enormous influence of the crown, and places the conduct and character of his Royal Highness in a very unfavorable point of view, does no credit to himself. Throughout the whole of the transaction that gave occasion to his pamphlet, he acted the part of a man perfectly willing to sacrifice his duty to his interests, and ready to betray any trust that might be reposed in him for an adequate compensation. On the public commiseration he has no other claim than that which may be granted to poverty, by whatever misconduct he may have drawn it upon himself; and though its sale may renumerate him for the labour of its composition, its circulation can have no tendency to redeem his character with the virtuous or respectable part of the community.

But whatever may be the feelings with which Major Davies's statement is received by the unambitious part of the public, it is both the duty and the interest of the members of the house of commons, and of every conspicuous individual engaged in the administration of public affairs, or mingling in the contests of political party, to espouse his cause and eulogize his virtues. In electioneering contests every artifice is fair; and how, therefore, can they suffer the major to be punished for an act which on their own principles was perfectly justified by its expedience? To sacrifice every feeling of duty and conscience to the purposes of personal ambition, is the acknowledged privilege of every politician; and why is infidelity to his employers more criminal in a Davies, than the purchase of boroughs in a Castlereagh, or the sacrifice of the catholics to party convenience in a Howick? To deceive and betray his constituents, is surely as wicked in a member of parliament, as to outwit the treasury; and the major had at least as plain a right to sell his personal services to the Duke of Cumberland, as Col. B. or the Hon. Mr. F. to transfer the voters on his estate to the disposal of Mr. Yorke.

He informs us that when the contested election took place for the county of Hampshire, in September 1806, he was the resident assistant barrack master general of that district, an office of great importance, trust and confidence, carrying with it the most considerable influence with the freeholders in every town where the barracks were erected.

This influence arose, in consequence of the different farmers and tradesmen furnishing supplies, either for building, or articles of every description used or consumed in a barrack, being considerably under his controul. At this period administration concluded that his active and personal exertions were necessary to secure the return of the two government candidates, Messrs. Thistlethwayte and Herbert.—Conclusively he received directions and *orders* (!) from the secretary of the treasury for effectually supporting the views and interests of the above-mentioned gentlemen: these orders were followed by various letters and official documents from general Hewitt, barrack master general, containing further and more complete instructions for his guidance to secure success to the administration. Thus fortified with his authorities, he proceeded vigilantly upon the canvass when he was stopped in his career by the arrival of his royal highness the duke of Cumberland at Winchester, who immediately commanded his attendance, with orders that he was not to remain an instant before he presented himself to him. The moment that he received the duke's commands he followed the orderly serjeant that brought them into the presence of his Royal Highness.

Major Davies asserts that in the conversations in this and the subsequent interviews, his royal highness told him " that he had been *playing the devil*—that he was *cursedly* vexed and angry—that by refusing to support Sir Henry Mildmay, the major was refusing his royal highness's protection? And that he promised, on condition of his delivering up the confidential papers committed to him by the treasury, to get him a better situation, to bear him harmless, and to bear on his *broad shoulders* the whole weight of the blame." On this last assurance the major delivered up the papers, and the duke " converted them to his own political views." Of the conversations, however, we have no other evidence than the testimony of the major himself, though his observations on the result give to his narration an air of probability. " Now is there one (military man) to be selected that can suppose I would of my own accord volunteer giving up documents so serious, the parting with which *must eventually* injure me, *must eventually* destroy my prospects of future advancement, and render my situation unpleasant by the loss of official confidence? No man in the kingdom can suppose me guilty of such matchless folly. I repeat and sacredly declare that the duke of Cumberland's *influence* and *pledges* induced me to act as I have done; and this *influence* over my actions was well known to every freeholder in Winchester. His royal highness's promises have been completely at variance with his actions: I became his dupe, and am now his victim."

His royal highness was now in possession of the details of Major Davies's interviews with the friends of the candidates, particularly Lords Caernarvon and Temple, and the directions given to him touching the places where he could be most useful; also as well as with copies of his correspondence and reports to the Barrack master general. In fact, every transaction that had occurred, from the commencement of his orders to that day, was laid open to Sir Henry; who thus obtained the opportunity of counteracting every plan that had been formed against him. Mr. Deverel, the agent for the government candidates for the election, and residing at Winchester, finding from the major that he had shewn the papers to the duke, earnestly requested that he would consign them to his charge; promising at the same time to place him out of the reach of the duke's displeasure, by enabling him to *retire on his full salary*. Lords Caernarvon and Temple advised him to burn every vestige of writing coming from government, and by no means to give them to the duke; for if he (said Lord Caernarvon) gets possession of them, we shall, I suppose, have a parliamentary squabble about their contents. With this advice, however, the major did not comply.

The duke requested him to deposit the papers with Mr. Rose at Cuffnells. This gentleman was at that time one of the *outs,* and therefore interested in their production: but on the subject being moved by Sir Henry Mildmay, the motion was lost, and no necessity found therefore for the presence of the major. On the return of the Pittites to office, they naturally felt that he who had betrayed their predecessors, would betray them, whenever it might accord with his interest or convenience. Discountenanced by government, the major lost perceptibly the confidence of the barrack-master general. He therefore informed his royal highness of the awkward and irritating state to which he was reduced, and requested his removal from that particular department. To this application the Duke returned for answer ", *the barrack people dare as well be damned as injure you.*"

At length after being subjected to many mortifications and discouragements the major was dismissed, on charges apparently frivolous in themselves, and only adduced at present, because to adduce them was convenient.

When he saw the Duke of Cumberland, and informed him of the uncommon transaction that had happened, he received many assurances of putting matters to rights. " It required no great effort, (he observes,) of his Royal Highness's interest, for I was so harrassed with ill health, and the combination of events so recently vexatious, that I only requested the lowest half-pay. The duke desired me to give him a petition, confessed the case was hard and mysterious, and requested me to leave the rest to him."

He gave the required document to his royal highness, and felt himself perfectly convinced of what he denominates " the vivacity of his assertion. *Patience* was recommended when he called at St. James's palace, and at the end of nine months he discovered his petition lying upon His Royal Highness's table in his study; where it had peaceably rested from the day of its delivery."

The major now applied to the Duke of Cambridge, who took upon himself to explain the subject of their interview; and the result of his Royal Highness's condescension was a command for the major's attendance at St. James's.

He accordingly obtained an interview. It was agreed to write a second petition, to which the Duke promised to pay more attention than to the first. *Eighteen months* wore away, yet he could obtain nothing satisfactory: his appeals, his letters, and his attendance on the duke were equally fruitless. At length he obtained permission to see Mr. Perceval, the chancellor of the Exchequer, to whom his royal highness had transmitted the petition. The minister informed him that the application had been nearly forgotten: that it was true the duke had put a paper into his hands, but it did not occur that there was any particular desire expressed by his royal highness to have it complied with! The duke had been ill, which had prevented of late any intercourse; he would however send an answer to St. James's in a day or two. A month arrived before this day or two elapsed; he then addressed Mr. Perceval by letter, and obtained an answer, in which for want of support his petition was refused. His Royal Highness appended to this unwelcome intelligence that he would do no more, or interfere in any shape whatever.

Such is a summary of the major's statement, expressed in his own language as nearly as brevity would admit; with as much delicacy towards all the parties concerned as is justified by the tenor of the narrative.

How superior the ministers themselves were to all corrupt and sordid considerations; how warmly they felt for the happiness of their country and the welfare of its people; how justly and generously they suffered the real merits of the major to outweigh his momentary and occasional errors; and with what eagerness they listened to any suggestion that might lend to alleviate our burthens and contribute to our security, their conduct subsequent to the exertions of the major in diminishing the expences of the department over which he possessed a jurisdiction, sufficiently evince. The barracks in the county of Durham were loaded with exorbitant rents. The disregard of economy in the expenditure of this department was glaring and wanton. To put an end to such wasteful and useless prodigality, he deemed it necessary to use his most strenuous efforts. By diligence and perseverance he succeeded, and brought the proprietors to take about one half of the original rents, though many of them were armed with leases or agreements. On this occasion what is the conduct of the board? So far from rewarding the major's past exertions, and encouraging him to perseverance by any marks of official attention, or any promise of future advancement, they were pleased to inflict on his conduct an oblique censure, and to inform him that he ought to have communicated with them before he had proceeded to alter the rents! His interference was never forgiven, and shortly afterwards he received a final *dismissal*.

Copy of the affidavit of His Royal Highness the Duke of Cumberland, on evidence at Westminster Hall, in an action of trover, for the recovery of the papers alluded to between Major Davies and the Right Hon. George Rose.

Times, July 16, 1811.

His royal highness the Duke of Cumberland said, that he was present at an interview between the parties at Cuffnells, five years ago, in September or October, 1806. His royal highness remembered that some papers were delivered to the defendant then, which the plaintiff had previously brought to the duke, knowing his royal highness was a friend of Sir Henry Mildmay. His royal highness told him it was utterly impossible for him as a peer of parliament to interfere in any election; but if the papers would be of any use to Sir H. Mildmay, the plaintiff might give them to the defendant —he did so, and told the defendant that he was at liberty to make what use of them he pleased. His R.

Winchester, Nov. 3*d.* 1806.

Sir,

I am desired to inform you, that St. Barbe, the banker at Lymington is a particular friend of Mr. Rose, and to desire you will be so good as to send here the names of the voters you have obtained at Lymington.

I am, Sir,

your obedient servant,

B. C. Stephenson,

(First Aid de Camp and Secretary to His R. Highness.)

Major Davies.

" His royal highness was in possession of the details of my interviews with the friends of the (ministerial) candidates, particularly Lords Caernarvon and Temple, and the directions given to me touching the places where I could be most useful, also copies of my correspondence, and reports to the barrack master general—in fine, every transaction that had occurred from the commencement of my orders to that day—this disclosure furnishing Sir Harry Mild-

H. was then the general commanding that district, and told the plaintiff he was going to call at the defendant's, and the plaintiff might meet his royal highness there.

His R. H. being asked as to the supposed paper of instructions to Major Davies, in what towns and places to canvass, said upon cross-examination that his directions to the major were to attend to his duty, and not to interfere in the election. His R. H. had been *two or three times* applied to, from the plaintiff to get him half-pay, but not *immediately from him:* since the action upon enquiry into the circumstances of his appliation it was not found practicable to grant it. This was twelve months ago.

There were no further applications to His Royal Highness, except for papers. At the same time that the plaintiff applied to the defendant, his R. H. had not one of the papers. *All that he had* were given to Sir Henry Mildmay lately deceased.

may with every plan formed against him," &c.&c.&c.
Statement, page 20.

In Major Davies's pamphlet, are published more than twenty letters addressed immediately to the Duke, of which the receipt is acknowledged by his private secretary. Of these the two following are extracted on account of then brevity.

St. James's,
July 11, 1810.

I am commanded by his Royal Highness the Duke of Cumberland, to acquaint you, that in conformity to your request, his Royal Highness is pleased to sanction your waiting on Mr. Percival to urge the prayer of your application,

I have the honor to be,
Sir,
Your very obedient servant,
Fred. B. Watson, Sec.

Windmill Street,
May 3d, 1810.
Sir,

This letter will bring before your Royal Highness the situation of a man and his family, now reduced to the lowest pitch of suffering: this picture must naturally occur to your Royal Highness, where such a length of time has elapsed since my resourceless state has been known to you: you have promised relief but this promise has been forgotten by your Royal Highness.

The horrors of want can no longer be concealed, distress will force my case to be public, and when known, every human mind will feel for a being sacrificed as I am.

With the most dutiful respect, I am,
your Royal Highnesses
most obedient servant,
J. SEYMOUR DAVIES.

To General H. R. H. the Duke of Cumberland.

On the general points of contradiction between the affidavit of his Royal Highness and the corroborated statement of Major Davies, any observation would be superfluous; but it is impossible to pass without remark, the discordance between the answers given by his Royal Highness on his direct and his cross examination. In the first he evidently leaves the court and jury to infer that he never received the papers, but rejected the offer of their acceptance, because it was " impossible as a peer of parliament to interfere in any election;"—in the second he admits that they were for some time in his possession, and that all *he had were (ultimately)* given to Sir Henry Mildmay.

By preventing the appearance of the present statement, the Duke of Cumberland would have performed an act of service to himself, and of duty to his family. The junior descendants of the house of —————— are of all men the most guilty or the most unfortunate. Whatever has been communicated to the English people of their actions and their characters is unfavorable. They possess no loftiness of principle, yet want the dignity of manners that embellishes vice and ennobles meanness; they are proverbially deficient in natural endowments, yet are destitute of that common-place discretion which evades contempt by retiring from observation, and is content to resign the honors of superior wisdom, if it be suffered to escape without the mortifications that are due to impertinent stupidity. How deeply would the bosom of a parent in humble life be afflicted were his children to resemble in character, or imitate in their pursuits the progeny of ———————————! Neither the dupe of an unprincipled libeller because he was first the slave of a vulgar and servile prostitute, nor the refugee from a foreign possession, because he had taught its soldiers to regard him with abhorrence, and its inhabitants to pronounce the name of England with regret, nor the —— who takes once more a discarded mistress to his arms, because the poor remember his brutality and the rich despise him, has any just occasion of complaint, if the liberty of the press be employed to its most ample extent in the exposition of his character. The expression of public opinion will not be restrained, and in proportion to the loyalty and affection of a public writer to the father, will be the watchfulness with which he regards, and the severity with which he endeavours to amend, the conduct of the children.

THE REVIEWER, No. VIII.

THE LIFE OF RICHARD CUMBERLAND, ESQ., &c.
BY WILLIAM MUDFORD.

To say that the author of this valuable publication has brought forward a work which can be read with interest, after the memoirs which Cumberland has left us of himself, is to confer no inconsiderable praise. "When" (he observes) "the memoirs of Cumberland were published, I was forcibly impressed with their insufficiency in all that regarded the estimation of his literary character; and while I found in them all that could be wished about the man, I was conscious that whenever his death should happen, an ample and interesting opportunity would occur for the union of his personal history, with a minute enquiry into the pretensions of the author." He has entered, therefore, into very minute and ingenious strictures on the most prominent of Cumberland's productions; and if he has added but little to the anecdotes of his personal character already known, he contributes to our instruction and entertainment, by making them the ground-work of moral and critical deduction.

The extent of Mr. Mudford's reading has enabled him to display a copiousness of illustration, and a felicity of comparison, that fully compensates for the want of personal acquaintance with the subject of his biography; and he possesses a manly independence of opinion, that without degenerating into perverseness, contributes to elevate his work above those stupid and common place repositories of critical dullness, which contentedly echo the opinions of the multitude; of which the compilers mistake timidity for candor, and regard the honest expression of an original sentiment, as unjust to the dead, and insulting to the living.

As a specimen of the entertaining matter with which his papers abound, we select the following anecdote:

"In No. 50, there is an attempt to illustrate the modern

mode of theatrical criticism, by an imaginary enquiry into the tragedy of *Othello*, supposed to be written the day after its first performance. The idea is ingenious, but the merit of invention does not belong to Cumberland: at last a similar conception occured to another writer, and was reduced to practice some years before the appearance of his *Observer*. This writer was Mr. Pinkerton, who published some verses in 1782 called " Rimes," and which he believed to be poetry. The critics thought otherwise, however, and told him so: but he was as little qualified to remain tranquil beneath the lash as Cumberland could be. By some accident the volume arrived at a second edition, and Mr. Pinkerton appeared armed for encounter with his opponents. In his advertisement he called them all dunces, but makes no attempt to prove them so: he utters the filthiest abuse and deems it humour; he dwells with the most offensive egotism upon his own praises, and calls it a vindication of himself. He does more also. To shame his enemies and to convince mankind that they are a race of hopeless blockheads, he gives a translation from a presumed Greek MS. " reposited in a leaden box and found in an ancient dunghill," which proves to be a critique upon the first Pythian Ode of Pindar, and is written with as much vulgarity and silliness as Mr. Pinkerton could devise. This was to assure the world that modern critics wrote with vulgarity and silliness: he supposes also another critique to be found (in the ruins of Herculaneum, and forming the cover to a pie, upon some of Horace's odes written just after their production, distinguished only for feeble malice and abortive wit. Nay he makes a third discovery, of some critical remarks upon Dryden's ode, which surpass in all that is despicable and insignificant, either of the preceding artificial antiquities. If the reader will forgive me for polluting my pages with such ineffable nonsense, he may be satisfied of what I say by reading the following paragraphs, which comprise the whole of this bastard progeny of resentment and dullness. It is supposed to be copied from a MS. dated May 16th, 1701.

Cryticall remarques upon Mr. Dryden's Odd called Alexandre's feast. By Burnaby Burman, Clarke of the parish of Cammerwell, A. M. A. S. S.

" Abracadabra. De profundis clamavi. Poeta nascitur non fit. Oratur fit non nascitur. Quæ masculis tribuuntur mascula sunto *(copied from bookes, so am shure they are richt spelt).* I quot these verses of the Greeke poetee, curteous reder, to shew thee that I am not unqualifyed for the tasque I have taken in hande, but on the contrarie am embued with pulite learninge.

This poeme beginnith thus: " Twas at the royal feste," &c. How wulgar is this, it resemblith a drinkinge songe. The author seemeth not to knowe the difference betwixt an odd and a songe, which is as followeth, viz. a long odd is a short song, and a long songe is a short odd. Now an odd should never be in a common stoile, but as we say in an odde stoile. Q. E. D.

That lyne, ' so should desert in arms be crowned,' is of verie bad example. If deserters be crowned, trew soldiers must be whipt in their place. So what is sauce for a goose is sauce for a gaunder.

' Happy, happy, happy paire,' might have been paired thus: ' Happy, three pair,' which would have saved wryting the word happy thrice over.—Qu. if it should not be nappy ?

' Timotheus placed on high,' read perched on high. For ' flying fingers' we ought surely to read ' frying fingers.' Annie flying fingers, I never chanced to see; frying fingers are common in playing on a wind instrument, such as the ancient harpe was.

' A dragon's fiery form belyed the god.' If a dragon gave a god the lye he ocht to have hadde his nose pulled, fiery as he was.

In the IV. handsau we read of slaying the slain thrice; a thing in my judgment not altogether possibil. We likewise rede the word ' fallen ' five times over. An egregious absurditie ! For if a man is once fallen he cannot fall again, till he has got on his legges. Now legges are not once mentioned.

In No. VI. we meet with ghosts, (Jesu protect me ; for as I lyve, I saw a ghost last nyghte at Peter Haynes's barne door,) that in battle were slayn. A ghost slayer ! Oh ! heaven what nonsense. The conclusion is mighty prettye. But upon the hole this piece is not equal to anie of the noble productions of a Mr. Thomas Durfey. Amen.

The intellectual character of Cumberland was not distinguished by grand or comprehensive features. He had more resemblance to the lynx than to the monarch of the forest. Within a certain boundary of vision his conceptions were at once vivid and distinct, but he was incapable of comprehensive observation, and destitute of that creative power which exalts the mean and aggrandizes the trivial. He was one of those writers whom the continually operating impulse of ambition cherished by opportunity will at any time produce. Had fortune denied him the preliminaries of education, he would not have risen to distinction by the force of original genius; had the operation of circumstances favorable to the developement and cultivation of literary taste, terminated with his departure from the university, though he might have written with the same perseverance and enthusiasm, that actually marked the progress of his literary career, he would not have risen about the successive thousands of the eighteenth century, whose effusions are only recorded in the columns of the reviews. Nature in her formation of his mind had done little, but that little was cultivated with exemplary care, and called into action by the rare concurrence of the most propitious circumstances. Compared with Johnson he bore the same resemblance to that celebrated man, which the block of marble polished and fashioned by the hand of the architect bears to the diamond. The value of the one is independent of the artist, who no otherwise contributes to its worth than by eliciting the inherent value of the native gem: whatever pleasure or admiration the other may excite is exclusively granted to the skill of the workman and the value of the workmanship: its beauties are adventitious to the original material, which is not admired for its abstract value, but for the form into which its uncouth proportions have been moulded, and the ornaments that embellish or diversify its surface.

There is no other instance of a writer obtaining an eminent name in literature, with so few pretensions to the more valuable powers of the mind, and the more poignant feelings of the heart. He is seldom animated and never eloquent; he was not remarkable for profundity of learning or delicacy of taste: he seldom attempted philosophical or metaphysical enquiry; and of wit and humour he was singularly destitute. He possessed no exuberance of imagination, nor any susceptibility of exciting the more pathetic emotions. Few men have written so much on the manners of the world, or so frequently depicted the passions of mankind, who have affected us so little. His readers seldom feel the ardor of enthusiasm, and never indulge in the luxury of grief. He never excites astonishment, or impatience, or laughter; in reading his works we sometimes smile, and usually approve; but to excite the complacence of his readers is generally all the merit that he can justly claim, and to do this is no evidence of extraordinary powers.

His real merits however are so great that with all these admissions he may claim a respectable place among the writers of the eighteenth century. That uncomprehensive minuteness of perception that formed the prominent feature of his intellectual character, contributed by its very circumscription to the excellence of his dramatic and biographical sketches. His field of view was circumscribed, but within its circle he saw with peculiar quickness and accuracy; by the exclusion of surrounding objects the images that came within his sphere of vision were presented to his eye in the most and appropriate hues and distinct proportions. When he attempts therefore to catch those minutiæ of manners which to abler men would have been invisible or evanescent, he is always successful. The operation of the same principle will account for the imperfection of his dramatic characters, and for the general excellence of his dialogue. In the invention of his *dramatis personæ* he was obliged to have recourse not to his memory but to fancy; instead of describing a particular individual whom he had seen, he is compelled to paint an ideal character with general habits, and possible peculiarities; and his imaginary portraits are therefore seldom any thing more than hasty and general outlines, without much expression of character, or dexterity of finishing. In dialogue he is only successful, when he appropriates the common language of middle life to the persons of his drama. When he endeavours to invent a characteristic phraseology for any of his dramatic favorites, he loses the fidelity of art, without exhibiting the creative felicity of nature.

As a scholar his knowledge was more classical than profound or various. To his acquaintance with the Greek dramatists, his translation from Aristophanes, bears honorable testimony; but his remembrance of the ancient writers was rather general than particular, and the minutiæ of classical criticism, had either never become the objects of his study, or had been dismissed from his attention during the later years of his life. He could quote Homer, and feel his spirit, and determine the meaning of his moral or playful passages with peculiar facility; but had any passage of that poet been adduced in his presence to illustrate a disputed point in the mythology or history of the ancients, he would have sunk into convenient inattention. No man was more able to draw a parallel between the similar passages of Pindar and Cowley; but to decide on a disputed point of metre, or to trace the history of English style, and poetical phraseology, he was more humbly qualified than thousands of contemporaries, to whom nature had denied even a trivial portion of his talents and attainments. He possessed, of course, a general intimacy with the belles lettres; but his stores of literary illustration, were neither copious nor original: he had seldom wandered beyond that regular path of reading, which is expected to be trod by every well bred man, who pretends to a taste for literature: he seldom delighted his companions by his exuberance, instructed them by his accuracy, or surprised them by his abstruseness.

These observations are not intended to depreciate the

character of Cumberland beyond their proper level; but to place his literary fame on the only basis by which its stability can be secured. If the writings of Cumberland be read as the productions of a sensible man mingling much with society, and observing its general forms, and the peculiarities of the individuals that composed it, with unusual quickness and distinctness of perception, their fame will be more lasting, and their utility more extensive, than if they were transmitted to posterity as the production of commanding genius, splendid learning, and irresistible vivacity. By all his compositions the learned may be instructed, the fastidious entertained, and the virtuous improved. Of this praise how few have been deserving, and how rare are the endowments that could entitle their possessor to a more exalted tribute of critical justice!

In the preface to Mr. Mudford's work, a letter is inserted from Sir James Bland Burgess, in which that gentleman observes, that " his great excellence was chiefly shewn in conversation, in which his entertaining powers were unequalled. Those who lived most with him, could best appreciate this: but this like Garrick's acting vanished with him, and no adequate representations of it can be conveyed to posterity." As a most appropriate comment on this passage, Mr. Mudford has quoted the opinion of Mr. Hewson Clarke, a gentleman connected with him in the London Review, and the confidential friend of Cumberland, and his intended biographer. That the vicissitudes of fortune should have prevented their intercourse for the last six months of his life, we fervently regret,

The colloquial efforts of Mr. Cumberland were in " no degree above the ordinary level. He was not peculiarly distinguished for the profundity of his detached observations, or the brilliance of his occasional repartees; to warm or extended argument he had an invincible aversion, and nature had denied him the polished fluency of his friend Sir James Bland Burgess. He never *led* the conversation of his social circle, or sustained its vigor by the animation of his influence. Yet his casual remarks, when they were not distinguished by acuteness or brilliance, were characterized by that terse felicity of expression which constitutes the chief excellence of his memoirs: if he did not predominate in conversation, he gave relief to the colloquial contests of more ambitious speakers; and if he seldom poured forth the treasures of his own intellectual stores, he displayed peculiar dexterity in the formation of hints, and the application of questions, that might call into display the natural or acquired endowments of his friends."

"It may account in some degree for the extent of his colloquial reputation, that his deportment was in the highest degree impressive and engaging. The smile that played upon his lip embellished many a common-place sentiment; and the graceful yet dignified elegance of his address, gave weight to opinions, that from a less favored speaker, would have been received with contemptuous silence, or acquiescent indifference. Though a Johnson might in the presence of Cumberland have felt his own superiority, he would not have ventured to display it: even while he unconsciously unveiled the less amiable features of his character, he averted the resentment of his auditors, or softened their dislike by the fascination of his manner; and those who could not but acknowledge his susceptibility to the minor vices, were astonished on reflection at the coldness of their dislike and the reluctance of their condemnation."

"He was so fond of flattery himself, that he believed it to be acceptable to his friends, even in the most disgusting form or the most exuberant proportions. He was the easy and delighted dupe of every juvenile parasite, who found it convenient to barter adulation for patronage: and the first number of the London Review bears melancholy evidence, that his own fame and the gratification of the public, were not of sufficient importance to outweigh the grateful drivelling, or the fawning meanness of a youthful protegé, who " melted his last guinea into a picture-frame, for his honored portrait to be hung as a reverential monitor above his chimney-piece."

That these observations are correct as far as they extend, the testimony of every friend, and the internal evidence of all his compositions conspire to prove: his pages are crowded with reciprocations of compliment, and with eulogies that have no apparent purpose but to court return. In proportion, likewise, as he valued praise, he was alive to censure: no man felt more acutely the sarcasms of the daily journalists, or the reproaches of criticism. To evade them, was the great business of his life; and his writings are therefore pervaded by a tone of candor and of tenderness towards others, which sometimes degenerates into affectation, and may sometimes be unjustly mistaken for hypocrisy. If in the contest with Lowth, and on one or two less important occasions, he ventured to expose himself to the hostility of literature, he did not forget, in any of these instances, that he came forth in a cause of all others the best calculated to awaken the sympathy and the gratitude of his contemporaries. The champion of a Bentley against the calumnies of jealousy and ignorance, no sooner advances to the charge, than he is hailed by the united welcome of the hosts of literature.

His desire of pleasing was indeed so strong, that scarcely an hour elapsed, in which its operation did not subject him to the charge of insincerity. He complimented every individual whom he met, without being conscious that he did so; and when he only exercised the common privilege of discussing the conduct and describing the characters of his casual acquaintances, he falsely appeared to be guilty of gross and deliberate hypocrisy. But there was no design in what he did: his compliments were like the superscriptions of his letters, matters of course; and his opinion of the individuals whom he censured were seldom regarded by the circle to whom they were addressed, as trespassing beyond the bounds of propriety and justice.

It appears to the writer of this article, however, that envy was no feature of his character. Allow him that praise to which he conceived his own attainments entitled; (and compared with the expectation of authors in general his claims were moderate,) he would readily confess the superiority of his literary contemporaries. His jealousy did not proceed from uneasiness at the success of others, but was the result of fear for himself: admit his own pretensions to the throne, and he cared not by how many rivals it might be shared.

Had Mr. Clarke been enabled to finish the sketch he has drawn, he would in all probability have relieved its darker tints, by many touches of an amiable character. In Cumberland the love of praise was only equalled by the warmth of his friendship and the ardor of his gratitude. His flatteries were at the command of every one; but his professions of service were never made but in the spirit of sincerity, nor without being followed by fulfilment. The enthusiasm with which he engaged in whatever could conduce to promote the fortunes or exalt the reputation of his friends, would have redeemed more numerous and less venial errors than those which entered into the composition of his character. His habits of life were a model of propriety to the gentleman and of elegance to the scholar. His piety was fervent without ostentation or austerity; and in his domestic relations he displayed a sensibility of feeling, and a constancy of affection struggling with ingratitude, that would have done honor to any character however ennobled by genius or by virtue.

It only remains for us to repeat our thanks to Mr. Mudford for the instruction and entertainment he has afforded us, and to recommend his volume to all who delight in critical speculation, to whom the literary history of the eighteenth century affords a subject of interesting enquiry, or who wish to add to their selection of literary anecdote.

STOCK JOBBING CLERKS.

Sir,

The examination of Ambrose Charles, by Mr. Garrow, on the late trial of Mr. Walsh, is probably within the recollection of all your commercial readers. On that occasion it appeared that although but a clerk in the Bank of England, his check for 20,000l. was paid into Walsh's bankers. The same person is principal adviser and acting broker to one of our present sheriffs. It would appear therefore that the following notices posted up in the Transfer offices and the Rotunda is merely exhibited to lull the people who frequent them into security, and without any intention of putting it in force.

" No clerk of the Bank of England is permitted to act as a broker or jobber in any of the public funds.

By order of the directors,

" T. Best, Secretary."

There is much more danger to be apprehended from the interference of the clerks in jobbing and brokerage transactions, than your readers might at first sight suspect they have access to the bank books, and of course have it in their power to inspect the accounts of every individual, and ascertain the value of their stock. This knowledge gives them a very unfair advantage in the market, and might possibly lead to the embezzlement in conjunction with confederates, of the unclaimed stock and dividends of others.

It is somewhat singular that the real or pretended disclosures of Mr. Charles respecting the stock transactions of Lord Moira, should never have become the regular subjects of public investigation. For some time we heard of nothing but vengeance against the unfortunate clerk, and indignant innocence on the part of his lordship; but the subject dropped without the punishment of the former: what its termination may have been with regard to the latter it is not for me or my brethren to conjecture.

A Citizen of London.

BENEVOLENT INSTITUTIONS.

Sir,

The old adage that charity begins at home, having at length been erased from the catalogue of English maxims, I beg leave to submit to your consideration the subjoined outline of a plan,* which promises to possess in a greater degree than any other which has been yet proposed, the necessary requisites of enormous expence, insurmountable difficulty, and decided inutility. To invent a scheme of charity that shall be easily executed, and productive in proportion to the sums expended in its prosecution, is within the power of common individuals; but to become the father of a project that possesses all the excellencies demanded by the benevolent and fashionable world, is a task beyond the powers of any man less versed in speculation than the individual who now addresses you. I have the honor, Sir, to be a member of the Missionary Society, a director to the Auxiliary Bible Society, one of the committee for Promoting Christianity in the East, and a coadjutor with the Rev. John Owen in many laudable undertakings. To elucidate the principles therefore, on which every successful project of benevolence is now conducted, you cannot but admit that I am qualified: and as in the multitude of your avocations, you may have been prevented from investigating this important subject, you will probably thank me for indulging at some length in its elucidation.

In the first place, Mr. Editor, in order to render a plan of benevolence acceptable to the public at large, or to the religious part of it in particular, it is absolutely necessary that it should be directed to the benefit of distant nations; to liberate our suffering fellow citizens from prison, or contribute to the relief of domestic distress, is unworthy the benevolence of men, whose philanthropy embraces the whole of created nature; who are as

---

* This plan does not appear to be original, or we should have inserted it. Ed.

much for a New Zealand savage as for a British artist struggling with adversity; who, excited by the noblest feelings of humanity, would rather subscribe to the spiritual necessities of a Laplander, than save an English beggar from perishing by hunger. To administer to the wants of the poor of our own country is a common, and vulgar practice: exalted minds own no distinction between their native soil and the dominions of a barbarian monarch, unless it be to the advantage of the latter. We are all brethren in the flesh; and why should one of our brethren be dearer than another?

2. No scheme of benevolence can be constructed on a *legitimate* plan, which does not sacrifice the most useful and attainable objects to those of which the benefit is problematical, and the success uncertain. Enterprize in a good cause is characteristic of genius and of virtue. In proportion to the degree of risk, is the energy by which any important object is conceived, and the intrepidity required to effect its execution. There is no merit in relieving virtue in distress by the benefaction of a five pound note, because this is a common duty, and easily performed. When an individual bestows his donation on a charitable institution for the circulation of religious books among the Hindoos, he is certain that he will never witness its effects, and doubtful whether it can ever be productive of substantial benefit. To the praise of magnanimity, therefore, and of a noble superiority to pecuniary considerations, he may justly advance his claim. Though thousands of our fellow Englishmen be immured in prison, and afflicted with disease and poverty; though our hospitals be crowded with the afflicted, and our alms-houses with the destitute; of what consequence is this to a fanatical philanthropist, whose nights are past in dreaming of the salvation of the Caffrees, and whose days are employed in shipping off new editions of the scriptures, that may by some miraculous event escape the dangers of the sea and the fury of the Bramins, to be admired for the beauty of their

characters, and serve to line the wicker boxes of the Hindoos? If many thousand pounds be expended in fruitless endeavours to convert the Hindoos to christianity, when a smaller sum would have diffused throughout our own country the means of present and of future happiness, who can deny to the subscribers, the praise of benevolence that stops not to consult with prudence, and enthusiasm, that leaves sight of its own country to visit on romantic wing the shores of Asia and the wilds of Africa?

3. But thirdly, no plan can be regarded as legitimate which does not testify the ardent attachment of its supporters to the established religion of their country. The filial piety of the members of the establishment is not testified at present by attendance on the sick, by friendly admonition to their less reverent parishioners, or by an unwearied and conscientious discharge of their duty as ministers. To attend a Bible society is more commendable than to visit the cottage of the poor; to harangue the committee of an institution that may possibly convert a heathen to christianity in less than twenty years, is thought more praiseworthy than to exert yourself honestly and effectually to excite the zeal and confirm the faith of those over whom you possess the authority of a pastor; and an incoherent speech from the chair, is a brighter testimony of your merits as a clergyman, than a sermon from the parish pulpit. If a reverend gentleman enters into the support of legitimate institutions with considerable warmth; if he leaves his parish to the guidance of a curate, and hastens to town to mingle in speculation and political controversy; if he writes letters to Lord Teignmouth when he ought to be expounding the catechism; he immediately becomes an elected champion of the church, and may look forward with certainty to a bishopric or a deanery.

4. From this it naturally results, that no benevolent institution is legitimate, that will not lead to a warm and extended controversy. Opposition excites attention to

the scheme, affords the projectors the wished-for opportunities of scriptural and oratorical displays, a plausible pretext for an appeal to the patriotism of the community, and the materials of strong and popular resolutions. The doctrines and principles that have been attacked in parliament may be defended from the pulpit: cruelty, injustice, persecution may be laid to the charge of the opposing party; and forbearance, intrepidity, christian charity, and compassion for infatuated infidelity, assumed by the legitimates.

Yours, truly,
CANTAB.

That many of the subscribers to the different societies for the promotion of christian knowledge and the circulation of the Bible are influenced by other motives than a regard for the interests of religion, or the welfare of mankind, it would be worse than affectation to deny; but that the majority of those who have chiefly distinguished themselves in their promotion and establishment are influenced by the noblest feelings of religion and benevolence we can assert from our personal knowledge of their characters. It is in the spirit of friendly remonstrance therefore, rather than of censure, that we would wish to recal them from the error of their ways. It appears to us that admitting the urgency of converting the Hindoos, or circulating the scriptures among the boors of Lapland and the savages of Russia, and supposing the possibility of executing these objects to an extent not utterly disproportionate to the exertion it demands, their prosecution is productive of evils more than counterbalancing any possible good that may arise from their success. The exertions of the Bible Society and of all similar institutions have an irresistible tendency to weaken the principles of practical benevolence, to dissipate in romantic and imposing schemes of extensive and universal charity, those feelings of sympathy in the sufferings and anxiety for the welfare of our fellow creatures, that would otherwise be testified in the relief of domestic misery, and the alleviation of that distress which daily and hourly occurs to individual observation.

The clergy are at present acting on those very principles that they once so honorably and rationally opposed when proceeding from the school of Godwin : they lose sight of that practical good which is immediately before them, in the pursuit of distant and possible advantages : in their love for mankind, they forget what is due to themselves, and to the unfortunate members of that community of which they are the spiritual teachers. It would excite our laughter, if it did not awaken our indignation, to observe that among the liberal subscribers to the Foreign Bible society, there are to be found more than one of those very clergymen of the diocese of Durham, who lately solicited the contributions of the public towards the education of the orphans of their deceased brethren, and who thought proper to reply to the spirited attacks of Mr. Burdon, by asserting their incompetence to support the charity without the public assistance. It is surely the duty of these gentlemen, and of many others whose conduct is marked by similar inconsistency, to look at their own parishes, and examine the state of their own funds, before they yield to the energy of enthusiasm for the spiritual welfare of the Hindoos: the clergyman who cannot spare his guinea, may fulfil the purposes of benevolence by the devotion of his time; and it would be more creditable to the profession, as a body, if the sons of the clergy were to be supported by their own contributions and exertions than by the benevolence of the christian laity. As the fact stands, however, the clergy combine to diffuse instruction among the Laplanders, and leave their own poor to be supported and educated by the bounty of the public.

Were we to estimate the intellectual character of the age by the principles upon which its exertions for the circulation of the scriptures professedly proceed, it would be natural to suppose that the English nation had reverted to its original ignorance, that any sophistry however fallacious was acceptable to the public mind, when its apparent tendency was to promote the interests of the clergy, and that the excellence of charity was not supposed to depend on the objects to which it was directed, or the means by which it was carried into effect, but exclusively on the enthusiasm of its promoters. That to circulate the Old and New Testament is to diffuse the knowledge of christianity, is the fundamental proposition on which all societies for the distribution of the scriptures necessarily rest their claims to public encouragement. Yet nothing but the blindness of frantic zeal could prevent them from discovering its absurdity. The Bible only contributes to the instruction and edification of mankind, when the reader is prepared for its examination by previous acquaintance with the authority from which it is derived and the purposes for which it was given to mankind, and directed to its most important doctrines and most useful precepts. To put the Bible into the hands of a savage is to make him a present of which he knows not the origin, abounding apparently in contradictory statements; containing innumerable allusions, histories, and discussions, which without other knowledge he cannot understand. His imagination will naturally be captivated by those portions of scripture that are the most marvellous in narration, and the most striking in effect: the exhortations of our Saviour will excite no interest compared with the death of Sampson, and the appearance of the spirit of Samuel; what is useful will awaken no enthusiasm, and the abstruse will be neglected for that which is entertaining. But if the Bible be accompanied by a preliminary address, stating that the scriptures are the gift of God, that our Saviour was born in the reign of Augustus, and other facts of equal importance, the necessity of auxiliary aids is at once admitted; and no Bible society should be established unless its funds are adequate not only to the circulation of explanatory books, but to the support and establishment of spiritual instructors. Were the directors of the present institutions however to confine their exertions to those parts of the world where the objects of their bounty have received the benefits of a christian education, and where the materials of instruction alone are wanted, their efforts would not be applicable to the censure that we have applied to their actual conduct; and could only be objected to on the general principle, that they should do what they are able at home, before they direct their exertions abroad. Let them remember that the individuals whose exertions chiefly contributed to any object that might justly have been regarded as paramount to every other the abolition of the slave trade, did not devote themselves to the emancipation of the suffering Africans till they had first fulfilled their duty to their neighbours; and that in the prosecution of their mighty undertaking they were never seduced to the neglect of those humble virtues that distinguish the genuine christian from the ostentatious philanthropist.

COUNTERPART TO THE WARM CHILD.

OUR readers will recollect we had to notice a few months back, the ill luck which befel a Nottinghamshire divine, in not being able after *seven* different summonses to perform the ceremony of baptism upon a child *while it was alive*, though the distance was not two hundred yards from his own door. We did not apply the *thong* on that occasion, hoping a gentle hint would have been sufficient. Contrary to expectation, however, it appears that a parishioner of his in the country being in the very last stage of mortality, wished for his consolatory attendance on the Sunday after the usual duty of the day had closed. The wish was imparted to him—No—he could not possibly stop then—had urgent business—to-morrow—to-morrow he would come on purpose.—To-morrow came—and with it also came the parson—he alighted, went into the house, and exclaimed—I am come at last.—*Come!* says the house-keeper in a tone and manner too emphatic to be misconceived; "Why—surely—I hope—dear me—I hope you don't blame me?" "Not blame you! ifeckins but I do," says the woman. " Well but—well but—can't I just

peep at him—perhaps—perhaps—" " None of your per-
hapsing here," says Margery; " I tell you he has been stiff
and cold these seven hours, and you should not play any
of your fool's tricks with him, poor soul, even if he *were
warm.*"

A NOTTINGHAMSHIRE MAGISTRATE.

THE APHRODISIAN SOCIETY,
COUNCIL-ROOM.

SIR,

THE opening speech at the beginning of the present
session has excited considerable attention among the admirers of the lovely marchioness. So neat and appropriate an oration has not been delivered within the
memory of woman. In eloquence it surpasses the speech
of the regent's commissioners, and its adaptation to the
present crisis of affairs is the subject of general admiration. Since my last report several interesting questions have become the subject of debate; but as it is my
purpose to contribute to your entertainment rather than
to weary you by a full detail of proceedings, I have
contented myself by transmitting you the opening
speech, and the substance of last night's debate.

Jan. 1st, 1812.

SPEECH OF THE PRIORESS OF ⸻, *ci-devant* PRINCESS
OF P⸻.*

The abbess has directed me to signify to you the
satisfaction with which she has observed that the exertions that have been made to extend the empire of
adultery, have proved completely effectual; and that on
several occasions in which the few remaining adherents
of virtue and modesty have continued to oppose her progress, the reputation already acquired by yourselves and
your companions, has been gloriously maintained.

The successful and brilliant enterprise which terminated in the conveyance of Lady A. to the habitation of

---

* See the opening speech of the present session of Parliament.

her paramour, is highly creditable to the exalted female under whose guidance it was conducted, and has contributed materially to obstruct the designs of those enemies to conjugal independence, whose operations had so lately excited apprehension and alarm.

The princess is assured that while you reflect with pride and satisfaction on the conduct of our fair coadjutors, and of our fashionable allies in these various and important services, you will render justice to the consummate skill displayed by the Duke of ——— at the opening of the campaign: not only has he conduced in a considerable degree to the defeat and discomfiture of the infatuated individuals who had sought for immediate safety under the banners of virtue and decency: but he has likewise contributed to the erection of an impenetrable barrier against the future introduction of those once formidable enemies into the immediate vicinity of our residence, and has laid the foundations of a general system of morals and religion, that may equally conduce to the universal emancipation of mankind, to the legitimate triumph of female freedom, and the firm and undisputed pre-eminence of adultery.

The princess trusts that you will concur with her in her anxiety for the establishment of her sister Licentiousness; she confides in your known attachment to her person, for the suggestion of such means as may contribute to her future splendour; and for the provision of such resources as may be sufficient to support the dignity of her crown, and the stability of her empire.

The princess has ordered the estimates of the current year to be laid before you. She confides in her faithful subjects for the grant of the requisite supplies, convinced that they must feel how much depends on the copiousness of her treasury, and the punctual fulfilment of her financial engagements. Great as have been the expences of legal contention, and enormous as have been the late demands on the compromising fund, she perceived with satisfaction that her calls on the fortunes of her subjects rather tended to stimulate them to more ardent and enthusiastic efforts in her service than to restrain their ardor or dispirit their enthusiasm.

The princess is fully satisfied that under whatever calamities her loving subjects may be doomed to exercise their fortitude, or to whatever privations they may be subjected by the chances and vicissitudes of war, they will on all occasions be ready to contribute to the support of their Irish allies, and always willing to remunerate their services. She feels herself the more confirmed in this from observing that the most distinguished of her beloved votaries have always been the warm advocates of Catholic emancipation from the tyranny of husbands, and the uniform friends of extreme unction and auricular confession.

Outlines of a Debate on a Motion of Lady H—— H——, that Females above the age of seventy-five years be hereafter declared incapable of election as Members of the Aphrodisian Society.

Her grace of ———— rose. She hoped that in rising to support the motion of her honorable friend, whatever might be refused on the score of incapacity, would be granted to experience. She had made the laws of intrigue the study of her life, and presumed to suppose that in their practical application, there were few whose exertions had been more unremitted or conspicuous. She could not but look back with a mingled feeling of sorrow and delight, to the period when her studies were guided by the experience of a Grosvenor, and her enquiries into the nature of man assisted by the practical sagacity of a Kennedy. She could not pretend to so long or so patient an investigation of abstract points, as some of the ladies who might feel disposed to continue the debate; but of things in general, she ventured to assert that not a single member of that honourable room could boast of a more perfect or more accurate acquaintance. To the privileges of woman, she had always been a decided friend; without the enjoyment of personal liberty existence was nothing better than a blank; it would be more desirable that the female part of the world should not exist at all, than be restrained by the tyranny of man from exerting their corporeal as well as their mental faculties to their utmost extent of action: slavery was more insupportable than death; and for her part, she would rather relinquish the name of woman, than consent to a paltry compromise of privileges which nature had bestowed, and nothing but the hand of death should take away.

It had indeed been objected to her as a member of the coterie, that she had already advanced to a period of life, when the activity of bodily exertion might appear in some degree disproportionate to her powers, when she might be expected to retire from the gaze of public admiration, and resign the hopes and fears, the gaieties and the sorrows of the amorous world, to younger and more blooming rivals. But she felt that it would be dishonourable to herself, and unjust to those individuals of an opposite sex, who had hitherto experienced the steady guidance of her friendly hand, and who reposed in unsuspecting confidence upon her, to withdraw herself at the present crisis from the service of the public. She confidently hoped that in that assembly no one could be found who would merely suffer the period of female exertion to be limited by the tyranny of man, or who would not fulfil the duties of her sex, so long as the vital spark gave animation to the frame, and the warmth of honest feeling circulated through the veins. No one in that assembly she was convinced had a more intimate acquaintance with mankind in general; and more perfectly ascertained how far on common occasions they were inclined to go; how great was the eagerness of the opposite sex to enter into the private affairs of unfortunate woman; how much they were inclined to lay upon them the most odious burthens. The lady who had just sat down, had very poetically assured the room that the couch of conjugal love was a bed of roses: for her part, she had been accustomed to beds of *down*, and *pah! tricks* had been played by her companions on camp beds within her recollection, but the couch of wedlock was rather a bed of thorns than a bed of roses; and it was only from the free and flowing wings of Cupid that she wished to pluck the materials of a bed of feathers. Old age stood in need of comfort and indulgence, rather than demanded those restraints which may be politically imposed on the young and inexperienced practisers of intrigue. Here her ladyship recapitulated the history of antiquated love, from the days of Semiramis to those of Ninon D'Enclos. She descanted with considerable warmth on the pertness and precocity of the present generation of female striplings; not indeed that she objected to any practices that might conduce to the extension of female freedom, but she felt it her duty strongly to object to a monopoly. She flattered herself that she had been able to *betstow* as much happiness in the young noviciates of the present day, as could be derived from communication with any of those youthful rivals who had attempted to appreciate her pretensions. She was certain that in selecting her as the object of his sarcasm, the Editor of the Scourge was in a great measure unacquainted with the extent of her capacity, or the warmth of her benevolence. She suspected that on these occasions he was apt to draw a long bow, and was convinced that had he felt the secret movements of her soul, his gratitude and his gallantry, would equally have precluded him from indulging in severities, that must necessarily compel her to deny him entrance to her premises; and she could not but observe, that the mention of herself might be a future bar to his own accommodation."

Here Lady A. arose and exclaimed I know not what the lady may mean by her allusion to female striplings, but this I know, and this I will assert, that little as I am, {I have a soul as superior to vulgar restraints as that lady herself, or any other member of this room, whatever may be the magnitude of her personal dimensions. It would ill become a female descendant of the house of ——— to shrink from competition with any female in the warfare of intrigue. My years are few, but my progress has been rapid; my stature is diminutive, but pigmy as I am, never have I seen nor ever do I expect to see the man, in whose presence I should be afraid! Under the auspices of my beloved mother, I studied the arts of intrigue, and with the sanction of my husband I have reduced them to practice. Let not the dowager of 70, therefore despise the bride of 23! let her follow her accustomed pursuits with the dignity that becomes her age and station, suffer me to proceed in her steps as fast as time and circumstances will permit. The question itself is in my opinion a very stupid one. It is worse than folly to debate on subjects that no one of our time conceives to be deserving of a moment's notice.

"Love free as air at sight of human ties,
Spreads his light wings, and in a moment flies."

Who now a day marries for love, or talks of fidelity as a virtue? Let every fashionable pair, regulate their lives by the principles that regulate myself and my husband, and farewell to jealousy, and all the miseries of marriage. His companions endeavour to obtain my favor, and can I do less than express my gratitude, by introducing him into the circle of my female friends? He is enraptured by the humble beauties of my female attendants, and I retain in return the privilege of trifling with his steward. When a damsel is sent to wait on my person, he is seated in my boudoir, and signifies by signs his approval or dissent. When he has occasion for a coachman, he consults my taste. Life glides away in all the felicity of reciprocal obligation; he is grateful for my services, I forget and forgive his infidelity."

The speech of Mrs. ——— was peculiarly effective. Ladies, (she exclaimed) it be all wrong. I do protest that it grates upon my feelings like the string of an untuned harpsichord. I hate people to be strumming on one instrument. I do love variety of pieces. I am quite willing to swear that it is the direst nonsense, no better than tweedle-dum-dee! a fiddlestick for the virtue. A very bad player. I care for not any body. My money is in all the funds, and no duchesses will have so much in a year, as I do use to have from that *Daily*. Mr. —— has got some French-horns. Softly sweet in Lydian measure. So my lady, the speakers all have crotchets, that is flat!

HISTORY OF THE ASPLAND HEIRESS.

Chapter I.

The house of Aspland had been for many ages distinguished above the other families of Europe for the bravery of its sons and the beauty and the virtue of its daughters. From the paltry vassal of a feudal tyrant, the first of the lords of Aspland rose by his own merits to precedence above every courtly rival, and from the lowest extremity of indigence, he succeeded in the acquisition of treasures more extensive than those which enriched the coffers of his sovereign. The bravery of his descendants extended the possessions he obtained, and the charms and accomplishments of the female branches of his family, secured by the ties of nuptial alliance whatever accessions of honor or of wealth might be the reward of hereditary valour. The last of the lords of Aspland succeeded, therefore, to his father's dignity undisturbed by competition, in the full and quiet possession of arbitrary power and exhaustless wealth: proud in the contemplation of his own security, and looking forward with the ardor of ambition to the extension of his own domains by incroachment on the possessions of his neighbours. For many years, however, he was doomed to repose in fretful inactivity: the nobles who surrounded him exhausted by former dissensions, and remembering with feelings of sorrow and humiliation the consequences of mutual variance, evaded every pretext of quarrel, and listened to his martial exhortations with sentiments of compassionate indifference.

At length the vassals of a neighbouring lord grated by the remembrance of wrongs inflicted on their ancestors, awakened to a sense of their rights as men, and emboldened by the easy and timid character of their master, arose as with one spontaneous impulse, demolished the prisons in which so many of their ancestors had expired, imprisoned their lord himself, and proclaimed the laws of subordination and the dependance of man on man, to be the productions of folly and the instruments of despotism.

The neighbouring lords alarmed at the progress of principles so dangerous to their own authority, and despising the undisciplined rabble who had thus torn from rank its splendor and from justice its insignia, marched forth at the head of their vassals to chastise the insurgents. The lord of Aspland was selected as the leader of their forces, and scarcely had he arrived at the borders of Lord Francis's domains before he published a proclamation denouncing the severest punishment on his rebellious retainers, unless they immediately returned to their allegiance; proclaiming vengeance against any of his vassals who should treat him with injury or insult, and assuring them that severity or kindness should be displayed by the bands who advanced to reduce his vassals to their former subservience, in proportion as they treated their unfortunate master with reverence or contumely. Irritated by so insulting a declaration, apparently inconsistent not only with their own declarations of independence, but with the common rights of mankind, all their enthusiasm was now directed to the expulsion of the hosts of their invaders: excited at once by the frenzy of revolutionary ardor and by the desperation natural to ignorance operated upon by fear, they sallied out from the palace that had been so lately the scene of their atrocities, and laying aside the badges of servitude for the weapons of the soldier, not only repelled their enemies from the boundary of their lord's domains, but carried a fierce and destructive warfare into the possessions of their enemies.

Immediately opposite to the main land, on which was erected the family seat of the house of Aspland, stood the paternal inheritance of a good old gentleman, whose ancestors had been unanimously invited by the owners of the land to live over them as guardians and protectors. This old gentleman was not like the lords of the main land, absolute master of the lives and properties of his tenants; but received a reasonable allowance from the produce of their labours for his care in watching over the general welfare, and his administration of equal justice between the rich and the poor, the haughty and the humble, among his tenants. He was blest with a large family, and his eldest son was now arrived at a time of life, when nuptial connection was likely to be productive of benefit to the family, and of happiness to himself. In a meeting, however, that was annually held between the old nobleman and his tenants, for the management of general affairs, and for promoting the good of the estate, it had been agreed that as the marriage of his lordship's offspring with the daughters of his tenants might be the occasion of much mischief and confusion, by elevating the tenants to an undue influence over their master, or by causing improper connection between the young noblemen, and the daughters of the yeomanry, no marriage should be contracted by them unless with the daughters of the nobility, whose estates laid along the shore; or stretched into the interior of the main land. This agreement, however plausible as it might seem in theory, had already been productive of many pernicious effects. Unable to marry the objects of their affections, the young lords either seduced, and then deserted them, or took them to their continued protection, and burthened the country with an illegitimate offspring. The morals of the tenantry were soon corrupted by their example, and have been in a progressive state of degeneration, since the promulgation of the compact.

The eldest son however of Lord G—— had involved himself in a debt beyond the prospect of extrication; when it occurred to his father's steward, that by the prospect of their liquidation, he might be induced to amend his manners, and consent to the formation of a matrimonial engagement. The proposal was made and accepted. The heiress of the house of Aspland was chosen as the partner of his bed; the steward was a man of great talents, and uncontrollable influence at the castle of W. He had persuaded his master to take an active part in the quarrel between the combined lords and the vassals of Lord Francis; he had witnessed with gratitude the zeal and bravery of the Lord of Aspland, though he regretted his discomfiture; and he thought that by the projected alliance he should give new life to the energies of the allied combatants, and reward the services of their most active leader.

One of his lordship's chaplains, therefore, was chosen as the messenger of the heir's proposals, which were received with joy by her father, and with acclamation by his vassals. But the heiress of Aspland felt no emotion but the anguish of despair. An Irish gentleman, a visitor at her father's palace, had long been the possessor of her affections: her father forbade the continuance of their intercourse, and her paramour was exiled from the domains of Aspland. But no terrors of human authority will dismay the courage or restrain the enterprize of love. Though her father had entrusted her to the care of an old and vigilant duenna, though her attendants were threatened with the severest visitations of his displeasure, should they be seduced by negligence or interest to the surrender of their trust, and though the appearance of B—— himself subjected him to the vengeance of a man whose personal intrepidity was only equalled by his insensibility to all the softer emotions of the heart, yet in the dead of night he found his way to the chamber of his mistress, persuaded her to assume the disguise of a page, and to fly on the wings of love and hope beyond the verge and the power of her father. Afraid of discovery, and conscious that their appearance on the highways would lead to immediate detection, they sought their course over desolate moors, and through almost pathless forests, till they had arrived within a few miles of the estate of a nobleman to whom B—— had long been endeared by his virtues, and whose favor he had secured by his various services. They had retired for repose beneath a woodmans shelter on the verge of the forest, when the emissaries of the lord of Aspland stole upon their slumbers, and regardless of the shrieks of the female and the bribes of her protector, bore them to the separate vehicles provided for their conveyance. Surrounded by guards, they were escorted to the palace of Aspland: on their return, the lover effected his escape. Between the period at which the messengers were dispatched and that of their return, the chaplain from the lord of the island had received his credentials: to silence the rumours of his vassals the princess appeared in the balcony of his palace, the chaplain was amused by tales of indisposition, even the officers of the castle believed the relation of the late adventure of the heiress of the house of Aspland to be the invention of calumny, or the offspring of romantic volubility.

The chaplain was a man of exemplary rectitude and of the most acute discrimination; his austerity of manners at once overawed and repelled the female into whose hands he had been commissioned to deliver his credentials; she repaid his apparent hauteur and incivility, by a cold and formal reception of his compliments; and though the chaplain remained in ignorance of her previous attachment, he transmitted to his friends a description of her person, that without forsaking every outline of resemblance, was at once the theme of disgust and ridicule to the ladies of their *island*. Among these the mistress of the heir and her antiquated friend, a female capable of any wickedness, and versed in every description of intrigue, were delighted by the chaplain's information; and resolved to convert it to the furtherance of their respective purposes. The titled matron obtained permission to proceed to the domains of Lord ——, for the purpose of attending the destined bride in the barge prepared for her for passage across the waters. She knew that she had to practice her arts on frankness, thoughtlessness and inexperience. Caroline though still impressed with the memory of B.——deserved every praise but that which is due to sexual purity. The commander of the barge was a personable man; the matron was skilful in the erection of opportunities; and the son of Neptune was said to have succeeded to the honors of the soldier. The matron concealed her discoveries, and patiently awaited till the time should arrive when the disclosure might be productive of benefit to the discarded mistress.

With what pomp the marriage ceremony was performed, or how loud and sincere were the testimonies of joy that resounded from every part of the domains of Aspland, the aged remember and the young have heard. The matron still continued her assiduous attendance on the bride; and under the pretext of exhibiting her to her destined husband in the most attractive form of insular beauty, she arrayed her person in all the display of studied deformity.

DOGGREL ATTACKS ON THE REGENT.

Sir,

Among the other absurdities which the present state of the law of libel involves, it is not the least remarkable that while beneath its sanction, the most trivial offences may be punished with severity, the most gross and infamous abuse of the liberty of the press may be committed without any fear of legal retribution. As the various statutes on this subject are now constructed, an individual may be imprisoned three years for a theoretical declamation on the subject of military flogging, while he may insult his sovereign and vilify the most exalted characters with impunity. If ever these observations required any proof of their correctness, they would be afforded by the undisturbed circulation of the infamous libels that under the titles of The Royal Sprain, the Three Royal Bloods, the Ghost of the Royal Stripes, &c. have lately obtained an extensive circulation among the lower orders of the people. To represent the prince as a coward and an adulterer; to persuade the subjects of his father that the court at Carlton-house is the receptacle of the vilest profligacy and the most disgusting indecorum; to extend the impression that every branch of the family is alike destitute of prudence and of virtue, is not only the evident design but the inevitable tendency of these compositions. They do not affect the language of remonstrance, they are not addressed to the intelligence of their readers, nor do they censure the conduct of the exalted persons whom they attack with that discriminative satire which admonishes without insult, and corrects without degrading: they forget even the courtesies of expression, and detail the supposed conduct of the Prince in terms as gross and vulgar and impertinent as if they sung the exploits of a Johnny Gilpin. But their effect is not to be measured by the degree of excellence they exhibit: they have a powerful influence on the lower classes; they render the names of our princes first familiar and then contemptible; they teach the peasant and the artizan to regard a court as a temple of debauchery, and the chief magistrate of the country as a drunken profligate, who passes his time in the violation of every moral duty; regardless of decency and destitute of shame.

The rapacity of booksellers and the necessities of the manufacturers of doggrel have no limits, and they have conspired therefore to invent for the edification of the people of England, an account of a pretended amour of the P——e Regent's, with L—— Y——; of the discovery of the parties in *flagrante delictu*, by his lordship, and of what they elegantly call a *milling match*, which terminated in the infliction of two *black eyes* on the heir apparent. The ignorance of these miserable scribblers, respecting the present situation of the Yarmouth family, is so deplorable as almost to surpass belief, and absorb anger in compassion. But the falsehood of their tales is beyond the reach of detection by those for whom their productions are intended; that they should be told *in print*, is sufficient to attract their curiosity; and the mischief of these works does not so directly proceed from the story itself, infamous and degrading as it must be considered, as from the language in which it is detailed, and the allusions by which it is accompanied.

The first, and decidedly the least disgusting of these productions, is entitled The Royal Sprain. How well it is calculated to accomplish the purposes I have described will appear from the subjoined extract.

> The Goddess wrapp'd the lovers in a cloud,
> And gently drew them from the pressing crowd,
> To rooms where mirth and noise dar'd not intrude,
> Sacred to solitude,
> Well suited for voluptuous joy—
> Paintings that would a Stoic warm,
> Where beauty stretched her naked form,
> And wantoned with the archer boy,
> Lighted anew the breast's impetuous fires,
> And gave new fuel to unquench'd desires.

The poet then tells us that there is a dame yclept Suspicion; and that,

> This lynx-eyed demon had possessed
> Poor Yarmouth's lordly breast;

He marked the progress of the cloud,
  By all besides unseen,
And slow and sullen left the brilliant crowd,
  For well he knew the Cyprian queen;
And as the goddess to the skies withdrew
  While the warm lovers nothing coy,
  Indulged in every wanton joy,
Indignant Yarmouth started to their view:
Not greater horror mark'd sad Jordan's face,
  When rumour told her that her prince was base;
  Not greater pangs the duke's round phiz distorted,
  When all his schemes on wealthy *Long* were thwarted;
  Not greater dread the murderer's breast can tell,
  Who sees the rough chalked gibbet in his cell,
  Than that which chill'd young Cæsar's ramping blood,
When his much injured *friend* beside him stood.
Yarmouth had lately gained much fame,
  Where Jackson daily holds levee,
And champion Crib, illustrious name,
  Plucks the ripe fruit from honor's tree.
Where pugilistic science deigns to sit,
  Teaching young sprigs of greatness how to hit.
Forgive your prince, affrighted Cæsar cries,
  And dropt upon his knee,
  With such becoming sweet humility,
  Well tim'd to check fierce indignation's flow,
  And turn a less relentless foe.
  Up! up! says Yarmouth, scurvy poacher,
  Mean, chicken-hearted, sly encroacher!
  Who under cloak of royalty
  Thus with protected game makes free!
  Give me redress —— d——your eyes!
Whether the Paphian goddess was afraid
  To meet the injured Peer's reproof,
Or at the key was picking up a shilling,
  She kept her lovely form aloof,

While the sad cause of all this sad transaction,
  Swiftly retreated from the scene of action,
And Jove the second *gain'd* (!) a decent *milling*.

The whole of this story it must be confessed is unusually edifying; but the description of Lord Y.'s supposed pursuits, and the preceding ascription of ardent friendship for such a man, to the prince, must have a pretty tendency to exalt the latter in the estimation of the people.

In one part of the work we are told with *a sneer*

  Of princesses, queens, and such like sacred things,
  Names which the vulgar greatly should regard.

The aforesaid Humphrey Hedge-hog is certainly the most decent animal of the three; yet though his quills have been shot at fashionable life, he evidently knows not the distinction between a *rout* and a suite of rooms.

  Young Cæsar (meaning your royal self no doubt,)
  Was pleased most kindly to attend a rout,
  A sort of fashionable court,
  To which nobility resort,
  A *place* which painted belles and titled wantons
    use,
  Not much unlike the vulgar stews.
  Yes! Yes! these routs are most convenient *places*,
  Teeming with rich varieties of faces.

The *Royal Bloods* presents us at the outset with a specimen of pastoral poetry.

  'Twas in the blooming season of the spring,
  When birds began to ply the busy wing,
  The shrill-ton'd lark up rose and loudly sung,
  As scarcely visible, he fluttering hung.
  The ploughman now began his daily toil,
  And travelled slowly o'er the rugged soil,
  Forth fondly musing on her sweetheart's vows,
  The rosy milkmaid seeks her lazy cows,

> And carrols out the song he loves to hear,
> When work is past, and evening skies appear;
> When at her parents' humble cottage door
> He tells the tale he oft has told before.

We are now introduced into the bed-chamber of the Duke of York, and entertained with a soliloquy, in which he pronounces his brothers to be fools and blockheads.

> Plain as a tradesman was his highness drest,
> Not e'en the glittering star upon his breast;
> The regimental clothes, his greatest pride,
> Had from *necessity* been laid aside;
> Necessity which cost the warrior dear,
> And changed his drink from claret to small beer,
> Reduced his equipage from twelve to six,
> And *played up* sundry other curious tricks.

He now pays a visit to the *Premier*, who advises him to oppose the restrictions, and thus regain the favour of the Prince.

In page 15, the opposition are represented as asking the Prince Regent not for places and pensions, but for the necessaries of life.

> Out at the elbows are our patriot suits,
> And much in want are we of shoes and boots;
> Worn are our breeches too to rags and tatters,
> That now they scarcely hide our private matters.
> Much do we wish our stock of shirts t'increase,
> Having amongst us scarcely one a piece;
> We therefore beg your highness will arrange
> That we your servants may receive a change.

The story now begins. The Prince is seen on his journey to Oatlands, in company with *feather-bed* M. M. who is converted into the medium of a puff to one of the author's former libels.

> And much ability did M. discover,
> In stabbing that new piece the R——l L——r;

> A work, quoth he, no more like Pindar's writing,
> Than volunteer reviews resemble fighting.

Dinner is announced, and among the party are L—— Y—— and his lady! The author of the Royal Bloods ventures in this part of his work to contend with the immortal writer of the Royal Sprain. But who shall decide between these sons of genius?

> Amongst the ladies who at O——ds dined,
> Was one whose person far excelled her mind;
> Fair as a lily was she to the view,
> And like a rose-bud tipt with morning dew.
> Upon the female, thoughtless, gay and young,
> The P——'s eyes with studied fondness hung;
> The lady though a married one too plain,
> Returned the R——t's amorous looks again.

The next stanza represents his R. H. as willing to sacrifice every law of honor, friendship and hospitality to the gratification of his passions.

> His highness saw whilst making his advances,
> By the soft intercourse of wishful glances,
> 'Twould not be difficult to *gain his ends*,
> If he could blind the husband and his friends.
> At length an opportunity is found,
> Whilst mirth among the company goes round;
> By stealth the lady and the Prince withdrew,
> A step which both have special cause to rue.
> Unnoticed Y—————— every motion eyes,
> Whilst in his breast the furious passions rise;
> At distance follows to a private place,
> Which proves the public scene of sad disgrace.
> Scarce had the P——, our virtuous R——t, prest
> The trembling female to his R——l breast,
> When with a sudden crash the fastenings flew,
> The door bursts open, Y—— stands in view.

To these stanzas succeeds a new version of the milling match, which rivals that of his predecessors in truth and eloquence. The brothers are sent for, and after due consultation,

> The plan's approved, and ushered to the papers,
> That G————'s pain proceeds from cutting capers;
> And now the R——t and his *love-sick* brother,
> With kindness strive to comfort one another.
> G————e listens to his brother's mournful tale,
> And feels his pity and his love prevail;
> Cl————e weeps over G————'s late defeat.
> And G———— makes Cl———— Admiral of the F————t.

The last of these productions is entitled " The Ghost of the Royal Stripes, which was prematurely stifled in its birth in January 1812.. By Jeremiah Juvenal." It is asserted by the friends of the bookseller, that a confidential friend of the exalted personage intended to be ridiculed, not only bought up the whole impression of the original work, but paid one hundred pounds for its suppression. The story is in every respect incredible, but the circulation of such tales is of some benefit to the vampers of catchpenny pamphlets, and may obtain for the rhymes of Mr. Juvenal a profitable circulation among the " cits of London and the boors of Middlesex."

Jeremiah Juvenal, Esquire, is resolved to imitate the example of his ancient name-sake, and to indulge in the description of wickedness, with a gust proportioned to its enormity. Not content with representing the R————t as a drunkard and an adulterer, he depicts him as a ravisher.

> The tables groan'd beneath the weight
> Of costly food, and costlier plate;
> And hungry lords and ladies seated
> With ready zest the dainties greeted.

En passant, that the lords and ladies did not stand during their meal is an important and curious *item* of information.

> At length the hour of bliss drew nigh,
> The hour of mirth and jollity;
> The glittering groups in pairs advance,
> Eager to twine the mazy dance.
> Apart the Prince surveyed the fun,
> And quizzed the beauties one by one,;
> But fairest of the dazzling fair
> Yarmouth's young dame still triumphed there.

In this part of the composition a confidential friend of the prince, a gentleman of high honor and accomplished manners, is introduced in the respectable character of a p———p.

> Now *Mac*, dear *Mac*, the Regent cried,
> Go lead my willing prize aside,
> That we may give a loose to pleasure,
> And beat quick time to love's soft measure.
> *Mac* sought the fair and led her strait,
> To rooms of solitary state,
> Where not a sound disturbed the scene,
> But all was silent and serene.
> Soft and sly G———e slunk away
> Homage at Cupid's throne to pay.
> Careless of honour, mirth and fame,
> Thoughtful alone of Yarmouth's dame.
> The dame afraid how she should fare,
> Had scarcely closed her secret prayer,
> When G——— rushed in, by love inspir'd,
> And *Mac* with modest bow retired.

After a long game at cross purposes, the P——— exclaims,

> Two ways appear, fair lady chuse,
> One you must take, or one refuse;

Be kind and speedy in your choice,
Your fate depends upon your voice.
I ask that love my hopes to bless,
Which I by force may soon possess;
Chuse then to give what I require,
Or strength shall second my desire.
The lady then astonished stood,
Regardless of the Royal Blood,
And said " for ever I shall scorn
On Y———h's brow to plant a horn."
" Then thus," at length the Regent cries,
" Thus will I seize my valued prize,"
He said, and in his pr———ly arms
He locked the dame and all her charms.
But careless of his rank and grace,
The lady scratched his royal face.
While thus the war of words ran high,
And anger flashed from every eye;
Sudden the door wide open flew,
And Y———h stood confessed to view.
The peer's indignant feelings rose,
And words were soon exchanged for blows,
No rebel eloquence he tries,
But boldly blacks the gallant's eyes.
Enraged the lover met his *doom*,
From Y———h's cane, unfriendly boon,
Till his bruis'd H———s, faint and sore,
Stretched his fine form on the floor.

Of Mr. Juvenal's scholarship let the reader judge from the following specimens:

Thy simple worth, dear *Mac*, alone
Outways the value of a throne.

In vain the P——— *assay'd* to eat;
His stomach loath'd the unsavoury meat.

On the whole this attempt at satire of Mr. Jeremiah Juvenal, is a very *Agg*-ravated *Agg*-ression on public decency.

Sir Robert Walpole was accustomed to say, " Give me the exclusive privilege of writing ballads for the people, and I care not who are their ministers." Pamphlets like the Royal Sprain and its successors, of which the purpose is to degrade the great, and vilify the good, afford abundant gratification to the discontented, who anticipate a change in the present order of things; to the envious, who would wish to see the great and the noble reduced to the same level with themselves, and to the wicked, whose convenience it may suit to divert the indignation of the world from their own vices, by directing it to the indiscretion of their superiors. That very absence of every poetical excellence which renders them so contemptible in the eyes of the educated classes recommends them to the vulgar, who are better pleased with the mere jingle of the rhyme, and the plain expression of scandalous assertions, than by all the embellishments of poetical fancy and classical allusion. That productions like these should be counteracted by other means than the terrors of legal vengeance, must be the wish of every rational patriot; but it is still more to be desired that the forbearance of the crown lawyers may be consistent, and that while they overlook the ribaldry of a deliberate libeller, they will not persecute the warmth of hasty but honest independence.

JUSTUS.

THE WIDOW FAIRBUR, or, DISCOVERY upon DISCOVERY.

SIR,

SINCE the far-famed exhibition of Mr. Coates, the whole town has been occupied in enquiries respecting the widow Fairbur. Mr. Coates himself is too disinterestedly benevolent to know any thing about the fair object of his charitable exertions: westward of Temple-bar no such lady has been seen, and it is certain that the receipts o the ever-memorable night were not expended in the city. The name of an unfortunate widow, who for any thing I knew might be both young and beautiful, and willing, called every feeling of gallantry into action in the bosom of your humble servant—I first sought her, therefore, at the boarding-schools, and proceeded regularly from the genteel seminary at Blackheath, to the polite academy at Putney; in this line of pursuit, however, my search was fruitless, and I then bethought me of the alms houses for clergymen's widows, but after having wearied myself and alarmed the sisterhood from one end of the town to the other, I received in return for my labours a most desperate flagellation from a young sprig of clerical whippism, who told me that poverty ought to be a protection from insult, and that my curiosity would be best rewarded by a visit to King's place, I took the hint, but even there they knew not where the widow Fairbur was to be found: a wag informed me that she was an *old woman*, and might be found among the magistrates; I went to Bow-street, and while listening to the examination of an unfortunate culprit, was equally astonished and delighted by hearing a person next me whisper to his friend, " there is the widow Fairbur." Breathless with " delighted impatience," I turned me round; but conceive my astonishment and mortification, when in the person of my wanton and buxom widow, I beheld a being drest in male attire, of a dark and malignant countenance, in the dress of a dirty fop, and with the manners of a pick pocket. Pray, said I, can you inform me what is the profession of that lady, or why she assumes the features (for I supposed them to be artificial) of a man. " As for the motives of the fair widow," he replied," there is no disguise that she will not assume for a few shillings; and with regard to her history you may satisfy your curiosity by calling at the Three Tuns in —— street, where she is the member of a literary society, and recites her productions every alternate evening to an assemblage of fashionable and literary characters."

On making the requisite enquiries, Mr. Editor, I found that the assemblage of fashionable and literary characters consists of a barber, a bricklayer, and the widow Fairbur. She is a constant attendant at the theatre, manufactures theatrical critiques for a morning newspaper, and recite them after they are composed, for the edification of her pair of auditors. She is very fond of introducing her children, by a lady named Thespis, to the attention of her social circle, (if circle that can be called which lies between two points,) and is sometimes so infatuated as to introduce their Pin-basket for the general amusement. Her first brats, though evidently bastards, were sprightly children enough; but the offspring of her later years have been miserable abortions: though their parent hugs their dead and deformed carcases with affectionate fondness, and is never so happy as when she can persuade a good-natured stranger to take a peep at the dear delightful progeny.

The widow Fairbur was once, I am informed, a painter of red lions and golden bulls for the Bonifaces of Middlesex: flattered by success in this department of the fine arts, she betook herself to the sketching of miniatures, and afterwards combined the skill of the painter with the taste and science of the dramatic critic. She was long notorious as a bully, and frightened those who were afraid of her criticisms into the purchase of her pictures. A gentleman named Gifford, however, came forth to chastise her knavery: the widow appealed to the protection of the law, but finding that her character was too well known to the gentlemen of the bar, she fled to America, where, strange to say! she married a wife, who she soon afterwards deserted, forgetting not, however, to take all imaginable care of the lady's property. She returned to England under the protection of a deluded watchmaker, and since her arrival has obtained the necessities of life, by "spunging on dirty w——s for dirty bread" (Epistle to Peter Pindar.); by extorting dinners and dollars from the dramatic performers; by flattering the follies and participating in the vices of theatrical coxcombs, and by all the other combined arts of puffing and cajollery.

She is a determined toper: gin and purl are her favorite liquors; cribbage her favorite game, licentiousness her favorite pursuit. Her person is filthy to an almost inconceivable degree, her habitation as uncleanly as her person, her mind as polluted as her habitation. Without honesty, shame, or decency, she has long been the outcast of mankind, and the object of disgust and contempt even to the mean and profligate wretches with whom she is condemned to enjoy her evening potations.

I am credibly informed Sir, that *she* has lately assumed the distinction of LL.D. and gives herself the airs and graces of a literary character. Into the nature of her pretensions I shall make a full and immediate enquiry, of which you shall be acquainted with the result; and for the present, in the hope that the preceding particulars will partly satisfy the public curiosity,

I remain,
Your very obedient servant,
London, January 29th, 1811.   INQUISITOR.

Mr. GILLET AND Mr. STOCKDALE.

In the fourth number of the Scourge we inserted an advertisement of Mr. John Stockdale, reflecting in very severe terms on the conduct of more than one individual connected with the premises destroyed by fire in Crown-court, and apparently insinuating certain unpleasant charges against Mr. Gillet in particular. That the remarks which accompanied this advertisement should have excited Mr. G. to commence an action against the supposed proprietors for a libel, will account in some degree not only for our subsequent return to the subject, but for the difficulties that opposed themselves to its investigation. It is with pleasure, however, that we now declare our firm conviction that the advertisement alluded to was not intended to apply to Mr. Gillet; that if it had been intended to apply to that gentleman, it would have been the vehicle of gross injustice; and that the actual loss of Mr. Gillet by the destruction of his premises, was nearly equal to treble the amount of his insurance.

To the Editor of the Scourge.

Sir,

In your last number of the Scourge, No. 13, Jan. 1, page 34, while reviewing a new quarterly publication, you have ventured to assume, " from internal evidence," and to announce to your readers, that I am a principal contributor to that review; and upon the strength of such assumption you have very kindly given me some friendly advice.

It is not in my power to make my acknowledgments for such advice, because it happens that your assumption is ill-founded. Neither shall I make a single observation upon the critical acuteness you have evinced in assigning to a particular individual any contribution to a work, which, to this hour, he has never seen.

My business is, therefore, necessarily of a more serious kind. Your positive assertion has not only done me *an actual injury* in my professional pursuits; but it is also calculated to do me much more among professional men. For it was made in *direct contradiction* to a solemn declaration made by myself, *two days* before your number appeared; wherein, on relinquishing my course as a periodical writer, I stated to the public, and for the information of gentlemen in the law, that I am totally unconnected, in any shape whatever, directly or indirectly, and that I intended inflexibly to maintain my determination, to remain for ever unconnected with any political or periodical literary work of any description whatsoever.

Now, Sir, your assertion goes to the extent of falsifying flatly what I have as flatly disclaimed, and therefore of impeaching my veracity. When I gave up the editorship of " the Weekly Political and Literary Review," in consequence of my having been called to the bar last term, I not only assigned the reasons why I deemed it improper to connect myself, thenceforward, with any political or periodical publication; but I also declared that from that day, I had no interest, share, property, or connection, directly or indirectly, in any such works; and that it was my inflexible determination never more to connect myself with them. Nevertheless you have roundly appointed me a principal contributor to this New Quarterly Review, which you have been criticizing. I have a right, therefore, to request, that you will, in your next number, do me the justice, which is the least you can do, to do away the ill impression which your paragraph has excited, of retracting your assertion; and that you will let the contradiction appear in as conspicuous a part of your work, as that in which your misinformation appeared.

To put the matter out of doubt, I here again declare, that the new review, to which you allude, I have never seen in my life; that I have never directly or indirectly written a single article or line for that review or for any other; and that I am as ignorant as a child unborn, who are the proprietors, editor, or contributors to it.

If I had designed to have told a direct falsehood to the public when I renounced my review, there are circumstances which have occurred, that would have made it impossible for me to have carried on such hypocrisy. For, besides the ill state of my health, for many months, incapacitating me from such pursuits; I am labouring under an heavy domestic loss, which altogether disqualifies me from embarking in such undertakings.

I trust, therefore, Sir, that you will not hesitate to give me an assurance, that the present representation, will be duly attended to in your next. I am, Sir,
Your obedient humble servant, H. R. YORKE.

THEATRICAL REVIEW.

Nullius addictus jurare in verba magistri;
Quo me cunque rapit tempestas deferor *hospes:*

Opera House and Pantheon.

THAT the Opera-house under its present system of management is merely an apology for a place of fashionable concourse, is acknowledged even by its most regular visitors, and cannot escape the attention of the most casual spectator. Without the ability to attend in person to the direction of the establishment, or the inclination to engage at a liberal salary subordinates of talent and experience: the management of the theatre has been long entrusted to a combination of meddling, superficial, and profligate individuals, who possess neither the requisite acquaintance with dramatic affairs, the property that might secure them from temptation, nor any motives to personal exertion. The only novelty that has appeared since the commencement of the season, had nearly been sacrificed to the emptiness of the treasury: the most delightful ballet that modern taste has produced, was robbed of its effect by the coarseness of the scenery, and the inaction of the machinist; and the progress of every stage exhibition, whether new or old, whether excellent or contemptible, is marked by a languor of movement, corresponding with the slow and uncertain application of the pecuniary stimuli.

Tremanzzani already acquainted with the necessity of positive stipulations, and determined to enforce their fulfilment, refused to appear until the manager should comply with his just demands. His place was supplied on the first night of the performance by Signor Righi, who appeared to as much advantage as could be reasonably expected. The critic of the Morning Post, however, resolving to testify how frequently he attends the theatre, and with how much impartiality his praises are bestowed, expressed the next morning his satisfaction at the performance of Tremazzani, a satisfaction only diminished by observing that he appeared to labour under some remains of his late indisposition. His perverseness has in all probability enabled him to accomplish his intentions, and he has now returned to that station which he has occupied in former seasons, to the gratification of the public, and to his own credit and emolument.

But besides that the expected reversion of the management to Mr. Waters, may remove every ground of immediate complaint, and render the Opera-house in the course of a few months in every respect worthy of the fashionable patronage, its present state affords no excuse for those who endeavour to impose on the credulity of the public by specious but unfounded pretexts, or are themselves the easy and deserved dupes to the artifices of necessitous adventurers. If the subscribers to the Pantheon and Mr. Greville himself be the victims of their own rashness, let them at once abandon the design instead of injuring the other theatre without any possibility of benefiting themselves; and let them not by wilful misstatements of the progress of the building incur the disgrace of falsehood, in addition to the disappointments attached to inconsiderate ambition. They cannot be ignorant that Mr. Greville obtained the supposed licence from the chamberlain's office on condition of returning it; that he forgot the condition; that admitting its validity it does not authorize the entertainments they have announced that it expires in July; that there is no prospect of its renewal, and that the building cannot be completed. They have no funds; nor if they had, could they proceed in their speculation without an act of parliament. Half of the space intended for the stage is tenanted by a lawyer: from this gentleman they purchased it for fifteen hundred pounds, of which they agreed to pay down one third, and the two remaining thirds at convenient intervals. When the time of paying the second instalment arrived they *were short of cash*; and in a day or two afterwards it was discovered that Mr. Mayo had misinterpreted the conditions of his lease and sold the property of others. An injunction has been issued by the real proprietor of the ground, and this " *national structure*" must be opened, if it be opened at all, with half a stage. With what deliberation and how profound a knowledge of the subject they have conducted their operations may be conjectured from the simple circumstance, that after the audience part of the theatre had been completed, they were obliged to request a celebrated architect to examine into its construction, and inform them whether it was likely to support the weight of a crowded audience!

It will be seen by the subjoined statement, which ought to be received with the caution that is due to *exparte* representations, that the subscribers lay great stress on the alledged acknowledgments of the Lord Chamberlain of the validity of the licence after it had been transferred to their disposal. But whatever may be thought of the expedience of the chamberlain's conduct, his right to demand the re-delivery of an informal document, or of a licence improperly obtained, cannot be disputed. He might be willing to wave this right, so long as no disposition was evinced on the part of its possessors to affix to it a meaning which it does not express, and beneath its sanction to encroach on the rights and injure the property of others. Observing as he must have done the willingness of the subscribers to stretch it as far as might suit their own convenience, he cannot be blamed if he at once reclaimed the document itself as the most effectual mode of preventing its abuse, and of evading the trouble and degradation of an epistolary contest.

In answer to a letter from the proprietors of the theatre, requesting a meeting with the vice chamberlain, the following letter was, we understand, received:—

"Hill-street, Jan. 11, 1811.

" Lord John Thynne presents his compliments to the proprietors of boxes at the Pantheon Theatre, who have honoured him with a letter, requesting to have some conversation with him on the subject of Mr. Greville's licence; but having been under the necessity of declaring it null and void, and it being impossible for him to know of any person concerned in it except Mr. Greville, to whom alone it is granted, no conversation could lead to any beneficial result. Nothing can be done until Mr. G. returns the licence to the Lord Chamberlain's office.

" The proprietors of property boxes at the Pantheon Theatre."

In answer to which, the proprietors sent his lordship the following reply:—

" Pantheon Theatre, Jan. 11, 1812.

" My Lord,—It was with great surprise that the proprietors of boxes at the Pantheon Theatre have learned from the answer your lordship did them the honour to give to their note of the 9th instant, that the licence granted by your lordship to Mr. Greville, you now consider null and void. Such a declaration coming after the correspondence which passed on the subject of the licence between your lordship and the proprietor of it, in which the powers and authority of the licence were repeatedly acknowledged and confirmed by your lordship, does appear to them to have been made without your having brought to your recollection that correspondence, and given sufficient consideration to the situation in which the proprietors have been placed in consequence of it. The proprietors therefore beg leave to make the following statement:

" That at a meeting of noblemen and gentlemen called for that purpose, Mr. Greville exhibited a licence obtained from the Lord Chamberlain's office, and to the following effect:

" I do hereby give leave and licence unto H. F. Greville, Esq. to have burlettas, music, and dancing; also dramatic entertainments performed by children, under the age of seventeen years, from the 30th day of July next to the 30th day of July, 1812, at the Pantheon in Oxford-street, within the liberties of Westminster.—Given under my hand and seal, this 29th day of June, in the 51st year of his Majesty's reign.

JOHN THYNNE, Vice-Chamberlain.

" ' Entered, William Martin.' "

Afterwards, from the explanation called for by Mr. Greville as to its powers, your lordship, in the following letters, gave to that licence a confirmation:

(EXTRACT.)

" Hill-street, July 15, 1811.

" Sir,—This result of the investigation has reinstated Mr. Mash in his office, and taken off the suspension of your licence, which I request you will consider now as again to be in full force. (Signed) J. THYNNE.

" H. F. Greville, Esq

(COPY.)

"Lord Chamberlain's Office, August 23, 1811.

"SIR,—I have the honour to acknowledge the receipt of your letter of this morning. As I cannot imagine that the terms of the licence granted to you are in any degree equivocal, I must beg to decline any explanation upon the subject, by referring you to the instrument itself for every information you can possibly want.—I am, &c.
(Signed) "T. B. MASH.
"H. F. Greville, Esq."

The noblemen and gentlemen, who were present at such meeting, with several others, on the faith of that licence, confirmed and strengthened as it was by the above explanatory correspondence, were satisfied with it as an authority under which they might safely advance their money. Mr. Greville is the sole proprietor of the licence; but upon the faith of that licence alone they have advanced considerable sums. The licence, therefore, now remains as the only security for the advances they have made, and which have been all expended under it.

From these circumstances they must submit it to the equity of your lordship, whether they can, at this distance of time, and after so much sacrifice and expence have been incurred, be called upon to surrender the only security they hold for the large advances they have made.
(Signed by the PROPRIETORS.)
Right Hon. Lord John Thynne, &c.

"Lord John Thynne presents his compliments to the proprietors of boxes at the Pantheon, in answer to their letter of the 11th instant; begs to inform them that his letter of the 15th of July, was written, during the time of Mr. Mash's suspension, and consequently, when he was ignorant of the circumstances under which the licence had been obtained. He has seen Mr. Mash, who informs him that his letter of 23d August, was written in answer to one from Mr. Greville, respecting the performance by children.

"Lord John Thynne can only repeat, that nothing can be done till the licence is returned to the Lord Chamberlain's office.---Hill-street, Jan. 13, 1812."

In answer to this from his lordship, the proprietors gave the following reply:

"Pantheon Theatre, 17th January 1812.

"MY LORD.---In answer to the letter we have had the honour of receiving from your lordship, we have to regret extremely, that we are under the necessity of again trespassing on your lordship's time; but the injury threatened to ourselves, and the ruin to so many others who have embarked such considerable sums on the faith of your lordship's authority, force it upon us as an imperious duty.

"We must ever regret, that from any circumstances, your lordship should have been deprived of the knowledge of the transactions of your office, and that even when one clerk was removed from that office, information should have been withheld from you by all others. But we must also deeply lament, that from the month of July, when Mr. Mash was restored, until the month of December, a period during which (as might naturally be expected) the whole capital now risked was embarked, there should have been no communication whatever made upon a subject threatening so much ruin to all interested, as the present declaration, that the authority which had existed for so long a period is null and void. Distressing as these circumstances must be felt by all of us; we cannot but exonerate ourselves from every species of blame. Unconnected with your lordship's office, and ignorant of its regulations, we could only look to the officers who filled its situations, as reponsible for the observance of its rules; and we could in no instance have conceived that we could be made sufferers for the non-observance in others of the serious duties imposed upon them. Contending, as we always must, that upon those officers alone is imposed the charge of observing that every regulation is complied with necessary to the valid issue of every instrument from the office, with which they are charged; or that if any should be issued, wanting in such compliance, that it should be immediately recalled, instead of being allowed to become a means of serious injury to all those who may give credit to its apparent validity. Whether the attention of Mr. Mash was directed by Mr. Greville to one of the powers of the licence, or to all, appears to us of no importance whatever. Mr. Mash's letter of 23d August, distinctly recognises the validity of the instrument to which he alludes, for your lordship will see the impossibility of that instrument's being valid in one sentence, and invalid in another.

"Having stated these circumstances, we must again call upon your lordship's equity and justice to reconsider the penalty now threatened upon us for having been guilty of no impropriety whatever: but on the contrary, for having only relied with implicit faith upon an instrument bearing your lordship's authority; and we must hope, that the justice, with which we feel satisfied we are pleading, may induce your lordship to consider the extent of injury you may inflict, and so relieve us from the necessity of surrendering the only security we are possessed of, for the large sums of money ourselves, and others have embarked upon the Pantheon Theatre. We are still forced to look to your lordship's letter of the 15th of July, as a distinct avowal of the validity of the licence to which it refers; for your lordship will hardly call upon us to take into consideration the omission of your lordship's deputies, or to consent that such omission should invalidate your own declaration, that from the date of that letter, the licence was to be considered as being in full force; but if more was necessary, we should beg leave to refer your lordship to your letter to Mr. Greville of the 23d of August, (one month after the reinstatement of Mr. Mash in his office, and two months after the period when the licence was granted,) in which your lordship states to Mr. Greville as follows:

" Bay Cliffe, August 23, 1811.

" SIR—The licence you have, is exactly similar to that which was granted you by Lord Dartmouth, in the year 1808, and consequently must give precisely the same powers.

I have the honour to be, &c.
(Signed) " J. THYNNE."
" H. F. Greville, Esq."

" We have always looked upon these letters from 'yourlordship, as a distinct confirmation of the valid existence of the licence. We have implicitly relied upon them as authorities upon which we might safely embark our money; it must now remain for your lordship to decide, whether we have properly placed our confidence. We have the honour to be, &c.

(Signed by the PROPRIETORS.)
" Right Hon. Lord John Thynne, &c."

There is something in the management of theatrical concerns well calculated to excite the petty ambition of all who have neither talents for any kind of business, nor credit sufficient to insure their reception into the confidence of more honorable men than the traders in patents. That the subscribers to the Pantheon are in general men of character, fortune, and abilities is known to every one; but that they have been cajoled or deceived by individuals whom no considerations of prudence can withhold from dramatic speculations, nor any sense of shame or gratitude divert from the most flagrant impositions on the public credulity is equally notorious. Were not the vain ambition of becoming the arbiters of national taste, and the directors of the national amusements, the predominant excitement to interference in theatrical concerns, we should not have occasion to witness so many deplorable examples of voluntary involvement in the multiplied difficulties that they so frequently induce.

A new opera was announced for this evening under the title of "the Virgin of the Sun," but the indisposition of Miss Smith has compelled its postponement till Friday. Its title implies that it is one of those splendid productions in which the dramatist yelds precedence to the scene-painter and the mechanist; and truth, nature, and morality are sacrificed to magnificence of scenery, and richness of decoration. We have often asserted, and must again repeat, that the introduction of *spectacle* on the stage of Covent-garden is more frequent and obtrusive than even expedience can justify. We are convinced that an adherence in a more considerable degree to the legitimate drama would remunerate the managers as liberally as their present system; and if it would not, the admission of the fact is at once an evidence of the evils of monopoly: it proves that instead of two large theatres many smaller ones ought to be erected; of which the exhibitions should be particularly specified. Even under the present patent we are assured by a law officer of eminence, that Mr. Astley or any other gentleman has the full power of obtaining an injunction against the introduction of living animals on the stages of Covent-garden or Drury; and if this be too invidious a task for a private individual, is it not within the jurisdiction, and would it not be creditable to the patriotism of the lord chamberlain?]

Of the dirty and obscene animal that is now exhibited on the stage of the " first theatre of the world," it need only be said, that by the majority of the audience its absence would gladly be dispensed with. Its odour does not remind the spectators of the fragrance of Arabian gales, and on this account, and from the disgust excited by its filthy appearance and unusual stupidity, their sentiments have been expressed in a manner the most general and unequivocal. To those who take delight in such a spectacle, we recommend a visit to the Surrey-theatre, of which the chief bestial performer is far more intelligent, cleanly, and entertaining than that of the Covent-garden boards.

CONTENTS.

TO CORRESPONDENTS, see back.
NEW MODES OF RAISING A REVENUE; OR, VICE v. TAXES 173
Infidelities in high life........ 174
Calculation of their number... 175
ON THE PAST AND PRESENT STATE OF OUR ECCLESIASTICAL ESTABLISHMENT. 176
Industry and zeal of the reformers 177
System of church preferment... 178
Distribution of patronage...... 179
Rise of Dr. M———........ 180
A reviewing parson............ 181
Modes of clerical preferment... 182
AN ENSORIAN ESSAY ON SOMETHING: MEANING ANY THING, AND PROVING NOTHING. 183
Distinction between queens and queans...................... ib.
Phiz-iological discoveries.... 184
Folly of teaching virtue 185
India proved to have no existence 186
Mr. Ensor's learning exemplified...................... 187
PUBLIC INSTITUTIONS. The Antiquarian Society......... 188
Ancient and modern antiquaries compared................. ib.
Mole-ism of Antiquaries..... 189
The Antiquarian Society described..... 190
Mr. Carlisle's merits as a secretary...................... 191
Dissertation on a tea-spoon.... 192
Proved to be of great antiquity. 193
THE WHIPS.—No. II.
The carnivorous Colonel 194
His travels from Wales 195
His military exploits......... 196
Col. Greville's courage......... 197
MISS RAFFLE'S PARTY, OR THE FESTIVITIES AT DOUGLAS HOUSE......... 198
A law lord's perplexities....... 199
A fashionable groupe........ 200
The hon. Mr. D to his love.... 201
The Marquis to his dearest Polly. 202
Her perfections............. 203
A ROYAL IMITATION...... ib.
A royal duet................ 204
THE REVIEWER. No. IX.. 205
Salmagundi: or the Whim Whams and Opinions of Lancelot Langstaff, Esquire, and others. Reprinted from the American edition, with an introductory Essay, and explanatory Notes, by John Lambert......... 205
Mr. Lambert on the American character................ 206
Merit of their prose compositions. 207
Mr. Langstaff's literary talents. 208
Character of an English traveller.................. 209
His reception in America..... 210
Rises to the summit of fashion. 211
Is sent to prison 212
Tommy Moore and the Americans 213
American fashions.......... 214
THE POLITICAL OBSERVER, No. VIII. Correspondence between the Prince Regent and the Duke of York..... 215
The Prince Regent......... ib.
His retention of Mr. Perceval.. 216
The sentiments of Lord Grey... 217
The Prince's proposal declined. 218
Motives of the Regent's conduct. 219
His change of sentiment accounted for............... 220
Pride of the Grenvilles........ 221
Policy of the Spanish wars. 222
Hypocrisy of opposition...... 223
A junction recommended...... 224
The Regent's conduct to the catholics................ 225
Lord Castlereagh............. 226
Sir Vicary Gibbs............ 227
The Pittite system........... 228
THE TEARS of SIR VICARY!! 229
Tyrants great weepers......... 230
The opposition lament......... 231
Friendly consolations......... 232
Lord Grenville's miseries...... 233
TO HIS GRACE THE LORD ARCHBISHOP OF YORK. 234
Dangers of the church......... 235
Clerical farming illegal........ 236
Ecclesiastical privileges........ 237
Appeal to the archbishops...... 238
RE-APPEARANCE of THOMAS PAINE 239
Paine redivivus............. ib.
Clio Rickman's policy......... 240
Disingenuousness of Paine. 241
His acuteness and veracity...... 242
CUMBRIAN TRANSFORMATIONS, or LOVE and METHODISM................ 243
Village adventures............ 244
An equivoque............... 245
Mr. Squintum's progress...... 246
Becomes a dear man.......... 247
Mr. Squintum's preacher...... 248
Youthful grace.............. 249
The infant Wesley............ 250
THEATRICAL REVIEW..... 251
State of New Drury........... ib.

NOTICE TO CORRESPONDENTS.

Veritas will very particularly oblige us by sending the longest of his communications at an early period of the month, as we wish to authenticate many of the topics necessarily introduced by a reference to historical documents. Will he do us the favor of appointing the time and place of interview, by a note addressed to X. Y. Z. at our publisher's?

The Duke of Norfolk turned Potatoe Merchant is inadmissible.

The memoirs to the Sicilian Courtezan have extended to a length so unexpected and inconvenient, that we must reluctantly postpone their insertion for another month.

The admirable Essay on Constitutional Fictions and the Errors of the Scotch Political Reformists, has no other fault than its prolixity. We shall be happy to return it for curtailment.

The paragraph from the Morning Chronicle, on the Canting Society; the case of Colonel Brown; Colonel M'Mahon and the Widow's Pensions; and Wellesley versus Canning, or Intrigue upon intrigue shall meet with attention adequate to their merits.

The collection of Inscriptions at the Seat of Alexander Davison, Esq., in Northumberland, is extremely imperfect, and contains nothing worthy to be submitted to the notice of our readers.

Lady A.'s enquiry was so evidently the offspring of other motives than curiosity, that we received her messenger with suspicion, that her subsequent explanation has had no tendency to allay: her gratification now depends on Mr. D—— himself.

The Royal Society, and the other Public Institutions, will become, in rotation, the subjects of our critical and political investigation.

We had expected to gratify our readers by a number of the Hypercritic, on the last Number of the Edinburgh Review; but it is beneath our censure: the falling-off is equally striking and unaccountable.

THE SCOURGE.

MARCH 1, 1812.

NEW MODES OF RAISING A REVENUE;
OR,
VICE *versus* TAXES.

SIR,

Your repeated attacks on the politics of the whig-leaders, have excited the most "vivid emotion" in the bosoms of themselves and their partizans. The friends of Lord Grenville assure the public that your observations are not *bottomed* on a good foundation; Mr. *Brand* is all on *fire*; Lord *Grey* never takes up your pamphlet without looking *blue*; the *Temple gates* are ordered to be shut against you; Mr. Sheridan (*mirabile dictu!*) eyes your pages in *sober* sadness; and it is no less true than pitiable, that your sheets have a very dull sale among the friends of the opposition; because they are of true British texture, without any intermixture of materials from Holland. Alarmed by the symptoms of despair that they have lately exhibited, and well aware that unless they return to power, they will never be able to afford out of their paltry sinecures of 20,000*l.* a year, or out of those reversionary grants which they so kindly condescended to accept from their gracious sovereign, even the most trifling remuneration to their faithful partizans; my thoughts have been long directed to the invention of a scheme, that might counterbalance in some measure the distrust of the Prince, and the hatred of the people. My labours (heaven be praised!)

have at length been rewarded by success, and I am enabled to submit to my patrons a proposal which shall not only command their immediate restoration to office, but secure its inheritance to them and their heirs in perpetuity.

It will appear, on a moderate calculation, that of the matrons of high life within the immediate circle of the opposition alone, about one fourth have been detected in conjugal infidelity: that of the *friends*, old and young, directly or collaterally connected with the opposition families, one third have violated their vows of chastity, or forgot to make them; that each married female has at least a new paramour weekly, and each virgin changes the object of her sighs and lamentations once a month. Now, Sir, since nothing can be done in this age of political and financial œconomy without the aid of arithmetical computation, let us suppose the number of matrons to be about 10,000, and that of the virgins, 36,000; dividing the former number by 4, and the latter by 3, we have the number of adultresses, 2500, and of unmarried incontinents, 12,000. Multiplying 2500 by 52, we have 130,000 for the number of *crim-con-ists* in a year; and performing the same operation with the figures 12,000 and 13, there arises a product of 156,000 for the number of simple *lovers*. Now, Sir, I beg leave to propose that it should be considered as a point of honor in the fashionable circles, that each matron should contribute to a fund established for the purpose, and called the Matron's Fund, 5*l*. before every change of her paramour; that 10*l*. be given to the " Spinster's Fund, " established on the same principle, on the same account; and that attached to the respective establishments, a licence office should be erected, at which should be kept a correct register of the names of the male and female parties, with the date of their commencement; and that 10*l*. be paid on admission at each of these institutions, and 5*l*. annually. After these suggestions have been attended to, Mr. Editor, and the expences of the buildings defrayed by public subscription, what remains but to devote the receipts to the purposes of bribery and corruption? Of the immensity of the revenue, permit me to convince you of the subjoined calculation.

Matrons. Changes. Fine.   { annual deposit in the
2,500 × 52 × 5l. = 650,000   matron's fund.
Virgins. Changes. Fine,   { annual deposit in the
12,000 × 13 × 10l.=1,560,000   spinster's fund.
               Total   ——————
                                                         2,210,000

Again:

         156,000 Simpletons.
         130,000 Crim. con.-ists.
           2,500 Matrons.
         12,000 Spinsters.
         ——————

Total   300,500 ×   10l. Admission = 3,005,000l.
Which suppose renewable only every four years,
                         and we have annually   750,125
Lastly 300,500 persons × 5l. annual licence = 1,502,500
                                                              ————
                        Total annual receipt £4,461,625

I need not suggest to you, Mr. Editor, that the preceding scheme is susceptible of many amendments and improvements. Penalties might be inflicted on the production of children; double-adulterers, or married men cohabiting with the wives of others, might pay double, &c. But imperfect as the system in its present state may be regarded, this hasty outline will shew the important consequences of which it may be rendered productive; and in the mean time recommending an enquiry of a similar nature into the resources of the ministry and the Burdettites,

         I remain, your obedient servant,
                                     CALCULATOR.

London, Feb. 12, 1812.

ON THE PAST AND PRESENT STATE OF OUR ECCLESIASTICAL ESTABLISHMENT.

WHATEVER may be the sentiments of a calm observer respecting the merits of Mr. Lancaster's system of education, or the means by which he has endeavoured to detract from the just praise of the gentleman on whose discoveries it is founded, he cannot be denied the merit of having incidentally contributed to arouse the established clergy from their habitual lethargy, and to excite them to the performance of their professional duties. Since the progress of the Lancasterian schools first threatened the safety of the establishment, the more respectable portion of the clerical body have displayed a zeal in the promotion of Christian knowledge, and a vigilance in resisting the encroachments of fanaticism, that a few years ago no one could have supposed to be compatible with their habits, or consistent with their established prejudices in favor of *quiescence*. It is to be regretted, indeed, that many of the objects to which they have lately directed their attention, are of a description so far removed from the sphere of common life, and present so little promise of practical utility. But it is better that the clergy should be employed in fruitless exertion, than that they should sink into their former inertness: that the spirit of activity should have been once awakened is gratifying to the public, and fortunate for themselves.

On looking over the histories of the early protestant clergy of this country, we are astonished at the labours and acquirements of those celebrated men. An unexampled industry in professional duties, seemed to have scarcely interfered with the toil and diligence of literary acquisition, which might itself have occupied the lives and worn out the vigor of men in full health and ease. Yet they made their acquisitions in the midst of dangers that must have been extremely prejudicial to the composedness of literary investigation. The student was not left to the quiet enjoyment of his study, nor the divine to the peaceable possession of his pulpit. Trying calamities not unfrequently broke in upon them; and those men whose leisure should have been guarded by national protection, for the furtherance of national good, were sought out, sometimes to suffer, always to struggle; urged from their books among turbulent and factious men, and in a day when superior excellence was only a mark for more decided unpopularity, driven to all the exigencies to which superior virtue will devote itself rather than embrace the evil cause. But their intercourse with the world, dangerous as it would have been to minds less firmly framed, appeared not to have stained the purity, or changed the habits of these eminent men. They retired from courts and councils to their libraries, and from their libraries returned into the active and bustling world, with the pure and noble minds that owed nothing to chance or situation, but every thing to principle. The history of these men, as revivors of theological learning in England, is that of excessive learning applied to one great and unchanging object. Deep researches into languages oriental and western, the most acute and philosophical investigations of nature, almost universal knowledge of ancient and modern history, a perfect acquaintance with the systems of theology delivered by the leaders of the most celebrated sects of their own and preceding ages, were the accomplishments of these extraordinary persons. We do not here speak of the higher qualities of zeal, devotedness to their cause and unimpeachable integrity, which made them the lights of the church, and the benefactors of their country.

The reflection that strikes us most painfully and most powerfully, on remembering those men, is the utter deficiency of the succession; the total falling off in all the great requisites of the clerical character, in those who have succeeded to the places from which the great reformists have gradually passed away to receive the only reward for which they laboured. Eminent as the reformers were, and dignified as their motives must appear, it is impossible that so regular an effect could have been produced on so extensive a scale, without the support of some one of those excitements, which are obviously sufficient to rouse common minds in the common intercourse of life to vigorous and continued exertion. If the more active and learned among the early clergy were more exposed to suffering, they were more cherished by their superiors. The rewards, which a wise and provident liberality had set apart for merit, were impartially and promptly bestowed: honor and emoluments were rigorously confined to the purposes of encouraging and remunerating virtue. It is recorded of some among the bishops, and that even in an age more nearly approaching to our own, that they looked through their dioceses for young men, whose habits and capacities gave the fairest hope of their future fitness for the church: that they took those young persons into their palaces, provided them with the instruction necessary to make them accomplished pastors, and finally placed them in situations that might at once reward their efforts, and give the most ample room for the exercise of the talents and virtues which might be expected from their education. We mean no irreverence to the prelacy of our day; but we will confess, that we do not expect any very sudden adoption of an example now grown obsolete along with the virtues that flowed from its existence; and we must express a sorrowful conviction, that the indolence and ignorance, the want of zeal, and deficiency of knowledge, which have degraded the national clergy in the eyes of the people, are to be traced almost exclusively to the vicious system by which preferment is administered. Distinguished merit may make its way, but is not sure of its reward; such merit must be rare, and its success has little connection with the general good to be derived from rewarding the inferior excellence which is to be found among inferior men, and required to be exercised in the humble ranks of the establishment.

It would, perhaps, be vain to hope that any signal change in the distribution of preferment can take place during the existence of parliamentary corruption. But numerous expedients might be found not unworthy the regard of those to whom the literature, and the purity of the church are still dear. The great means by which knowledge and usefulness in all other professions have been promoted, is competition : to promote this object, a fair field must be thrown open for the honorable rivalry of intellect and acquirement. This has given us eminent lawyers, able men, of business, physicians who have extended the dominion of their art to nearly its utmost boundary, philosophers who have exalted the reputation of their country and contributed to enlighten and benefit the world. This principle applied even in an humbler degree to the church, would produce effects more extensive than its adherents have dared to calculate. Some of our nobles have the presentation of from ten to one hundred benefices; some of our bishops have a patronage more than sufficient to reward all the merit that can arise within their dioceses. If only one of the numerous livings within their gift, were annually offered to the competition of the curates, a different spirit would soon be observed to pervade the subordinate orders of the clergy. Only the weak, the servile, and the ignorant would fawn, and cringe, and flatter for that which appeared within the reach of fair and honorable competition. The meritorious candidates who might be unsuccessful on one occasion, would look forward with confidence to future opportunities of trial; and even the unworthy would either refrain from engaging in the contest, or would be taught by its result in what light to estimate their own acquisitions and abilities.

Under the present constitution of the church, its most valuable livings are left to the disposal of grooms and prostitutes. The chere amie of some weak and amorous nobleman, persuades him in a moment of licentious dalliance, to promise a reversion to her " college friend;" and my Lord Pot-8-o's agrees to match his bay mare against Jack Highflyer's chesnut gelding, for a thousand guineas, on condition that their common friend Tom Tandem have the next presentation to some good fat thing within his lordship's gift. The cousin or nephew of a bishop marries into a family of middling circumstances; the son and heir, intended by nature for a hopeful tradesman, is sent to college with the *particular approbation* of his lordship; he learns at the university (what indeed may be learned any where) to drink and wench, and drive a tandem; but still he is allied by marriage to the bishop, and must therefore become the possessor of a benefice. If sacrifices like this to family connection, be necessary, let their evident effects be in some degree counteracted by some general and regular provision.

We have before us the portrait of a dignitary of the church, who rose to his present eminence, not by the display of superior talents, or the practice of superior virtue, but by the intemperate and unnecessary combination of the politician with the priest. Distinguished at the college over which he now possesses supreme dominion, by nothing but the indolence and intemperance of his habits; without any pretensions to scholastic or mathematical knowledge, and possessing a very slight acquaintance with English literature, he might have passed through life unnoticed and unknown, but for his accidental interference in the political disputes that agitated the university of which he was a graduate. An assemblage of the townsmen having been called to consider the propriety of petitioning his majesty for the dismissal of ministers, he delivered a long and scurrilous harangue. His zeal was reported to the minister. The mastership of his college fell vacant, and Mr. Pitt exalted him above the heads of his seniors in age, and his superiors in learning. The influence that he thus obtained, he naturally and even laudably devoted to the furtherance of his patron's schemes, and the support of his interest. Mr. Perceval on assuming the office of prime minister, foresaw the importance of his attachment, and recommended him to his sovereign as the most proper person to be inducted to the see of B——. These are circumstances which reflect not so much discredit on Dr.—— himself, as on the system by which they are sanctioned: that he should accept the dignities conferred upon him was to be expected; that it should have been consistent with the usual practice to confer them, demonstrates the necessity of some reform in ecclesiastical discipline.

A graduate of the university of Oxford disgraces his college and his profession by indulgence in the most depraved pursuits, and the most intemperate habits. He is compelled to leave the university, and obtains in London the character of a popular preacher. Dowagers of rank invite him to their parties; he becomes at once a man of intrigue and gallantry; devotes to cards the leisure that ought to be employed in the exercise of his professional duties; and during the melancholy interval between September and January, dissipates the solitary hours, in the composition of burlesques on the religion of which he is a minister, and on the establishment of which he shares the honors and emoluments. He indulges his revengeful feelings in satirical attacks upon the individuals who contributed to his expulsion from college, and on the university that his conduct has disgraced. The presentation of a valuable living devolves on his patroness: the curate, a venerable and learned servant of the church, applies to obtain the fulfilment of her promise, and learns that it has been violated in favor of the card-table fop, the advocate of infidelity, the libeller of exalted worth, and the secret enemy of our religious establishment.

A living of nearly eight thousand per annum, is in

the gift of a particular family, and were the system of church preferment such as it ought to be, a prize so valuable would be the reward of extensive learning and exemplary virtue. But the younger son is just of an age to be sent to college. He is entered therefore at Oxford, where he spends three years of academical probation in every variety of juvenile dissipation. When he presents himself before the bishop, it is found that he can construe the first chapter of St. John; and he is therefore, according to the usual practice, entitled to ordination. His theological knowledge is confined to Blair's Sermons; in the *Belles Lettres,* he is acquainted with Enfield's Speaker, and his classical acquirements extend to the remembrance of a few lines in Propria quæ maribus. But in shooting, hunting, swearing, drinking, and wenching, he may bid defiance to the rivalry of his contemporaries. Instead of attending therefore to the spiritual welfare of his parish, he devotes his mornings to the chase or the shooting party, his evenings to the seduction of the village maidens, and his nights to the orgies of Bacchus. As he becomes old and indolent and gouty, he acquires the moroseness of a tyrant, and displays the avarice of a miser: he distresses his tenants, abuses his authority as a magistrate, annoys and oppresses his parishioners by continual litigation, and dies of drunkenness and vexation, loaded with the execrations of that community, of which he had been appointed the teacher and the guardian.

If the majority of the beneficed clergy be thus dissolute and illiterate, it affords only a feeble ground of exultation that there are to be found among them many individuals of extensive learning, and exemplary manners. The safety of the church, and the religion of the people, depend on the character of our spiritual instructors as a body: to say that to effect a moderate reform in the system of preferment would be impossible, is to libel the constitution of our ecclesiastical establishment; and to admit that it is possible, without coming forward to co-operate in the prosecution of so desirable an object, is to sacrifice existence to tranquillity, and in the enjoyment of luxurious repose to suffer the sleep of death to chill the heart and paralyze he limbs.

AN ENSORIAN ESSAY ON SOMETHING;
MEANING ANY THING, AND PROVING NOTHING.

When the great Chrononhotonthologos (see that play written by Fielding) was missing, Aldiborontiphoscophormio, was asked where he might be found. Why this enquiry was made, the reader may discover by referring to Athenæus: it argues that I have a right to make a similar enquiry respecting truth, as Archimedes cried *Eureka* in the time of Hiero, King of Syracuse. Does the reader wish to know more of kings; I will refer him to the memoirs of πιππιν; or does he feel any curiosity respecting queens, let him look at τομ θυμ Q. A. φηλδινγ; Δολαλα loquitur. *Queens* indeed are usually *queans*, a proof that in our language there is yet great need of a synonymical dictionary. On the subject of queans I recollect a curious passage in Suidas too long to be quoted. Macrobius says something of a similar nature, but Philoxenus apud Stobæum is of a different opinion. After this argument it would be a waste of time to contend with the bigots who believe in hell—a place that may be proved by the accounts of the Siamese, to have no existence but in vulgar superstition. Would you wish to learn what the ancients thought of this, refer to Diogen. Laert. or that admirable work, the theme of my constant meditation, Ramanha, written by one of the scribes of Sandracottus, who clearly shews that hell is a corruption of Bel the Dragon, a fit prototype for our Dr. Bell, whose impudence astonishes me and the nation, and makes him a fit companion for the Belzebub of the priests.

These things smell of the filth out of which they come. Is it your desire to know what I think of such idioms, I shall say in the words of a sublime poet,

Θη μωρ Υ κρι Θη λε; Υ ΠΙΣ.

A profound and philosophical observation, displaying an accurate acquaintance with phisiology, not to mention *phiz*-iology, and betokening an investigation into causes and effects. Not less dangerous, however, on that account to the craft of the priests, and those subtle impostors the bishops and guardians of our church, who should never think of a jordan without shame for those predecessors in church juggling of ancient time, who persuaded the poor Jews to leave the streets of Jericho to be drowned in the river. The great Popius indeed calls them

Λαιτς οφ θη Χυρχ;

but they are in fact ΠΡΗΣΤΣ or in still more expressive terms ΡΩΓΣ: men who have no objection, *bibere* as well as *mingere*, and who are never at a loss to think if they do not actually exclaim,

Ιφ αι 'αδ α γυδ συχ, αι κυδ ταακ ιτ νε.

Is there any piety in the clergy? If you are anxious to know, look to the history of Dr. Dodd; was he not executed for *forgery*? a crime which he merely learned from his predecessors, who had practiced it from time immemorial, and given their blundering forgeries—forgeries that the meanest apprehensions could detect to the world, under the name of the scriptures: are you desirous to know of their sobriety? Does not the Vicar and Moses fully describe their pretensions to that virtue; Was there not great debauchery practised by the ancient priests? as some one relates in a certain passage, though I recollect that his contemporary seemed to suppose that his descriptions were exaggerated, while his commentator boldly supports them. Who has not heard of Ann Brownrigg and Dr. Faustus (Annal. Germ. Curios. Ch. 1. Page 976), and John Kemble? than whom no stronger proofs can be afforded of the abominable tendency of the christian religion. Did not the first whip her apprentices to death, evidently hoping that they would go to heaven, an idea that would never have occurred to her, had it not been for the shocking falsehoods of the christian priests; nor would Dr. Faustus have preyed on the credulity of the poor Dutchman, but for the notion of a devil; nor Mr. Kemble been called Black Jack, but for some supposed resemblance to Old Nick.

As for what the learned have thought of education, there are many ingenious though false maxims contained in the following collectanea, which I have brought together with great industry and research.

Ωυατ ισ γοτ ωρ θε Δεφιλς ϲαν ισ ςπεντ υνδερ `ισ ϲελε.
Κνω ευρ `ανδς φρόμ πικιγγ ανδ ςτηλιγγ.

But is it not plain, that if you teach a boy to be honest in early youth, he is honest merely because he has imbibed certain prejudices, and been accustomed to certain actions? There can be no merit in abstaining from theft, if abstinence be involuntary. I am therefore of opinion, that to instil any description of morality into the youthful mind is in the highest degree improper and injudicious. Let our youth be left to themselves, and when they grow up their errors are their own, and if they act rightly no one can detract from their merit, by saying that their goodness was involuntary. Besides, how can the parent know whether the principles that he instils into his son, if he does instil any, be correct? Have not philosophers of all ages been disputing about virtue, and are not their disputes still undetermined? To avoid doing wrong the safest way is to do nothing. In Otaheite (and why are not the Otaheitans as wise as we?) chastity is considered as a disgrace: among the Spartans (pity that the morals of antiquity are not more duly studied!) theft was regarded as a virtue; and why is not the opinion of that great people, as consistent with *the nature of things, and the laws of immutable truth* as our own?

But I am weary of contention with stupidity: so was Cicero, as may be seen in his writings; but when men pretend to speak of what they have never seen, as things existing: when they tell us of a place called India, and this India containing elephants, and these elephants carrying castles on their backs; and that this India was conquered by Alexander, and that we puny and foolish Englishmen have actually obtained the empire once governed by the Macedonian: and when they talk of palanquins, and not only of palanquins, but of palanquins containing Europeans, and those Europeans carried in those palanquins, of these Europeans the same and at the same time snoring: and heavens and earth! such things said of a place that possibly does not exist, and for our glory, is it not enough to make a philosopher mad, and when made to *make him make* himself ridiculous?

———

P.

That the preceding essay of our ingenious correspondent is after an existing model, and does great credit to his imitative talents, our readers will demand no other proof than the following extracts from Ensor's Essay on National Education. " Are kings and their ministers judges of the arts? Was Peter of Medici, who employed Michael Angelo in forming a statue of snow, or &c. &c. &c. or Louis the 14th, who asked the Duke de Louvois, *mais a quoi sert de lire,* or his minister. Louvois, who piqued himself on never opening a book, for which of course he was praised, and particularly by La Bruyere, or Bute, who Cumberland says had a disposition to be a Mæcenas, or Mæcenas himself? I suppose not, for on the authority of Seneca, Suetonius and Tacitus, we must repute him a most affected writer. Or to reascend from ministers to potentates, was Hadrian a judge or lover of the arts, or could he foster them? Yet he in fact originated our endowed colleges and academies. I say, he could not.

" Are you a poet, and would you chuse Charles the Ninth, of France, for a patron. He said poets were to be fed, not fatted; or Dionysius of Syracuse: this man patronized Philoxenus, who censured some of the king's poetry, for which he was condemned to the quarries. Would you chuse a vice-roy for your patron, and be knighted with John Carr, &c. * * * * Would you have some private but opulent patrician for your patron, as Calvicius, Sabrinius, &c. &c."

Our correspondent appears in his concluding paragraph to have imitated a paragraph in Mr. Ensor's essay respecting devils ; but the copy is far surpassed in ludicrous peculiarities by the original.

Mr. Ensor is one of those men who dabble in every thing, without understanding any thing. He quotes Stobæus, yet misconstrues the plainest passages of Homer, and speaks of Quinctilian in a page that contains about a dozen instances of ungrammatical construction. He comes forward as a teacher of philosophy, and displays the dogmatism of the pedant, without the learning of the scholar, or the subtlety of the humble logician: he mistakes a knowledge of names and titles for learning, and supposes that to be obscure is to be profound, and to be quaint is to be original. To say what has never been said before, is an easy task to the writer who espouses opinions because of their absurdity; to shock the feelings of the devout, requires no qualities more exalted than impiety and impudence. The rational and conscientious deist would for his own sake observe the most scrupulous delicacy to what he might consider as the prejudices of mankind ; truth itself meets with reluctant reception from the lips of a jester or a bully ; the feelings of the community at large are not to be tamely exposed to laceration even by the conscientious enthusiasm of an individual who may possibly be right, but to whom even the certainty of being in the right gives no dominion over the sensations of his fellow creatures, and who, *à priori* must be regarded as a mistaken zealot. Were we to argue against Mahometanism in a Mahometan country, we should treat the prejudices of its adherents with respect, and should not venture to call in the alliance of ridicule, till truth had prepared the way for its reception; till it became a legitimate weapon in the hands of the majority, and those alone who defied its stroke, were insensible to its keenness.

PUBLIC INSTITUTIONS.

THE ANTIQUARIAN SOCIETY.

Whoever has cast even a hasty glance over the labours of our first great leaders in the prosecution of antiquarian enquiries, must have been impressed with mingled feelings of astonishment at their industry, and of reverence for their talents. A single page of the merest drudge of the age of Elizabeth, contains as much philosophy, and embraces as large a proportion of historical and classical knowledge, as is sprinkled through the volumes of a Lysons or a Caster. They excited the amazement of their contemporaries by the magnitude of their designs, and the extent of their researches, and displayed no consciousness of the miracles they had performed: undertakings that would have occupied the life of a modern antiquarian, without approaching to completion, they regarded only as preliminaries to greater and more extensive efforts: and works which under the superintendance of a privileged dealer in antiquarian lumber, would have been presented to modern readers in a dozen folios, embellished with engravings, were dropped casually from the press, as the mere amusements of literary leisure, or as preliminary memoranda for the use of more able and industrious lovers of antiquarian science.

In a professed and legitimate antiquarian of the present day, neither the learning of the scholar, nor the judgment of the critic, is required or expected. The discoverer of a rusty key, the possessor of an illegible inscription, men whose knowledge is confined to a suspicion that Augustus was not the contemporary of Thomas A.

quinas, but who can speak with garrulous enthusiasm of mullions, and transepts, and side-arches, and crypts, and pilasters, are the *viri laudati* of a society established for the purpose of elucidating our national history, and contributing to the advancement of useful knowledge. Were they to descend indeed to the minutiæ of Gothic or Saxon antiquities, with any reference to the formation of architectural taste, or to the illustration of architectural history: did they endeavour by their researches, to elucidate the progress of our national manners, or the history of those political revolutions which preceded every change of architectural style in the buildings of our ancestors, their labours would be productive of substantial benefit to the public, and of the most exquisite gratification to those who at present regard their pursuits with no other sentiment than derision. But a true antiquarian feels no interest in any subject that may conduce to the extension of our knowledge, the improvement of our taste, or the gratification of rational curiosity. It is sufficient for him, that a church is ruinous, that a coin is rusty, that a pitcher is broken, that an inscription is obliterated, or a manuscript illegible. With him one remnant of the antique is as much an object of admiration as another. The comparative interest excited by two ancient structures is not dependant on the relative beauty of their workmanship, or even on the respective singularity of their proportions, but on the date of their erection. If a miserable hovel obtaining the name of a parish church, has stood twenty years longer than Westminster Abbey, it is by twenty years the more valuable structure of the two. If two pieces of parchment be presented to the society, the question is not what do they contain, or which of them throws the most important light on any subject of scientific or historical enquiry, but which is the oldest and most illegible. Selection and system, the great instruments of successful progress in every other object of human research, are rejected by the great body of antiquarians as useless and troublesome auxiliaries.

They collect materials without any regard to their utility, and without attempting to facilitate the study of antiquities, by arranging them in classes, and by pointing out their dependance on each other, or their connection with collateral branches of investigation.

To enter the rooms of the Antiquarian Society with a faint expectation of being repaid for the recurrence of half an hour to our favorite pursuits, our readers will admit to have been natural and reasonable: we knew that the society was richly endowed, and that every year augmented its revenues; we remembered the names of Strutt and Whitaker, and willingly indulged in the persuasion that the associates of such men must be well qualified to astonish by their learning, and enlighten by the splendor of their philosophy. We could not but suppose that at the weekly meetings of the society, the unconnected facts communicated by individual members, would be collected into one luminous system, that they would be applied by the labour of some superior mind to the elucidation of important difficulties, and to the deduction of useful and ingenious conclusions. To give life and beauty, and utility to the mass of heterogeneous materials drawn together by the minute and patient labours of distant and insulated members, would evidently be a duty of easy performance to the president, and, productive of the most important advantages to antiquarian science.

How far our expectations were gratified will be most easily determined from a narrative of their proceedings. About fifty members were present. The president, Sir Harry Inglefield, called over the names of several candidates for admission as fellows of the society. The ballot box was sent round for the first on the list, and during its progress round the room, Mr. Carlisle the secretary, was pleased to read to the society the first of several communications of its associates. This learned and important paper had been transmitted from the country, and was interspersed with several references to a plate of antiquities about two feet wide, and one foot high, posted at the end of the room opposite to the president; and in the first place let it be observed, that as the mouldings, &c. by which the orders of architecture were distinguished, occupied a minute portion of columns scarcely exceeding the height of from one to two inches, and as the members were *all seated* sideways towards these drawings, they must have been singularly delighted and edified by Mr.-—'s communications. In spite, however, of the smallness of the drawings, Mr. Carlisle began: and in a monotonous, vulgar, drawling, unimpressive tone, favoured the society with its contents. From the manner in which it was read, and from the frequent interruptions, we were prevented from committing it to paper, in such a form as would have been pleasing or satisfactory to our readers, nor if they feel the same indifference with ourselves to minuteness without accuracy, and insipidity without erudition, can they justly regret the circumstance. The account was that of a church which seemed to have no other recommendations to the notice of the society than that it was old and shapeless. It informed us that the arches were oval, that through the transept might be seen an arch, that mullions were observable, that the side-aisles were long, and the buttresses fallen to decay. What circumstance in the history of architecture, in the annals of our country, or in the progress of science, these facts were intended to elucidate, we must remain in ignorance. The writer of the communication forgot to inform us, in what respect *his* church was different from any other ruinous structure, and its utility, therefore, remains to be discovered by the society.

Suppose that *we* were members of the Antiquarian Society, and were stimulated by the love of age and ugliness to favor its secretary with important communications. Suppose too, as on this occasion, that a drawing of the object of our researches was affixed to one end of the room, and that the ballot box had been sent round for the admission of Mr. Rowland Hunt; suppose, in the last place, that Mr. Carlisle, after due preparation, begins as follows:

Mr. Carlisle. Copy of a communication received from Mr. —— of ——, dated July 16, 1812.

Sir, I beg leave to submit to *you* as secretary of the Society of Antiquaries, the following description of a rare, curious, and I flatter myself singularly interesting ancient object, found by me lately as I was walking and musing among the ruinous fragments of the ruins in Wild-street, which, Sir, should you think them worthy of your attention, you will be kind enough to communicate to the Society of Antiquaries in London. This curious relique seems to be of pure silver, four inches long: the form is extremely curious. What I believe I may with propriety ———

The President. Gentlemen, I have the honour to inform you that Mr. Rowland Hunt, is elected a member of this society. I have in addition to inform you that Mr. A. B. is recommended to this society as a gentleman of extensive and profound acquaintance with the antiquities of England. Recommended by C. D. E. F. and G. H.—— Pass round the box.

Mr. Carlisle.—Propriety call the head, is of a shape something between a circle and an oval—of equal thickness throughout; consequently though hollow on one side, equally protuberant on the other. I think I cannot better illustrate this to the respectable Society of Antiquaries, than by requesting them to observe the moon on its third or fourth day, and suppose the concave part to be scooped out. From the head a shaft rises, having great resemblance in shape to the expanding part of the gothic pillar, as it proximates to the arch. This shaft, as you will perceive by the annexed drawing, expands as its length increases. End circular, flat, bent back, plain. On reverse a nebulus attaching shaft to head. Towards the end a curious compartment containing a Basso ——

Mr. President. Gentlemen, I beg leave to announce that Mr. B. is elected a member of this society.

Mr. Carlisle.—Relievo. First compartment, a wild beast—no doubt a lion. Second compartment, a large L. I beg leave to suggest to the society the probability that this letter contains the date of this valuable relic of antiquity. Third compartment, a portrait of fine execution: laurel round the hair, probably a relievo of Augustus. Immediately on one side these compartments are two letters curiously engraven in the metal, a proof that the ancients knew much more of the art of engraving, than many are disposed to admit. The letters are M. O. meaning, I have no doubt, as applied to Augustus, Magister Orbis—the master of the world.*—If the society think this account of a very curious article worthy even of a moment's attention, I shall consider myself as well rewarded for all my trouble and perseverance in its discovery and explanation: and remain,

Sir,
With the most profound respect,
Yours, very truly,
P. P.

Now from this description of a *silver spoon*, we have no doubt that as much advantage would arise to the arts and literature of our native country, as from any one of the communications submitted to the society on Thursday evening. In our mode of expression, we have imitated their contents with conscientious accuracy: and if such be the compositions that occupy the time, and furnish the cabinet of the society, what wonder can be excited, that a Lysons should distract its councils by intrigue, and every exertion be employed to prevent the possible reelection of the present learned and respectable president?

---

* The *curious article* here described is a silver spoon, with the inspector's stamp, viz. a lion, his majesty's profile, and the numeral letter. The initials M. O. are for Mary Osborne.

Such exhibitions as that which we were condemned to witness, have not only a negative effect, but are positively and extensively injurious to the interests of literature. An intelligent foreigner admitted into what he had been taught to regard as one of the first among our literary societies, and forming his opinion of our advancement in antiquarian knowlege from the proceedings on Thursday evening, would retire from the rooms with the most profound contempt for our literary character. His grace of Norfolk we do not suppose to be peculiarly versed in the history and antiquities of his country; but on seeing him enter the room, we could not but imagine to ourselves the impression of the scene before us on the mind of a Chatham or a Fox. It is unfortunate for the interests of learning, that its professors should ever be exhibited to the great, the powerful, or the eminent, in a point of view either repulsive or ridiculous; and we are unable to conceive any exhibition more unfortunately calculated to excite the derision of a statesman, or the pity of a philosopher, than a meeting of the Society of Antiquarians.

THE WHIPS. No. II.

THE CARNIVOROUS COLONEL.

In our number for the month of January, we delineated the character of the Barouche Captain, or as he is called in his house, by way of contradistinction from his brother, "*the Member!*"—We have now to present our readers with anecdotes of his most intimate friend, who although not a *driving* member, only *an eating one,* as being the constant box companion of the Captain, is well worthy the honour of following his principal. *The Colonel,* is the son of an apothecary, at Haverfordwest, in South Wales. His poor father passed the best part of his life in the various duties of trituration at the mortar, teeth-drawing, blood-letting, both to man and horse, and in the other little concomitant comforts, which all country apothecaries, but most especially a Welch apothecary, enjoy. Our present subject, the Colonel, not having talents sufficient for even the manufacture of pills for man, or balls for horse, received his *congé* from his father, and was sent into the wide world to seek his fortune. With Dick Dowlass's wardrobe, his all, his whole worldly estate, in an old pocket handkerchief of his uncle's, the town *farrier*, he found himself, one fine morning, with a heart as heavy as his head, on the road to Bristol. Walking all day, and taking his rest in the barns, and other outward accommodations of the Welch villages he passed through, he made the tour from his native town to the great and flourishing city of Bristol: where his natural stupidity was, in as great a degree as his heavy nature will admit, somewhat roused by the active scene which he witnessed. But here his talents could not procure him even that portion of bread, which his inordinate appetite required: he was literally starving, when a tailor took him into his service to carry out clothes to his customers. This, his first patron, he served for near a year; but unfortunately being detected in a criminal intercourse with a shoulder of mutton in his master's pantry, he was dismissed the service with ignominy. Once again on the wide world, London, that grand source of wealth and honor, appeared to him to be his best object. Again therefore he commenced Peripatetic, and with the occasional help of good natured return chaise-boys, he arrived safe and sound in the metropolis. His first employment was as an assistant to a baker in Whitechapel, where he was universally beloved for the punctuality with which his rolls were daily dispensed on the first delivery, even of the coldest mornings. Near two years he passed in this occupation, but martial fire inspired him; and he sighed for the glories of war. With this feeling, he most gallantly eloped from his good friend the baker, and enlisted into a regiment of heavy dragoons, then quartered at Canterbury. Here he first found himself in the military costume. It would be tiresome and unnecessary to dwell upon the three or four years of his noviciate as a soldier, nor is it material to accompany him through the various gradations of private, corporal, serjeant, and quarter-master; it is sufficient to say, that having passed through these *ranks of the army*, he contrived to get acquainted with the kept-mistress of a Lieut. Colonel of ————, through whose means he obtained his first commission in that corps. One circumstance we cannot pass over in silence: his old misfortune, the cravings of his appetite, having induced him to purloin the mess of his comrade, he was tried by a regimental court-martial for the offence, and received two hundred lashes as his reward. A reference to his back, which still blushes in recollection of this untoward event, will at once decide this fact.

Here we have our hero in the glorious regiment of ————, where his acquaintance with the "*Member Captain*," owed its happy origin. Their friendship has been long and mutual: once indeed a fatal misunderstanding had nearly taken place, owing again to his old complaint, his most insatiable appetite. It happened very unfortunately that he was detected by an officer of the corps in receiving an apron-full of table remnantss from a cook maid at Brompton, whose scraps from her master's table he paid for, by sacrificing with her at the altar of Venus. This affair reaching the ear of Colonel, now General O'————, he placed the gallant Colonel in arrest, in which he continued for four days, and then obtained his release, solely because Lord H———— did not chuse to let an officer of his regiment appear before the public in so disgraceful a situation. It was on this occasion, that the "*Member Captain*" and the "*Carnivorous Colonel*" had an unhappy misunderstanding: the former had purchase for him his promotion: to him, therefore, he owed his rank and its attendant glories. "*The Member*" thought proper to remonstrate with him upon the fatal indulgence of his appetite; "*the Colonel*" replied,—the Member rejoined, and a separation was nearly the consequence: but their mutual knowledge of each other, convinced them of the necessity of compromising their differences, and like their amiable predecessors, Peachum and Lockitt, they embraced, and swore fresh oaths of inviolable friendship.

Since the Member's union with the daughter of *Lindamira*, "*the Colonel*" has another table at which he has occasional access; but their attachment stands but on a fragile basis, for the Colonel was formerly one of the loudest of her enemies, and the captain's alliance was formed in opposition to his most urgent remonstrances: nor can she forget the anxious zeal with which the colonel was accustomed to propagate the following anecdote. When Colonel Greville first formed the Argyle Institution, *Lindamira* contrived to have her name introduced among the ladies, subscribers, and paid her money accordingly. The committee of ladies, on looking over the list, objected to her, and Colonel Greville was desired to let her know that she could not be admitted. He did so, and returned her the subscription she had paid: she wrote him a most violent and angry letter, insisting upon knowing, how, and in what, she was objectionable. To this Colonel Greville, according to *his own account*, very plainly replied, that he could not explain these matters *to her*, but that he should most willingly give every satisfaction to either *Mr. or Master———!* This he asserts was final—the money was kept, and nothing farther said!

The circumscription of our limits, and the pressure of other interesting matter, oblige us to defer the continuation of this article to our next; when it will be resumed; and the Colonel's fair fame done every justice to.

MISS RAFFLE's PARTY, or the FESTIVITIES AT DOUGLAS HOUSE.

On the fourteenth of February, dedicated from time immemorial to love and festivity, arrived the fifth anniversary of that auspicious day, when the most noble the Marquis of ——— and Miss Polly Raffle exchanged their vows of mutual passion, and their protestations of eternal fidelity. The most masterly and tasteful arrangements had been made beneath the immediate superintendance of the noble Marquis himself, for the due observance of so joyful an occasion. An appropriate statue of his lordship in the character of Apollo, adorned the grand staircase of the mansion, and a bust of the fair and accomplished hostess, accompanied by the attributes of Diana, was conspicuously prominent amidst several beautiful engravings, commemorative of the Mahratta war, and the discomfiture of the Indian princes by the united policy and valour of two illustrious brothers. The preparations were for some time retarded by the unexpected difficulties that impeded his lordship in his endeavours to raise the necessary supplies: financial operations are too frequently attended by delay: to redeem the plate of a noble family is not so easy as to pledge it: W——— is at an inconvenient distance from the Horse-guards; and it was not till half past six o'clock, that a messenger arrived with the long expected conveniences: including besides several articles of more elegance than utility, many dozens of knives and forks, and bank notes to the amount of a neat fifty. Polly received them with rapture, and with unparalleled condescension returned a one pound note to his lordship, informing him that pocket-money might be useful. The company now began to crowd the staircase, and Miss Polly resumed her smiles, and prepared to display her accustomed grace and condescension in the performance of her duty as mistress of the ceremonies. The first and most welcome of her visitors, was the gallant and accomplished Lord H——, tenderly supporting the timid and trembling foosteps of the agile N——a; to these succeeded a law lord of oratorical celebrity, not less famed for talking in his youth, than in his old age for desperate incontinence. The *lady* who had graciously accepted the offer of his arm, as he rambled through one of the alleys of Soho, appeared in distant perspective to be arrayed in very elegant and becoming attire; but as she approached the fair hostess, her mantle was discovered to be a cloak of red duffel; her pumps, though slander itself could not have denied the nicety of their adaptation to the foot of the wearer, exhibited on a nearer view evident indications of the length and fidelity of their services.

> The shoe's black leather battered and decayed,
> Lets in the dirt through chinks that time has made.

Her stockings had once been pure as the chastity of their wearer, but were now as *holy* as the conversation of her seducer. Her bonnet exhibited the dignity of age; her lily neck displayed the whiteness of the purest cerusse, and her cheeks were flushed with all the blooming beauty of red lead. Miss Raffle was absolutely petrified with vexation and astonishment; and as for her attendants,

> Each Miss straight exclaimed, while she turned up her snout,
> "Ma'am, your cloak isn't fit to be seen;"
> The *beaux* they ran in and the *belles* they ran out,
> And nothing was heard but confusion and rout,
> While the hosstess addressed SALLY GREEN.

The war of words was long and loud: the protector of the unfortunate stranger *advocated* her cause with his usual eloquence, and even the M——s ventured to express his sympathy in the fair one's peculiar situation. Such ingratitude was too much for the gentle Polly; in the fury of jealous rage she seized the ci-devant ruler of millions by the forelock, and benighted England might at the moment in which we are inditing this true and important history, have bewailed the loss of her brightest luminary, had not the damsel of Soho with equal alacrity and courage rescued him from the hands of his exasperated mistress. The attention of Miss Raffle was now diverted from her protector to the " trollop of a visitor." Expert in the mysteries of scratching, and observing the stranger's bonnet to be an effectual protection against her usual mode of attack, she directed all her force against this " capital covering," and by one courageous snatch effected its capture. But scarcely had she accomplished her purpose before she retreated many paces in mute astonishment; thrice did she measure the height of the stranger with her eye, and thrice did she advance towards her with an expression of wonder in her countenance, and of kindness in her attitude. At the fourth approach she sprung into her arms, exclaiming in tones of joyous agony, " Oh! my sister! it is my sister! I know it by her wig!"—Great was the surprise of the spectators, the pleasure of the Marquis, and the exultation of Lord —— at this discovery! The females, recovered from their alarm, crowded round her, to congratulate the fair one on her arrival; but her sister observing her agitation, reflecting that a few moments would be necessary to restore her to her first composure, and anxious that a " sister of the Douglas clan" should not disgrace the family by mean habiliments, conducted her to her wardrobe, where she was soon attired in all the splendor of a fairy queen.

Among the rest of the company present we observed the Duke of C. and Mrs. Jordan; Lord P—— and Lady A—— W——, Lady A——l and Sir H. D——e, the Duke of S—— and Mrs. B————, with a great variety of other fashionables. The festivities of the evening were such as magnificence alone inspired by taste, could have exhibited. The meats, the jellys, and the wines were universally admired: the wit of the fair hostess was the general theme of wonder and delight: her sister astonished the circle by the splendor of her beauty; and the noble host intermingled the most engaging courtesies to his guests, with the most obsequious attention to his mistress. Among the favourite tunes, were the "Black Joke;" " A fig for the parson. cries Paddy O'Lea;" " Though mortals may prate about wedlock and stuff;" " The Self," and " the Dandy O."—So numerous, however, and so various were the modes of entertainment, that we must reluctantly confine ourselves to the description of an amusement which was not less productive of wit and entertainment, than appropriate to this auspicious anniversary. The amusement to which we allude was the composition of valentines, a species of production in which the subjoined specimens will prove that many of the fair and noble assemblage were destined by nature to arrive at unusual excellence.

THE HON. MR. D. TO HIS LOVE.

My dearest love, I've got such things to say,
   You'll scarce believe—why Lord its shocking!
Half the club has run away,
   All on account of Mr. Scourge's mocking:
It is I'm sure a deuced pity,
   D——e but I'm half distracted!
Such a business ne'er was acted
In this great, great, great, great city:
   Why sure you do not think I tell a flam,
D—— me, the club's no longer worth a d——n
And what is worse, they've all forgot to pay,
So dearest I must run away;
   Or sure as I am here,
They'll come upon me for the bills last year,
And then by ——
   Your Billy goes to quod,
And will be forced to put a long lean phiz on
Within the King's Bench prison.
It's b——d vexing, and I'd sooner hang up,
Than pay a guinea for a brother bang up.

I'm h——ly inclined to cut my throat,
　　But if I die
　　No friendly eye,
Will curry Maypole, or rub down Tom Tit;
　My bay-off horse besides has got the glanders,
　And now is under cure with Tommy Sanders;
　And sure it would be monstrous cruel
　　To leave the poor dear jewel
Without a master to look after it.
　Besides, my darling, what becomes of you,
If your true lover kicks the bucket?
　For oh, my lovely dearest Prue,
I cannot leave by will a single ducat:
And what is worse than all I've got a wife,
　And she and sister Bab might take to crying,
If husband were to take away his life:
So just at present I'll not think of dying.
Not that I care a farthing for the pain,
　As I will prove in any court of justice:—
So what the use can any one explain,
　I'd like to know, in kicking up a dust is.
　And as for *bums*, why Lord! its all my eye
　And Betty Martin, I won't pay not I;
　But sweetest dear, and dearest sweet,
　　I will keep you in the Fleet,
　Or if my darling loves the Bench,
　She there shall live as gay as Tommy's wench;
　For d——n me if a girl so fine,
　　Shall want a jolly Valentine.

THE MARQUIS TO MISS POLLY RAFFLE.

As when the obedient band sonorous sound
　The clarion hoarse, and touch the warbling fife;
The mingled music breathes delight around,
　And sooths the languor of an Indian life:

So sweet, so soothing flow the accents sweet,
  From Polly's fragrant lips, and youthful tongue,
Then why with oaths and curses so replete
  Does Poll receive her swain; as cruel as she's young?

'Twas but the other day, that from the *house*
  I urged my amorous way, of rapture full,
Crept up the stair-case, softly as a mouse,
  And heard her cry, *I'll break the rascal's scull!*
Trembling, I entered; she with rage received me;
  And swore "by hell" 'twas more than half-past three;
Exclaimed,"you villain oft you've thus deceived me,"
  And drenched me with a scalding cup of tea.

Pure as the eastern sky her lily hands,
  And white her fingers as the precious Ghee;
But were they yellower than Golcondo's sands,
  Sweeter their *colour* than their *weight* to me!
For oh! how often round the room she knocks me,
  How often on the carpet lays me sprawling,
And spite of cries, about the ears doth box me;
  Unkind unkind return for all my caterwauling!

Light are her nimble feet, her ancles taper,
  And oh! her legs what eye but mine has seen them!
But still since she can kick as well as caper,
  Less safe I am *before them* than *between them*.
Yet as no longer kicks inflict disgrace,
  I'll not attempt to put restrictions on her,
A Prince may kick a Marquis out of place,
  And to a *quean* I'll yield my *seat of honor*!

A ROYAL IMITATION.
Cl———

Of all the fair damsels that flaunt in the Park,
  Or in tandem or curricle shew off;
Not a sweeter than *Long* I've been able to mark,
  Nor a heiress so rich do I know of.

A royal duet.

J———

I've toyed and I've prattled with fifty bold men,
   And doomed to despair fifty more;
But O—the Narcissus of three-score and ten,
   Is the swain whom alone I adore.

Cl———

Tho' Tilney's not much of a wit, nor her face
   Adorned by the bloom of D———n's rosy belle,
Gaily sparkles her wealth, and if rubies dont grace
   Her cheeks, they embellish her casket, as well.

J———

Tho' my lover be wrinkled, and crooked, and grim,
   And the rheum from his eyelids in driblets distil,
Yet the oaks on his grounds are still older than him
   And a fig for his *powers*, if I have the WILL!

Cl———

Since Tilney's hard heart is so flinty and stony,
   I'll resign her---because I'm unable to win her;
And if J——— should deign to forgive her old crony,
   On his knees he will thank her---a sorrowful sinner!

J———

I'll consent if from W——— in requisite splendor,
   To see my sweet daughters the *ladies* may come;
If when Polly falls sick, brother K——— will attend her,
   And the servants at B---y be *under my thumb*.

Cl———

'Tis granted; your children at all public places,
   Shall out-elbow the virgins and laugh at the matrons;
At the offspring of virtue, your sons make wry faces
   The bishops their friends, and the princes their patrons!

THE REVIEWER.—No. IX.

Salmagundi; or the Whim Whams and Opinions of Lancelot Langstaff, Esquire, and others.
Reprinted from the American Edition, with an introductory Essay, and explanatory Notes, by John Lambert. London. Richardson, Cornhill, 2 vols. 12mo.

THE present is the only collection of American essays that we have read without feelings of surprise at their tameness or disgust at their vulgarity. Grossness is the peculiar characteristic of American wit, and insipidity the usual accompaniment of transatlantic elegance. When an essayist of the new world is told that his diction is coarse, and his stile ungraceful, he endeavours to improve it by the repression of those very exuberances that alone contributed to his excellence, and by which exclusively his productions were rendered worthy the trouble of correction. The great body, therefore, of Mr. Langstaff's brethren may be divided into the two distinct classes of the dull and the vulgar; of those who are too stupid to be read by the community, and those who cannot be read by the critic without exciting less pleasure than disgust.

That Mr. Lambert's opinions of American literature are more favourable than ours, will appear from the subjoined explanation of his sentiments. His introductory essay, indeed, is devoted to a favourable delineation of the moral political character of the Americans, and to the obviation of those prejudices which he supposes to prevail against them among his countrymen. He has conducted the discussion with great temper and ingenuity, and if the reader do not rise from its perusal with a firm conviction that the Americans are a great, and virtuous, and happy people, it will not be owing to the deficiencies of their advocate.

To the Editor of the SCOURGE.

Sir, London, 13th Feb. 1812.

My attention was particularly directed in the last number of the SCOURGE, to your observations on American poetry; which though in some respects different from my own sentiments on the subject, I was, yet, much gratified to find in such a publication. When I first heard of your work, I was apprehensive that its pages would be too much occupied in exposing the vices and frivolities of society, to admit of any grave and serious discussions on the manners, customs and literature of the age; but I must confess that I have been very agreeably disappointed in the perusal of several essays, which have afforded me as much solid satisfaction, as the lighter parts have entertainment. The blending of the serious with the gay, is, I think, the most likely mode of pleasing the various tastes of your readers—at the same time that it contributes to the estimation of the work, in the minds of those, who are too apt to regard the mere effusions of satire, as the offspring of malevolence.

Having visited the United States, and paid considerable attention to the character of the American people, I perused your observations on the poetry of that country with much pleasure, particularly as the manners and literature of the people, in that quarter of the globe, are so seldom discussed in the periodical works of this country. I agree in many of your reasons for believing that a soil so barren of all those delusive charms, and witcheries of fable, which constitute the soul of poetry, is by no means favourable to American genius. But I cannot think the actual contemplation of the "pomp of courts"—and "the pride and circumstance of war," however it may contribute to the imagination, is at all an indispensable requisite of the poet. How many of our best poets never partook of the splendour of a palace —the fatigues of a campaign—or the horrors of a battle— otherwise than through the medium of books?—and how many never contemplated the venerable remains of ancient grandeur—otherwise than through the medium of the prints which covered the walls of their prisons? Yet these men have produced inimitable productions!— I will not say, that if they had lived in America, it is likely they would have written so successfully, or even at all; as it is probable their minds would have been wholly occupied in providing a maintenance for themselves and families. In that country they could not have lived on the precarious bounty of rich and noble patrons; and of course could not have followed that idle and dissipated life so prevalent with men of genius. Necessity would have compelled them to follow the plough, rather than the muses: the same powerful motive influences the Americans now, and will continue so to do for years to come.

For this reason, therefore, I am of opinion that the paucity of transatlantic literature is not so much occasioned by a dearth of those romantic and chivalrous objects of the imagination, which abound in the old countries of Europe and Asia—as owing to the peculiar state of American society, which has not yet approached that crisis, when a considerable portion of the community is fostered by the patronage of the affluent; and when the man of genius and talent, can contrive to dine upon the produce of his literary efforts.

Your arguments, Sir, are, however, more forcible in their application to the poetry of America, than to any other branch of its literature. The subject of a poem, at least of the epic kind, requires to be surrounded with that species of romantic scenery and action, which can only be drawn from distant ages, and from countries remarkable for the antiquity of their origin, and the obscurity of their annals---whereas, works in prose are more generally constructed upon matters of fact, or upon the events of modern times. The requisites, therefore, for a good American poet, are not always necessary to the prose writer: and the latter, if blest with sufficient genius, may equal, and even surpass the most celebrated writers of the old world.

I do not by this, mean to imply that such is the case at present, or even that it is likely to happen for ages to come; but merely that it is not impossible.—As some proof, in justification of my opinion of the literary talent of America, and as a kind of conciliatory shake of the hand, from your brother *satirists* in that country—I have accompanied this letter with a copy of an ingenious little production, entitled *Salmagundi*. It is considered by all who have perused it, as possessing considerable merit. Some trifling errors are apparent; yet considering the peculiarities of the nation from whence it has sprung, I am surprised there are so few. If you have not met with the work before, it will, I think, afford you no mean idea of the native talent of the Americans; and enable you to judge whether their soil is more congenial to prose writing than to poetry.

I am, Sir,
Your very obedient servant,
JOHN LAMBERT.

The opinions of Launcelot Langstaff are of a character somewhat superior to the compositions of his periodical rivals. His satire is more various and more humorous, and his vulgarity less obtrusive. Yet every page reminds the critic of the shop, or the counting house: the wit is of a *tradesmanlike order;* and the general character of its style, resembles that which might be expected from a Portsmouth contractor, who should devote the leisure that remained, from his cables and his tar-barrels, to "learning and the muses." Even the very appellations employed to designate the objects of satirical remark, are characteristic of a nation too earnestly occupied in commercial pursuits, to cultivate with labour or solicitude the pursuits of literature. Straddle, Cockloft, and Giblets, are the most memorable of the personages introduced into Mr. Langstaff's lucubrations; and we thing that the portrait of the first of those individuals, while it evinces the talents of its author, affords a fair but striking exemplification of the faults that we have attempted to describe.

"Straddle had just arrived in an importation of hardware fresh from the city of Birmingham, or rather as the most learned English would call it, Brummagem, so famous for its manufactories of gimblets, penknives, and pepper boxes, and where they make buttons and beaux enough to inundate our whole country. He was a young man of considerable standing in the manufactory at Birmingham, sometimes had the honour to hand his master's daughters into a tim whisky, was the oracle of the tavern he frequented on Sundays, and could beat all his associates if you would take his word for it in boxing, beer drinking, jumping over chairs, and imitating cats in a gutter and opera singers. Straddle was moreover a member of a catch club, and was a great hand at ringing bob-majors; he was of course a complete connoisseur in music, and entitled to assume that character at all performances in the art. He was likewise a member of a spouting club, had seen a company of strolling actors perform in a barn, and had even, like Abel Drugger, " enacted" the part of Major Sturgeon with considerable applause; he was consequently a profound critic, and fully authorised to turn up his nose at any American performances. He had twice partaken of annual dinners given by the head manufactures of Birmingham, where he had the good fortune to get a taste of turbot and turtle, and a smack of champagne and burgundy, and he had heard a vast deal of the roast beef of old England; he was therefore epicure enough to condemn every dish and every glass of wine he had tasted in America, though at the same time he was as voracious an animal as ever crossed the Atlantic. Straddle had been splashed half a dozen times by the carriages of nobility, and had once the superlative felicity of being kicked out of doors by the footman of a noble duke—he could, therefore, talk of nobility, and despise the untitled plebeians of America. In short, Straddle was one of those dapper, bustling, florid, round, self-important ' *gemmen*' who bounce upon us half beau, half button-maker,—undertake to give us the polish of the *bon-ton,* and endeavour to inspire us with a proper and dignified contempt of our native country.

"It is certain that he kept his tailor, and shoemaker constantly employed for a month before his departure, equipped himself with a smart crooked stick, about eighteen inches long, a pair of breeches of most unheard-of length, a little short pair of Hoby's white topped boots, that seemed to stand on tipto to reach his breeches, and his hat had the true transatlantic declination towards his right ear. The fact was, nor did he make any secret of it, he was determined to "astonish the natives a few."

"Straddle was not a little disappointed, on his arrival, to find the Americans were rather more civilized than he had imagined—he was suffered to walk to his lodgings unmolested by a crowd, and even unnoticed by a single individual.—No love letters came pouring in upon him, no rivals lay in wait to assassinate him; his very dress excited no attention, for there were many fools dressed equally ridiculously with himself. This was mortifying indeed to an aspring youth who had come out with the idea of astonishing and captivating. He was equally unfortunate in his pretensions to the character of critic, connoisseur and boxer: he condemned our whole dramatic corps, and every thing appertaining to the theatre; but his critical abilities were ridiculed; he found fault with old Cockloft's dinner, not even sparing his wine, and was never invited to the house afterwards. He scoured the streets at night, and was cudgelled by a sturdy watchman; he hoaxed an honest mechanic, and was soundly kicked: thus disappointed in all his attempts at notoriety, Straddle hit on the expedient which was resorted to by the

Giblets——he determined to take the town by storm. He accordingly bought horses and equipages, and made a furious dash at *style in a gig and tandem.*

"Straddle was equally successful with the Giblets as may be supposed, for though pedestrian merit may strive in vain to become fashionable in Gotham, yet a candidate in an equipage is always recognized, and like Philip's ass laden with gold, will gain admittance every where Mounted in his curricle or his gig, the candidate is like a statute elevated on a high pedestal; his merits are discernible from afar, and strike the dullest optics. O Gotham! Gotham! most enlightened of cities, how does my heart swell with delight when I behold your (thy) sapient inhabitants lavishing their attention with such wonderful discernment.

"Thus Straddle became quite a man of ton, and was caressed, and courted, and invited to dinners and balls. Whatever was absurd or ridiculous in him before, was now declared to be the style. He criticised our theatres and was listened to with reverence. He pronounced our musical entertainments barbarous, and the judgment of Apollo himself would not have been more decisive. He abused our dinners, and the god of eating, if there be any such deity, seemed to speak through his organs: he became at once a man of taste, for he put his malediction on every thing. And his arguments were conclusive, because he supported every assertion with a bet. He was likewise pronounced by the learned of the fashionable world, a young man of deep research and deep observation, for he had sent home as natural curiosities an ear of Indian corn, a pair of moccassons, a belt of wampum, and a four-leaved clover. He had taken great pains to enrich this curious collection with an Indian and a *cataract*, but without success. In fine the people talked of Straddle and his equipage, and Straddle talked of his horses, until it was impossible for the most critical observer to pronounce whether Straddle or his horses were most admired, or whether Straddle admired himself or his horses most. Straddle was now in the zenith of his glory. He swaggered about parlours and drawing rooms with the same unceremonious conduct he used to display in the taverns of Birmingham. He accosted a lady as he would a bar-maid; and this was pronounced a certain proof that he had been used to better company in Birmingham. He became the great man of all the taverns between New York and Haerlem: and no one stood a chance of being accommodated until Straddle and his horses were perfectly satisfied. He bullied the landlords and waiters with the best air in the world, and accosted them with true gentlemanly familiarity. He staggered from the dinner-table to the play, entered the box like a tempest, and staid long enough to be bored to death, and to bore all those who had the misfortune to be near him. From thence he dashed off to a ball, time enough to flounder through a cotillion, tear half a dozen gowns, commit a number of other depredations, and make the whole company sensible of his infinite condescension in coming amongst them. The people of Gotham thought him a prodigious fine fellow: the young bucks cultivated his acquaintance with the most persevering assiduity, and his retainers were sometimes complimented with a seat in his curricle, or a ride on one of his fine horses. The belles were delighted with the attentions of such a fashionable gentleman, and struck with astonishment at his fashionable distinctions between *wrought scissars* and those of *cast-steel*, together with his profound dissertations on buttons and horse-flesh. The rich merchants courted his acquaintance because he was an *Englishman*, and their wives treated him with great defference, because he had come beyond seas. I cannot help here observing that salt water is a marvellous great sharpener of men's wits, and I intend to recommend it to some of my acquaintance in a particular essay."

The career of Straddle terminates by his "*going smash*" into the limits (*rules*) of a prison.

As we understand that Mr. Langstaff's productions are

very highly valued by his countrymen themselves, for the correctness with which he delineates their national manners, there can be no injustice in forming our opinion of the state of American society from his account of Mr. Straddle. It gives us a view of transatlantic refinement as unexpected as unpleasing, to be told, that a *Brummagem* traveller, a fellow who amused the tea-table by dissertations on the manufacture of scissors, a connoisseur in " gimblets and penknives," should obtain by simply assuming the airs of a tavern bully, admission to the circles of " fashionable" society. Nor does it convey a very exalted idea of the decorum or elegance of their public assemblies, that a vulgar and boisterous coxcomb, with the language and manners of a menial, should be entitled by the mere sporting of an equipage, to " tear half a dozen gowns of the American *belles*," not merely with impunity, but with the humble admiration of the " young bucks" of " Gotham." In England, a character like Straddle, would only obtain by his " smashes" the reputation of a swindler, or by his indecorum the castigation that is due to vulgar and impertinent obtrusion.

The poems of Anacreon Moore appear to have obtained as extensive a circulation among the virgins of New York, as among the daughters of our English gentry.

" I hate the loose insidious jest,
To beauty's modest ear addrest,
And hold that frowns should never fail
To check each smooth but fulsome tale,
But he whose impious pen should dare
Invade the morals of the fair;
To taint that purity divine,
Which should each female heart enshrine;
Though soft his vicious strains should swell,
As those which erst from Gabriel fell;
Should yet be held aloft from shame,
And foul dishonour shade his name.

Judge then, my friends, of my surprise,
The ire that kindled in my eyes,
When I relate that t'other day,
I went a morning call to pay,
On two young nieces just come down,
To take the polish of the town;
By which I mean no more nor less,
Than *a la française* to undress,
To whirl the modest Waltz's rounds,
Taught by Dupont for snug ten pounds:
To thump and thunder through a song,
Play *fortes* soft and *dolces* long:
Exhibit loud *piano* feats,
Caught from that crotchet hero Meetz;
To drive the rose-bloom from the face,
And fix the lily in its place;
To doff the white, and in its stead
To bounce about in brazen red.
While in the parlour I delayed
Till they their persons had arrayed,
A dapper volume caught my eye,
That on the window chanced to lie.
A book's a friend—I always choose
To turn its pages and peruse;
It prov'd those poems, known to fame
For praising every Cyprian dame,—
The bantlings of a dapper youth,
Renowned for *gratitude* and *truth*;
A little poet hight TOMMY MOORE,
Who hopped and skipped our country o'er;
Who supped on tea and lived on sops,
Revelled on syllabubs and slops.
And when his brain of cobweb fine,
Was *fuddled with five drops* of wine,
Would all his puny love rehearse,
And many a maid debauch in verse.
Surprized to meet in open view,
A book of such lascivious hue,

I chid my nieces, but they say,
'Tis all the passion of the day;
That many a fashionable *belle*
Will with enraptured accents dwell
On the sweet *morceaux* she has found,
In this delicious cursed compound.

It is evident from the preceding verses, that the Americans are not more successful in the cultivation of satirical than of didactic or descriptive poetry. The metrical compositions of Mr. Langstaff are inferior to the magazine poetry of their parent nation; and the good sense by which his writings are distinguished, never appears under a less pleasing form than when encumbered by the shackles of an imperfect metre, or when the plain and simple accents of truth are lost in the jingle of Hudibrastic rhyme.

THE POLITICAL OBSERVER, No. VIII.

Correspondence between the Prince Regent and the Duke of York.

To H. R. H. the Duke of York.

My dearest brother,

As the restrictions on the exercise of the royal authority will shortly expire, when I must make my arrangements for the future administration of the powers with which I am invested; I think it right to communicate those sentiments, which I was withheld from expressing at an earlier period of the session, by my warmest desire that the expected motion on the affairs of Ireland might undergo the deliberate discussion of parliament unmixed with any other consideration.

I think it hardly necessary to call your recollection to the recent circumstances under which I assumed the authority delegated to me by parliament. My sense of duty to our royal father solely decided that choice, and every private feeling gave way to considerations, which admitted of no doubt or hesitation. I trust I acted, in that respect, as the genuine representative of the august person, whose functions I was appointed to discharge; and I have the satisfaction of knowing, that such was the opinion of persons, for whose judgment and honorable feelings I entertain the highest respect in various instances. When the law of last session left me at full liberty, I waved, as you well know, any personal gratification in order that his majesty might resume, on his restoration to health, every power and prerogative belonging to his crown. I certainly am the last person in the kingdom to whom it can be admitted to despair of our royal father's recovery. A new era is now arrived, and I cannot but reflect with satisfaction on the events which have distinguished the short period of my restricted regency. Instead of suffering in the loss of her possessions by the gigantic force which has been employed against them, Great Britain has added most important acquisitions to her empire. The national faith has been preserved inviolable towards our allies, and if character is strength as applied to a nation, the increased and increasing reputation of his majesty's arms, will shew to the nations of the continent how much they may atchieve, when animated by a glorious spirit of resistance to a foreign yoke. In the critical situation of the war in the Peninsula, I shall be most anxious to avoid any measure which can lead my allies to suppose that I mean to depart from the present system. Perseverance alone can atchieve the great object in question; and I cannot withhold my approbation from those who have honorably distinguished themselves in support of it. I have no predilections to indulge, no resentments to gratify; no objects to attain, but such as are common to the whole empire. If such is the leading principle of my conduct, and I can appeal to the past as evidence of what the future will be, I flatter myself that I shall meet with the support of parliament, and of a candid and enlightened nation. Having made this communication of my sentiments in this new and extraordinary crisis of our affairs, I cannot conclude without expressing the gratification I should feel, if some of those persons with whom the early habits of my public life were formed, would strengthen my hands and constitute a part of my government. With such support, and aided by a vigorous and enlightened administration, formed on the most liberal basis, I shall look with additional confidence to a prosperous issue of the most arduous contest in which Great Britain was ever engaged. You are authorised to communicate these sentiments to Lord Grey, who I have no doubt will make them known to Lord Grenville.

I am always, my dearest Frederic,
Your ever affectionate brother,
(Signed) GEORGE, P. R.

Carlton-House, February 13th, 1812.

P. S. I shall send a copy of this letter immediately to Mr. Perceval.

To H. R. H. the Duke of York.
February 15, 1812.

SIR,

We beg leave most humbly to express to your Royal Highness our dutiful acknowledgments for the gracious and condescending manner in which you have had the goodness to communicate to us the letter of his Royal Highness the Prince Regent, on the subject of the arrangements to be now made for the future administration of the public affairs; and we take the liberty of availing ourselves of your gracious permission, to address to your Royal Highness in this form what has occurred to us in consequence of that communication. The Prince Regent, after expressing to your Royal Highness in that letter, his sentiments on various public matters, has, in the concluding paragraph, condescended to intimate his wish that some of those persons with whom the early habits of his public life were formed, would strengthen his Royal Highness's hands, and constitute a part of his government: and his Royal Highness is pleased to add that with such support, aided by a vigorous and united administration, formed on the most liberal basis, he would look with additional confidence to a prosperous issue of the most arduous contest in which Great Britain has ever been engaged. On the other parts of his Royal Highness's letter we do not presume to offer any observations; but in the concluding paragraph, in so far as we may venture to suppose ourselves included in the gracious wish which it expresses, we owe it, in obedience and duty to his Royal Highness, to explain ourselves, with frankness and sincerity. We beg leave most earnestly to assure his Royal Highness, that no sacrifices, except those of honour and duty, could appear to us too great to be made, for the purpose of healing the divisions of our country, and uniting both its government and its people. All personal exclusion we entirely disclaim: we rest on public measures; and it is on this ground alone that we must express, without reserve, the impossibility of our uniting with the present government. Our differences of opinion are too many and too important to admit of such an union. His Royal Highness will, we are confident, do us the justice to remember, that we have twice already acted on this impression: in 1809, on the proposition then made to us under his majesty's authority; and last year, when his Royal Highness was pleased to require our advice respecting the formation of a new government. The reasons which we then humbly submitted to him are strengthened by the increasing dangers of the times: nor has there, down to this moment, appeared even any approximation towards such an agreement of opinion on the public interests, as can alone form a basis for the honorable union of parties previously opposed to each other. Into the detail of those differences we are unwilling to enter; they embrace almost all the leading features of the present policy of the empire; but his Royal Highness has, himself, been pleased to advert to the late deliberations of parliament on the affairs of Ireland. This is a subject, above all others, important in itself, and connected with the most pressing dangers. Far from concurring in the sentiments which his majesty's ministers have, on that occasion so recently expressed, we entertain opinions directly opposite; we are firmly persuaded of the necessity of a total change in the present system of that country, and of the immediate repeal of those civil disabilities under which so large a portion of his majesty's subjects still labour on account of their religious opinions. To recommend to parliament this repeal, is the first advice which it would be our duty to offer to His Royal Highness, could we, even for the shortest time, make ourselves responsible for any farther delay in the prospect of a measure, without which we could entertain no hope of rendering ourselves useful to His Royal Highness, or to the country. We have only further to beg your Royal Highness to lay before his Royal Highness the Prince Regent, the expression of our humble duty, and the sincere and respectful assurance of our earnest wishes for whatever may best promote the ease, honour, and advantage of his Royal Highness's government, and the success of his endeavours for the public welfare. We have the honour to be, &c.

(Signed) " GREY.
" GRENVILLE."

It will appear from the preceding correspondence that the conduct of the Prince Regent, whatever may be thought of its wisdom or expedience, has been precisely that which in our repeated strictures* on the language of the opposition journalists, we ventured to anticipate. The

---

* See more particularly No. VII. Art. 1. in which we anticipated the change that has taken place in the views of the Prince Regent.

chief magistrate of the nation is evidently a convert to the Pittites on every subject of vital importance to the interests of the state. He has declared his intention to persevere in the war of the Peninsula, and we shall endeavour to prove in the course of our observations that his opinions on the catholic question are decidedly hostile to the claims of that large proportion of the community which has looked up to his accession with the warmest feelings of anticipated gratitude.

That such would be the bias of his opinions on his elevation to unrestricted power we ventured to foretel without any reference to their justice or expedience. No ground of prophecy respecting the intentions of a monarch can be more fallacious than his declarations as a prince. The political opinions of the Regent's friends, are of a nature to captivate the fancy and awaken the enthusiasm of a youthful and ardent mind, unvitiated by intrigue, and naturally predisposed to the reception of pleasing visions of futurity. The doctrines of universal toleration, and the principles of unrestricted liberty were peculiarly acceptable to a Prince of Wales, who had some right to consider himself as a martyr to the rigid and cautious policy of his father. But he has now attained a period of life at which the generous passions have subsided into quiescence, and when the first motive of action is convenience. His very acquaintance with the fundamental principles of the Lambes and the Moiras must have taught him how little they are congenial to the habits of a court, and how little their diffusion must contribute to the gratification of a sovereign. It is natural and consistent with rational expectation, that the chief magistrate of a great nation should be most firmly attached to that party of which the principles are most decidedly hostile to the encroachments of the people. A ministry that pledges itself to the support of whatever is established, who deem it a preliminary objection to any measure, however inconsistent with justice or expedience, that it encroaches on the prerogatives of the crown, and who shudder at the slightest progress towards the most necessary reform, must be on the general principles of moral deduction, and without any reference to personal character, the favoured and confidential servants of a limited monarch.

It may be asserted indeed that the aristocracy of the Grenvilles has never been disputed, and that their reverence for hereditary honors, and the *hauteur* of exalted birth, are not less visible in their political measures than their personal habits. But the pride of the Grenvilles has too much of the *baronial* character: its reference to the immediate fountain of hereditary honor, is less conspicuous than its independent and inherent dignity; and the principles in which alone they could act with the appearance of consistency, have been too plainly relaxed by their necessary intercourse with the " lower Foxites" under the guidance of Mr. Sheridan.

It was to be presumed, therefore, *à priori*, that the Prince of Wales, as soon as he should enter on the unrestricted exercise of the royal authority, would consult his own gratification as a monarch, by the retention of the present ministers in office. But whatever predisposition he might feel towards this line of conduct, would be animated and confirmed, by the advantages arising to the sovereign from their peculiar system of foreign policy. The influence of the crown must be augmented or diminished in proportion as we augment or diminish our relations with foreign states, and our preparations for foreign warfare. Fraternal attachment may be supposed to have some influence on the Regent; and it is impossible not to perceive how much the power and the reputation of the Duke of York, have risen above their ordinary level, since we first engaged in the defence of the Peninsula.

The amount of the patronage exercised by the crown, in the appointments to the commissariat, in the selection of persons to fill the more important departments connected with our military arrangements, and in the grant of titular or pecuniary reward to the officers who distinguish themselves by their bravery, or to the negociators who fulfil to the satisfaction of their royal master the instructions with which they are honored, is beyond all estimate; and not only this extensive addition to the influence of the crown, but all that might arise from the continuance of our relations with Sicily, or the formation of future continental alliances, would be abstracted from its possession, by the admission of Lord Grey and his party into the Regent's councils.

We do not mean by these observations to insinuate, that the war of the Peninsula would not have been persisted in by the Prince Regent, on the ground of its expedience. We have always endeavoured to defend our first cooperation with the Spaniards; and even were we now to admit the original impolicy of the war, it would be impossible to retreat with honor or safety. Were our troops to be withdrawn from the Peninsula at the present moment, we should never regain our natural rank among the nations of Europe. We have stimulated Spain to perseverance in the contest: confiding in our assurances of protection, she has defied the power, and exasperated the malignant passions of her invader; and who but a political poltroon would advise his sovereign to desert her cause, and to bring irretrievable disgrace on the English character, by the violation of the most sacred engagements, and by the sacrifice of a brave and generous nation to that power which we taught them to defy, and that revenge which our own provocations have contributed to excite?

The country is too well acquainted with the Grenvilles, to believe that their opposition to the war of the Peninsula has proceeded from any motive of purer patriotism than the hope of distressing its projectors. In their observations on our foreign policy, and on the conduct of Lord Wellington, the whig-leaders have neither been consistent with themselves, nor with each other: they derided and traduced Lord Wellington, till they were taught by the expression of the public sentiment, that they carried their hypocrisy too far; they are now content to dwell on the distinction between the measures pursued, and the means employed to carry them into execution: a distinction just in itself, but which they chose not to perceive, till Lord Wellington's fame had soared above the reach of party detraction. The editor of the Morning Chronicle, forgetting all the sneers and inuendos in which he so eagerly indulged till the beginning of the last campaign, is now too happy if his readers will give him credit for the uniformity with which he has confessed, and the enthusiasm with which he has admired, our commander's merts. On recurring to the speeches of the opposition members, and the comments of their literary partizans, it is impossible not to perceive that if the ministers had not engaged in the defence of the peninsula, they would have been as much abused by their opponents for inaction, as they are now censured for their profusion and temerity. The charge of imbecility would have been re-echoed from one part of the kingdom to another: Lord Temple would have declaimed on the madness of losing the only opportunity that providence had thrown in our way of contributing to the recovery of European independence; Mr. Whitbread would have called for the vengeance of the country upon men who could leave a brave, generous, and patriotic people to contend, unaided, in unequal content against the invasion of a foreign tyrant; and the Edinburgh Reviewers, " humbly submitting themselves to the lords and gentlemen in parliament assembled," would have ventured " to hint a doubt" whether France might not be more effectually attacked through the intervention of Spain, than by the capture of an Indian sp ce island. Where ministers must be censured, any side of a question may be assumed as the right one; of the old topics of attack, some were too hacknied for repetition, and others could not be employed without inconvenience to themselves. Moderate reform was a very useful subject of declamation, but it was difficult to use it in debate without affording some ground of advantage or exultation to the Burdettites: the catholic question had been so frequently debated that the ministers were ready at reply, and the people weary of its discussion; and no temporary subject could be found of so much abstract importance, or implying so heavy and immediate a responsibility on the part of ministers, as the war in the Peninsula.

But whatever might be the real sentiments of the leaders of opposition on this important subject, the Prince could only judge of the system they might pursue, in case of their accession to power, by their previous declarations: to call them to the undivided possession of the cabinet would have been therefore to relinquish a policy to which we have shewn that his situation must have rendered him partial, and which he declares to be conformable to his feelings of honour and expedience. But he had just reason to expect that he should be able to form an administration which while it should not abandon the cause of the Peninsula, would be collectively more favourably disposed towards the catholics of Ireland, and less decidedly hostile to the Americans, than the cabinet as it was composed at the moment of his accession to unrestricted power. An understanding among the members of a ministry chosen from opposite parties is neither unusual nor unnatural. Something might have been yielded and something obtained, on both sides. If the leaders of two great parties must never coalesce, the nation must always be hurried to extremes. The wise and virtuous principles of one party can never be acted upon without equal perseverance in the furtherance of injustice and impolicy; every change of policy consequent on a change of ministry must be radical: the good must be overturned with the bad: and on the dismissal of Mr. Perceval and his friends, the opposition could not emancipate the Irish Catholics, without recalling the orders in council, and withdrawing our troops from the Peninsula. Suppose for a moment that one of these measures might be foolish, and the rest judicious, what is the policy or plausibility of a system of government that subjects the Prince Regent to the necessity of chusing a cabinet that if it does one right action, must commit two wrong ones? If the Prince Regent is unable out of all the parties of which the two houses are composed, to form an administration, that shall judge of every measure by no other criterion than its justice and expedience, what have we to hope from the talents or virtues of the sovereign?

After having retained the servants of his father, because the war of the Peninsula could not be conducted without them, it may at first sight appear that the Prince was compelled to sacrifice, what in his opinion might appear a lesser object to a greater; and that the expression of his sentiments in favor of the catholic claims, is only deferred to a more propitious opportunity. But the language of his communication to Lord Grey, excludes the possibility of this conjecture: by leaving the question on the state of Ireland to be debated and determined, without his interference, to what higher praise can he aspire, than that of having left the house of commons at the mercy of Mr. Perceval? His Royal Highness must have known that the ministers would, independently of the justice of their cause, obtain a majority; and if he felt any sympathy, therefore, in the sufferings of the catholics, he would have thrown at least so much of his personal influence into the favourable scale, as to outweigh the undue weight of ministerial ascendancy. But it is superfluous to draw any conclusions from the language of the Prince, when it is in our power to judge of his future policy by his political acts. The return of Lord Castlereagh to the secretaryship of war, is a virtual declaration of hostility towards the claims of the catholics: whether the refusal of those claims be an injury, is a question on which the country will always be divided; but that the recal of such a man to the councils of the sovereign, is not only a declaration of unchangeable opposition to those claims on the part of the Regent, but a gross and *gratuitous* insult to the nation at large, and the catholics in particular, who but his lordship himself, would have the folly to deny? Whatever sorrow and astonishment may be felt by the Irish catholics, at the disappointment of those hopes that they had so long and so warmly cherished of the decisive interference of the heir apparent in the prosecution of their claims, must be aggravated to a dangerous degree by the immediate restoration to the cabinet of an individual, as inveterately hostile to their efforts, and so universally *distrusted* (to use no *libellous term*) by every rank and description of society, whatever may be their political bias, or their religious persuasion. It is indeed a bitter satire on the public men of this country, that out of the ministerial party, no other person could be found to fulfil the duties of the secretary at war, than an individual who of all others had proved himself to be incompetent to the office, whose incapacity had already wasted our resources, sacrificed many thousands of our troops, and rendered us the scorn and the opprobrium of Europe. What conclusion can even the most ardent admirers of a great personage deduce from the recal of such a man to power, but that the future acts of *his ministry* will be marked by the same indifference to the opinion of the nation; that impotence, vanity, and deceit, will continue to flourish beneath the sway of the idol of the people; and that beneath the auspices of Mr. Perceval, no wickedness shall be so enormous, nor any incapacity so evident, as to exclude its possessor from exercising the functions of an office immediately connected with the prosperity and safety of the empire?

And if the appointment of Lord Castlereagh to the responsible situation of secretary at war, be expedient, on the part of the Regent's ministers, what can be thought of his lordship's acquiescence? To brave the scorn and indignation of the community, is only possible to him whose energies are fortified by the confidence of virtue, to whom nature has denied the instructive feelings of manhood, whose sensations have been hardened by perpetual attrition, against every impulse of shame, or whose avarice overpowers every generous and honorable sentiment. If Lord Castlereagh be satisfied with the testimony of his own conscience, we exhort him to commit the grounds of his self-satisfaction to the world: to repress the uneasiness that the report of his reinstatement has excited, and avert the dangers that it may not improbably occasion, are acts of duty to that gracious master whose councils he has been called to enlighten by his wisdom and whose dominions he is expected to extend and consolidate by his vigor.

It is evident that in the retention of his father's counsellors, the Regent was not prevented from the dismissal of the subordinate and obnoxious officers of state. Sir Samuel Romilly might have been called to succeed the present Attorney-General to the satisfaction of the country, and without any disarrangement in the construction or system of government. The dismissal of Sir Vicary would have been hailed by every class of society, as a pledge on the part of the Regent of his respect for the liberty of the press, and his deference to the opinion of his subjects. It has been said that to deprive the Attorney-General of his present dignity, would be to dismiss a zealous and worthy servant at the command of the multitude. This assertion means nothing more, than that the zeal of a state officer however misapplied or injudicious is deserving of reward, that the feelings of a man in authority are to be of more weight with his sovereign than the liberty of the subject, and that the British public is a clamorous and unthinking rabble. While such a man retains the power of issuing *ex officio* informations, it is impossible to discuss any political question without stopping to calculate at the conclusion of every paragraph, whether it does or does not contain a sentence that may subject its writer to an imprisonment of two years in a distant gaol. That the law of libel is in itself imperfect and unjust, we admit; but till it be amended let its administration be committed to other men than those who weep over the misfortunes of convicted traitors, while they pursue with unrelenting rigor the *verba ardentia* of the literary advocates of national independence.

While we are decidedly of opinion, therefore, that the Prince Regent by the retention of his present ministers has acted more wisely and more consistent with the interests of the nation than if he had called the opposite party into unconditional power, we cannot but regret most deeply that he should have displayed such early and positive indications of attachment to the obnoxious as well as the beneficial features of their system; that he should have considered the retention of Mr. Perceval and his coadjutors as a pledge for his acquiescence in their wishes with regard to every obnoxious or subordinate department in the state, and for a coincidence in their sentiments on every subject of national importance. We should have thought it possible that without any material interference with the present arrangements, the catholic question might have been left open to further discussion, that some pledges might have been given for the observance of the liberty of the press, and for the abolition of obnoxious sinecures, and that those politicians of the day who had given decided and repeated proofs of incapacity, malignity, and folly, would have been dismissed or excluded from office. But as the case now stands the system of the Pittites is not only triumphant in its general principles, but in its minute details: the most obnoxious creatures of the ministry are suffered to enjoy the fruits of their subservience in undisturbed tranquillity, and the dreams of the sanguine and the hopes of the good, are more distant from fulfilment than when a Bowles stood forth as the champion of his sovereign.

THE TEARS OF SIR VICARY!!!

Sir,

The sensibility displayed by Sir Vicary Gibbs, before the court of Special Commission, has excited no less surprize among his brethren of the long robe, than among his unprofessional auditors. The tears of an Attorney General are acknowledged by every one to be "exceeding great" curiosities; but the tears of Sir Vicary surpass, in rarity and value, the stream that flowed from the Princess Periwitta, or the gems that adorn the cabinets of the British Museum. The Regent's palace instead of being supported by vulgar Caryatides, may now be embellished with the heads of his Chancellors and Attorney Generals, and the statues of Niobe give place to the bust of a weeping *Gibbs*.

Such is the abstract value of these memorable effusions; but as indications of the moral and intellectual qualities, their claim to confidence or admiration will be more reluctantly admitted. In my professional capacity I have had occasion to observe that among children the most angry, ill-tempered, and malicious little urchins, are most susceptible of lachrymal irritation; and that in adults a propensity towards the indulgence of "tearful" effusions is more frequently the characteristic of nervous irritability, than of sensibility or benevolence. I need not recal to your recollection that many of the most profligate and malignant tyrants of antiquity were remarkable for their expertness at shedding tears; that Agathocles occupied many successive hours in the amusement of crying, and that *Xerxes* proceeding with an army of slaves to overwhelm the liberties of Greece, was moved to tears by the reflection that out of the innumerable legions subservient to his sway, not one survivor would remain to witness the termination of another century. The Duchess of Guise, who planned the massacre of St. Bartholomew, and assisted at its execution, was much given to weeping; and Lord Chancellor Jeffries is credibly reported to have been detected more than once in the act of crying.

Reasoning from appearances, therefore, the late exhibition of Sir Vicary afforded no satisfactory evidence of his tenderness or humanity; and we must refer to the general tenor of his conduct, and to other important epochs in his professional career, for the materials of just conclusion. It does not appear that the warmest of his admirers, or the most devoted of his friends, suspected him, previous to the appointment of the Special Commission, of harbouring an inconvenient portion of the milk of human kindness. But many subjects are involved in darkness till information brings them to light; and it is no proof of Sir Vicary's insensibility or cruelty, that his friends have not been able to discover in his composition any indication of the contrary qualities. Yet there are occasions on which forbearance would have done as much credit to Sir Vicary's humanity, as commiseration in the instance before us. I cannot persuade myself, that he has learned to regard every punishment that falls short of death, as too trifling to demand his personal sympathy: that in sending an individual for two or three years to a distant gaol, he believes himself to be performing an act of professional kindness; and would say to the objects of his visitations, if the expression of his sentiments were permitted, " be thankful that you are not brought to the gallows or the scaffold! You may ascribe it to the peculiar mildness of my temper, that you are suffered to languish in a prison!" Yet unless this be the spirit in which he acts, and the feeling by which he is impelled, on what principle can we account for the number and activity of his prosecutions for libel, while he is affected to tears by the condemnation of a traitor? If the persons tried under the authority of the Commission, be worthy of the royal mercy, they will obtain it, the tears of Sir Vicary were perfectly gratuitous; and if they be found not to deserve the Regent's commiseration, it would be difficult to tell in what respect their claim on the sympathy of an Attorney General is more powerful, than that of the unfortunate individuals who have been drawn from the successful prosecution of their professional pursuits, and sentenced to long and lingering confinement, because in their zeal for the liberties of their country, their prudence was less conspicuous than their enthusiasm.

The tears of the great and eminent, whatever may be the objects that excite them, are always worthy of poetic celebration: and I was about to try my hand at a duet, between the crying Attorney General and the weeping Chancellor, when it fortunately occurred to me, that lawyers are very formidable persons, that in the eye of the law eulogy is not clearly distinguishable from libel, and that to satirize the *outs* was much more safe and laudable than to celebrate the *ins*. Lord Grenville's disappointment became the theme of my condolence, and with the aid of Hamilton of Bangor, I have composed a ballad, which may not be entirely unworthy of your notice. I need not point out to you the simple, pathetic, and pastoral effect communicated to the dialogue by the introduction of the Scottish dialect. P. S.

THE OPPOSITION LAMENT.
* *Tune* (the *Braes* of Yarrow.)

Perceval. Weep on! weep on! thou haughty peer,
   Weep on! weep on! with lamentation;
  Weep on! weep on! no more thou'lt see,
   The Regent of this gallant nation.

 Gr. Oh where gat ye that bonny bonny star;
   And where gat ye that ribbon blue?

M——a. I gat it where ye mun ne come near,
   Frae the blyth prince for service true.

Perceval. Weep on! weep on! thou flouted loon,
   Weep on! weep on! thou gowky doodle!
  Or if thou'rt shamed at hame to stay,
   Gang eat thy mess wi' Yankey Doodle.

---

* See the beautiful ballad beginning " Busk, busk ye, my bonny bride."

Friend. Why does he weep, that portly portly lord,
    Why does he weep wi' lamentation?
  And why maun he nae mair be seen
    Wi' the Regent o' this gallant nation?

Per. Lang maun he weep, lang maun, lang maun he weep,
    Lang maun he weep wi' dule and sorrow;
  For he has tint the Treasury dear,
    And Castlereagh returns to-morrow.

Friend. Why look, oh Stow! thy towers so brown,
    Why is thy hall so sad, so gloomy;
  And why such melancholious sounds,
    Thro' mansions rich, and light, and roomy?

Gren. Curse ye, oh curse ye that veto veto sad,
    The hand that wrought the mournful letter;
  The fatal pen that scrawled his name,
    I could ha' borne death's warrant better!

Friend. Did I not warn thee, not not to speak,
    And warn from talk of toleration?
  But rashly bauld, thou would'st gae rave
    Of catholic emancipation.

  Sweet sweet is power, indeed 'tis sweet,
    And tempting tempting the Exchequer,
  And nobly flies ambition's steed,
    No powerfu' rival nigh to check her.

  Is power so sweet? as sweet the peace
    Of mind, fra' conscious right arising:
  Tempting is wealth? no golden treasure
    Compar'd with virtue's worth thy prizing.

  Cheer up! cheer up! thou portly portly lord,
    Cheer up! cheer up! and eat thy dinner!
  Leave the flunky squad to their ain sweet selves,
    And pardon gi' to the royal sinner.

Gren. How can I cheer up! a portly portly lord,
    Or! how for grief, fa' to my dinner;
Or how, distent wi' muckle wae
    Forget, forgive the royal sinner?

The Prince put on his royal royal robes,
    His regent's crown and dofft his feather,
Ah! wretched me, I little little kenned,
    What storms would follow sunshine weather.

The Prince drove out with his milk-white milk-
    white steeds,
Unheedful of my dule and sorrow;
And ne'er from Hertford-house return'd,
    Till early dawning o' the morrow.

Much I rejoiced that waeful waeful day,
    I quoted Horace, *ad Pisonem*,
But lang 'ere night the letter came,
    And Grey *in condolationem*.

My happy rivals may be, may be proud,
    With cruel and ungentle scoffin',
While from my coach the fringe is torn;
    And from my wig the bag is doffin'!

Oh, prince unkind, Oh! cruel cruel prince;
    How could'st thou tempt me to self-slaughter?
Thou kenn'st if thee I cannot serve,
    I wi' not live to serve thy daughter.

But thirty thousand I yearly yearly take
    Frae the public purse, and I take care on't;
And I had hoped, O cruel cruel prince,
    To hae full fifty thousand mair on't.

Friend. Return, return, Oh! portly portly lord,
    The Regent heeds not of thy greeting,
Return up stairs, thy friends so gay,
    And a' thy woes forget in eating.

TO HIS GRACE THE LORD ARCHBISHOP OF YORK.

"England expects every man to do his duty."

NELSON.

My Lord,

These memorable words were the last orders of the greatest man in his profession that ever graced the annals of British maritime warfare: a man who acted firmly up to the extent of the most capacious ideas, who suffered not any opportunity to escape him; who was not contented with merely directing, but by the vigor of his personal exertions animated the drooping spirits of his friends, and appalled the hearts of the bravest of his enemies. It was true, he might not, at certain times, seem to possess the wisdom of the serpent; his measures were of that truly bold and decisive cast, of which the puny mind of the wary logician has not the least conception; but then, on the other hand, he was never known supinely to watch the augmentation of a torrent for the mere purpose of shewing his adroitness in subterfuge, by an endeavour to stifle its impetus by *lateral incision*.

I offer no apology, my Lord, for thus addressing you. I do believe you to be a wise and virtuous man, and trust I shall deport myself with all due respect for your person, and exalted station, clothing the not unwelcome truths I have to utter in becoming language—further, I have good reasons for supposing, will not be required of me—the soul of a *Vernon* would sicken at the incense of flattery.

The times, my Lord, are portentous; the prospect around us sombre in the extreme; menaced from without by a cold-blooded, calculating, persevering enemy, an enemy who has not for years back averted his political eye from one stated point; who steadily, as the basilisk, flashes (hitherto impotent) destruction towards us; who estimates our subversion as the key-stone of that arch, which is designed to support the vast unwieldy fabric of his impious usurpations. Wonderful, indeed, has been the success attendant upon the enterprizes of this hitherto seemingly favored mortal! Whether he be an agent in the hand of Providence to drain the vial of its wrath upon the continent of Europe to the very dregs; or whether his unparalleled atchievements arise from taking a more than lynx-eyed view into the springs and dependencies of human actions, is not perhaps easily determined; nevertheless, his gigantic career cannot wisely be viewed with that *affectation of indifference,* which, more than probably, has ill concealed cowardice for its basis. The ever restless activity of his mind, combined with his comparatively inexhaustible resources, must in time, erect a machine of which the ponderosity will excite a sensation somewhat different from *contempt.*

Suffer me, my Lord, from the pinnacle of that venerable edifice, the established Church of England, on which you are so worthily, and I hope propitiously seated, to direct your eyes downward for a moment. View the wild mass of waters rolling round its base—hark how the surges dash the spray, till it even moistens the border of your vestments—the sapped foundation, ever-saturated, regorges the insidious element deeply tinged with its remotest particles.---My Lord!---It shrinks---it totters under you! Heaven shield your lordship, and all good men, from the momentum of such a descending mass! In the pages of the Scourge, for January ast, I pointed out, by an humble address to the *ergy,* the means most likely to obviate those difficulties. with which we are entirely surrounded. Had it fortunately been of any avail, your Lordship would not, in this instance, have been approached by an obscure unlettered lay-man. But no---either total disregard, or the deepest obloquy have been hurled at its author. I confess I augur a better fate to this appeal to their *superior*. Cast but a single glance, my Lord, round the pale the line of circumvallation, of that establishment of which you are so nearly the head. View but the chasms from whence issue herds of agriculturalists---boards of commissioners (their motive for qualifying, to which, God, their own consciences and some few of their fellow subjects well know! —public and private drunkards and avaricious gamblers) Well may the dissenters increase! In vain, my Lord, are exclusive systems of national education: the effect and fate of Sunday schools too clearly prove the futility of every effort of that nature, unaided by *a radical reformation* in the lives and manners of the clergy. What are canons, if not to bind *that body?* What are statutes, if *magistrates* brave them to the very teeth? In order to shew that this is not merely chimerical, I will lightly touch on a few instances by way of exemplification. By 43 Geo. 3, Ch. 84, Sec. 4. it is enacted " that such clerical persons as have not sufficient glebe, may with the consent and approbation of the bishop of the diocese signified in writing, for a limited term of years, take any farm or farms, lands, tenements, or hereditaments, that may, under all the circumstances, appear to such bishop proper to be taken, held, or occupied by any such spiritual person *for the convenience and accommodation of his household and hospitality only.*" And by Sec. 5. " Such clerical persons may hold estates as property, but not any farm for cultivation, unless under a lease granted on or before *Jan.* 1. 1803, or by consent of the bishop signified in writing as aforesaid. This is the positive law of the land; and yet, within less than a day's ride from this spot, hundreds of acres are occupied in sheer defiance of its power. Would your Lordship think it possible for a *magistrate* thus to err? Can you imagine any active *vigilant magistrate*, adorned with the cobwebs brushed from the precious lumber of James and Elizabeth, (just as applicable to the present state of society in Britain, as they would be to the natives of Otaheite) so far to forget his situation---his oath---his function, as to be incited by a thirst of gain *to violate the statute law of the land*--- those statutes of which he is the sworn administrator? My Lord, instances are not wanting of *after-dinner boastings* of the annual hundreds cleared by permissions obtained under the special circumstance of a *deficiency in glebe,* and granted expressly *in aid thereto,* for the convenience and accommodation of the clergyman's household and hospitality *only:* but that your lordship ever willingly authorized so palpable, so gross a dereliction, I will not, I dare not, for one moment believe, and I hold it a most foul calumny in any one to assert it. It is possible the illegal occupation is not absolutely without approbation in writing; for it were no difficult matter, on an emergency of that nature, after a description of the premises, to couch the request in the humble interrogative used of old by Lot "*is it not a little one?*" Also by Canon 75, " No ecclesiastical person shall at any time, other than for their honest necessities, resort to any taverns or alehouses, neither shall they board or lodge in any such place. Furthermore they shall not give themselves to any base or servile labour, or to drinking or riot, spending their time idly by day or by night, playing dice, cards or tables, or any other unlawful game; but at all times convenient, they shall hear or read somewhat of the holy scriptures, or shall occupy themselves with some other honest study or exercise, always doing the things which shall appertain to honesty," &c. &c. &c. Yet notwithstanding this most pointed, this total prohibition, many are the places where clergymen of various descriptions, *magisterial* ones included, in public rooms every evening (Sundays to be for the present excepted) spend their hours in gambling at cards, and some not without being strongly suspected of swerving occasionally *from the things which appertain to honesty.* My

Lord, may I presume to ask you one serious question? Is it possible those open infractions of duty can escape the observance of the *laity*? It does not require either fine sense or exalted sense to discover such flagrant breaches of rectitude---no, my Lord, the common *day labourer---the chimney sweeper*, shake the head at it---the very *scavenger* employed under their window openly comments upon them! While the stream flows thus polluted, in vain are systems of national education. In all the resolutions I have hitherto read issuing from that source, not a single word occurs, not the most distant hint is suffered to escape of the least necessity for any rectification of conduct in the clergy; no, it is quite sufficient to collect a number of children belonging to the labouring poor and take them to church---the thing, my Lord, has already been tried: *the Sunday schools are a case in point*, from them have the rank of the Dissenters been amply, yea over amply swelled. That aliment which to a hale and vigorous constitution would afford the greatest nutriment and support, would to an infirm an emaciated frame operate as a deadly poison. Your Lordship well knows no succedaneum is to be found for the honest, the conscientious discharge of a clergyman's duty. Much has been said on the subject of a *general* diffusion of knowledge; this in every stage of society must be partially dependant on circumstances; in a common way, where a *general* invitation is given to *inspect* any thing whatever, care is *generally* taken to render the *object* and every thing *appertaining* thereunto, *as fit to be seen as possible*. Truth and honesty, my Lord, will always bear the strictest scrutiny of day-light---truth needs not the arm of power---the lash of coercion to support it---truth courts enquiry, and rectitude will ever glory in the diffusion of information. All may yet be well if the clergy will condescend to *allure* the seceders to their deserted fold; but if a pertinacious adherence to those courses which they certainly know are inimical to their spiritual calling, is to be persisted in, then (merely upon the first principle in nature) let every nerve be strained hermetically to seal *the fount of knowledge*---let the *veil of ignorance* be augmented by the triply opake web of Egyptian tangible obscurity! The time is even now come when ENGLAND EXPECTS EVERY MAN TO DO HIS DUTY; let but the clergy of the established church of England punctiliously perform theirs, and, in allusion to any foreign invader, each Briton may apostrophize in the nervous language of the poet,

" Oh sons of earth! attempt ye still to rise,
" By mountains pil'd on mountains to the skies?
" Heav'n still with laughter the vain toil surveys,
" And buries mad men in the heaps they rise."

A FRIEND TO THE ESTABLISHED CHURCH.
Southwell, February 20*th*, 1812.

RE-APPEARANCE OF THOMAS PAINE.

SIR,

As a stedfast and persevering champion of the public morals, and a zealous advocate of the national religion, I had fully expected to find in the last number of your work, some strictures on an infamous pamphlet, entitled " The Age of Reason, Part the third; being an examination of the Passages in the New Testament, quoted from the Old, and containing Prophecies, concerning Jesus Christ. By Thomas Paine, &c.; published by Daniel Isaac Eaton," the ci-devant Bibliopolist of Jacobinism, at a place which he denominates " the Ratiocinatory, or Magazine for Truth and Goodsense, *Ave Maria Lane!* The preface, I have reason to believe, was written by the unfortunate Clio Rickman, and contains nothing more than the hacknied quibble on the word " Apology" prefixed to the title of Bishop Watson's answer to the former parts of the Age of Reason. The concluding paragraph, however, is worthy of attention. In the Antijacobin Review, the Gentleman's Magazine, and in many other periodical works, there has been circulated a long account of the last moments of Paine, in which a most deplorable picture is exhibited of the infidel's last moments. The account itself, however, bears very evident marks of fanatical origin; and the writer of the preface to the work now before me, assures us, on the authority of many persons now living in England and America, that the relation is a contemptible farrago of falsehood and nonsense. The result of my own enquiries has brought me to the same conclusion; and as infidelity is more frequently hardened to insensibility than awakened to a conviction of its danger, what can we say of the advocates of religion, who could descend to so contemptible an imposition, but that their zeal was greater than their prudence, and their hypocrisy more evident than their honesty?

The most curious part of the " introductory matter" is " an impromptu to the memory of Thomas Paine," apparently by the writer of the preface.

> Whilst reviling foes, who knew thee not,
>   Employ their tongues in *vain*;
> Who no one virtue having got
>   Love others to *defame*.
> Whilst bigots curse and rogues revile
>   This great man now no more;
> Who would in pity, if alive,
>   Their want of sense deplore.
> Whilst vile reports* of his last breath
>   The liar's mouth still fill;
> Truth will at last rise up supreme,
>   And choak the villain's skill.

" * See Times newspaper. Falsehood with some addition taken from the Baptist Magazine. The parson or preacher in that work informs his readers that he had it from the portfolio of a brother minister, alias preacher, who might perhaps have dreamed like unto Joseph, who had so many dreams, but never dreamed about christianity, nor ever attended his son's lectures."

> Whilst princes, judges, bishops, peers,
>   His head and heart condemn,
> He is, my friend, as plain appears,
>   A god compared to them.

After this " farrago of nonsense and falsehood," we are favored with an address from Paine himself, to the ministers and preachers of all denominations of religion, in which he endeavours to prove the folly of religious belief, from the disputes and dissentions that have always divided the christian world. " One set of preachers (he observes) make salvation to consist in believing: they tell their congregations, that if they believe in Christ, their sins shall be forgiven. This in the first place is an encouragement to sin, in a similar manner, as when a prodigal young fellow is told his father will pay all his debts, he runs into debt the faster, and becomes the more extravagant. Daddy, says he, pays all, and on he goes. Just so in the other case, Christ pays all, and on goes the sinner."

" Another set of preachers tell their congregation that God predestinated and selected from all eternity, a certain number to be saved, and a certain number to be damned eternally. If this were true, the day of judgment is past, their preaching is in vain, and they had better work at some useful calling for their livelihood. Can a bad man be reformed by telling him that if he is one of those who *was* decreed to be damned before he was born, his reformation will do him no good; and that if he was decreed to be saved, he will be saved, whether he believes it or not, for this is the result of the doctrine? such preaching and such preachers do injury to the moral world. They had better be at the plough."

These extracts afford a just view, not only of the mode of reasoning by which Paine and his disciples attack the strong holds of religion; but of the manner in which they obtrude themselves on the notice of their fellow creatures. When an infidel is spoken of, he expects to be treated with all imaginable courtesy; when he speaks himself, he applies to all who are not prepared for the reception of his sentiments, the epithets of fools and rascals. He forgets, that among multitudes he stands alone; that in such a situation some doubt of the correctness of his own opinions, and some moderation in their expressions is not only prudent, but necessary, if his cause be just, to its favorable reception: he stops not to enquire, whether if his fellow creatures be the dupes of prejudice, that prejudice may not contribute to their happiness; and he forgets that if the multitude, by possibility, be right, he has cruelly and gratuitously lacerated its most sacred feelings, and weakened even the salutary authority of imperishable truth.

That Paine was a man of considerable talents, is confessed by the Bishop of Landaff, and is evident from the present publication. He excels in the art of putting ingenious sophistries into the homely garb of humble common sense. In his Appendix he says "I do not believe because a man and woman make a child, that it imposes on the Creator the unavoidable obligation of keeping the being so made in eternal existence hereafter." By the general reader, this sentence will be received as the concise expression of a plain and rational opinion; it will not occur to one purchaser of the book out of ten, that the power of bringing other beings into the world, was conferred by the Almighty power, and its future operation predetermined.

It would appear, from the concluding paragraph, that the vanity of Thomas Paine was at least commensurate with his talents. "This," says he, " is my opinion. It is consistent with my idea of God's justice, and with the reason he has given me; *and I gratefully know he has given me a large share of that divine gift.*" It is not my intention, however, to enter into a minute analysis of his posthumous attacks on the christian religion. To engage in controversy with the infidel, unless in detail, is worse than unprofitable; nor should I have obtruded even thus far on your patience, had not I been anxious to direct your future attention to the productions of Mr. Eaton's manufactory. I remain, with great respect,

Orchard-street, Feb. 18, 1812. J. L. BUTLER, M. D.

CUMBRIAN TRANSFORMATIONS, or LOVE and METHODISM.

Sir,

In the parish of which your present correspondent is the oldest inhabitant, lived Mr. Tunbelly, a respectable publican, the master of the Goose and Gridiron, and the fortunate possessor of a mate, whose waist exceeded his barrels in rotundity, whose cheeks were more ruby than his wine, and whose temper was more crooked than her corkscrew. In his own person he bore no other indication of his profession than a nasal prominence resembling in form the map of Italy, and emitting as much light and heat as the burning end of his kitchen poker. In height he was just five feet three inches; lean as the hack that conveyed his lady and himself on Easter Monday to the neighbouring fair; his voice had a scrannel tone; of his legs one had by nature been bent inwards, the other was straight and symmetrical, and did great credit to the skill of the village joiner. He had worn from time immemorial a brown bob wig, a grass-green coat, a cocked hat, capacious ruffles, a buckle six inches in diameter, red worsted stockings, and buckskin breeches. I am thus particular in the description of his dress, because it is characteristic of " auld lang syne," of times that never will return, when individual character put forth all its luxuriance, at a distance from the assimilating hot-bed of the metropolis, where professional habits obliterate every indication of personal character, and fashion restrains the bias of eccentricity. For twelve long years had this happy couple been joined together in the bonds of holy wedlock, and participated in the fashionable luxuries of every decent village in Cumberland, negus and scandal. If their visits to church were not very frequent on their own parts, their zeal for religion was plainly testified by the monthly attendance of Dorothy their bar-maid; and if their own quarrels were the theme of wondering curiosity to all the hamlet, Mrs. Tunbelly repaid the obligation by active interference in the domestic concerns of her neighbours. She was, it must be confessed, a notable woman; could make herself a welcome and useful visitor at every christening, and possessed undivided sway throughout the parish as the arbitress of fashion.

About the year 1783 a pedestrian of a comely person but mean appearance, arrived at the Blue Lion. A dirty pocket handkerchief contained all his worldly riches, consisting of a shaving-box, a pair of worsted stockings and a volume of Wesley's sermons. Mrs. Tunbelly was accustomed to regard a trunk in the "Blue room," and a hack in the stable, as her best security for the due payment of her bill, and the dress and manner of Mr. Toogood were not calculated to remove her ancient prepossessions. The husband, however, was of opinion that before they refused him refreshment, it would be prudent to make some enquiries respecting his condition and pursuits.

Having ordered the gentleman therefore to be shewn into the back parlour, he began according to his usual manner to descant on the fineness of the weather, the oppression of taxes, and other favorite topics of conversation; to all his remarks, however, the stranger only replied by a succession of sighs and groans. At length he found the necessity of coming to the point, and the following is a correct report of the dialogue.

Tunbelly. I suppose you come here on business?

Stranger. Yes, my Lord has given me a call---thanks to his name!

Tunbelly. Why I suppose your Lord is a goodish kind of a person then—mayhap?

Stranger. Yes, friend—he has fed and cloathed me even from my youth up, and hath been very gracious unto his servant.

Tunbelly. Oh! oh! then I suppose you have a jolly time of it among you. Pray what may be your allowance; how many noggins of rum have you a day, if it be fair to ask?

Stranger. I thirst for no other liquor than the water of life.

Tunbelly. Aye, let me tell you *aqua vitæ* is no such bad thing. But pray if it be so that you can tell me, without offence, what did his lordship give you a call about?

Stranger. Verily he told me that the lost sheep of Ashwell had gone astray, and sent me to draw them from the path that leadeth to destruction.

Tunbelly. Well, I'll be *hanged* if I recollect any sheep that run away since farmer Dixon's; but, however, I'll make enquiries among my neighbours, and perhaps I may find some for you—so you are a shepherd, it seems?

Stranger. Yea, verily, an unworthy one; the meanest on the Hill of Sion.

The last word of the stranger put an end to Tunbelly's inquiries. Sion!—Sion! he exclaimed as he returned to his wife; why sure enough, he's shepherd to old Senhouse, at Sion Lodge, who sleeps in the blue room twice a year. This conclusion he communicated to his helpmate, but she was not satisfied with his report of the conversation, and resolved to investigate the stranger's history for herself. He had ordered a glass of brandy and water, and she now took it in her hand, resolved to bring it back, if she were not satisfied. The exact particulars of the conversation that ensued, I have not been able to ascertain; but certain it is that on her return she left the brandy and water behind her, that the village schoolroom was engaged by Mr. Tunbelly himself for the approaching night; and the bellman sent round to inform " all friends and neighbours" that a prayer meeting would be held, at which every christian brother was exhorted to appear. In this distant and obscure part of the country methodism was little more than the shadow of a name. The fame of Mr. Wesley had reached Ashwell, but none of his emissaries had yet regarded it as a fruitful vineyard. Curiosity therefore drew together the old and the young, the devout and the profane. Sighs and groans, and exclamations, gave audible evidence to the powers of the itinerant; the congregation was excited to enthusiasm, and the punch-bowl provided by Mr. Tunbelly for the occasion overflowed with sixpences.

Among the audience were Mrs. and Mr. Tunbelly. Mrs. Tunbelly had several private wrestlings with the " dear man" (for the cant of methodism is easily diffused;) when the number of proselytes had become so numerous that Mr. Squintum's weekly visit from Whitehaven was insufficient to satisfy every yearning soul, he condescended to bestow on Mr. Tunbelly the gifts and attributes of a local preacher, reserving for himself a stipulated sum out of the profits of his labours. The vaults, the bar, and the stable, were neglected by the enthusiastic publican for the pulpit; and his preaching was soon remarked, in spite of the more prudent sanctity of the wife, to be more palatable than his ale.

The progress of Squintum and his coadjutor in the work of conversion, had now successfully continued for two years, when the prospects of the one were obscured, and the zeal of the other provoked to madness, by the appearance of a competitor in the trade of methodism. A Manchester traveller and his wife, had witnessed with envy, the facility with which the Cumbrian preachers transferred the money of the industrious poor to their own pockets. At the suggestion of the wife, the husband resolved to try how far it was possible to share the spoils of vulgar credulity. Bills were circulated, therefore, throughout the village, intimating that a genuine disciple of Mr. Whitfield was about to pay a spiritual visit to the faithful at Ashwell, and that a female proselyte would not only " exhort," but listen to the confessions of the female backsliders. *Such* a notice what firmness could resist? On the first night of the appearance of the female *holder*-forth, the rooms of the opposite party were deserted, and the female orator proved herself to be the most " *divine*" of women; the husband descanted very sweetly on the winding-up the thread of life, and wrapping up the soul in the broadcloth of righteousness. He told his auditors, that though a man's sins should be more indelible than the nankeen dye, by his assistance they should be washed as white as the purest calico; that he hoped they would become well cut patterns of faith everlasting, that they would do well to purchase the treasure of great price, without the cloak of hypocrisy, or the veil of pretended sanctity; and that he should be sorry if they imagined that the truths he had told, were the manufacture of his own brain. His eloquence was triumphant, and the victory was completed by the bankruptcy of Tunbelly, and the elopement of his rib with the holy Wesleyite!

Mr. H. remained among us for several months, extending the progress of fanaticism; and enriching himself from the presents bestowed upon his wife, by the infatuated dupes of his hypocrisy. The women sold their furniture, that they might purchase trinkets and china for the dear woman, their sister and mistress in the faith; and pigs and poultry found their way by most miraculous instinct from the farms and yards of his neighbours into the preacher's kitchen. In the very height of his glory, however, he was taken from us, by an unexpected visitation. As he was holding forth on the vanity of all earthly treasures, he was arrested in the midst of his congregation by two police officers, from Bow-street, on a charge of embezzling the goods and money of his Manchester employer. He was taken away the next morning, amidst the mingled curses and lamentations of the multitude; and has since been transported to New South Wales.

A few of his disciples regarded this misfortune as nothing to be lamented, seeing that it was a trial of righteousness; but the greater number were ashamed of their infatuation, and returned to their former habits of attendance at church, and affection for their families. Methodism, however, is always on the watch for the gratification of its avarice; we soon had another preacher to watch over the select few, who still continued in the ways of grace: his congregation was too small to admit of luxurious ostentation; but with the adjacent circuit, he contrived to " pick up" a comfortable living.

This personage, a dapper being, aged forty-five, of portly but diminutive person, with a face more remarkable for the rotundity that indicates luxurious eating, than the glow of health, or the efflorescence of the wine-bibber; with a pug nose, and eyes expressive of perfect self-complacency, was in reality a good-hearted little being; destitute of solid principle, but of friendly habits, and good humoured eccentricities. Like many more important characters, he would commit actions of a tendency the most deplorable in their ultimate consequences; while he would have shrunk with abhorrence from the commission of any act, that could have occasioned even the immediate uneasiness of a fellow creature. He looked not beyond the moment before him, and thought any mode of obtaining a livelihood, that was not in the common acceptation of that term dishonest, or did no immediate harm to any body, was perfectly fair and laudable. In the early part of his life he had been a surgeon's mate; having been lost among the taverns at Plymouth he was left behind, while the vessel proceeded on her voyage with his purse and wardrobe; he began, therefore, to practice as a quack doctor among the nymphs of that chaste and refined town; but he found that there were too many rivals already in possession of the good graces of the fair, to admit of his obtaining a precarious subsistence, and he engaged himself as tapster and factotum to the buxom landlady of the Rose and Crown. Here he lived in clover for many years, and might have continued to do so still, had not Mr. Whitfield himself condescended to hold forth in the long room, and had not Mr. Pearson been an attentive auditor. Being a man of humour, he himself held forth on the ensuing evening to an amazed auditory consisting of his former patients, and of the ostler and his fellows. What he had done so well in jest, it occurred to him that he might do in earnest. His widow began to be old and peevish; she had a niece too proud to marry him, and too poor not to expect the widow's savings. He made his serious debut among the sailors on ship-board; and so much edified the captain of a collier just dismissed from the transport service, that he gave him a free passage to Whitehaven, and by his interest obtained him the mastership of the Mariner's Charity-school.

This school, however, was a sinecure, and he took up his abode amongst the good folks of Ashwell. Though the sixpences fell in with sufficient frequency to pay for his daily feast and his nightly purl, his congregation was never very numerous. He had very little of the whine, he indulged more frequently in the relation of extraordinary adventures on ship-board, and among the bears of the North Pole, than in the explanation of the scriptures; and what was worse than all, he played at cribbage. This their former instructors had told them was very sinful, and would be productive of eternal damnation. When the village elect were informed, therefore, that Dr. Pearson had been impressed as a surgeon, and conveyed on board one of his majesty's ships, the mourners consisted only of the barber, the exciseman, and the successor of Mr. Tunbelly.

But the period was now approaching when fanaticism should revive in all its enthusiasm, and the business and property of the unfortunate tradesman and mechanics of the town should *go to the d———l,* that their souls might be saved from " H———ll."—The critics who applauded master Betty on his first appearance had never witnessed, or had forgotten the labours of many an infant preacher, who arose at the end of the eighteenth century, to enlighten the darkness of a benighted generation. A youth of fifteen, the son of a strolling player, was conveyed on a methodistical speculation to the coast of Cumberland. He had the scriptures by heart, and had been tutored with so much diligence that he could expound their obscurities, and enforce their precepts with considerable fluency. The fame of such a prodigy was rumoured from one extremity of the coast to another---it was found impossible that any room should contain the numbers who flocked together to behold the phenomenon of early inspiration. When the youth appeared, all the females were in raptures with the beauty of his countenance: his infantile lisp contributed by the effect of contrast to place in a still more extraordinary light his talents of exhortation. The village declared with one voice that the dear youth was inspired: nothing was witnessed in the decent families of the place, but contention which should first be favored with the honor of a visit: matrons sighed for his private exhortations, and virgins made him their confessor, and received in return such advice as seemed best calculated to fortify their innocence. It was found that the boy was fond of sugar-plums, and messengers were dispatched to Carlisle to obtain those luxuries. Miss Banks, the bookseller's daughter, and in Ashwell a lady of great importance, not only made him tippets of the finest cambric, but tied them on with her own fair hands. At length the mania extended to the country round, and the youthful preacher was invited twice a week to exhort and sleep at a female boarding-school. His wrestlings at this " seminary of education" were too successful. In a few months symptoms of something very different from old maidism, appeared in one of the oldest pupils. The governess was alarmed, and resolved to detect the offender, and rushing unexpectedly on a moonlight evening into the chamber, she found the righteous cherub in bed, between the pregnant lady and her own daughter. The discovery was too complete for subterfuge, and Augustus Mountjoy took a precipitate departure to the Isle of Man.

Such, Sir, is an authentic history of the revolutions in our methodistical establishment up to the year 1796: when the village committed itself to the spiritual guidance of its apothecary. From that year to the present time, I shall continue my sketch, at an early opportunity. You will perceive, even from this hasty outline, how cruelly the people of the remotest districts of this country have been deceived and tormented by their lank-haired fanatics. Your exertions in the support of rational religion against the encroachments of designing hypocrisy, or superstitious enthusiasm, deserve the thanks of the community, and are peculiarly grateful to him who subscribes himself with great truth and sincerity,

Your affectionate friend,

A CUMBERLAND MAGISTRATE.

—— Hall, near Mary Port,
Feb. 16th, 1812.

THEATRICAL REVIEW.

Nullius addictus jurare in verba magistri;
Quo me cunque rapit tempestas deferor hospes.

THAT New Drury will be opened for the entertainment of the public either under an accumulation of debt, or by its transference to other proprietors, there is now no reason to dispute; and we own that our sympathy in the distresses of Mr. Sheridan is so much less powerful than our partiality to the legitimate drama, that our pleasure at the representation of Hamlet or the School for scandal would not be in the least degree interrupted by any reflections on the embarrassment of theatrical speculators. If the house be opened, and the public receive an equivalent for its money, the subscribers may divide the profits as they please. We are not called upon to pity the tradesmen attached to the theatre, because if they credit the concern after the warnings they have received, they must be very foolish or very avaricious; and of the subscribers themselves we are convinced that one half regard the sums paid down as distributed in benevolence, and have no expectation of receiving either principle or interest.

We have been favored with explanations of the principles on which the theatre is erected, and gladly express our opinion that much ingenuity is displayed in their application by Mr. Wyatt to the purpose immediately before him.

It cannot be denied, he observes, that the largest return which can be obtained consistently with a due attention to the interests of the public, is the legitimate right of the proprietors: and consequently that after having determined the width of the stage opening on a suitable scale, the most capacious form which can possibly be constructed to admit of distinct vision and sound is the form which ought to be chosen.

It appears to be a very popular notion at present, that our theatres ought to be very small; but if that popular notion be suffered to proceed too far, it will tend in every way to deteriorate our dramatic performances, by depriving the proprietors of that revenue, which is indispensable to defray the expences of such a concern, and to leave a reasonable profit to those whose property may be embarked in the undertaking.

It must be evident to every one conversant with the heavy expences incident to such an establishment, that no principal theatre in London, can be so managed as to afford to the public any advantage equal to, and certainly none beyond, what it has already been accustomed to receive, unless that theatre shall be capable of accommodating to the amount of not less than 600l. (exclusive of private boxes) at one time: calculating at the prices subsequently to the opening of the new theatre in Covent Garden.

Assuming the boundary, which has been described as the limit of the stage opening, and confining the front boxes, which is absolutely necessary for purposes of vision and sound, within a given distance from the front line of the stage, it is quite unquestionable that a segment of a circle, including three-fourths, of an entire circle, contains the most capacious area, which can be formed within those given points; and therefore if that form be also one which is well adapted to distinct vision, it ought, upon the principle before stated, to be chosen in preference to any other.

A theatre consisting of three fourths of a circle with a proscenium, which shall limit the stage, opening to 35 feet, will contain in four different heights, 78 boxes, holding 1004 persons; with four boxes, of larger size than the rest next to the stage, on each side of the theatre, capable of containing 188 spectators, in addition to the 1004, before mentioned, amounting in the aggregate to 1192 persons;

	£.	s.	d.
or	417	4	0
A pit capable of containing 911 persons, or	159	8	6
A two shilling gallery, for 482 persons, or	48	4	0
A one shilling gallery, for 284 persons or	14	4	0
Making together the sum of	£639	0	6

exclusive of four private boxes in the proscenium and 14 in the basement of the theatre, immediately under the dress boxes. Supposing the four private boxes in the proscenium to be appropriated to the managers, and certain other persons connected with the theatre, who shall pay no rent for those boxes, the remaining 14 private boxes will let as follows; namely, the twelve smaller ones, for 500l. each, for the season, being at the rate of 23l. per night for 200 nights, which together with the foregoing amount produces an aggregate total of 662l. 0s. 6d.

Comparing his own experiments with those of Mr. Sanders. Mr. Wyatt is led to conclude, that the natural expansion of the human voice when moderately exerted, will be in the proportion of about two ninths further in a direct line than it will laterally, and that the voice being distinctly audible on each side of the speaker at a distance of seventy-five feet, it will be as plainly heard at a distance of ninety-two feet in front of the speaker: declining in strength behind him, so as not to be clearly heard at a much more thirty feet from his back. Now it is evident that as the space between the front line of the stage the boxes immediately facing that line may at times constitute the lateral direction of the voice, the utmost distance from the front of the stage to the back wall of the boxes facing the stage ought not to exceed seventy-five feet. Upon this principle Mr. W. has confined the distance from the front of the stage to the back wall of the boxes facing the stage, to fifty-three feet nine inches, or twenty-one feet three inches within the expansion of the voice in its lateral direction. After having determined the longitudinal distance he completes upon it three fourths of a circle; he justly objects to the semicircle as too much widening the stage opening, and to the oval and horse-shoe as extending the longitudinal distance. He insists also on the necessity of making the depth from the front to the back of the boxes of an equal magnitude, throughout the house, in order to facilitate the uniform diffusion of the sound.

Mr. Wyatt has sprung the proscenium from the back instead of from the front of the boxes, and rounded off the fronts of the boxes nearest the stage until they join the wall which separates the proscenium from what he chooses to call) the *spectatory*. By this means he has contrived to display the scene to the very last seats in the stage box, without increasing the stage opening beyond its legitimate length.

"In the theatre at Parma, (he observes,) which is particularly celebrated both for sound and vision, the frontispiece of the stage opening is placed at a distance of no less than forty feet from the termination of the spectatory, for the purpose of opening a view of the scene to the spectators nearest to the stage; and the width of the stage opening in that theatre with a view to the same desirable object is extended to thirty-nine feet, exceeding by four feet the width which is given to that opening in my design.

He then observes that even by this contrivance the spectators in the back seats of the theatre at Parma, have not the same advantages of vision as the visitors of New Drury.

For the facility of ingress, and egress whatever doors of entrance, staircases, or avenues are provided for one side of the house, are provided for the other side. He has separated the doors from each other as much as possible, and has made them extremely wide. He has taken off all angles upon the landings, making those landings throughout, of exactly the same length with the steps. In the great staircases leading to the boxes, the ascent is first in one flight, and then in two, and so on alternately to the top: the centre flights being exactly double the width of the side flights throughout, and the staircases are capable of containing upon *their own steps and landings* a greater number of persons by one third than the *whole* of the boxes can contain.

Adverting to the respectability of many persons, who occasionally go to the theatre at the second price; and considering the inconvenience to which such persons have been hitherto exposed, by waiting for the time of admission, either *out of doors*, or among the servants in the hall, he has been led to provide a remedy for this inconvenience; and has in his plan made an arrangement for admitting those persons, at any period of the performance, to a well-aired comfortable room; where after having paid their money, they may be at liberty to wait the time of what is called the half price; an accommodation which is estimated by persons well acquainted with these matters, to be capable of attracting an additional twenty pounds per night, which for 200 nights, is 4000*l.* per annum.

And lastly he proposes to place the saloon in the second tier to embellish it in such a way, that the luxurious, the idle, and the dissolute may prefer it to any other part of the house, to have no baskets, and thus to secure, without any invidious distinction, the dress boxes from improper intrusion or interruption.

Covent Garden.

The Virgin of the Sun is, as we concluded from its title, one of those splendid productions in which the dramatist yields precedence to the scene-painter and the mechanist. The object of a modern dramatist is not to " shew the age and body of the time, its form and pressure;" " to hold the mirror up to nature," but to scribble dialogues that may naturally lead to affective situations. The judgment scene of this piece, for instance, is introduced by Mr. Reynolds, not because it is requisite to the " better carrying on of the plot," but because it exhibits an actor in a picturesque attitude, and affords occasion for the introduction of the splendid scenery. Were Shakespeare now alive, he would find it necessary to wind up all his tragedies with a " flourish of trumpets, a grand march, a monarch on his throne, and a procession of courtiers." As a spectacle the piece surpasses all that ingenuity had before produced ; and Mr. Reynolds may claim the merit of writing for the scene painter more successfully than any contemporary dramatist. In the introduction of Liston alone he has been unfortunate : the part of Diego is wholly ineffective.

It is impossible to determine whether the language of the Virgin of the Sun be intended to creep in prose, or hobble in blank verse : One of Ataliba's speeches does both ; we have placed the verses within inverted commas :

Ataliba. I see—and whatsoe'er may be my private feelings,
 " As trusted guardian of the state, and well
 " Convinced a sovereign faithful to his duty
 " Is the best image of our god on earth,
 " I will while I exist uphold my nation's"
laws, and when I die restore as I received them. Now perform your office.

Miss Smith, with great natural talents, and the most perfect acquaintance with all the arts of her profession, appeared to much disadvantage in the part of Cora. There is nothing of female loveliness in the contour of her face, or of female tenderness in the expression of her countenance. She bears about her the genuine features of *old-maidism;* and ought if she wishes to rise in the estimation of the public, to refrain from appearing in parts of youthful, animated, and amiable passion. She is formed by nature to worship the severer muses, and is as unequal to the personation of a love-sick nymph, as Mr. Young to the representation of an amorous Adonis.

Our pity has seldom been more fervently excited, than by the *exhibition* of Mr. Huntley in the part of Alonzo. This gentleman is not deficient in natural genius ; but his countenance is only expressive of meanness or insipidity. If there be any situation in this world, in which a man may be hopelessly miserable, unvisited by the infliction of bodly pain, it is that of an actor enthusiastic in the study of his art, and endowed by nature with the most perfect powers of conception, while he is unable to appear before an audience, without exciting the contempt of the judicious, and the derision of the unfeeling.

That Mr. Kemble retires from Covent-garden after the termination of the present season, is positively asserted by his friends: and that he has formed an engagement with the ostensible managers of New Drury is insinuated by the friends of Mr. Sheridan; with every feeling respect, however, for his personal and professional character, we cannot but express our opinion that he would act most wisely by following the example of his sister. To retire in time is the first wisdom of a successful actor. Mr. Kemble is not what he has been; since the commencement of the present season, his voice has undergone a perceptible alteration, and the ' horse crock of Kemble's foggy throat,' it does not require the alertness of the Satirist to discover. As a proof, if any proof were required, that we offer these observations in the spirit of genuine friendship, we insert the following eulogium on Mr. Kemble as he was, by a man whose opinions on dramatic subjects can seldom be disputed without danger or injustice.

"As an actor (says Mr. Cumberland) who in the decline of our national taste stands firm in the support of the legitimate drama, Mr. Kemble has my most sincere respect: and when I bear this unprejudiced testimony to his merit, I am moved to it by no other consideration but as I think it due from me being the conductor of a work devoted to the interests of fair criticism and contemporary genius. If he is evidently cautious how he lends himself to great variety of character, he very probably acts wisely for his fame and prudently for his health; but I am far from sure that we have seen him in the whole capacity of his powers: nor does it follow, because he has never stepped beyond the boundaries of his genius, that he has absolutely stepped up to them. I rather think that if he chose to sally from his entrenchments he might take new ground, and post himself very strongly on it. I have watched him in *Leon*, and will venture to say that his fatuity in that character is more highly coloured than that of Garrick's was. I dare say my readers can recollect certain parts in which his unimpassioned recitation that would hang so heavy in the hands of others, has a charm that never wearies us in his. I am satisfied that he might considerably enlarge his compass if he would. Nevertheless, we must confess the stamp of nature is upon him as the tragic hero: and when we add to that the habits he has acquired by the study of his art, and probably by the disposition also of his mind, he has a right if he sees fit to be seen in none but the gravest and most dignified situations. Nay although it were allowed on all hands, and he himself were conscious, that such were the true compass and determined limitation of his powers, yet Mr. Kemble would have no right to arraign the liberality of nature, because she did not give him feature as flexible and a frame as plastic as she gave to Garrick: what is great and solemn and sublime she has qualified him to express: and though her gifts, as such alone, had not been very various, they surely may be called extremely valuable: But I adhere to my conjecture," * * * * " Upon this arduous part, (Hamlet,) Mr. Kemble enters with attributes in some respects happier and more auspicious than those with which Garrick was by nature armed. The dignity of the Prince is in his form, the moody silence, meditative look, repulsive coldness, and taunting ridicule cast on the creatures of the court who besiege him, are peculiarly his own: in the judicious management of soliloquy, so little understood by some, he is not to be surpassed by any: and in the interviews with the apparition of his father, no actor can be more impressive. The present stage while possessed of Mr. Kemble, has to boast of a performer more deeply scientific, more learned, and more laborious in his profession, than is probably to be found in the annals of the British theatre."

During the present month the innocent and ingenuous Mr. Taylor has been unusually active. Into his conduct towards Mr. Alexander Read, against whom he had preferred a charge of perjury, and whose honor and integrity he fully established by his own evidence, we shall enter in our next number at considerable length. The opening of the Pantheon having been announced for Thursday next, Mr. Taylor resolved to shew its managers how little he dreaded their competition, and actually postponed the Opera from the accustomed Tuesday till Thursday. Last night, therefore, there was no performance: nor could he have devised a more effectual way of sending all the visitors of the Opera to the Pantheon.

February 25th, 1812.

THE SCOURGE.

APRIL 1, 1812.

CONTENTS.

TO CORRESPONDENTS, see back.

THE POLITICAL OBSERVER,
No. IX. The Prince Regent
and the Opposition 259
Opposition honesty exemplified.. 260
Their humility 261
Participators in princely follies. 262
The Regent's visits 263
Fallacy of excuses 264
The Morning Chronicle's consistency 265
Swindling and highway robbery. 266

THE NOBLE ADULTERER .. 267
His conjugal injustice 268
A governor degenerated into a slave 269
Loans from his mistress 270

CUMBERLAND METHODISTS ib.
Caleb Quotem the first 271
Becomes Methodist preacher ... 272
Mr. Sparkle's debut 273
Wedding preparations 274
A clerical pickler of herrings ... 275

PUBLIC INSTITUTIONS
Royal Academy 277
Defects of the academical lectures 277
Mr. Flaxman's piety 278

ARCHITECTURAL QUACKERY.
Lugar's Architectural Sketches for Cottages, Rural Dwellings, Villas, &c. &c. 279
Dangerous nature of their plans. 280
Professions! 281
Performances 282

DR. HALLORAN and GENERAL GREY 283
Fracas at Cape Town .... ib.
Dr. Halloran's spirited conduct. 284
Falls under General Grey's displeasure 285
A poetical bugbear 286
Midnight horrors 287
Dr. Halloran's imprudence 288
Gen. Grey's vindictiveness 289
The Dr. sentenced to be banished 290
Brutally forced from his family.. 291
Prejudication of a military charge 292
British humanity abroad 293

MISS ELIZABETH'S JOURNAL. Extract the first 294

Freddy as a soldier 295
George's chere amie 296

MRS. WYNDHAM AND COL. GREVILLE 297
A male gossip 298
Proposes to sell Mrs. Wyndham a share 299
Her alarm 300
And ultimate disappointment... 301
Recriminatory correspondence.. 302
Col. Greville's fidgets 303
Domestic altercations 304
Pantheon licence 305

THE REVIEWER. No. X ... 306
Childe Harold's Pilgrimage, a Romaunt, by Lord Byron .... ib.
Its want of interest 307
Examples of inanity 308
Compared with Walter Scott 309
Thelwall and rhythmus 310
Description of Portuguese scenery 311
The Maid of Saragoza 312

THE H—— DYNASTY, or the EMPIRE OF THE NAIRS ... 313
Wedlock exploded 314
Advantages of promiscuous love 315
Good effects of libidinous writings 316
A procession 317
The Salique law revoked 318
A female jacobin 319
Her lover is guillotined 320
The valet turned gentleman 321
The elopée discovered 322

THE P——SS OF W—— 323
The princess's income .... ib.
The delicate enquiry 324
Contents of the documents..... 325
Peculiarity of her situation 326
Dr. Busby and Apollo 327
The philosophy of Lucretius ... 328
Master Busby's recitations 329
Beauties and defects of the translation 330

POLITICAL HINTS 331
Mr Crevey and Col. M'Mahon 332
Military flogging 333

A STAUNCH DOG AT A FAULT 334
Clerical dignity 335
Devotional drapery 336
Cream of violets 337

THEATRICAL REVIEW 338

NOTICE TO CORRESPONDENTS.

IT will be seen by the present number that our pages are always open to the reception of cases of oppression, appeals from the victims of tyranny or injustice, to the public, and other articles of a similar description. It is necessary, however, that they should be accompanied by satisfactory documents, or by reference to the persons by whose evidence they may be substantiated.

Lady A. is at liberty to proceed as her advisers may direct her.

We have received a letter from Clio Rickman, disclaiming in positive terms any concern in the publication of the Third Part of the Age of Reason. The lines quoted by Mr. Butler, (page 240,) he asserts to have been made some years ago *impromptu*.

We have received many communications respecting a poem called the CAPITAL. It appears from the extracts enclosed, to be a tissue of blasphemy and nonsense; but as its stupidity will prevent its doing much mischief, we have thought it prudent to dismiss it in a note. The same reasons have dissuaded us from the insertion of Forum Impiety.

The author of the "Conduct of Man" has mistaken his talent. He has thought much and deeply, but will never be a poet.

The Carpet War; a Prince in a Pickle; the Carlton House Gazette; A Review of Wharton's Roncevalles; Stroehling the Painter, and his Grecian Quackery; Poetical Biography, No. 2; on ancient abuses compared with Modern Innovation; and Yarmouth, an Ode, shall meet with an attentive examination.

To our Piccadilly correspondent (a personal friend if we mistake not), we labour under particular obligations; and beg leave to suggest the coronation of the Empress as a fit sequel to the other. The individual pictures should be distinct.

The transmission of interesting Pamphlets as *soon as published*, is particularly requested.

THE SCOURGE.

APRIL 1, 1812.

THE POLITICAL OBSERVER, No. IX.

THE PRINCE REGENT AND THE OPPOSITION.

THAT without consenting to the immediate abandonment of our allies, and to an unconditional change in all the principles of our foreign policy, it was impossible for the Prince Regent to call the whig party to his councils, is evident from a *prima facie* examination of the correspondence between his Royal Highness and the leaders of opposition. Whether by granting those conditions his Royal Highness would have fulfilled most effectually his duty to his subjects, is a question upon which the opinions of the nation, as upon every other momentous topic of public inquiry, must be necessarily divided; but should it hereafter appear that one part of the ministerial policy was right, and that much might have been gained by reciprocal concession, let it be remembered that the opposition leaders refused in limine every advance to satisfactory explanation; that they bluntly and decidedly pronounced themselves to be infallible, and demanded from the Regent a pledge of future acquiescence, not in one particular measure, or in one important principle of national policy, but in all the opinions that, as members of opposition, they had hastily formed, or conveniently embraced.

But whatever may be the ultimate decision of the public respecting the answer of the whig leaders to his Royal Highness's overture, there can be but one opinion of the conduct of themselves and their partizans, since the accession of the Prince Regent to unrestricted power.

Disappointed in their expectations of uncontrolled authority over the persons and opinions of the first magistrate, they forget even the common decorum of expression that would be due to a private individual, and address his Royal Highness in language as scurrilous and offensive, as during the whole period of his private career, it was fulsome and adulatory. Admitting it possible that the Prince should deserve the epithets applied to him, or be guilty of the follies of which he is accused, the admission only aggravates the guilt and the indecency of their present language. It cannot be denied, that for thirty years, during which the object of their attacks indulged in indiscretions as offensive, and follies as ludicrous, as those which are now imputed to him, they persisted in proclaiming him to be all that was great, and good, and generous, and magnanimous; that without any reference whatever to his political opinions they pronounced him to be a perfect gentleman, embued with every manly feeling, possessed of the most extensive knowledge and the most brilliant accomplishments, and uniting the dignity of the prince with the ardor of the friend.

Only one little month has elapsed and what is the picture they afford of his mental endowments and his personal habits? The salacity of a Nero, the caprice of a Caligula, and the fatuity of a ——— are ascribed to their former idol, by his former eulogists. Language that, addressed to a humble citizen, would demand the infliction of legal punishment, and to the soldier or the man of honor, could not be expiated but with life, is poured forth against the ruler of the English nation, in a torrent at once destructive and inexhaustible; overwhelming every established boundary of decorum, and sweeping away every legitimate barrier, that had hitherto protected the sanctity of a court from the noise and turbulence of political commotion.

In these observations we allude more particularly to the regular organ of opposition, the Morning Chronicle. The satires of the Examiner cannot be included in the list, because his opinion of the Prince has been consistent, and he has never pledged himself for his wisdom, his magnanimity, or his virtue. On the same plea we ourselves must rest our defence of whatever observations on the conduct and character of the Prince Regent, it may be our future duty to advance. It is of the opposition, as compared with themselves, that we complain:—of their participation in every folly, and their eulogies of every vice, committed by the Prince, the evidence is in the recollection of every one, and may be found in any file of the Morning Chronicle up to February 18th, 1812: of their subsequent injustice and indecency, we shall only pollute our pages with one short extract.

> " But he, tho' half his life was o'er,
> Was *loose* and *silly* as before;
> In him all youth's unbridled rage
> Was blended with the *fraud of age.*
> Onward with headlong speed he rushed,
> And poor old friendship wholly crushed."

Now unless the opposition expect that every ancient principle of moral deduction is to be abandoned in their favor, this sudden change in their language either arises from the rage of personal disappointment that consults its own gratification without any regard to the sovereign whom they obey, or the people whose confidence they have betrayed, or it is the language of a party of political bullies, endeavouring to obtain that ascendancy by abuse, which they are unable to command by the legitimate exercise of their talents. By whatever excuses they may wish to palliate their conduct, or in whatever disguise they may attempt to deceive our observation---the truth is, that so long as they expected power, they were the most fulsome and subservient of literary parasites; and that immediately after the disappointment of their hopes, they became the most scurrilous vilifiers of the object of their former adulation. This is a fact of which no explanation can do away the impression: it stamps at once the character of the party, and affords to the Prince and the people a guide by which to estimate their present declarations and their future promises.

But the opposition will reply:—when we indulged in all the extravagances of the prince; when we lent him money to devote to his licentiousness, and consented to become his companions and associates in the orgies of Bacchus, and the mysteries of Venus; when we extolled his daily visits to Sam Chiffney, as proofs of a great and generous mind, superior to petty distinctions and cold formalities; and when we excused his intercourse with Mrs. Fitzherbert as the natural consequence of his peculiar situation, the Prince was *young!* Something might be forgiven to the impetuosity of youth, and something to the occasional observations of a prince exposed to all the temptations that bestrew the path of rank and inexperience. But if this language have any meaning, as applied to their conduct, it must imply that the age of youth is from twenty to fifty, and that the Prince of Wales has been hurried away by the exuberance of boyish passion, till the assumption of his regency. If something was to be forgiven to the exuberance of youth, how happens it that they never reproved the salacity of age? They say *now* that the Prince is lascivious: it is notorious that he is not more lascivious at present than he has been for the last ten years; and by what strange chance does it happen, that they did not discover salacity till the present moment? The answer of the public is easy; till the present moment they were in expectation of place: their former language, or forbearance, was the language or forbearance of expecting parasites; their present scurrility is the offspring of imbecility excited by revenge.

But (it may again be asserted) " we had nothing to do with the amours of the Prince, except as regarded their political influence. If we never censured the Prince's connection with Mrs. Fitzherbert, it was because their intercourse had no perceptible influence on the public happiness. It was not our province to censure the Prince's visits to ——— House, till their consequences became manifest, and till it was evident that the influence there exerted was prejudicial to the interest of his early friends." In other words, (supposing their representation of the Prince's conduct to be correct, and for that they only are responsible,) " we have no objection that the Prince should be a shameless adulterer, or the slave of a prostitute, so long as his vices are not productive of injury to ourselves: he may while away his hours in ——— square, and yet be a very virtuous and magnanimous prince, if he will leave to us the unmolested management of his political arrangements; but if his visits be inimical to the interests of opposition, we cannot do less than stigmatize him as the slave of a prostitute, and the tool of a ' *tame cuckoo*.'"—It is observable that the visits of the Prince Regent to ——— House, were not less frequent during the period of the restrictions than during the last month. Yet while some faint hopes of return to office still remained, and the views of the H———rd coterie were not fully developed, not a murmur escaped the lips of the " early friends," that could indicate the most faint or casual emotion of disgust.

From charges like these, however, the Morning Chronicle endeavours to exculpate his party, by observations, that if he had indulged in political discussion would have been relevant and forcible, but have no meaning whatever as applied to the defence of personal abuse. " The ministerial papers are filled with indignation at the change of our language on the subject of the Prince Regent. They forget that the praises we have bestowed on the Prince of Wales, whether justly conferred or not, were a tribute to qualities of which we can no longer discern the trace, or hear the profession. We praised in the Prince of Wales the declared adherent to the principles and party that placed his family on the throne, the friend and admirer of Mr. Fox, the self-proclaimed instructor of his daughter in the principles of that illustrious statesman, the professed enemy of peculation and corruption, of war, violence, and injustice, the liberal supporter of religious toleration, the future conciliator of Ireland. It is not our practice to contaminate our pages with scandal, or attract attention to our columns by indecent topics of animadversion." Dismissing for a moment the consideration of this paragraph as a defence of the language of the Morning Chronicle, we cannot but admire the facility with which it takes for granted whatever may conduce to the advantage of the party. That the opposition are the sole and infallible judges of the accordance of the Prince's conduct with his professions, that the principles acted on at present by Lord Grenville are those of Mr. Fox, and that they have at any period of their lives distinguished themselves as the enemies of peculation and corruption, are positions of which some are notoriously false, and the rest require some other proof than the assertion of the Morning Chronicle. Nor as they contribute to his own defence, are the preceding observations less unfortunate. *It is not the political, but the personal character* of the Prince, that was at one time the object of its editor's eulogy, and is now the constant theme of his abuse. If the editor of the Morning Chronicle never contaminated his pages with scandal or scurrility, then to assert that his prince unites the lust of youth to the fraud of age is loyal and decorous; to stigmatize Lord ―――― as a " tame cuckoo" is decent and respectful; and even after this interpretation of his language, has been admitted, the question again arises, why this mode of testifying respect was not displayed before the 18th of February? The Prince, we humbly presume, is not more silly though certainly more *loose* than before the expiration of the restrictions; and if those epithets be now applicable to his habits or his mind, the vision of Mr. Perry (whom, as Mr. Perry, we admire and respect) must have been assisted by the intellectual telescopes of his friends.

It may indeed appear to those who are unwilling to believe that public virtue is something more than a name, that the attacks on the Prince Regent are the mistaken and unauthorised effusions of the opposition journalists, without the participation or the knowledge of the leaders of the party. But a series of scurrilous articles in their official journal, might be begun, but could not be continued without their approbation. It is surely ascribing nothing unworthy to Mr. Perry to suppose that no hint from the leaders of the party that he so zealously and conscientiously espoused would be attended to; and the opposition, we are inclined to hope, do not rest their defence on a verbal distinction between *approval* and *quiescence*. Besides, Mr. P. is in habits of daily intercourse with the persons whose sentiments he is on most occasions supposed to express; his literary co-operation must be in some degree directed by the tone in which they discuss the conduct and character of the Prince Regent; and the public acts neither uncandidly nor unwisely in judging of its asperity, by the sarcastic poetry of the Morning Chronicle. But we do not rest our opinion on presumptive evidence. If we are not grossly mis-informed, some of the articles in the Chronicle, and many of those that have appeared elsewhere, (particularly the " Prince of Whales" in the Examiner), are the productions of the Prince's early friends; of those who are now the most willing to revile him as a monster of ingratitude, and affect to be indignant at his forgetfulness of former attachments!

Nor is it necessary to rest the justice of our charge on the supposed connections of the editor of the Morning Chronicle. So enthusiastic and imprudent is the malignity of the opposition, that though the editor of the SCOURGE has uniformly been distinguished by his hostility to the whigs, they have not been ashamed to furnish him with materials of attack against the exalted personage, among whose early friends they are eager to be numbered.

Let it be remembered that by the preceding observations we do not pledge ourselves to a different opinion of his Royal Highness from that which the opposition now express. Our only object is to shew, that with them, the Prince is a god or a devil, an angel or a monster, as best suits the purposes of the moment, or according to the fluctuations of their feelings between hope and disappointment. We do not deny the visits of the Prince to ———— House, but we assume the right of asking the opposition, why these visits remained unobserved till their exclusion from power? We can conceive it to be possible that his Royal Highness should be indolent and capricious, but should like to be informed why his vices and his follies were so laudable till the expiration of the restrictions? When the opposition are able to answer these questions, to the satisfaction of the public, they may possibly regain a trivial proportion of their early popularity. At present, much as the people detest Lord Castlereagh, and despise the puppets who have been selected to fill the vacancies that might have been occupied by an Erskine or a Grey, they would rather obey the worst and most venial of the present ministry, than witness the *unconditional* return of the whigs. The colleagues of Perceval have at least the merit of honest impudence: the opposition have as much dishonesty, and a larger portion of hypocrisy; they are * * * *s without courage; and their depredations on the public purse differ only from those of the Percevalites in nature and degree, as SWINDLING differs from HIGHWAY ROBBERY.

THE NOBLE ADULTERER.

Our allusion to the pecuniary distresses of a noble —— has excited more than one of his political friends to the most unguarded indications of angry and intemperate zeal. They are well aware that acknowledged poverty is an insuperable bar to the progress of ambition, and that many who would forgive the conjugal infidelities of their noble master, would withdraw from his service as soon as they should discover the extent of his embarrassments. To the family itself the concealment of his distresses from the knowledge of the public, was an object of essential importance: the marriage of his nephew may be prevented by the suspicion that any part of the funded property of his destined bride, is intended to replenish the coffers of the uncle; and the collateral branches of the house of —— might find their reception in the money market less welcome than it is, were the insolvency of their principal generally known.

Yet notwithstanding his endeavours to conceal the state of his affairs, his situation is pretty correctly understood by all who have any interest in their prosperity or decline. Even the heiress of unnumbered thousands is well aware that some portion of her treasures may hereafter contribute to gratify the avarice or the luxury of his favorite Polly; and the emissaries of John King are by no means decided that a premium of twenty-five per cent should counterbalance the objection of suspicious securities. It is known too well that the apparently exhaustless treasures obtained in a distant clime, have long been squandered in political intrigue, or lascivious indiscretion, and that no hope of retrieving the ruined fortunes of his lordship now remains but his return to some official situation of emolument, or another voyage to the regions of oriental wealth.

That the conduct of such a man is the fit subject of

public observation, cannot be disputed. His embarrassments are not only productive of inconvenience to himself, but may hereafter be brought forward as proving his claims on the public generosity. We may be told at no very distant period that to leave an old and deserving servant, to lament in aged indigence the ingratitude of his country, would be unjust in the executive power, and disgraceful to the people whose glory he had extended, and whose empire he had consolidated; a pension of ten thousand pounds a-year may then be proposed as a remuneration for his services; and like many other individuals whose private follies have been paid for out of the public purse, and whose political intrigues have been rendered subservient to their personal vices, he may employ the spoils obtained from weakness and credulity, in fortifying the outworks of corruption, and extending the encroachments of ministerial power on the liberties of the people.

Let it be remembered, therefore, when an appeal of this kind shall be made to the generosity of the country, that the fortune expended by the —— has not been devoted to the pursuit of any laudable object, or of any virtuous purpose; that it has not contributed to the becoming splendor of his domestic establishment, or to the gratification of an accomplished and affectionate wife, but has been squandered away in facilitating the licentious pleasures of a prostitute. The —— is driven from her home to take refuge among her early friends, that a vulgar and abandoned woman, may be left to the undisturbed enjoyment of the paternal mansion—the sums that ought to have been divided among his lordship's creditors, have been squandered in the decoration of a country seat for the object of his lascivious attachment, and the —— is deprived of her box at the opera, that Polly may be drawn into her native village by four milk-white geldings!

Here with her sister, she lives in all the splendor of meretricious infamy; her parents, originally labourers, reside in a snug cottage, adjacent to her villa, express the most unbounded gratitude for the favor conferred upon them by the protection of their daughter. The visits of this ci-devant monarch, are neither accompanied by the magnificence, nor received with the courtesy, that would best become the rank, and accord with the ardor of her noble admirer. Neither the pelting of the pitiless storm, nor the obstacles opposed to his pedestrian progress by the dirtiness of the pathway, or the intricacies of the natural labyrinth that leads to the back door of his Polly's residence, can impede the frequency of his excursions. Twice a week at least does he court the pleasure of being hurled headlong by the enraged virago from the top to the bottom of his own staircase; and the tributary journals, whose lucubrations are supposed to be indited beneath his own immediate superintendance, might add to their already copious stock of abusive epithets from the exhaustless store of their patron's mistress.

The omnipotence of sensual passion has seldom been more strikingly displayed than in the conduct of our leading politician. The ci-devant governor of millions, the terror of ———, and the idol of an extensive empire, retires from the gaze of multitudes, to supplicate the compassion, or patiently suffer the revilings and the insults of a harlot, whom he himself has transplanted from the hovel to the palace. A nobleman of arbitrary principles, and stately habits, distinguished for his virulence in political contention, and professing a lofty independence of the parties that solicit his co-operation, hastens from the scene of his parliamentary duty to become the slave or the plaything of an abandoned female. Were the follies of the nobleman whom we have now introduced on our satirical canvas, injurious only to himself, his insensibility would not be less deserving of compassion, than his vices of reprobation; but his conduct admits of no such palliation. While his mistress revels in all the luxuries that a doubtful credit, or the loans of the money-brokers can command, the ——— laments in solitary indigence, the infidelity of her husband and the miseries of dependence consequent on his desertion; and we have no doubt that as soon as the nuptial contract between the heiress and the simpleton shall be ratified, the treasures amassed by commercial industry, and augmented by the silent operation of time, will be in due proportion conveyed to the habitation of Miss Polly Raffle, there to gladden the eyes of her milliners, and contribute to the boundless ecstacies of her keeper by the occasional loan from his generous and condescending mistress, of a ONE POUND NOTE.

M. S.

CUMBERLAND METHODISTS.

Sir,

Having brought up the history of village fanaticism till the year 1793, it might be supposed that few characters could have exhibited since that time on the stage of methodism, and that few vicissitudes could have occurred in the fortunes of the rising sect. But the disciples of Wesley have not, even at the present moment, attained such a solid ascendancy over the minds and habits of the villagers, as to levy their contributions with unvarying regularity, or to secure, by the allurements of Rumford stoves, and Persian cushions, the perpetual attachment of those who once have ventured within the pale of Methodistic sanctity. The neighbouring squire, therefore, whose word is a law to half the gentry of his neighbourhood, still slumbers in his curtained pew, and subscribes his annual guinea to the bell-ringers. How long these distinctions may remain, it would be idle to conjecture: it has been whispered, however, that an evangelical clergyman has purchased the incumbency of Ashwell; and if the report be true, it may be presumed that the church and the meeting will be consolidated; that christianity will be superseded by the canting system, and groans be regarded as more certain indications of religious principle than good works.

The superiority of the church, however, in the rank, if not in the number of its visitors, has hitherto prevented the village of Ashwell from sinking into a mere district of the Wesleyan empire. The spiritual guides of the multitude have been itinerant mountebanks rather than regular quacks, and have therefore exhibited a variety of character, and succeeded each other with a rapidity of movement, that could not have occurred to observation, in the legitimate evangelists.

No sooner had Augustus Mountjoy escaped on shipboard, from the vengeance of an injured parent, and the pursuit of the parish officers, than William Hodgson (a name long to be remembered in the village of Ashwell) was excited by the love of righteousness to combine with his other callings, the profession of Methodist preacher. He is now a respectable surgeon and man-midwife at Sunderland, in the county of Durham : in what particular branch of business he was most distinguished at the period of which I am writing, it would be difficult even for those who knew him best to determine. He was in reality the very Caleb Quotum, whom many of your readers may have supposed, and whom I myself believe, to be the offspring of Mr. Colman's imagination. The coincidence between the ideal and the existing character, at once evinces the genius, and the knowledge of the world of the author of the "Review." Mr. Hodgson was positively, and of my own knowledge, a public baker, a schoolmaster, a grocer, an auctioneer, a druggist, a barber, a surgeon, an apothecary, and, connected with these, a cutter of corns. He was bell-man, chapel-clerk, and sexton; he dealt in crockery ware; and was celebrated for his skill in the art of dying. To pursue all these avocations, and yet find leisure to hold forth three times a week to a Methodist society, required some degree of talent and activity. He was in fact an honest little fellow; I used to contemplate his sharp and sallow countenance, and his bent body, curved by continual stooping across his counter, and over the Reading made Easy's of his scholars, with more admiration than contempt. His methodistic zeal was, I am convinced, sincere: he did little harm in the pulpit, and his exertions were not entirely unproductive of good. He understood too little of the scriptures to indulge in the cant of methodistical phraseology; his discourses, if discourses they could be called, were uniformly practical: what he said was as familiar to the mind of his hearers, as what he sold was familiar to their senses; and they put their money into the plate as an act of benevolence to an industrious fellow townsman, rather than as a payment to a privileged instructor.

I have before observed that Mr. Hodgson was clerk to the village church, and bellman general. The last of these offices required his attendance at a moment's warning, and at all hours of the day or night. If a child was lost, or a purse stolen, or a cellar opening determined on at the Queen's Head, or an illumination called for by the Squire, it was the province of *Dr.* Hodgson to proclaim it. But the most important and arduous duty attached to his calling was beneath the immediate superintendence of the curate. When a villager of Ashwell departed this life, the bellman is sent round to toll that same bell that announces an auction or a dance. This is done with adequate solemnity, and as soon as a crowd has been collected, he pronounces with solemn emphasis the following sentence. "All friends and neighbours—I desire you to attend the funeral of our deceased brother A. B., who departed this life at half-past three o'clock this afternoon, and will be buried at three o'clock on Wednesday next." Nor did the labours of Mr. Hodgson terminate here. As chapel-clerk it was his duty to precede the corpse, usually accompanied by more than an hundred people in regular procession, and to give out the particular staves of the 114th Psalm, and then to chaunt the first line, as a guide to the choral efforts of the whole company. Now it often happened that a villager expired in the very middle of his sermon, and uncourteously subjected him to the necessity of dismounting his rostrum; and when the funeral happened to set off more late than usual, what with the covering of the grave, the distribution of gloves, and other important parts of his official duty, he was detained too late to edify the assembled brethren. These circumstances gradually diminished his importance in the eyes of the Methodists; and his attention to the Methodists rendered his *church* patients dissatisfied. The curate too observed the impropriety of permitting a Methodist preacher to officiate as a servant of the established church, and his place was given to a rival schoolmaster. Hodgson, however, had paid the Squire for his situation, and refused to resign it—the curate was afraid of offending his worship, and left the affair to be decided between the rival candidates. For six months the *christians* of Ashwell were amused with races between those worthy rivals, from the vestry to the pulpit, and with two parties of Psalm-singers, posted at opposite sides of the church, one pouring forth in vocal melody the homely strains of Sternhold and Hopkins, beneath the auspices of the intruder, and the other attempting to tune the more polished verses of Tate and Brady, under the direction of Dr. Hodgson. But while the contest proceeded, the *Doctor* was losing his patients, his customers, his scholars, and his disciples; another dear man was invited from Whitehaven, the village bookseller announced his intention to deal in drugs, and Hodgson left his ungrateful flock to exercise his professional skill among the good people of Sunderland.

The "dear" man who condescended to accept our invitation, was one of those sanctified coxcombs who unite the fop with the divine, and never astonish by the brilliance of their discourses without taking care that their fair auditors should admire the whiteness of their teeth, and the lustre of their rings.

Mr. Sparkle would not play at cards, but he had no objection to tea and supper parties. It was in the performance of the duties of the fire-side, that he captivated the hearts of the young, and flattered the vanity of the old. No man could display more grace or expertness in the distribution of the wine and cakes, or in the *presentation* of the toast. The petty attentions in which he excelled were received with more marked respect as coming from a teacher of religion; and the complacency excited by his manners, accompanied him from the parlor to the meeting-house. The old and the young were equally delighted with his gentleness of tone, his continual smirk, his artificial lisp, and the grace with which his lilywhite fingers meandered through the pages of his hot-pressed Bible. To hear the methodist *beau*, the milliner forsook her needle, and the jointured widow deserted the church. On the fourteenth of February the table of the *sweet gentleman* was covered with valentines, intermingling impiety with frivolity; and expressing the emotions of lasciviousness in the language of the Scriptures. At length this paragon of fanatical *grace* condescended to repay the attentions of Miss Biddy Langstaff, a fair maiden of forty-three, who had been captivated at first sight by the air with which he performed the honors of the snuff-box.

Every preparation was now made for the celebration of the joyful ceremony. The laces of the youthful damsel were new set, her closets rummaged for the roses and lilies of silk and worsted, that had adorned the bridal dress of her deceased "mama." Eringo comfits, with all the parapharnalia of pies and puddings, were arranged in the back parlor after the customary form; and Miss Biddy Longstaff might at this moment have been the joyful mother of a hopeful family, but for the capricious cruelty of fate, who, a few days before that appointed for her nuptials, unkindly drove an Irish lady and her waiting-maid on a bathing expedition to the vicinity of Ashwell. Excited by curiosity Mrs. Abigail attended the scene of Sparkle's glory, but scarcely had the preacher ascended the pulpit before she exclaimed, "Oh! my husband!" and burst into tears. The exclamation of the female, and the confusion of Sparkle were not unobserved by the destined bride. She took the stranger aside, and there learnt the full extent of her calamities. Half in resentment and half without reflection, the afflicted damsel communicated to Miss Biddy Longstaff, that Mr. Sparkle had been *valet* to her master at Dublin, a few weeks before whose death they had been married; that for a short time he was as attentive as husbands usually are, but that during the bustle and confusion of her master's funeral, he had disappeared, and taken along with him a handsome wardrobe, and whatever moveables were at once valuable and portable. The conversation was interrupted by the appearance of the husband, who falling on his knees alternately soothed the one and supplicated the other. Miss Biddy was inexorable; but Mrs. Sparkle was happy to have her husband restored to her arms at any rate; and willingly consented, on condition of his future constancy, to implore the forbearance of his injured mistress.

It might have been supposed that the detection of the frauds of this unhappy impostor, would have awakened the votaries of fanaticism to a sense of their own folly and credulity. But since his flight the harvest of methodism has been more productive than ever, and the poor inhabitants of Ashwell are now the willing and enthusiastic worshippers of a pickler of herrings. But I have, it is to be feared, already trespassed on your patience; and shall defer the portrait of our spiritual guide, till I have learned whether the information I have already transmitted affords you amusement proportioned to its length.

    I remain, dear Sir,
     Your faithful friend,
      A Cumberland Magistrate.

———— *Hall, near Mary-Port,*
 March 19th, 1812.

THE ROYAL ACADEMY.

Of the intrigues that distract the councils of this institution, and the abuses by which the beneficial tendency of its statutes are impeded, we are preparing an extended and elaborate exposure; convinced that whatever may be the abstract utility of academical establishments, the conduct of the individuals connected with our English school of art, has been in the highest and most extensive degree injurious to the very interests that it was their duty to promote. At the present season, however, the lectures are the chief objects of attention to the students, and of curiosity with the public; and various considerations induce us to precede our more general remarks, by some casual strictures on the PROFESSOR OF SCULPTURE.

The voice of Mr. Flaxman is unusually powerful, his articulation distinct, and his enunciation forcible and deliberate. When compared with Turner or Fuseli, he as far excels those celebrated painters in the *art of reading* as he is confessedly inferior to the latter in every intellectual qualification. But his excellence as a mere reciter of written composition, only renders his appearance as a lecturer more injurious to the interests of art, and more dangerous to the students who submit their habits and opinions to his guidance. Delighted by the distinctness and fluency that characterize the delivery of his lectures, they listen with reluctance to compositions of a nobler order, communicated in a less pleasing form, or requiring that attention to the matter, which by the admirers of Mr. Flaxman is awakened and detained by a correct and forcible elocution. Were the *contents* of his discourses, indeed, remarkable for their intelligence and philosophy, his qualifications as a reader would be invaluable; but his discourses are nothing more than an imperfect and desultory history of sculpture, inferior in correctness to that which is contained in the French Encyclopedia, and written in a style, of which the only merit is grammatical correctness. Of the philosophy of sculpture, of the metaphysical questions that apply to the subject before him, or even of the mechanical principles on which the expression of what has been happily conceived, must chiefly depend, he is either unwilling or unable to expatiate. To demonstrate his piety, he deduces the origin of sculpture from Moses; to testify his learning, he enumerates the names of the sculptors employed in the temple of Minerva; and to evince his taste, he exhibits the casts and models of several celebrated specimens of art. But *in what* the beauty of these specimens consist; why the Apollo Belvidere is more beautiful than any similar effort of human genius; or on what principles of the art, the *nates* of the Venus *de Medicis* deserve the eulogium of Winckelman, the student is left to discover from his own inquiries. Now, we had humbly ventured to conceive that the objects of the lectures at the Academy, were to correct the mistakes, and facilitate the professional studies of the junior artists: it might have been expected, therefore, without any unreasonable fastidiousness, that something should have been said by Mr. Flaxman on the merits and defects of the *ancient* masters of his art; that instead of telling us, as Lempriere had told us before, that the statue of Jupiter by Phidias, was of stupendous magnitude, he would have informed us in what consisted the difference so observable between the styles of that great sculptor and Praxiteles; and that in quoting the assertions of a foreign critic, that every merit of a celebrated statue was counterbalanced by the "want of truth in the attitude," he would have discussed the justice of the censure, and have explained to them in what the "*falseness*" of the attitude consisted.

We have expressed ourselves the more freely on the merits of Mr. Flaxman, because he is himself a niggard of his praise; because, not content with legitimate applause, he suffers no opportunity to pass unemployed, of courting the suffrages of the weak or the ignorant; and still more strongly, because his lectures have a tendency to diffuse that affectation of magazine-learning, and that contentment with the mere information to be gathered from the pages of an encyclopedia, which has already repressed the energies of youthful enthusiasm, and reduced those who might have become the luminaries of literature, into mere repositories of dictionary knowledge, DABBLING IN EVERY THING, AND UNDERSTANDING NOTHING. Whatever three-fourths of the visitors whom Mr. Flaxman receives at the Academy with so gratifying a display of disinterested courtesy, may imagine, we beg leave to express our decided opinion that nothing can be easier than to collect from a classical dictionary a convenient number of dates and names, and to intersperse them among the detached notices respecting the progress of sculpture, that *any book* pretending to the elucidation of the fine arts, must, on the most cursory examination, supply.

The *piety of Mr. Flaxman*, we should have left to its own reward, had not its praises, in conjunction with the most fulsome eulogies on every other part of his lectures, been bandied about from one editor of a Sunday paper to another. Even the Morning Advertiser, a journal that disclaims any attention but to the useful pursuits of the lower classes of society, is crowded with accounts of the lectures of Mr. Flaxman; accounts that must be less intelligible to the mariners of Wapping, and the satin-stitch damsels of Goswell-street, than the history of Sandracottus, or Lord Monboddo's Ancient Metaphysics. We had hoped that long before this time the affectation, (we shall not dignify it by the name of *superstition*,) that discovered all that was great, and awful, and beautiful, in the Holy Scriptures; which pronounced the clothing of a horse's neck with thunder, to be the most sublime of images, and stoutly resisted the erazure from the text of Longinus, of the passage in which he quotes the first chapter of Genesis had been shamed into silence. The Scriptures were not given to the nations of the earth as models of composition, or as the repositories of scientific research, and historical knowledge; but as the vehicles of truths, compared with which all that the scholar could learn, or the philosopher discover, fade into insignificance. When Mr. Flaxman informs us, therefore, that "all that can be said of sculpture, or deduced respecting it, may be found in the holy book, the Bible," we can neither admit the truth of his position, nor admire the spirit in which it was conceived. On this subject we beg leave to submit to his attention the words of a correspondent. "True piety is modest and unobtrusive—absorbed in religious feeling, or reposing in the tranquil serenity of hope, it retires from the gaze of multitudes to enjoy in secret the raptures of communion with its Creator: or if the duties of common life call it forth to public observation, it appears not with the countenance of sanctimonious enthusiasm, but of chearful dignity and calm benevolence."

ARCHITECTURAL QUACKERY.

Our attention has been called to this important subject of satirical observation, by the perusal of a work entitled,

Architectural Sketches for Cottages, Rural Dwellings, and Villas, in the Grecian, Gothic, and Fancy Styles; with Plans suitable to Persons of genteel Life, and moderate Fortune: preceded by some Observations on Scenery and Character proper for picturesque Buildings. By R. Lugar, Architect and Land Surveyor.

Though works of this description seldom or ever come under the notice of a satirical work, from the supposed unimportance and harmless tendency of their doctrines upon the morals of the people; yet as poison may be administered in honey, and its effects in the course of time be found equally destructive, though disguised in a specious form which allures the eye and delights the taste, only to *deceive* the judgment; it forms a part of our painful duty to the public to seek into all the mysterious avenues of human cunning and QUACKERY, in order to expose *imposture*, whether in the conduct and professions of a minister of state, or in the more humble and tranquil exertions of an architectural draftsman!

As every nation is applauded in proportion as it affords encouragement to the polite arts, in which building forms a prominent feature, and gives scope to a tasteful display of design, where the *utile duci* may be said to be found, the English have advanced considerably in the love of ornamental architecture. This passion for building has, within these few years, become so *epidemic* that all comfortable old family mansions, are now turned into temples and Roman villas, or razed from their ancient and venerable *sites* to make room for a fanciful cottage after the design of some *imposing* draftsman, who, though less useful than the medical character, *lives* and *fattens* upon the present public mania for building.

Books, therefore, that have for their object a design upon the public purse, under whatever name or form they may be published, come into our hands in a very questionable shape, and demand of us a steady and faithful exertion of our censorial duty.

This painful part of our province can only be performed under the cheerful reflection, that though we may *wound* the ambition of the author, and tarnish his fancied honors, we are doing a [great and essential service to thousands of the British gentry, who indulge in architectural improvements, and decorative buildings, from the recommendation and allurement of a set of *charlatans*, who call themselves architects, but are nothing more than geometrical decoy-ducks.

Money, drawn out of the pocket of the public, by these *seemingly harmless* productions, which seduce the reader into building, at the promise of much *beauty* and great economy, and afterwards leave him pennyless; produces a train of individual and national evils, that calls for such castigation that will lead us to hope that, our literary exposition of pasteboard and pencil builders, will have a salutary effect upon the public, in guarding it from imposition and plunder!

The author of the work before us proceeds to say, amidst a vast variety of *pretty things** not founded on truth, that——

"Hitherto, it has been my good fortune to meet with persons possessing mind too liberal and sensible, to be *offended at* a respectful inquiry—What sum could be conveniently spared to carry their intentions into effect? when the inquiry had for *its sole object the best interest of my employers*; and I hope it will not savour too much *of self-praise* in me to say, that I have at all times endeavoured, *not* only *to encourage any waste of money, by* allowing gentlemen *to over build*, and by that means incurring an endless expense in supporting a large establishment, to procure every thing in suitable order, but to confine the cost and quantity of building within the limits proposed; maturely considering, in the first instance, what sum would be absolutely necessary to be laid out, to give the required advantages and at the least charge; and not lead them to erect spacious buildings, to gratify *my own* vanity in the display of fancied taste and ability, and thereby draw *public* attention to my works by improper means."

Setting aside the negligence and inelegance which are manifest in this specimen of our author's composition, for the consideration of the more important feature of *motive* which gives birth to such publications, we must be allowed to observe that we are acquainted with several instances of that want of *honorable* economy, so highly

---

* See page 9 of the book.

coloured as the *leading principle* of this new description of authors.

What will become of such professions of economy when we inform the public that one of these pasteboard architects lately gave in an estimate to build a cottage for something under three thousand pounds, and when it was finished, he made a demand of *near seven* thousand, upon the gentleman who was unfortunately seduced into *building*, under the *specious* assurances of economy, which have been just quoted, and the still more *specious* sketches, which only amuse the eye as a bait to entrap the understanding of their too credulous victims.

If this declaration be true, *as we are assured* it is— then the reader must see that we have not unfairly taken up such dangerous works, as a proper subject of critical castigation, while the *economical professions of* these *pseudo* architects, will, in time, become as *light* as the flimsy material upon which they have too long impressed falsehood and deception, for purposes alike injurious and destructive of individual prosperity and national happiness.

Felix quem facient aliena pericula Cautum.

With the hope, that the reader will become *alive* to the philosophy of this advice, we shall venture to caution him how he places a confidence in architects, who only introduce themselves to the notice of the public, by those kind of works, that exhibit picturesque sketches of villas; cottages orneés, &c. &c. which being well engraved, shew a deception of light and shadow, that give a relievo much bolder than is consistent with the laws or economy of nature, and consequently an unjust and unfair effect to the pictorial representation of the proposed future elevation.

It is to be remembered, that whatever is began in deception, is not likely to terminate in honor; and therefore we regret to say that it is a fact, beyond the necessity of further demonstration, that the various frivolous works of this description have been powerfully instrumental in vitiating the public taste, and may be said to possess the same mischievous tendency as those books bearing the title of " Every Man his own Lawyer," or " Every Man his own Physician,"—each eminently ruinous to the client as deleterious to the patient—unsuspectingly conducting their admirers to Chancery and the grave.

DR. HALLORAN AND GENERAL GREY.

In the beginning of the year 1810, a duel was fought in the garrison of Cape Town, between Captain Ryan, and Paymaster Patullo of the 93d regiment: the latter attended by Captain Hitchins of the same regiment, the former by Captain W. Burke Nicholls of the 72d regiment. In this rencontre, Mr. Patullo was slightly wounded, and the affair was considered as terminated; but a few hours subsequent to the meeting, Captains Ryan and Nicholls were put under arrest by the commander of the forces, and a court martial was ordered to assemble for their trial. The parties above-mentioned had alone been privy to the transaction, and independently of the mutually implied compact of confidence on such occasions, a reciprocal pledge of secrecy upon honor was exchanged on the ground. When the court had assembled, Major Dale of the 93d regiment appeared as prosecutor, and Paymaster Patullo and Captain Hitchins as evidence for the prosecution. Major Dale had pre-engaged the assistance of the only barrister in the colony, and Captains Ryan and Nicholls were thus left destitute of all legal advice or assistance for the conduct of their defence. These gentlemen had long been Dr. Halloran's most intimate and valued friends. They applied to him surrounded by several mutual friends to write their defence; and he, in the true spirit of honorable friendship complied with their request. Immediately after the close of the court martial, and while its sentence was yet unknown, Mr. Patullo was proposed by Major Dale as a candidate for admission to the Cape Town Subscription Society; an institution at which newspapers, pamphlets, reviews, &c. were provided for the members. At the ballot twelve persons only were present, of whom five were English, and seven Dutch gentlemen. By the former Mr. Patullo was unanimously rejected; by the latter, who knew nothing of him but through the medium of Major Dale, he was accepted. On hearing this, Dr. Halloran addressed himself to one individual director desiring to withdraw his name, and immediately after transmitted a letter to the committee of directors, informing them that he could not permit his name to appear associated with that of a person who stood decidedly and indelibly disgraced as a military man and a gentleman, and who was not admitted to any military mess in the garrison, except that of his own regiment. This circumstance, coupled with Dr. Halloran's assistance in the defence of his military friends, appears to have excited emotions in the bosom of Lieutenant-General H. Grey, of rather an ungovernable description; and in less than a week after the transmission of Dr. Halloran's intimation to the directors of the society, the General addressed to him a long and angry letter, removing him from the brigade in Cape Town, to out-quarters. It will appear from the preceding statement, substantiated by the evidence adduced, that Dr. Halloran only addressed the society through the medium of a letter; but the General, either too idle or too prejudiced to arrive at the truth, informs him, that his removal " is in consequence of his addressing a public assembly, and endeavouring to exclude from society an officer for what he did in support of him." He concludes with the following remarkable expressions :

" Perhaps it may save you some trouble to add that the threat you have so often and so improperly held out, of publicity, is a bug-bear I do not fear; on the contrary I wish every act of mine, as commander of this army, to be as public as possible; and I shall now myself send to the Commander in Chief a full statement of every thing that has passed relative to you, since you were attached to this army; which I have hitherto avoided doing, not wishing, in times like the present, when there is so much important business to attend to, to plague government with circumstances of this nature, and hoping that you would have seen your error, and not have gone such lengths as you have done."

In reply to this letter Dr. Halloran informed General Grey, that he had accepted his commission, expressly on condition of being attached to the brigade at Cape Town; but on receiving a second and peremptory order of removal, he preferred the alternative of resigning his commission, to that of enduring more aggravated insult, and resigning the scholastic and other establishments that his talents and industry had created at Cape Town. To rebut an insinuation of General Grey respecting the performance of his professional duties, he produced the testimony of the most respectable English residents; and to facilitate, as far as depended on him, the accommodation of the misunderstanding between the General and himself, he transmitted through a common friend a declaration " that in objecting to the admission of Paymaster Patullo, he had not the remotest intention or idea, directly or indirectly, of setting the Commander's authority at defiance," and expressing his sorrow that any misconstruction of his conduct should have prevented the success of his endeavours to conciliate his friendship. This application was ineffectual, and Dr. Halloran irritated by the mode in which his conduct had been noticed, and by the virtual inflictions of a severe and disgraceful punishment, for an act neither improper in itself, nor committed in his professional or responsible capacity, was excited to the composition of several poetical satires on the General's character and habits. Previous, however, to the appearance of the first of these, several anonymous and personal strictures had been transmitted to the General, and ascribed by him (on what grounds we are unable to discover) to Dr. Halloran. These letters the Doctor solemnly disavows, asserting " most unequivocally and solemnly that he had not at any time composed, or copied, or dictated, or transmitted, directly or indirectly, any letter or other paper, without his legitimate signature." This communication concluded with the following words. "You have told me in your letter of the 18th ult.—'your threat of publicity is a *bug-bear* I am not afraid of; on the contrary, I wish every act of mine as commander of this army to be made as public as possible;'—I admire the manliness of the sentiment, and I have taken you at your word! I have, I candidly tell you, written for publication, several poetical bug-bears, as well as prose strictures on various parts of your conduct both public and private; which, if you possess sufficient magnanimity, you are welcome to peruse, and I enclose one of the number for that purpose," &c.

This enclosure consisted of a poem, with the subjoined title, and of which the annexed passages are extracts.

" For publication.

" Vincam, vel superatus, non *sine sanguine* vinear!
" Αιμα μελαινον, black blood, viz. ink."

Bugbear, No. 1, or, Hamilton's Ghost.

Monstrum horrendum, et truci formidabile, Graio!

On his downy couch reclining,
To rest by opiates composed;
The midnight moon obscurely shining;
The Grey friar and his nun reposed.

Howled the tempest round his dwelling,
Gleamed the sky with meteors red;
When arose with hideous yelling,
Spectres of the injured dead.

Midnight horrors.

From their gloomy cearments breaking,
On the noon of night they glide,
 With immortal anguish waking,
While all nature slept beside.

These the Grey friar's couch surrounding,
On his feverish visions broke;
 When in conscience' voice astounding,
Thus a grisly spectre spoke.

Need I tell my fatal story,
I am *Hamilton's* sad ghost,
 Nipp'd in the career of glory,
By oppression's blighting frost.

In the prime of youth I perished;
Wretch, by thee to madness driven;
 When, my soul had mercy cherished,
Still that soul had bloomed for heaven.

Ever shall my spectre haunt thee,
Flashing on thy conscious mind;
 In the dance or banquet daunt thee,
In thy dark recesses find.

In conscience' still small voice affright thee,
When deep darkness wraps the pole;
 And to fate in thunders cite thee,
When the storms of battle roll.

When the dreadful groans of nature,
Earth's convulsive fabric shook;
 On the clouds with giant stature,
Her throne immortal justice took.

Then, thy cheek was blanched with terrors,
When this awful voice was heard;
 Who—for nature's venial errors,
As himself had never erred.

By relentless fury guided,
My eternal dictates spurns;
 And the sword to him confided,
On the unhappy victim turns.

> Him by this dire presage daunted,
> I summon to my equal throne,
> When the mercy he has granted,
> Shall be the measure of his own.
>
> But on thee, thou foe to merit,
> Her balm shall Pity never shed;
> Remorse shall rack thy living spirit,
> And direr pangs await thee, dead.

" The circumstances," says Dr. Halloran, " on which these charges are founded, are briefly these:—A young officer of good family and education, had committed several juvenile errors, which called, however, for reprehension from his superiors; and accordingly the officer commanding at the Cape, sent him into exile at *Hout's* bay. While he was there some near relations of his, returning from India, touched at the Cape, whom he made repeated but ineffectual applications for permission to visit. On the departure of the fleet without such permission for a mutual interview, the unhappy youth destroyed himself."

Up to the transmission of the preceding verses, the conduct of Dr. Halloran had been characterized by a spirit of manly independence, tempered with the prudence that was due to himself, and the respect demanded by the rank of his oppressor. But no circumstances of irritation will entirely excuse so gross and uncalled for an attack on the commander of his majesty's forces. To await, in dignified silence, the fiat of his sovereign, would have been most advantageous to his interests, and most becoming his sacred profession, as well as the relation in which he stood to the author of his wrongs. Nor, should it be admitted that the composition of the *Bug-bear*, was excusable in an individual, whose feelings had been wantonly lacerated, and whose fortunes malignantly destroyed, can the same apology be made for his avowal to General Grey, that he had received several anonymous and slanderous productions animadverting on the General's private and public conduct, which he was resolved to transmit to England. Of all the individuals at the Cape, he was the last who ought to have chosen such an office: to the mind of General Grey his readiness to fulfil it must have conveyed the impression of persevering and resolute hostility; by the enemies of Dr. Halloran, his proceeding would be censured as revengeful, and by his friends it must have been regarded as indelicate.

But the warmth of the Doctor's language would have been forgiven by a generous mind, as the phrenzied ebullition of feelings stimulated to expression by the prospect of disgrace and poverty; and the indelicacy to be reprobated in the transmission of the papers, might be the just object of regret to Dr. Halloran's friends, but could only excite the vindictive resentment of a mind so weak as to be agitated by the most trivial causes, or a conscience so tender as to be susceptible of laceration by the most light and fragile instruments. Up to the institution of legal proceedings, the motives of reciprocal resentment appear to have been so equally balanced as to leave no legitimate plea of injury to the General; and even admitting that exemplary patience was displayed on the part of the soldier and the most unworthy virulence on the part of the divine, the punishment of the latter had already (supposing it to be sanctioned by his majesty) been sufficiently rigorous and exemplary. " A generous enemy," says the Doctor, " my sufferings should surely have disarmed—for even in hatred there are distinctions; and the direst foes moderate their aversion and hostility, towards a disarmed and prostrate adversary."

A spirit very different, however, from that of magnanimity, appears to have directed the progress, and influenced the issue of the proceedings. Immediately on their commencement, Dr. Halloran appealed in a letter couched in language, which even the legal authorities of England would have pronounced to be regular and correct, against the jurisdiction of the Dutch court. For *transcribing* this letter, Dr. Halloran's amanuensis, Mr. F. H. Staedhall, who, even if the letter had been in the highest degree irregular or offensive, could not have shared in its criminality, since he was unacquainted with the English language, was prosecuted by his majesty's fiscal " for having *written a libel;*" with claim for twelve months imprisonment in the common gaol, and costs of suit; and he was actually cast in the costs, and sentenced to three months imprisonment by the *soi-disant* court of justice at the Cape. It is not our intention to detail the various forms of legal proceeding, or to enumerate the appeals and objections on one side, and the replications on the other. Prolix and tedious as the forms of English courts are usually considered, they are far exceeded in formality and tautology by the proceedings before the Dutch judicature. At length, on the 15th of December, 1810, they pronounced the following sentence; " the court has banished the defendant, declared him to have fallen under the terms of the proclamation of the 3d of September, 1792; and conformable thereto condemned him in a penalty of fifty-six rix dollars, and also to be confined in the public prison, there to remain at his (*own*) expence till there may be an opportunity of putting the said sentence of banishment against the defendant into execution."

On the delivery of the sentence Dr. Halloran lodged an appeal in the proper court, which immediately affirmed the former judgment. He then earnestly solicited the indulgence of being liberated from his confinement until the period of his embarkation, for the consolation of his family, and the settlement of his affairs, on giving bail to the amount of twenty thousand pounds, for his appearance when called upon. The governor, Lord Caledon, having rejected this request, Dr. Halloran entreated that he might be allowed, on finding bail to the amount already specified, to visit his family from seven till nine o'clock in the evening. This application also was refused, so that from the date of the sentence to the period of Dr. Halloran's arrival in England, he had no communication with his wife and children. Of the concluding scene, a scene that would have disgraced the most barbarous people, it is difficult to express our sentiments without subjecting *ourselves* to the brutality that we would wish to hold up to public execration. Having protested against the legality of the sentence, he was conveyed from prison by a force of thirteen armed men to a boat lying near the dock-yard. He immediately dispatched his servant boy, who happened to be in attendance on him, to desire Mrs. Halloran and his daughters to meet him, and receive his parting embrace and benediction. His messenger speedily returned in breathless haste to announce their approach; but the boat was not allowed by the fiscal's officers to wait their arrival! His family are still retained in that remote colony in the most distressing circumstances, and without the means of return. His applications for redress have hitherto been unavailing, and his petition for a passage to this country, and suitable accommodation for his family, has received only a cold and formal reply. Nor has he any other support under these multiplied afflictions, but the confidence that those, who in the moment of distress came forward to relieve the husband and the parent, will not now forget the matron and her children.

When it is considered on the very day the general's order of removal from Cape Town was given, Dr. Halloran had entered into a legal engagement to retain the appointment of rector of the grammar school for five years, that he had formed an establishment for the purposes of general education at an expence of more than two thousand pounds, and that he had engaged to himself an extensive circle of respectable and honourable friends, who loved him for his virtues and reverenced him for his great and various attainments, and that his situation justified the most pleasing anticipations of permanent prosperity; the cruelty of the sentence, and its disproportion to the crime committed, even supposing its commission to have been attended with no palliating circumstances, must strike the most unobserving with wonder, and the most unfeeling with abhorrence. And when it is known that this sentence was directed by external influence, that none of the proceedings were free or independent, and that Major Watson refused to attend the court in favour of Dr. Halloran, because it might expose him to the open hostility or private resentment of General Grey, by whose *power and influence* his professional prospects, with regard both to advantage and employment, might in consequence be materially obstructed, or deteriorated; every patriot and every man of feeling will indulge a hope, that the result of the gracious promise of the Prince Regent, that the case shall be taken into consideration, will not only terminate in the restoration of Dr. Halloran to his former affluence, but in the disgrace of the individuals who have abused their authority for the purposes of oppression.

In the mean time, as a proof of the spirit in which General Grey fulfilled the duties of his station, we beg leave to lay before our readers the subjoined general order. A production more disgraceful to its authors, or more illegal in its construction, we do not remember to have seen; and we are certain that had it issued from the escrutoire of any officer on an *European* station, he would have been cashiered.

General Orders, previous to the Sitting of the Court.

Head Quarters, 28th Dec. 1809.

"A General Court Martial to assemble on Thursday the 4th of January, at ten o'clock in the morning, in the Castle, for the trial of Capt. Ryan, of the 93d regiment, and Capt. Nicolls of the 72d regiment; the former for having sent, and the latter for having delivered, a challenge to the Paymaster of the 93d regiment. Capt. Ryan, having been before tried for the same offence, it is needless to make any observations on his conduct. But the Commander of the Forces must express his extreme surprize, that any officer from another corps should have been found to interfere in the disgraceful *dissensions*, which have so long prevailed in the 93d regiment; and he feels convinced, that Capt. Nicolls, of the 72d regiment, is the only officer of this army, who would have acted such a part, which can only be considered as setting at defiance the approbation of his superiors.

"With whatever art these gentlemen may think they have conducted themselves in this transaction, and whatever the result of the Court Martial may be, the proceedings will at least place their characters in a true point of view, to his Majesty, and the Commander in Chief.

"The conduct of Captains Ryan and Nicolls upon this occasion, is farther aggravated by the supposed offence on the part of the Paymaster having been on a point of duty, and of the most trifling nature; and the Commander of the Forces is convinced, that every officer, who has the good of the service at heart, will feel with him the necessity of checking the idea, "that officers in the execution of their duty are to be personally responsible to every man who chooses to pique himself on the reputation of a duellist."

If a case may be thus prejudged, because the object of accusation is at a distance from his country; if oppression be sanctioned by the British court, because it is committed in a foreign land; and a people who pride themselves on the justice of their laws, and the impartiality with which they are administered, regard with indifference the injuries of a fellow-subject, because they have been inflicted in a tropical latitude, of what avail have been the wisdom of our statesmen, or the fortitude of our patriots? If many cases like that of Dr. Halloran have occurred in our distant possessions, the sum of happiness at home bears no proportion to the miseries that our fellow-Englishmen have sustained by the mal-administration of justice abroad; and tyranny is only driven from our shores, to rage with tenfold fury on the plains of Asia, and in the deserts of Africa.

MISS ELIZABETH'S JOURNAL.

EXTRACT THE FIRST.

" How dull and dreary are the chambers of celibacy ! Seventeen years have now glided away since I became a resident of this gloomy mansion, nor during that long long period have I ventured to indulge in one expression of natural feeling, or to smile approval on the spontaneous attentions of those whom my peculiarity of situation alone prevented from becoming the most ardent and faithful lovers! Often as I have contemplated from the terrace casement the declension of the evening sun, the unrestricted intercourse of the crowds below has excited my envy, and impressed on my remembrance sentiments of indelible regret. Alas! to me no smile is visible but the smile of self-complacency : I hear the language of flattery, but am never addressed in the accents of tenderness; love is banished from the habitation of my father, and futurity presents a gloomy prospect of joyless *maidenhood*. Agitated by contending emotions I sometimes weep in the anguish of a broken spirit, and sometimes regard the beings who surround me with sentiments bordering on revenge. But the scenes of this day have taught me that the only feeling they are worthy of exciting is derision: I am not so *quixotic* as to feel resentment or anger at the evolutions of a set of puppets, the slaves of accident and ceremony ; but to laugh at the oddness of their construction and their movements may perhaps be amusing, and is certainly excusable."

* * * * * *

" I never supposed Freddy to be overburthened with good sense, but he has more of his father's temperament than the rest of the family, and never leaves his reason in the delirium of pleasure. His passions are too strong to be restrained by a sense of propriety, yet his habits of caution so predominant, that he never gives himself up with any degree of zest even to his most favorite indulgences. If his mistress demanded, as the price of her consent, a thousand pounds, he would give it rather than lose her, yet would trick her in the *counting* by a one pound note. I really think that there is no scene of licentiousness in which he would not consent to become a partner; yet during the hours of enjoyment, he would think to himself " what would be thought should my father discover me?" I should care nothing about his meanness, for I have few opportunities of seeing it, but his manner is so unpleasing, that I cannot endure him. Every attitude, and every motion, and every look, is expressive of selfishness: even when he wishes to look affectionately at us, he seems to say, you are dear to me, because you are *my* sisters; you derive all your claims on my love from your relation to my person: as Elizabeth and Sophia, you are so! so! girls; but as the daughters of my father, you have some claim to my attention and good offices." But this is the fault of his education and not of his heart; he is really a very affectionate and well-meaning man; would to heaven his wisdom was equal to his goodness! I am not able to judge of his qualities as a soldier, but I well remember the curious dialogue that passed between papa and him on his return from Holland."

Freddy was sulky, my dear papa was afflicted and shed tears; I pitied them both, and should have pitied Freddy more, if he had not appeared as proud of himself as if he had been a second Alexander. I could not refrain from smiling, when just as my brother began to swell into consequence at the remembrance of his exploits, papa exclaimed, ' Hold your tongue! hold your tongue! you have been a bad boy, a bad boy! go to bed! go to bed! and say your prayers! do! do!' "

Tuesday.

" B—— has this morning given me an account of poor George's *chere amie.* She was the daughter of Mr. S. a gentleman in ————shire, and was married, not at a malpropos moment to a Mr. F. a poor weak mortal, who indulged all her whims, and was the silent witness of all her follies. She led him a weary life, and sent him to the grave by downright cruelty.---I hate the woman. She assumes all the elegancies of the virtuous female, and though she knows that she is publicly regarded as a shameless profligate, appears to demand from us, the respect that none of us *can* pay to any one but a legitimate sister-in-law. How poor George can live with her, heaven has not enabled me to guess; but his friends have persuaded him that every feeling of his soul is of the noblest kind, and that he is born to command, and need only look to overawe. He chuses old and matronly women, while he prefers the young, the sparkling and the unsophisticated, to shew his predominance over the most masculine spirits, and his ability to control the most unmanageable tempers. Dear dear George! If a statue of vanity were erected on the earth, it ought to be in thy image and with thy attributes. Thou art a philosopher, without the power of stringing together three connected ideas; an orator, just able to ask a jockey how he does, and bid thy mistress a fine morning; a soldier, whose martial prowess consists in having conquered three fencing masters, who *gave* thee the victory; a man of great and generous sentiments, whose expansive soul extends to the contraction of debts never intended to be paid, and the seduction of mistresses whom thou art not destined to enjoy. My poor brother has no regular pursuit nor any accomplishment in which he particularly excels. He sings a little, dances a little, and scribbles a little, and eats and drinks a great deal. One quarter of an hour he devotes to his book, another to S——, another to F—— the fighting master, three hours to dinner, the evening to his wine, and the night to Mrs. F."

MRS. WYNDHAM AND COLONEL GREVILLE.

An appeal to the gentlemen of England from a *ci-devant* pupil of Mrs. W―――― against a colonel and a man of family, is almost as extraordinary as the elevation of a *pot girl* at the *queen's larder* to the possession of a handsome establishment in Argyle-street. When men of family pledge themselves, however, to the introduction of a female friend into the fashionable institutions over which they are licensed to preside, they have no right to be angry if the gay world listens with delight to any statement that has a tendency to render them the objects of derision.

Infirmity of body, if it may be received as an excuse for indiscretion, cannot justly be advanced as an apology for guilt; and whatever sentiments of compassion formerly dissuaded us from a full and satisfactory exposition of the various arts by which Colonel Greville has endeavoured to repair a ruined fortune at the expence of the public, have been dissipated by the publication of his conduct to a lady, who independent of her peculiar claims on his personal gratitude, deserves the support of every man of honour not totally insensible to the charms of beauty. If the statement of Mrs. Wyndham be true, Colonel Greville can no longer claim the rank or character of a gentleman; that it is *false*, he has not ventured to assert; and supposing him to be guiltless of the chief point of accusation, that of having cajoled her by false representations into the payment of three hundred pounds, which together with other sums he has refused to return, it tends to place his conduct in a very ridiculous, and his character in a very unamiable light. To live upon the friends, whom it is his daily and favourite employment to abuse, is not the practice of a man of honor; to obtain their money and then laugh at their credulity, is equally inconsistent with the principles of rectitude, and the feelings of a gentleman.

Mrs. Wyndham first met Colonel Greville at a party in Holles-street, and having heard that he was a very handsome man, and a great favourite with the fair sex, she felt much shocked at the alteration time and sickness had made in him. His appearance and plausible manner interested her much. About a month afterwards she found that he lodged opposite her house, and seeing his dejected state, and apparently deserted by all those who had courted his acquaintance, she gave him a general invitation to her house and table. She had the gratification to find both his health and spirits mend from the comfort and attention it was in her power to bestow on him; in other respects, however, she repented of her good-natured offer, for the Colonel made her house his home, and went so far as to see his friends and tradespeople there, instead of his own lodgings. Not content with this, he thought proper to enquire into her circumstances with very impertinent, and at *that time* unaccountable minuteness, and added to his other offences the meanness of clandestinely endeavouring to persuade Mrs. Wyndham's man servant to leave his mistress, a design in which he so far succeeded as to make him totally regardless of her, and attentive only to the Colonel.

From a man of Greville's disposition, and so constantly at Mrs. Wyndham's house, it was impossible wholly to conceal her affairs. She had sold some property, and in part payment had taken some notes to the amount of four hundred pounds. Having been in the city to get them discounted, she had kept Colonel Greville waiting dinner, and as an excuse for so doing told him what business had detained her, and that she had been unsuccessful. He upbraided her for her closeness towards him, and offered to *get them* done for her, at a much less loss than would be possible in case of her own negociation. The result of this business was a balance of fifty pounds due from Mrs. Wyndham to Colonel Greville, which was paid soon after her return from a short trip to Brighton. Being almost worn to death, however, by Colonel Greville's continual *worry* about his affairs and his health, she was obliged to seek relief by again going to that place. On her return to town in ten days, he was constantly painting the Pantheon scheme to her in the brightest colours, and tried to persuade her that if she entered into the concern she would make her fortune. " The more" (he observes in one of his letters), the more I consider the business of the Pantheon, the more I admire and approve of the scheme; nor is it because it *was* my own original *ideas,* and intended three years ago for my own institution in Argyle-street, that I am partial to it, but from a conviction that nothing can paralyze its immense advantage, but the misfortune of being in obscure hands. Convinced and satisfied as I am that if with what they have got, they can command a couple of thousands, the gains will be enormous, while not the smallest risk attends the undertaking. *I certainly shall not part with my share,* and strongly advise you, if y u can, to procure a thousand pounds—if you do, the two proprietors have offered me to relinquish a portion of their shares, which, with the half of mine, I shall with pleasure make over to you; but recollect this must be entirely between you and me. I've no doubts five or 6000*l.* will be coming in. Let me know your final decision, and pray at any rate be mum."

Mrs. Wyndham had at this time such a perfect reliance upon his honor, that if she could have raised the money she certainly would have yielded to his representations; but finding that she could not obtain the requisite sum, she declined having any thing to do with the speculation. *On this* the Colonel began to complain that the badness of his health, and the other schemes he had in view, made it impossible for him to bestow those attentions and exertions that the institution required; and as nothing now could prevent the success of it, he would, as some return for the kindnesses bestowed upon him by Mrs. Wyndham, agree to assign over his right to her, on condition that she paid certain sums he had answered for, and allow him five *per cent* out of the emoluments she might derive from the concern. For the first part an assignment was to pass between them, and for the five *per cent*, he would be satisfied if Mrs. Wyndham took an oath on the Bible, that she would pay it him or his family.

After the exchange of assignments she lent him 100*l.* in performance of a former promise towards the payment of 200*l.* to Mr. Morton the solicitor. Soon after this transaction Colonel Greville called as his friend was dressing, and as she could not see him, he sent up a letter he had received, and the following piece of paper:

"Mr. Bonner has just sent me this—what a scrape we shall get into,—and what an atrocious villain. Taylor has bribed him."

Mrs. Wyndham does not exactly remember the contents of the letter, but it went to state that the institution was totally ruined. At first this intelligence was regarded by Mrs. Wyndham with indifference; but she was informed by the Colonel that they meant to bring him in a partner, that as he had sold his share to her, *she* must be responsible, that there was a likelihood of its becoming a bankruptcy, and in that case she would lose the whole of her property and be completely ruined. After the dreadfull alarm into which she was thrown, he calmed her in some degree, by telling her that if she could let him have 300*l.* he would " *let her off*," on the additional understanding that in case of any lawsuit being commenced against him, she should be at one half the expence. In these conditions Mrs. Wyndham gladly acquiesced, and had they been much more distressing, they would have obtained her compliance.

After this he informed her that he had asked his solicitor, and found that they could not make him a bankrupt; that the business was settled much better than he had expected, that he had satisfied a few of the worst by the money she gave him, and that the others could only bring actions, which with her assistance in paying half the costs, he should be able to defend. He told her that 500*l.* advanced to the institution, he borrowed of a Mr. Withers or Villiers; this money he had to pay about May. He asked her if she could lend him 150*l.* or get any one to do so without his name appearing in it: she could not do this herself, but obtained in her own name 120*l.* for which she was to give a premium of 10*l.* It will be observed that this sum, with the three hundred pounds obtained by alarming Mrs. Wyndham with the prospect of becoming a partner in the Pantheon bankruptcy, and the 100*l.* lent makes a sum total of 530*l.*——After more than one apology for non-payment, and some marks of coldness on the part of Mrs. Wyndham, he became a less assiduous visitor. After an absence of some duration, she was informed that he had gone abroad; she began to be alarmed. She now made some fruitless applications for his address, and her patience being at length exhausted, she mentioned for the first time his having borrowed the money. Her astonishment may be easily conceived, at learning, in return, that he had borrowed 300*l.* of a Mrs. Finch, a lady who had come from the country to Mrs. Wyndham's house, for the purpose of consulting the London physicians on the state of her health. This determined Mrs. Wyndham to write to his family, but having been informed of his return, she delayed the transmission of her note, in the hopes of seeing him. Having waited in vain, she began to think that delicacy on her part was superfluous, and on going down to dinner was " thunder-struck" to find that Mrs. Finch had received a letter from him, in which he promised the repayment of her money, but assured her at the same time by every thing that was sacred that he was not indebted to Mrs. Wyndham, nor ever had been, and that no money transactions whatever had passed between Mrs. W. and him, except his once letting her have 300*l.*! He admitted that Mrs. Wyndham had been very kind to him, but thought he had amply repaid her by making her a present of some trinkets! Those trinkets Mrs. W. informs us, were presented to her with so much formality, that she fully expected to receive a casket of diamonds, but their value was in fact not more than three guineas, a noble remuneration for the comforts and conveniences of a respectable establishment, the attentions of a sympathizing friend, and all the cares and assiduities that restored his health, and soothed the habitual infirmities of a distracted intellect!

In consequence of the Colonel's letter to Mrs. Finch, Mrs. Wyndham wrote to inform him of her conviction that he intended to " swindle" her out of the 530l., and demanding, on pain of immediate publicity, either the money itself, or a note indorsed by his family. To this application he returned the following extraordinary answer, which of itself we conceive fully substantiates all Mrs. Wyndham's assertions, and exhibits a singular specimen of jesuitical subterfuge.

" Madam,

" I am not aware that I expressed any sentiment in my note to Mrs. Finch, that could authorise you to call it rascally and mean. With respect to the one I have received from you, containing a threat of exposure and prosecution, unless I this day pay you 530l. which you state you lent me, I have only to reply that if unhappily my character is privately or publicly libelled, I must submit to all the vexations which the defending of it must occasion me; and the greatest of which will be the grief of having to call Mrs. Wyndham my accuser. In the mean time I will thank you to favor me with an account of *when, how, and where* the money was advanced by you; and if you can inform me who the people are whom I have traduced, and who the ladies are whom I have swindled, you will much oblige your humble servant,

H. F. GREVILLE."

With this letter terminated their correspondence, and (we are afraid) Mrs. Wyndham's prospects of repayment.

Nor is the mere loss of the money the only cause of her regret: she has too much reason to believe that during the time of the Colonel's residence at her house, he employed himself in traducing her character to her female friends, and that the kindness with which he was received and the sisterly amenity with which she endeavoured to soothe his afflictions, and recover his infirmities, were received without sensibility, and repaid by the most wanton ingratitude.

That Colonel Greville, indeed, is a man not easily deterred from trespassing on the kindness or forbearance of his friends, is sufficiently evident from many instances of his conduct during the period of the preceding transactions. Two days, (says Mrs. Wyndham,) after I came from Brighton, his servant came to me to beg for God's sake, that I would allow Colonel Greville to sleep at my house, as his own was so damp that it would kill him to be there. I sent him for answer that I had no room I could possibly offer to him. The servant returned, and pointed out a room that was not occupied next my dining parlor. This I determined not to let him have, as I disliked having a sick person so near my eating-room. Wishing to put an end to his request altogether, I said I had no apartment but a garret that was fitted up for a little girl I had adopted, not supposing it possible he would accept of this. To my utter astonishment, in two hours after, a coach drew up, loaded with all sorts of dressing utensils, &c. &c. I expected to see lashed behind it the celebrated slipper-bath, Mr. Dick used laughing to say, he *addled* himself in whilst receiving his morning visitors. So far from feeling himself obliged to me for the inconvenience he was likely to put me to, he seemed to be inclined to quarrel the whole of dinner-time, for my not giving him the room he wanted. As my dining parlor is large for the size of the house, and knowing he was accustomed to have a good many morning visitors, I gave it him to receive them in. This, I conceived, would only put me out of the way for a short time, as I expected he meant to take a lodging as soon as he could meet with one that would suit him.

"A few days after this as I was passing the parlor in my way to the carriage, I knocked at the door to ask after his health. He spoke to me in the most impetuous maner, complaining loudly that he could not have the room an instant to himself: my servant was constantly in and out preparing the sideboard for dinner. He said he had twenty people that morning upon secret business, and it was really not to be borne. I was almost dumb with astonishment at his impudence, and coolly answered, I was sorry it was not in my power to make him more comfortable. On my return I could scarcely get into my passage for trunks, books, &c. On enquiring the cause of all this bustle, I was informed Colonel Greville was going. I went to him, and said, though an untruth, that I was sorry he was going in such a hurry. He absolutely flew into a rage with me. "Mrs. Wyndham," said he, " I must and will always have a room to myself—I left my own wife because I could not have my own way." Seeing the lady who was with me, ready to burst at his speech, I felt quite angry, and said, " Very likely, Colonel Greville ; but as I have never aspired to the honor of being either your wife or your mistress, you must excuse me if I say your conduct is very improper, and I feel quite delighted at your resolution of leaving my house:" we parted, and the next time we met, without any apology, were as good friends as ever; I appeal *even to the Greville party* whether this does not look a little like madness."

That the freedom with which we have expressed our opinions of his conduct and character should excite the anger of Colonel Greville is impossible. He will surely allow to others the same liberty of speech, that he has exercised himself; and if, therefore, we were to say of him as he said of Mr. Arnold, that " he has not a mind larger than a pigeon's," or were to pronounce, as he has pronounced of Mr. Bonner, that he is " an atrocious villain," what possible apology could he adduce for complaining of our freedom? A man so open to attack, should be careful how he traduces the characters of others; but if he must gratify his passion for abuse, prudence at least should dissuade him from committing his sentiments to those, whom conscience must teach him to regard in prospective as his inveterate enemies. At the time that he was borrowing Mrs. Wyndham's money he should have remembered that the time of payment would arrive, and that exposure would be the natural result of his refusal to perform his promise. Had his foresight therefore been equal to his cunning, he would have written nothing, that when disclosed should not contribute to his advantage. In the present case, his indiscretions have placed him at the mercy of a speculator, to whom his deportment was always of the most obsequious character, of a manager whose interest is necessary to the prosecution of his plans, and of a nobleman, (Lord Headfort,) whose countenance may be necessary to his retention in certain circles of society.

But (to emulate his learning) *experientia docet*, and we hope that when his extraordinary conduct respecting the Pantheon licence, under which Messrs. Cundy and Caldas opened the establishment, shall call for copies of his correspondence, it will not be found to contain the most gross abuse of his " dearest" friends, and the most servile adulation of those whom he privately professes to pity or detest.

THE REVIEWER, No. X.

Childe Harold's Pilgrimage, a Romaunt, by Lord Byron. 4to. 1l. 10s. Murray.

WE have waited for the appearance of the production before us, with an anxiety only equalled by the disappointment we have felt at our inability to bestow upon it that warm and unmingled praise which would alone secure us, in the mind of his lordship, from the suspicion of being guided in our criticism by any feeling of personal resentment. Selected as the most prominent objects of that abuse by which his lordship's retaliatory poem was so pre-eminently distinguished, we have retorted his attack with the manly openness of an honorable combatant; and though the javelin of this literary Hector fell pointless before the shield of truth, we hail with no unnatural exultation every public and splendid evidence of the worthiness of the hand that directed its threatening but harmless flight. That Lord Byron, as a didactic poet has surpassed the majority of his predecessors, and far excels the most celebrated of his contemporaries, we were among the first to admit; and though it must be confessed that he makes too unsparing a use of the language and sentiments of his predecessors, yet there are parts of the "English Bards and Scotch Reviewers," from which if we abstract the ascription of originality we cannot withhold the praise of classical elegance. But he is more elegant than spirited, and rather ingenious than splendid. All that labour, directed by taste, and operating on a moderate portion of materials, could accomplish, he has performed; but he possesses no luxuriance of fancy, or enthusiasm of sentiment: the images of a poetical creation do not crowd upon his mind, but present themselves before him in formal and regular succession, adorned with no ideal attributes, and apparelled in the homely and unattractive drapery of daily life. His stanzas do not seem to be the unpremeditated effusions of exuberant thought laboring for expression, but the manufacture of mechanical exertion endeavouring to contribute by regularity of ornament for the worthlessness of the original material. He is not at a loss for words to express his ideas, but for ideas to sustain the weight of a verbal superstructure. He observes indeed that the stanza of Spenser admits of every variety, and quotes Dr. Beattie to prove that in his measure, "you may be either droll or pathetic, descriptive or sentimental, tender or satirical as the humour strikes you;" but he ought to have remembered that to do any of these things with great effect in the stanza of Spenser, demands an originality of genius, and a versatility of talent, of which no one can presume himself to be the possessor, whose vanity is not fully equal to his prudence. The couplet of Pope is adapted to those of whom the elegance is more remarkable than the genius; the stanza of Spenser ought to be selected by him alone, whose ideas swell into exuberance, or whose sentiments expand into unpremeditated expression.

That these remarks are neither uncandid nor gratuitous, might be proved from every stanza of the Pilgrimage. But the great defect of the poem is its want of purpose to reward attention, or of interest to excite it. It is in reality a descriptive poem, but the descriptions are connected together by no stronger tie than the locomotive caprice of Childe Harolde. If the "Childe" resolves to travel into Phrygia, Phrygia is described; if Albania detains him for a few weeks, the reader is detained to dwell upon its beauties, through a proportionate number of stanzas. The book may be laid down at the termination of any passage, without reluctance or inconvenience; the reader of page 23 has no motive, independently of the possible beauty of composition, to turn over to page 24; and at the end of the two preliminary cantos published in the volume before us, it would be impossible to determine why the poem is not as technically complete, as if a dozen cantos were to succeed them.

The interest of the work is much diminished by its appearance under the form of a romaunt. A *romaunt*, if it implies any thing, implies a poem descriptive of manners long since past, composed at a time coeval with the existence of those manners, and in language appropriate to the scenes and persons introduced. But the Pilgrimage of Childe Harolde, by Lord Byron, contains allusions to the tyranny of Napoleon, descriptions of the modern boundaries of Spain and Portugal, and a poetical eulogy on the Maid of Saragoza! The language and phraseology of Spenser is only so far imitated as it affords a licence to error, and a plea for indolence. It admits of the employment of *do* and *did* whenever the introduction of the expletive may seem convenient, and affords a tolerable rhime where modern words might be found untractable. The author of a *romaunt* after the manner of Lord Byron, has no task more arduous, than first to write his poem in decent English, and then to substitute a few convenient, and a few antiquated words, for more modern or less sonorous synonymes. *Ee* will then become an easy substitute for *eye*, *ne* for *no* and *nor*, *right* for *old*, and any thing else that is convenient for any thing else that is correct. The subjoined stanzas afford a fair example of Lord Byron's defects of thought and manner.

15.

O Christ it is a *goodly* sight to see,
What heaven hath done for this delicious land,
  What fruits of fragrance blush on every tree,
What *goodly* prospects o'er the hills expand!
But man would mar them with an impious hand.
  And when the Almighty lifts his fiercest scourge,
'Gainst those who most transgress his high command,
  With treble vengeance will his hot shafts urge,
Gaul's locust host, and earth from fellest foeman *purge*.

16.

What beauties doth Lisboa first unfold,
Her image floating on that noble tide,
  Which Poets vainly pave with sands of gold,
But now whereon a thousand keels *did* ride,
Of mighty strength since Albion was allied,
  And to the Lusians *did* her aid afford;
A nation swollen with ignorance and pride,
  Who lick yet loath the hand that waves the sword,
To save them from the wrath of Gaul's unsparing lord.

17.

But whoso entereth within the town,
That sheening far celestial seems to be,
Disconsolate will wander up and down,
'Mid many things unsightly to strange ee,
For hut and palace show like filthily;
The dingy denizens are reared in dirt,
Ne personage of high or mean degree,
Doth care for cleanness of surtout or shirt,
Though shent with Egypt's plague, unkempt, unwashed, unhurt.

In the first of these stanzas the quaintness of the exclamation, and the conversion of heaven's thunderbolts into a dose of physic; in the second the uncouth and unnecessary repetition of the expletive; and in the third the substitution of sheening and ne, for modern words more accordant with the phraseology of the sentence, and more expressive in their meaning, are particularly offensive. But the verbal faults of the stanzas are not so observable as the general disproportion between the copiousness of the words, and with the paucity of the ideas.

When he subjects himself to an involuntary comparison with the only contemporary writer who has celebrated the Spanish contest in a similar measure, his imperfections as a versifier are not less conspicuous than his deficiencies as a poet. Compare, for instance, the exuberant, varied and melodious swell of the subjoined extract from Don Roderic, with the tame succession of syllables in which Lord Byron endeavours to pour forth ideas of a similar character.

For they might spy beyond that mighty breach,
Realms as of Spain in visioned prospect laid,
Castles and towers, in due proportion each,
As by some skilful artist's hand pourtrayed,
Here crossed by many a wild sierra's shade;

And boundless plains that tire the traveller's eye,
There rich with vineyard and with olive glade,
  Or deep embrown'd with forest huge and high,
  Or washed by mighty streams that slowly murmured by.

Rearing their crests amidst the cloudless skies,
And darkly clustering in the pale moon-light,
  Toledo's holy towers and spires arise,
As from a trembling lake of silver white,
Their mingled shadows intercept the sight
  Of the broad burial ground outstretched below,
And nought disturbs the silence of the night,
  All sleeps in sullen shade or silver glow,
All save the heavy swell of Tejo's ceaseless flow.
SCOTT.

Compared with the last of these lines, merely as an example of metrical excellence, the favorite passages of Thelwall, introduced with so much pomp to elucidate an erroneous and imperfect theory of rhythmus, are the sing-song playthings of literary infants.

Where Lusitania and her sister meet,
Ween ye what bounds the rival realms divide,
  Or ere the jealous queens of nature meet,
Doth Tayo interpose his mighty tide?
Or dark Sierras rise in craggy pride?
  Or fence of art, like China's vasty wall?
Ne barrier wall, *ne* river deep and wide,
  Ne horrid craggs, nor mountains dark and tall,
Rise like the rocks that part Hispania's land from Gaul.
BYRON, stanza 32.

His attempts at humour are singularly unsuccessful; but we must now hasten to gratify our readers by an extract or two from the more fortunate passages of the work, and shall leave the stanzas on the Cintra convention, to be read by those who delight in the contemplation of deformity.

The subjoined description of the most prominent objects constituting a Portuguese landscape, do credit to his lordship's accuracy as an observer of nature, and to his judgment as a metrical painter.

> The horrid craggs by toppling convents crowned,
> The cork trees hoar that clothe the shaggy steep,
> The mountain moss by scorching skies embrowned,
> The sunken glen, whose sunless shrubs must weep.
> The tender azure of the unruffled deep,
> The orange tints that gild the greenest bough,
> The torrents that from cliff to valley leap,
> The vine on high, the willow branch below,
> Mixed in one mighty scene, with varied beauty glow.
> 19.

His minor poems are only distinguished from the similar productions in the Hours of Idleness, by the interspersion of classical names, and Romaic quotations. But the *good night* in the first canto possesses greater merit than he usually displays, when he employs the alternate, or ballad measure. The Romaic vocabulary and *fac simile* may be objects of pleasing curiosity to the dilletanti travellers, who love to revive their recollections of an interesting subject of scholastic speculation. From one of the notes, however, explanatory of this part of his work, it is evident that the severity of the Edinburgh Reviewers towards his minor publications, has left on his mind an impression of resentment as permanent as injudicious.

The following stanzas are of an order so superior to what could be expected from a mere poetaster, that were not Lord Byron's talents so peculiarly adapted to didactic poetry, they would afford no inadequate excuse for assuming the lofty tone and portly march of Spenser and Campbell. The poet has displayed considerable felicity in the portraiture of Childe Harolde, who having run through sin's long labyrinth, till beauty had lost its charms, and wine its exhilirating power, resolves to fly from the haunts of early dissipation, to distant and unpolluted scenes.

Childe Harolde basked him in the noon-tide ray,
Disporting there like any other fly;
  Nor deemed before his little day was done,
One blast might chill him into misery.
But long ere scarce a third of his past by,
  Worse than adversity the Childe befel;
He felt the fulness of satiety;
  Then loathed he in his native land to dwell,
Which seemed to him more lone than Eremite's sad cell.

We shall conclude our extracts with the stanzas devoted to the celebration of the Maid of Saragoza.

54.

Is it for this the Spanish maid, aroused,
Hangs on the willow her unstrung guitar,
  And all unsexed the Anlace hath espoused,
Sung the loud song, and dared the deed of war?
And she, whom once the semblance of a scar
  Appalled, an owlet's larum chilled with dread,
Now views the column scattering bay'net jar,
  The falchion flash, and o'er the yet warm dead,
Stalks with Minerva's step, where Mars might quake to
  tread.

55.

Ye who shall marvel when you hear her tale,
Oh! had you known her in her softer hour,
  Marked her black eye, that mocks her coal black veil,
Heard her light lively tones in Lady's bower,
Seen her long locks that foil the painter's power,
  Her fairy form, with more than female grace,
Scarce would you deem that Saragoza's tower,
  Beheld her smile in danger's gorgon face,
Thin the closed ranks, and lead in glory's cheerful pace.

56.

> Her lover sinks—she sheds no ill-timed tear;
> Her chief is slain, she fills his fatal post;
> Her fellows flee—she checks their base career;
> The foe retires—she heads the sallying host;
> Who can appease like her a lover's ghost?
> Who can avenge so well a leader's fall?
> What maid retrieve when man's flushed hope is lost?
> Who hang so fiercely on the flying Gaul;
> Foil'd by a woman's hand, before a battered wall?

In spite of the various talent displayed in this production, it is impossible to rise from its perusal without lamenting that the labour employed in its composition was not devoted to some more congenial subject of didactic poetry. As it is, in attempting to astonish, his lordship has voluntarily resigned the power to delight: his attempts at brilliance of description, or grandeur of expression, resembles the tiptoe flutterings of the ostrich, rather than the towering and adventurous soarings of the Mæonian eagle. He was born to write with elegance: "to wake to extacy the living lyre," is as far above the reach of his ambition, as the music of the spheres transcends the warbling of a Greatorex.

The H—— Dynasty, or the Empire of the Nairs.

> Ye dames of Albion listen to my song,
> To you the youthful poet's lays belong,
> And 'tis for you that gallantry prepares,
> Utopian fields, the empire of the Nairs.
> See from the learned north a sage appear,
> The Phœnix knight, to courtly lewdness dear;
> To him Anacreon and the Monk give place,
> Compared with him Dutens' a babe of grace;
> Where Gottingen has long her sceptics bred
> On reason nurtured, and on sr crout fed,

He learned philosophy from Dr. Blincker,
A ceaseless smoker and an arch freethinker,
And long he quaff'd where streams of wisdom flow,
From Wieland, Schiller, Kotzebue, and Co.,
But since like Plato he has ceased to roam,
A huge portfolio brings his harvest home.

And who shall hail him on his native land?
Shall London send the beauties of the Strand,
Or Madame D——ville lead her blooming train,
To inquire if *business* flourish on the Seine?
No! hapless Windsor* tremble for thy fate,
Vice has no temples in the Utopian state;
For mercenary love is banished far,
Where nature holds her court in Malabar;
There the heart yields unbribed and undismayed,
And Love's a sentiment and not a trade.

"Ladies!" he cries, " the pupils of my school,
Laugh at each law, and scoff at every rule;
The German wits triumphantly declare
That modesty's a bubble in the air,
And she who sense of decency defies,
Has learned divinely to philosophise.
Where'er I've roamed true gallantry I've found,
It only languishes on British ground;
Haste then! beneath auspicious Love's commands,
To break of cold formality the bands,
And strive with tenfold warmth to cherish here
The freedom of another hemisphere:
Gay be your days and rapturous your nights,
The book I've written is your bill of rights;
And would you know your privileges run
To Hookham's shop and pay your one pound one.
Yours like the sun's impartial rays should fall,
To all you give yet have enough for all;

---

* N.B. To prevent mistakes we must observe that this word is not meant to denote a *castle* but a *lady.*

Advantages of promiscuous love.

All nature burns with unrestricted fire,
The lion roves in limitless desire,
Birds in the air, and fishes in the sea,
Proclaim with nature's voice that love is free;
Then why should man the lord of the creation,
Submit to marriage—'tis an INNOVATION."

" Learn from the noble Nairs of *Malabar*,
Woman was made for love and man for war;
He formed for danger, enterprize and arms,
And she for all a mother's soft alarms;
He firm and dauntless as the god of Thrace,
And she the parent of a numerous race;
The man who knocks a foe upon the head,
And the fair citizen who's brought to bed;
Each, tho' by different ways they seek applause,
Is crowned with laurels in a nation's cause;
If two foes fall, the country doubly wins,
And doubly too, if she produces twins.
Whoe'er the father from whose loins they came,
From A or Y or X, 'tis just the same;
Onward they come a brave promiscuous set,
She the great W of the alphabet;
About the father, wherefore make a pother?
The country knows enough that knows the mother.
Heroes can not like tortoises and snails,
Crawl with their goods and chattels at their tails,
So while the brothers march like valiant *Nairs*,
Their sisters stay at home and bring them heirs,
And when the youths return permit their brothers,
For one man murdered to beget two others."

* 'Tis thus the Phœnix knight extolls his wares;
Each buys and reads the EMPIRE of the NAIRS;

---

* See a bombastic imitation of Ossian, written by James Lawrence, a knight of Malta, entitled the Empire of the Nairs. He endeavours to prove that the promiscuous intercourse is most congenial to

From mouth to mouth the rapturous plaudit runs,
Long live the Nairs, long live the MOTHERS SONS!
Bang-up the Nairs, exclaim the four-in-hand,
Too glad to read what they can understand,
B—— scarce broken to the marriage state,
Sighs that the system has appeared too late,
The literary Captain takes it down,
T' improve the misses in the country town;
It soothes the spendthrift in the surgeon's ward,
And polishes the youths of Stanhope's yard;
The young Etonian stares in speechless trance
To find himself the hero of romance,
Or reads with tranquil air and steady hand,
A youthful Lovelace in his cup and band;
" Beware!" the matron cries, " 'tis bad indeed,
The virgin's ruined who should dare to read;"
While as with all a parent's warmth she speaks,
The conscious blushes dye the damsel's cheeks.
When last in golden dreams she prest her bed,
The guilty volume lay beneath her head,
Sure *she* might read what her mama had read!
But hark! mine ear, what distant music greets?
What proud procession moves along the streets?

---

nature, and most consistent with the principles of reason. We are afraid there are other princes than those of Malabar, to whom we might appeal for the practical illustrations of his opinions. " The Nairs, (says Mr. Lawrence,) are the nobility of the Malabar coast, and affirm that they are the oldest in the world. It is the privilege of the Nair lady to choose and change her lover; when he visits her, he walks round the house, and strikes with his sabre on his buckler, as a signal of his approach. To announce his presence to any rival, he, if admitted, leaves a domestic with his arms in a kind of porch The mother only has the charge of the children, and even the Samorin and the other princes have no other heirs than the children of their sisters, that having no family, they may be always ready to march against an enemy. The name of a father is unknown to a Nair child; he speaks of the lovers of his mother, and of his uncle, but never of his father. Marriage is a domestic yoke, the Nair system the freedom of nature."

Each restless dame, who novelty admires,
Whom conscience troubles, or whom passion fires,
Whom fashion flatters, or whom scandal quotes,
And all philosophers in petticoats,
Are with the Phœnix for their polar-star,
Resolved to emigrate to *Malabar*.
They now like simple Nairesses are seen,
In robes of cobweb and in girdles green:
Lo! by the hand a noble Countess takes,
A mighty Duchess in the land of cakes,
A Scotch Civilian ever good at need,
Had just unyoked them on the banks of Tweed,
Yet in their titles they conceive a flaw,
And fly, where love predominates o'er law.
See B—— whose name was hawk'd about the street,
Or A——— whose waiting-woman prov'd discreet,
And the frail L—— who in desperate case,
Renounced her jointure to avoid disgrace,
And W———, ever kind, whose wit extends
To count her conquests on her finger ends,
Last ———, doomed to bid the land adieu,
Led by her valet, beaten black and blue;
For dames at Calicut without disgrace,
Distinguish merit under livery-lace.
A duke's bright dowager without compeer,
And formed for conquests in her fiftieth year,
This English Ninon leads the gallant throng,
To where the king of rivers rolls along,
And bids them like Semiramis of old
Cast in the silver stream their *rings of gold*.

When suddenly where Mona's bridge extends,
A carriage passes, and a dame descends;
To her all duchesses had once given place,
And Brighton hail'd her as a future grace;
She stops the uplifted hands in act to throw
The badge of slavery in the stream below;

" Keep, keep your ring!" the dame impatient cries,
While disappointment fired her jealous eye,
Of slavery's chain, no nuptial ring's a link,
Since foreign wits have taught our sex to think,
Leave not the country! this auspicious day
Submits three kingdoms to the ———'s sway;
No female ever could resist his smile,
The first bred gentleman in Britain's isle,
If such a prince no amorous warmth inspire,
Tho' love be silent, let ambition fire!
Restrictions cease, and she whose lucky hand
Catches the handkerchief shall rule the land,
All acts of state shall issue from her bower,
Her *grace* the only avenue to power!
Methinks I see the mighty change begin,
The saints are fled, the rakes the battle win,
No musty matrimonial rules restrain,
The court where love and BACCHUS jointly reign;
Her sovereign will this paradise prepares,
And ENGLAND proves the EMPIRE OF THE NAIRS.

THE WHIPS, No. III.

THE GAMBLING CORNUTO.

IN the suite of M. Chauvelin there was a young man of family and considerable expectations, whom temporary embarrassments had reduced to practice the profession of a surgeon, and who in that capacity obtained admission to the house of Mr. B———, one of the most enthusiastic advocates of Gallic principles, and an ardent supporter of every principle of jacobinism. Tired of remaining in this ruined and oppressed country, where no Robespierres arise to interrupt the monotony of life, and rouse the energies of the multitude, he obtained from our government permission to depart for Holland, from whence he continued his journey to the capital of universal freedom. At Paris the intercourse between young S. and his family was resumed: the person of S. was at least equal to his other recommendations, and captivated the affections of Miss B——, who in the true spirit of female liberty, and in conformity to the rights of woman, delivered up her person to his desires, without any formal and superstitious appeal to the sanction of the church. She was a character not easily impressed with the milder or more amiable feelings: tall in her form, and ardent in her passions, had she ventured to wade through the blood of the unfortunate victims to the guillotine, her majestic stride and infuriated countenance would have far exceeded in picturesque effect, the more feminine appearance of Helen Maria Williams. She yielded to the embraces of S. with the freedom of a woman, resolved to do as she thought fit, rather than with the feminine reluctance of virtue overcome; for a few months the ardor of S. was reciprocal, but he received a command to join the army of Dumouriez with the less reluctance, because it tore him from her presence, and Miss B. could only bewail with the tones and tears of a second " Huncamunca," the departure of a lover whom if she did not love, she at least preferred for his personal endowments to his companions. There *are* ladies, however, who rather than have no lover at all, content themselves with the second *best*; and to this philosophical expedient, Miss B. on this occasion thought proper to resort: in a fit of political vexation Miss Helen had discarded her favorite; Miss B. liked him not the less because he was a name-sake, and at the sight of a box of trinkets, totally forgot the absent surgeon; who in the mean time forsook the medical for the military profession, and was promoted by Gen. D., as he declared to the writer of this article, for the authority that his tall stature and soldier-like appearance gave him over the straggling ragamuffins, who formed the less efficient portion of his troops. Miss B. lived for some time with her dear namesake in a voluptuous alternation of Bacchanalian and Paphian enjoyments; her dear papa was too much of a citizen to restrain his daughter's freedom, and he received the visits of her paramour with as warm a welcome as that which he now grants to the lovers of his titled wife. His discretion abroad, however, was not equal to his magnanimity at home. By appearing with too much activity as the friend of Robespierre, he attracted the notice of the opposite party, and on the fall of the tyrant, he and his daughter, and B—— were conveyed to the guillotine. A friend of Danton, captivated by the person of Miss B. prevailed on that turbulent demagogue to spare her life and that of her parent. Her paramour was not equally fortunate, he was beheaded in the presence of his liberated mistress; but dead men have neither trinkets nor kisses to bestow on the objects of their living affections, and Miss B. with true philosophical calmness, retired from the scene to share without remorse the embraces of her deliverer.

Among those who were drawn to the entertainments of her protector by the love of good-living, the *ci-devant* valet of the Marquis le Fayette, was a very conspicuous personage. He was an Englishman, and had served the republicans by garbled extracts from Hume and Bolinbroke, published in such a form as to be accessible to the vulgar. He took advantage of the rage for equality, and in spite of the practice of those who professed to support it in theory forced himself into all companies, and intermeddled in every kind of business. His volubility recommended him to the Duchess de B. a lady who had no other pretensions to the title, than a residence of seven years as the *chere amie* of an unfortunate nobleman. She first took him into her *service*, and after the formation of another connection, paid him a handsome sum for his absence and his silence. His person and his country recommended him to Miss B. and he in his turn was by no means averse to the cultivation of her friendship. He had left England as a servant; the connections of Miss B. might assist him in conjunction with the money of his late mistress, to gain a footing in respectable society: to his taste there was nothing unpleasant in the masculine roughness of her voice, or the rubicund splendor of her countenance; her coarseness he dignified by the appellation of portliness, and the glow of intemperance he mistook for the bloom of health. He offered her his hand, and we need not add that Miss B. accepted it. After the nuptial ceremony, Mr. H. returned with his fair bride to London, where he took a house in Bruton-street, and by adding at the gaming tables to his former accession of Parisian wealth, was enabled to sport a carriage, and rival the most experienced and the wealthiest of the Whips in the splendor and number of his stud. His lady rivalled Miles Peter Andrews himself, in the costly inanity of her routs; for at the present day wealth governs fashion, and takes precedence of virtue. In process of time, he erected a villa in the neighbourhood of Litchfield, where the country round admired at once his folly and his magnificence. For several years they lived like other fashionable couples, in the most perfect indifference towards each other, and the most profound contempt for every body else. In the autumn of last year Mrs. H. prevailed on her husband to take an excursion to Buxton; they tasted the waters, outrivalled all the other occupiers of the Crescent in extravagance; and after rendering themselves the object of universal envy and dislike, returned to town. On the night of Madame Bertinotti *Radicati's* first appearance: Mrs. H. attended only by her servant, visited the Opera. At twelve o'clock, at which hour she ordered the carriage to return, no Mrs. H. was to be found! It was in vain that they waited till the closing of the doors—their mistress was lost, and they were obliged to return homewards with the empty carriage. The next morning on enquiry for his lady, and hearing the story of the servants, Mr. H. was distracted. He cared nothing for his wife himself, but his indifference did not render him less insensible to the disgrace he had sustained. On searching her apartment it was discovered that she had taken along with her all the jewels and trinkets that it was possible to secrete about her person. Mr. B. was not unmindful of the advantages that might be made of her elopement. " If (he thought) her paramour should happen to be a man of fortune, twenty thousand pounds would be no bad thing; cash runs short, and that sum would repay me both for the loss and the disgrace." He sent his emissaries, therefore, in every direction that could probably lead to her retreat; but their inquiries were in vain, and Mr. H. was condemned for some time to all the anguish of unrequited celibacy.

Sometime afterwards, the coachman of Mr. H. having driven his master to Mr. Thelwall's lecture, returned with the carriage to Steele's livery stables, near Gray's Inn, and leaving his horses to the care of the groom, retired to a place of vulgar resort in the neighbourhood. They had not been long seated, before their conversation was interrupted by the noise of a scuffle in the lobby, and on rushing out they discovered two police officers in the act of arresting a gentlemanly looking person, whom they knew by his accent to be a Frenchman. The landlord told them that *Mounseer* was an officer that had broke his parole, who had lived at his house some time, and who seemed to have no want of money. " He has," continued Boniface, " a lady with him, as fine a woman as you'd wish to see." " Has he!" replied the officer, " then we must secure her as evidence!" While one of the officers and the host secured the General below, his companion along with Mr. H.'s footman, and the rest of the crowd, proceeded in search of the lady above: they found her beneath the bed, and dragged her from her lurking-place, and lights being introduced, the surprize of the servants may easily be conceived at discovering, in the wife of the French General, their long lost mistress. They immediately proceeded to Mr. H.

with intelligence of the discovery, and the husband proceeded to the police office, reclaimed his wife, and finding that General S.(whose identity with her youthful seducer the reader has no doubt discovered,) could pay no damages, again received the disconsolate fair one to his arms. The General was first sent into close confinement, and then permitted to return to his original station of parole, in the neighbourhood of Buxton, where his acquaintance with the fair one had been renewed, and the happy couple whom this *rencontre* has separated for a time, now live together in all the tranquillity of domestic harmony.

W———M.

THE P———SS OF W———.

In the House of Commons, some pointed questions were put to Mr. Percival, respecting the Princess of Wales, to which the answers are variously reported. According to the Morning Chronicle, he declared that neither as minister nor as counsel to her Royal Highness, could he take it upon himself to give any explanation on the subject introduced: according to the *Times,* however, he distinctly avowed that in the course of his professional inquiries on the investigation, nothing occurred to him that could attach any share of blame to her Royal Highness's conduct. Entertaining as we do, a decided conviction, that this assertion must be erroneous; it becomes our duty at the same time to point out the difficulties in which it must involve the Prince Regent, supposing it to be true; and the necessity, supposing it to be false, of some final arrangement that may be equally beneficial and satisfactory to the country.

If, in the progress of the investigation, no circumstances arose that could tend to criminate her Royal Highness, it must then be admitted that she is an injured and persecuted woman. Because without any legal ground of separation, the Prince refuses to make her the partner of his bed, she is to be deserted by the people, over whom she has been called to share the sovereignty, and suffered to remain in comparative destitution. For any thing that appears to the contrary, her neglect may be the mere result of princely caprice; it is possible that her presence is only unwelcome, because it would be a check on the career of licentious pleasure, that might be pursued by the heir apparent to the throne; and it is equally inconsistent with justice and propriety, that a female who as Mr. Tierney observed, would in case of the king's demise, be as much the queen of these realms, as the Prince Regent would be king, left to the mercy of a husband, who may dislike her for the very virtues that contribute most powerfully to domestic happiness.

But it may be asserted that though no legal evidence can be obtained of the Princess's indiscretions; yet that they have been so undisguised as to produce on the mind of the Prince, a moral conviction of her unworthiness; that there are levities which justify suspicion, though the act of criminality cannot be proved to the satisfaction of a judicial tribunal; and that as a husband the Prince Regent may be determined into his present system of conduct, by circumstances which he alone has the right or power to appreciate. But though these observations may justify the coldness of the Prince as a husband, they do not palliate his neglect as a sovereign, or deprive the Princess of any claim on the justice or liberality of the nation. If the British people refuse their money to confugal infidelity, or sexual indiscretion, they ought to refuse their grants to the male as well as the female branches of the family. If one common occasions the infidelity of the female be more criminal than that of the other sex; there are cases in which the licentiousness of the husband, is not only an apology for the indiscretions of the wife, but far surpass them in degree. If virtue therefore be the only claim on the pecuniary liberality of the English nation, there are other personages than the Princess of Wales to whom assistance of that nature ought to be refused. Nor can it be disputed that out of the present civil list, parliament has a right to appropriate any sum to the support of the Prince Regent's consort; unless a separation can be obtained, she has a full and important claim on our justice and liberality; and if the legal grounds of a separation *do* exist, it is due to the nation that they should be avowed.

We have had an opportunity of seeing the documents themselves, and were impressed with the conviction, that though the singular coincidence of suspicious circumstances might be susceptible of satisfactory explanation, the *prima facie* evidence was such as to justify the most public and the most solemn investigation. That circumstances transpired in the collection of this evidence, of which the possession contributed to Mr. Percival's political ascendancy, and is *at present the best security for his continuance in office*, is too well known to the junior branches of the royal family; and that the concealment of these circumstances was regarded as of so much importance by the person chiefly interested, as to draw from his privy purse very considerable sums, his treasurer will long remember with regret. In plain terms, if much indiscretion was displayed on one side, much provocation was exhibited on the other; if frailty characterised the wife, deliberate insult, and open violation of the decencies of life, distinguished the husband: the evidence adduced was calculated to liberate the complaining party at the expence of his own character, and by the exposure of circumstances which might render his own situation as precarious as that of the exalted personage, whose errors had become the subject of Mr. Percival's investigation.

It is due to the nation, however, as well as to themselves that their conduct should be manly and decided. If they are of opinion that the result of a public investigation would be successful, and that the advantages of a separation, would counterbalance the disclosures of the criminated party, let them come boldly forward and perform their duty; but if considerations of self-regard, or any doubts of the legitimacy of the evidence before them, restrain them from that open mode of procedure which can alone afford an opportunity to the weaker party of a fair and open defence, and place her on a level with her accusers, let them not assume that forbearance as a virtue, which is dictated by a sense of their own guilt, or a conviction of the ———'s innocence. And if they are so far insensible to the claims of honor or of prudence, as to aggravate the distresses of the object of their insinuations by pecuniary embarrassments, it may at least be expected of the British people, that their sentiments shall be expressed with a boldness that cannot be mistaken; that they will not suffer one female to be oppressed, on the plea of indiscretion, while so many of her relatives are closing a long career of meretricious infamy, in all the enjoyments that can be purchased by the treasures of a wealthy people, and that they will not stand tamely by, while the R——— lavishes those riches on a H——— which properly employed would contribute to the happiness of the legitimate partner of his throne.

THE NOCTES ATTICÆ of DR. BUSBY.

When we were some time ago favoured with a card requesting our attendance at recitations from a new translation of Lucretius, we must confess that we were alarmed rather than delighted. We remembered the lassitude that overpowered us in our early attempts to obtain an imperfect acquaintance with the philosophical poet of antiquity; and the specimen of the translation contained in Dr. Busby's prospectus was little calculated to seduce us into a new investigation of the seminal system.

Our ticket, therefore, might have still reposed in as profound an oblivion as that which awaits the Doctor's labours, had not our curiosity been excited by a paragraph in the Morning Post, in which the learned writer regrets that the *Noctes Atticæ* of Dr. Busby have not become the objects of general imitation among the " exalted circles of society." We now began to conjecture that recitation could only be a part of the evening's entertainment; the title of *Noctes Atticæ* recalled to our minds the taste of Pericles, the wisdom of Socrates, and the eloquence of Demosthenes; we remembered with how much rapture the sages and orators of antiquity, describe the intellectual luxuries of these convivial assemblies, in which the circulation of the goblet only contributed to animate the eloquence of wisdom, and add lustre to the brilliance of chaste and legitimate wit. Had the cards of invitation proceeded from a female, we should have ascribed to her in imagination the attributes of Aspasia; but as it was, we contemplated in Thomas Busby, Mus. Doct. the presiding Apollo of a temple of the muses; his son presented himself to our fancy in the resemblance of a second Orpheus equally expert at charming the attentive ear, by his divine enchanting ravishment, and of erecting another Thebes, when a race of Bœotians shall arise to remunerate his labours. With these impressions we hastened to Queen Anne Street West, and though our astonishment was great at finding in the Magnus Apollo of his own temple, a thin, dapper, talkative little gentleman about five feet four inches in height: though instead of a second Esculapius, we found a *doctor of medicine* without practice, and though *goddesses* were precluded from listening to the doctor's illustrations *de nature rerum,* we took our place composedly on the sopha, and *then*' like Jove reclining on his couch of clouds, surveyed in silent astonishment the scene before us.

A long interval of silence, however, permitted us to return to the common business of life: we remembered our duty as periodical judges of the taste and manners of the time, and were at a loss by what means to reconcile our obligations to Dr. Busby with our duty to the public. He had very handsomely invited us to witness what he conceives to be a very gratifying exhibition, and how could we consistently with the laws of honor or hospitality, express in our official capacity any feeling of disapprobation or derision, with which we may possibly be affected? While employed in these reflections we cast a glance at the prospectus, and recollected that the first object of these recitations, was to gain subscriptions for the Doctor's book. We resolved to subscribe for a copy of the new translation of Lucretius, and now conceive ourselves to be entitled to all the privileges of criticism.

At 9 o'clock Master Busby took his seat and read the contents of the book with so much calmness and propriety, that we supposed the word recitation to have been employed by mistake, and flattered ourselves that Lucretius would be *read*. To recite a philosophical poem (if recitation imply violent motion of the hands, or violent gesture of the body,) is of all absurdities the most gross: throughout the whole of Lucretius, there is scarcely a single expression of ardent passion, or pathetic feeling; he excludes human actions and emotions from his poem; the pictures that he introduces are either delineations of inanimate nature, or of collective groups seen in distant action, and viewed with the eye of the landscape painter without any interest in their contentions. The major part of the poem is devoted to the most frigid, if not the most abstruse disquisition on seeds and seminal principles, and the action of corpuscles, and primædial causes. Mr. Busby was alive to the absurdity of accompanying these inquiries with any violence of action, and he therefore read them from his chair; but the strictures of Lucretius, as where he describes the appearance of distant armies in actual contest, are equally unadapted to recitation; they should proceed like every other part of the work, from the philosopher at his desk, and not from the orator on his rostrum.

It must be confessed, however, that Master Busby has been admirably drilled; his elocution was distinct and harmonious without monotony; and the only fault of his action was its display of the rules on which it was formed, and the labour with which it had been cultivated. When he uttered the word " grasp" or "embrace," his arms were regularly folded : when he talked of the globe suspended in the air, his left hand was sent out on a voyage of discovery into "high air," while the right, on a level with his chest, supported the imaginary sphere; and when the regions of illimitable space were described, we anticipated a flying leap into the middle of the room. He was not deficient in grace, and might become a model of useful imitation to his rival declaimers Messrs. Claremont and Barrymore. How much is it to be regretted, that the pains bestowed on the cultivation of acquirements so superficial and so useless, have not been directed to the cultivation of his mind. It is really distressing to hear the son of Thomas Busby, Mus. Doct. and an architect, speak before a listening company, of *sumpshous* (sumptuous) halls, and chimœr-O's dire. Of the poem itself we have already expressed our sentiments as far as we were able to judge from the prospectus; and though it must be acknowledged that the exhibition we have witnessed, has exalted our opinion of its merits, yet we are still afraid that it is more remarkable for lisping effeminacy than nervous elegance. The appearance of effeminacy, however, may be owing exclusively to the perpetual employment of the word sweet—sweet peace, sweet flowers, sweet hues, sweet sun, and phrases of a similar description occur in almost every page of the composition. The rhymes *prove* and *move* continually recur, and once we believe *move* rhymes to itself. He is too apt to fill up his lines with two words expressing emotions too nearly resembling each other, to be frequently conjoined in the language of poetry. " To fill his soul with pleasure and delight," and "saw its fall with rapture and delight." "With grief and sorrow bowed,"&c.&c. are instances of a fault of all others the most injurious to poetical effect. " In lines of a description similar to the following, the first noun in italic had better give place to an epithet belonging to the second. " Such as with tears bedewed their *cheeks* and *eyes*." Though the Latin poet is accustomed to indulge in repetition, the translated language of the repetitions should be varied. In the original they are relieved by the introduction of a spondee or a dactyle changing the measure; in the English they can only be varied by the substitution of synonymous words.

" more,
As proved by any arguments advanced before"—

is a couplet returning with unpleasing frequency.

We have been the more candid and minute, in these observations, because the plan adopted by Dr. Busby affords him at least all the advantages that can be obtained from the suggestions of others. To an individual engaged in so important an undertaking, candor is the most valuable friendship, and had we respected him less, we should have held our peace.

POLITICAL HINTS.

MR. EDITOR,

Hitherto I have only been a constant reader of your monthly publication, with which though in some points I reluctantly disagree, I verily believe to be strictly impartial.

Feelings of indignation at some recent political events, to which I am persuaded you do not require my feeble aid to call your attention, have impelled me to undertake a task to which I am so unaccustomed, and to which I feel myself so unable.

Whatever may be the faults or whatever the excellencies of the present advisers of the Regent, will have no relation whatever to the present subject. It is to the conduct of the major part of their opponents since the lamented illness of his majesty, that my attempts shall tend to refer—Bitter as was their opposition, and virulent their animosity against the Duke of York upon the discovery of those disgraceful abuses, still fresh in recollection, it was but reasonable to suppose that his speedy reinstation would call forth some strong remonstrances on their part—But no; it was then understood to be the Prince's pleasure, and consequently the leaders of the opposition refused to sanction any motion questioning its propriety—On the late discussion on the Regency Household Bill, not only was a large sum of money, exclusive of the civil list voted to the Regent, without any reprehension on their part; but we beheld this body of patriots, these opposers of inordinate grants of the public money, who had always hitherto felt so much compunction in laying fresh burdens on the people, complaining of the deprivation of a revenue from the Duchy of Cornwall.

But now the time approached when they who had

made so great sacrifices of political principle at the altar of self-interest, had reason to expect an ample remuneration. Various were the arrangements for a new administration, and various the persons on, whom the chancellorship of the exchequer was bestowed. But lo! Time at length evinced that the Regent had been consistent enough to choose for himself, and his letter proclaimed that though he wished that some of the early friends of his public life, would constitute a *part* of his government, it was his decided opinion that the course of policy pursued by the Pittites was more conducive to the welfare of the empire, than that which would be embraced by their opponents.

Intelligence so diametrically opposite to what their ardent imaginations had suggested, acted like a thunderbolt upon them. Their disappointment and anger may with facility be traced from the period when Mr. Percival informed Mr. Creevey " that if he knew any thing of the matter the golden dreams of the right honourable gentleman were not likely to be realised." From this time their virulent aspersions on the Regent have been as apparent as their former subservience. Every matter is brought to light that may in any way distress the Prince, or perplex his advisers. Colonel M'Mahon was the first on whom they wreaked their vengeance, and no sooner was he ejected from his first situation, (perhaps justly too,) and his master had compassionately presented him another, than the propriety of the office of private secretary is called in question, and the Colonel is in a fair way of losing the second.

It appears to have occurred too, for the first time, a few nights ago, to these patriots that something ought to be done for the Princess of Wales. " Why," it is asked, " is she neglected? She is Princess Regent; she ought to have an establishment like the queen. We have no proof of any misconduct on her part. Why does she live privately and separated?" Few persons are not of opinion that some eclaircissement on this subject should take place; but it is sufficiently obvious, Mr. Editor, that arrangements of this nature should have been made during the passing of the Regency bills for the support of her majesty's household, and that of the Prince Regent; but at that period any discussion on that subject might have been disagreeable in a certain quarter, and therefore was not to be thought of by the Right Honourable Gentlemen.

It is painful, Mr. Editor, to every well-wisher to his country to behold the height to which party spirit is now carried. How despicable and disgraceful does it appear to hear men in the British House of Commons* magnifying the distress of the country, and asserting that many thousands, (I think fifteen) of the labouring classes in the commercial towns were supported by public subscription, though it was afterwards proved that they had included the families of workmen in employ, who had derived assistance from a soup dispensary.

Forgive me, if I trespass longer on your patience by directing your attention to the motions of Sir Francis Burdett for the abolition of military flogging. If the hon. baronet's intentions are good, his pertinacity argues meanly of his sense, for the military men of all parties in the House of Commons have candidly declared the impracticability of the measure; while by its discussion it tends to raise expectations among the soldiers which cannot be realised, and by its rejection serves to create discouragement and discontent.

Should any of the preceding humble observations afford you the least hint in the infliction of your lash, the writer will be abundantly recompensed. I am, Sir,

most respectfuly,

Westminster, March 25, 1812.   MEMMIUS.

---

* We shall endeavour in a future article to shew that the mistake is on the side of our correspondent.

A STAUNCH DOG AT A FAULT;

OR,

THE DOCTOR RUNNING COUNTER.

"What a piece of work is man! how noble in reason! how infinite in faculties! in form and moving, how express and admirable! in action how like an angel!" Amazingly sublime are these sentiments, said my grandmother, laying down the book and taking off her spectacles—" how grand, how exalted—in action how like *an angel?*" Looking at me with the most inquisitive earnestness. As she was the very best of old women, I made it a point seldom to contradict her, more especially when a case was doubtful as they certainly was; for though I myself had never seen an angel; yet I could not be quite sure but my good grandmother might: she had been in existence nearly a century, and times are much altered. I must, however, freely confess I mentally set the admired sentiments down in estimation among many others of like sublimity and exaltation, and ranked them as canting, blasphemous lies. Assuredly there is much more fuss made about man's perceptions than the thing itself will justify; man, as an animal, is a mere noodle (ask his wife else) outdone in point of sagacity by every beast about him. Change but the ribband on his child of a month old, and all recognition ceases. Poor *instructive* old Argus, though at the very verge of death affectionately hailed the return of his long lost master Ulysses.

> " Thus near the gates conferring as they drew,
> Argus, the dog, his ancient master knew;
> He not unconscious, of the voice and tread,
> Lifts to the sound his ear, and rears his head.
> He knew his lord; he knew and strove to meet,
> In vain he strove to crawl, and kiss his feet;
> Yet (all he could) his tail, his ears, his eyes,
> Salute his master, and confess his joys.

The dog, whom fate had granted to behold
His lord, when twenty tedious years had roll'd,
Takes a last look, and having seen him, dies;
So clos'd for ever faithful Argus' eyes!"

While *reasoning* Penelope experienced not one sympathetic throb—not one twinge of feeling in any part of her whole frame. Nay, the *seal*, that almost shapeless lump of fat and flesh, can discover her still more hideous offspring, although involved in doubled and twisted myriads. Nevertheless, man in his natural state, though possibly he may be now and then given to thieving, where nuts, crabs, and such like *monkey provender* is concerned, is not a downright rogue—that he has to thank cultivation for: the *brutism* of a *Caliban* is far from being nearly so pernicious as the *logic* of a *Paley*.

In good days of yore; the *man* was known by his *coat* doublets and hose were pricked, printed, and trimmed only as by law established. A good safe way this: men knew then what was what; whether they now do so we will presently examine.

In a certain ancient place of public worship, not twenty miles from hence, some few months since, after his sabbath day's dinner, in full and flowing uniform was seated a sage and reverend doctor. Truly orthodox in all the statutes and ordinances of the church, was this goodly pillar; and though he might be somewhat doubtful of the correctness in translation of the sentence, " money is the root of all evil," and could not be brought cordially to subscribe to the trite idea that pride was sinful; yet was he looked upon in general, as good a christian as might reasonably be expected, under such potent drawbacks as tithe pigs, gentility of the times, expiring leases, and pluralities. During the time the doctor was absorbed in heavenly musings, or perhaps calculating in minutiæ, the amount of renewal on Donkey Grange, a very decently attired young man entered the church, apparently a stranger; he hesitated some little time and then with modest unassuming piety, placed himself in the next sitting place to the reverentissimo. It is a custom with the eastern lamas to have a curtain let down before them when sitting; by which manœuvre their votaries are handed over wholesale to the dominion of imagination; we do things better. In order to obstruct the side-long insidious glance, which none but a squinting parson could detect, the flanks of the doctor's capital were defended by two green baize curtains, which, forming a recess, displayed to the utmost advantage the front view only of prebendal beatitude. Shielded by this accommodating screen, the youth had for some time pursued his devotions, when unluckily the doctor's carnal part of vision being attracted by a most bewitching fold in the drapery of his right arm, he thought he perceived a shade thrown upon his outworks; an involuntary start, followed up by a stricter scrutiny, convinced him some substance had segmentized his sphere : amazement and indignation were now visibly disputing the palm on the field of countenance; the Doctor's *alabaster* insensibly receded, and the highest *fawn colour* advanced, the muscles were swollen, the nose sharpened, and the vengeful arm in the act of rising, when lo! the reader utters with an audible voice, " *For there is no respect of persons with God."* (Rom. ch. ii. v. 11.) An internal response created a momentary pause; but, fully determined to give convincing proof of his open hostility to all *levelling precepts* without distinction, he roughly snatches back the curtain and with the most indignant avaunt of the hands motions the astonished intruder to take the *lowest place.* With the most benign resignation the young man bowed the head, took up his hat and retired, the curtain was restored, and a triumphant vindictive lour thrown over he auditory, in which was visibly pourtrayed, *insolent, to obtrude upon* ME!!! I have before observed that man is not that " all in all" piece of business he is held up, for, as neither from animal sagacity, cultivation by learning, experience obtained by eel-like wriggling to superiors, and foaming sharkism to inferiors, nor even by the well timed hit of the reporter of St. Paul, could this infatuated victim of clerical pomposity, discover that his offensive neighbour was neither more nor less than " the nephew of one of our highest dignitaries in the law," who had been on a visit in the neighbourhood about a fortnight. Previously, however, to the next Sunday, admiration at the conduct of the one, and reprobation of the behaviour of the other had been so loudly bandied in the parish, that the doctor clearly perceived he had been calculating under a wrong latitude; yet dependance on his acknowledged powers in blandishment and courtesy prevented his spirits from being too deeply depressed. Accordingly on that day after seating himself in his recess, he stole a sly peep to ascertain whether matters remained in statu quo, and most propitiously to his wishes, spied the young gentleman, quietly reclining in the corner, to which his former mandate had consigned him. Reader, thou hast heard of *cream of violets*, and a long string of nostrums of the cosmetic tribe; but these separately or jointly would have been puerile in effect to the assumed placidity diffused over the doctor's countenance for the time being, with the hand gently raised, the elbow making an angle of just nineteen degrees with the horizon, the thumb and fore-finger finely bowed, and the little one displaying a brilliant loftily elevated, the rings of the curtain were most softly touched, and moved along the rod slow, silent and smoothly: full on the nephew of the learned lord, and graciously he smiled, laid a most elegant book on the before *prohibited desk*, and with the most winning affability beckoned him to his side. The excellent young man tacitly acknowledging neither time nor place were fitted for resentment, accepted his invitation; but notwithstanding his well-bred effort to suppress it there was a look—a look which spoke volumes.

CASTIGATOR.

Newark, 10*th March*, 1812.

THEATRICAL REVIEW.

*Nullius addictus jurare in verba magistri;
Quo me cunque rapit tempestas deferor hospes.*

We had intended to enter into a minute exposition of Mr. Taylor's conduct, as a prosecutor, and a witness in the case of Mr. Alexander Read; but on referring to the trial itself, we have found the cross-examination so curious and satisfactory, as to supersede the necessity of further observation; and shall only observe on one part of the evidence, that on the 13th of June, when Mr. Taylor declares himself to have been at Hungerford fishing for *trout*, he was in reality secreted at Battersea, from the pursuit of the *gudgeons* of the laws. That the chaste and faithful Mrs. Dunn, accompanied Mr. *Turf* on this occasion, the visitors of the Opera will easily believe.

The Pantheon after going through all the regular revolutions of theatrical property—after being built without money, managed without discretion, and at last consigned to the care of chancery, has been shut up in consequence of Colonel Greville's withdrawing his licence on the plea of insecurity. For what reason, however, this plea was not advanced before, notwithstanding the positive opinions of Messrs. Soane and Cockerell, the gentleman with whom Colonel Greville has been in daily habits of pecuniary negociation, are best able to explain. It is disgraceful to the Lord Chamberlain, that the public amusements of this metropolis, and the fate of a large establishment should be subject to the whims of a capricious and needy individual; mean in poverty, and wayward in prosperity, without constancy of temper, or firmness of principle.

Mr. Kenney, the author of the World and of Raising the

Wind, has surprised and afflicted his friends, by the production of one of the lowest pieces of buffoonery, that even the present generation of authors so fertile in nonsense and absurdity have produced.

The farce of " Raising the Wind" may be numbered among the most fortunate productions of dramatic genius. The principal character is drawn with equal fidelity of observation and originality of conception: he is so natural as to recal in idea the scenes of daily intercourse, yet more effective than if he had been the illegitimate offspring of dramatic fancy. But the farce of " Turn out" exhibits nothing more worthy of praise than paltry copies of well-known originals. The founsdation of Restive's character is evidently the Quidnunc of Foote's Upholsterer, and to this foundation Mr. Kenney has only superadded some of that irritability which distinguishes the character of Sir Willoughby Worrett, and of which Dowton above all other actors is peculiarly successful in the expression. Somerville is only Mr. Phillips in the dress of a gentleman. Gregory is Giles Scroggins dramatized; and no one who has read or seen the " Citizen" of Murphy will be at any loss to discover the original of *Marian Ramsay* (Miss Duncan). The dialogue of the piece deserves neither praise nor censure; it neither disgusts in the delivery, nor retains any impression on the memory. The jests are of the most trite and hackneyed order: Restive is interrupted in a plan for the liquidation of the national debt, and mourns over the necessity of leaving his country in the midst of its difficulties, and an ineffectual attempt is made at crossreading by the intervention of Gregory, who finishes a Ciceronian oration of his master, by repeating to himself the first sentence of a love-letter to Sally Smallfry. Yet the conception of many of the incidents and the plan of the interlocutory parts display so much ingenuity that we regret the more forcibly the inadequacy of their execution. Marian's idea, for instance, of disgusting Dr. Truckle by the affectation of romantic feelings is susceptible of the most ludicrous effect; but how imperfectly the language that proceeds from her lips does justice to his conception, Mr. Kenny himself will best be able to determine, if he has the intrepidity to refer to the farce of Polly Honeycombe.

The *post* has thought proper to assure us that many of the songs were *encored* on account of their intrinsic merits. Of the degree of taste to be attributed to the audience, if this assertion be true, let the reader judge.

SONG.

I'm Marian Ramsay, from Scotland I come,
    All adown the green dale where the violets are springing,
And much I should grieve from dear Scotland to part,
But I'm come to the south, sir, to get a sweetheart,
    With my fal la la la, while the birds are a singing.

They say my relation's a mighty odd man,
    All away from the dale, &c.
'Tis you, sir, I'm sure, for, the truth to reveal,
As we say in the north, you're a comical cheel,
    With my fa la la la, &c.

So get me my sweetheart and wish me good bye,
    All away to the dale, &c.
If the bonny lad's willing, I'm now in my prime,
And sure, 'tis a pity to lose any time,
    With my fa la la la, &c.

Of the comic songs the following is the only one that has any claim to mediocrity, and even of this we should like to understand the concluding stanza. (page 37).

Love and poverty's fate is turn out! turn out!
Love and poverty's fate is turn out!
    But the rich blockhead's store,
    Alas! opens the door,

Through which merit, if poor, must turn out, turn out,
Through which merit, if poor, must turn out.

Great statesmen, when doom'd to turn out, turn out,
Great statesmen, when doom'd to turn out,
  Though full of their graces,
  When snug in their places,
With very wry faces turn out, turn out,
With very wry faces turn out.

Our foe would their neighbours turn out, turn out,
Our foe would their neighbours turn out;
  But John Bull is so queer,
  He'll sometimes interfere,
Just to trouble Mounseer to turn out, turn out,
Just to trouble Mounseer to turn out.

In the playhouse they often turn out, turn out;
In the playhouse they often turn out;
  And is'n't it boring,
  To hear them encoring,
While others are roaring, " Turn out! turn out!"
While others are roaring, " Turn out!"

Poor poets must often turn out, turn out;
Poor poets are often turn'd out:
  'Tis e'en thus with the great;
  So the poet must wait,
To know if his fate is, " Turn out! turn out!"
To know if his fate is, " Turn out!"

If Mr. Kenney be resolved to sacrifice the prospect of a permanent and legitimate reputation, to pecuniary gains, or temporary popularity, he has acted wisely in bringing out the present farrago of stupidity and buffoonery: we are not sure that the " World" or " Raising the Wind" is listened to with half the pleasure that is testified at the exhibition of his last production; and if we mistake not, though the hopes of the critics have ended in disappointment, the present is likely to *turn out* a profitable speculation.

 To that cold and comfortless temple of stupidity, the

Lyceum, we seldom venture except when our literary duty compel us to endure the mingled miseries of nastiness and nonsense. Our acquaintance, therefore, with Mr. Lewis was far from intimate; and our surprize at his appearance in Belcour in the West Indian, was only equalled by our amazement at the fatuity of the manager, who could permit him to attempt the part. Of all the heroes of the stage Belcour is most indelibly marked with the character of a gentleman; the native elegance of his manner is only equalled by the ardor of his temperament, and the glowing sensibility of his feelings. His haste and irritation are not the result of weakness excited to passion by trivial circumstances, or of fatuity degenerating into restlessness, but of generous and noble passion expanding into expression. But if there be any word that peculiarly characterises Mr. Lewis as an actor it is *hardness:* he is stiff when he wishes to be dignified, and abrupt when he ought to be transported by the omnipotence of ungovernable feeling. His words " *trip off* " his tongue with the pert and abrupt volubility of a tavern-waiter; yet his vulgarity is fully equalled by his pedantry, and his pedantry by his ignorance. If he must pronounce horizon with a short i— why will he pronounce the first syllable of PART-icular, as if it was a distinct word?— How would Cumberland have been distressed had he witnessed the murder of his favourite child, by the ruthless hands of this tormentor!

Mr. G. Wyatt has published his design for a third theatre. Like Mr. Benjamin Wyatt, the architect of Drury, he rounds off the front of the boxes nearest to the stage so that the sight may not be interrupted by a dead wall, with this difference only that the contrary flexure or divergence of the circle begins in Mr. George Wyatt's plan, at a point not far distant from the semicircle, and in the other after three-fourths of the circle have been completed. The present plan like that of New Drury, removes the saloon from the first to the second tier; the dress boxes are still further secured from intrusion by the indirectness of the communication between them and the other parts of the house. It is proposed also, there being no basket, that ten of the front boxes, containing nine persons each, should be let out by the night *only*, and in the event of which a private passage may separate them from the public lobby, and the partitions which divide them may be continued up to the ceiling. No inconvenience to the view of the stage would arise from this, the situation being immediately opposite to it, and not too far removed from the reach of an actor's voice. It is presumed by Mr. Wyatt that an arrangement of this nature will obviate all the objections and afford all the advantages of what are called private or annual boxes. We cannot agree with him in opinion. Were his plan adopted, no individual, the weight of whose purse was not equal to his fondness for dramatic amusements would ever be able to obtain the best situation in the house. Without the payment of three guineas a seat in these dress boxes could not be obtained even supposing them to be unoccupied for the evening. At present a *single* individual has a fair chance of taking an eligible seat in any part of the house; Mr. Wyatt would exclude from the best part of it all who could not afford, or would not wish to form one of a theatrical party. To attach a higher price of admission to this part of the house would be less unjust and invidious and equally productive.

The width along the front of the stage as represented in these plans (63 feet) is much greater than has been usual in the theatres of this country. The cause (observes Mr. Wyatt,) as well as the consequences will be obvious on a little attention. The general form of the house produced by the fronts of the boxes, is first of all that of a complete semi-circle, but instead of afterwards taking a *converging* direction it is made to expand, thereby placing the spectators in each of the two end boxes, with their faces fronting the stage, and affording a more complete view of it than has generally been obtained in such situations. No stage doors have been admitted as fixtures in the Proscenium, for it is obvious that when they are wanted they should form a part of the illusion which the whole scenery is intended to convey to the mind, rather than of the form through which that illusion is to be viewed, and in which character the proscenium ought always to be considered. Stage-boxes Mr. Wyatt conceives to be equally improper, and are excluded from his plans, unless one or two may be placed for the stage manager behind the trellis-work of the sides of the proscenium, (which he has made elliptical) in the same manner as the *loges grillees* of the French theatres. Its extent is totally inconsistent with the professions of the supporters of a third theatre, who have always rested part of their case on the " overgrown magnitude of the established and the projected houses." The difference in size between Mr. George Wyatt's theatre and New Drury, is too trifling to justify the language so lately employed.—It is evident that the idea of springing the proscenium from the back of the boxes, cannot have suggested itself to both the architects at the same time, and as Mr. George Wyatt's plan has been published subsequent to the other, it is but fair to regard him as the copyist.

Of Julius Cesar it would be equally useless to speak to those who have seen it, and those who have not. *Mrs. Siddons* and the *horses* are announced for reappearance during the Easter holidays. The combination reminds us of two of the most conspicuous proverbs in Bailey's Dictionary.

" Money makes the mare to go ;"

And

" Money makes the old wife trot."

MAY 1, 1812.

CONTENTS.

TO CORRESPONDENTS, see back.
THE REVIEWER. No. XI.... 345
The Treasury Poets, and Wharton's Roncesvalles............ ib.
Croker and Rose.............. 346
The dignity of John Fuller, Esq. 347
On the rage for describing battles 348
Mr. Wharton's poetry........ 349
Imitation of the Italian........ 350
The death of Ferrau......... 351
Mr. Wharton's treasury exploits 352
THE WHIPS, No. IV.
An exalted invalid............ 353
Love and music 354
His ———'s poetical talents.... 355
ON PROSECUTION for LIBELS,
and the PRINCE REGENT. 356
Hunt and the Attorney-General ib.
Convenience of subscriptions... 357
Utility of the public press...... 358
Libellers the most loyal writers. 359
Influence of courtly vice...... 360
CUMBERLAND VICARS..... ib.
A parson from college........ 361
A cribbage-playing clergyman.. 362
A priggish parson............ 363
Degenerates into a pot-house
buffoon.................... 364
A political parson............ 365
A novel-writing parson........ 366
Ashwell clericals............. 367
EPIGRAMS................... 368
On the Manchester riots....... ib.
On seeing Pasquin, alias Dr.
Williams, in a very shabby
coat, parading the Park with
his patron Romeo........... ib.
On the same................. ib.
The widow Fairbin's benefit... 369
A tart reply................. ib.
Predilections................ ib.
A CATALOGUE OF QUACKS.. 370
Architectural quacks.......... 371
Coffin-making quacks......... 372
Female quacks............... 373
BARON GERAMB; STROEHLING THE ARTIST, AND
PROFESSOR VON FEINAGLE..................... 374
Foreign impostors............ ib.
Baron Geramb's depredations.. 375
Italian castratos.............. 376
Dubost and Stroehling........ 377
Professor Von Feinagle........ 378
Mnemonics—Professor Poison.. 379
THE HYPERCRITIC. No. VI. 380
The General Chronicle, and the
Inquisition .... ib.

Miracles on miracles.......... 381
Virtues of the rosary......... 382
Eden the scene of an auto-da fe 383
Abraham an inquisitor........ 384
Origin of the Portuguese inquisition........................ 385
Established by a swindler...... 386
His exploits.................. 387
The General Chronicle 388
DUCAL SEDUCTION, or CORRESPONDENCE EXTRAORDINARY................. 389
Dastardly conduct of a noble
colonel..................... ib.
The extraordinary violation of
honor...................... 390
A " lovely letter"............. 391
His amatory correspondence.... 392
Love letters, and an assignation 393
Singular system of intrigue..... 394
His ——— declines a challenge.. 395
The adulterer's debts.......... 396
THE POLITICAL OBSERVER,
No. X.
To the Editor of the Scourge... ib.
The Percevalites examined.... 397
Responsibility of the Morning
Chronicle.................. 398
War in the Peninsula.......... 399
Consistency of the Whigs...... 400
The public subjected to a choice
of difficulties............... 401
On the Peninsular war........ 402
Re-appointment of Lord Castlereagh...................... 403
Burthen of taxes............. 404
Paper currency.............. 405
Its advantages and evils....... 406
ENGLISH INQUISITORS..... 407
The suppressors............. ib.
Shaving on Sundays prohibited. 408
Skittles an abomination....... 409
Lists of suppressions, &c...... 410
Private entrances............ 411
Mrs. Allen's sofas............ 412
CLERICAL ATHEISM...... 413
Precepts best enforced by example 414
A jolly parson............... 415
Jenny and her master......... 416
The clergy as a body.......... 417
O'KELLY THE FIRST....... ib.
Becomes a tapster........... 418
And afterwards an ensign 419
His legacies................. 420
CARICATURES............ 421
The Morning Post and Gilray. 422
THEATRICAL REVIEW.... 423

NOTICE TO CORRESPONDENTS.

The idea of the Caricature is taken from Milton's description of the mariners casting anchor in the scaly rind of the huge Leviathan. The characters are as follow, from the left: The Tortoise, Lord G. A Water-Spaniel, Lord G. The Rhinoceros, Mr. S.; Col. M. M.; Lord and Lady ———. A Shark, Lord C. A Porpoise, Lord T. Mr. P. A Gudgeon, Lord S. A Flat-fish, Lord M——. The two Rats, Lord W. and Mr. C. The Oyster, Bishop of B. The Great Seal, Lord E.

We can no more be regarded as responsible for the Political Satires exhibited for sale at the shop of our Publisher, than for the Evangelical Pamphlets of which he is the monthly distributor. "A little Reason and a great Regent, by Ambrose Dryswitch" has been claimed, we understand, by Anthony Pasquin; and to him be attributed whatever honor may attach to its composition.

We had hoped to receive a communication from Veritas, and from the poetical friend of Mr. Lawrence.

A correspondent informs us that Mr. Messenger Bell has announced a portrait of Mrs. Billington, in the character of SAINT Cécilia, and requests us to point out the particulars in which they resemble each other. We shall comply with his request.

The History of the House of Aspland should have been inserted, had not our number been devoted, in a fair proportion, to a similar subject.

The "names of the officers who put out the eyes of a Bear, and then bailed it," transmitted by a Brighton correspondent, should have been inserted, but for the very natural antipathy of the Editor, towards *a three years' confinement* for speaking the truth.

We thank Dr. Halloran for his good opinion, and hope with great sincerity that he may yet be enabled to rise above the persecutions of his enemies.

Wilkie's Exhibition shall be reviewed in our next number.

The *Chelsea Job* shall meet with due attention.

The correspondence between Mr. P. and an exalted personage requires to be authenticated by the submission of the originals to an inspection, or by a personal pledge on the part of our correspondent to substantiate the correctness of the copies.

Our subject of the Manchester article is no longer interesting.

In our last number among some less important errors, page 262, line 16, 'observations' are printed for 'aberrations.'

In the present, page 401, line 5, for 'claims' read 'pretensions,' line 30, for 'the' read 'their.'

THE SCOURGE.

MAY 1, 1812.

THE REVIEWER, No. XI.

THE TREASURY POETS, AND WHARTON'S RONCES-VALLES.

TILL the establishment of Mr. Perceval and his friends in the lucrative offices of state, poverty was supposed to be a necessary stimulus to genius, and abstinence the best companion of poetical as well as religious inspiration. But in these happier days, the garret must yield precedence to the office, and the luxurious providers of treasury dinners, to the porrage and porter inhabitants of Grub-street. It is now admitted that the possession of office, and the prospect of a sinecure, have by no means an invariable tendency to repress the vigor or circumscribe the flights of a poetical imagination; that the portly owner of a carriage-and-four may gain the summit of Parnassus with as much facility as the ragged and pennyless pedestrian; and that to have your doors besieged by dependant suitors, is a much more pleasing interruption to the slumber of mental inactivity, than the daily visits of the harpies of the law.

In the praise of their country indeed who are so likely to excel as those who partake in the most extensive degree of the *good things* that it produces? Who can be expected to sing the exploits of Lord Wellington with more fervent enthusiasm, than they who accumulate the means of enjoyment at home, by supplying the necessities of his troops abroad; what individual is able so feelingly to record the exhaustless wealth of the British nation, as he who by annual experiment determines the weight of its purse, and the extent of its generosity; or to whom can the task of celebrating our naval glory be committed with so much propriety as to him who supplies our dock-yards with cordage? When personal interest and personal observation combine to animate and direct the patriotism of a native poet, how cold, compared with *his*, must be the effusions of patriotism that flow from the pen of a Virgil and a Dryden!

We are not without hope, therefore, that the example so ably led by Mr. Croker and followed by the authors of various battles, after the manner of Mr. Scott, will continue to excite the rest of the treasury writers to enter the field of poetical competition. Who would not resign for ever the works of Milton, to have the pleasure of reading an ode to philosophy by Mr. Yorke, or a didactic poem by Mr. Stephen on the charms of independence? The world would be equally astonished and edified by an ode to wisdom from Lord Castlereagh; and the fame of Cowper would fade away before a translation of Casimir to his Ass by Mr. Rose. So great indeed is the emulation already excited among many worthy gentlemen connected with the public offices, that we are not without some hope of being enabled in our next number, to favor our readers with several of their most spirited and appropriate productions. Even the ardor of emulation, has extended from the treasury to the palace, and we have already in our possession a sonnet to chastity, by Lord Yarmouth, and a poetical comparison between Alexander and a great personage, by Aristotle the second, alias Mr. Bidlake.

We are surprized, however, that the authors of the Battles of Talavera, Albuera, and Barrosa, should have thought it necessary to take a poetical voyage to foreign kingdoms, when there are so many and to them so much more interesting themes of celebration within their personal observation or remembrance. The battles of the senate, and the intrigues of the back-stairs would supply them with copious materials of description and expression. Character and incident, the great requisites of poetical excellence, would to the bard of domestic contest, be always at hand: the virtuous Sheridan, whose genius would have shone forth, with still more radiant lustre, but for that amiable modesty which counteracted the full developement of his powers: the Prince himself, in whom the sternness of philosophy was subdued by native benignity of disposition, and the severity of virtue attempered by gentleness of deportment; and John Fuller, Esq. M. P. for Suffolk, a man indeed of whom it may be doubted, whether wisdom did more supremely guide his head, or dignity exalt him in all outward proportions above his fellows—these, it is to be presumed, would furnish the poet with no common selection of heroes. For incidents no man of genius could be at a loss, who has witnessed the battle of the 18th of April, between the godlike Perceval, and the sublime Whitbread; or who has had the felicity of seeing a royal an princely leg in all the majesty of *clouts! Scenery* could not be wanting to those who have once enjoyed the honor of a smile, from that most gentlemanly and intelligent personage,—— Cooke, Esq. secretary to Lord Castlereagh, or who have been honored with a sight of the Regent's bathing tub. Nor would the language of Mr. Scott, be less appropriate to subjects like these, than to " the battle blare," " On Stadelaw's unsightly wall, and ivy-circled tower," especially as there would be no danger in the description of domestic scenes, of planting ivy on a newly constructed fortification, and calling a very elegant battery, *a la Vallancey*, by the epithet unsightly. With what propriety indeed the adjectives " mild" and " merciful," could be transferred from Francis to Sir Vicary Gibbs, or " loveliest of thy sainted sex," be applied to the marchioness of a certain square, the heads of the treasury are best qualified to determine.

It is not without pleasure, however, that we confess the claim of the *treasury writers*, (for to that name we conceive the authors of the battles of Talavera, the battles of the Danube and Barrosa, the battles of Albuera, Portugal a poem, and Roncesvalles, are equally entitled to some degree of praise, after making a liberal allowance for the peculiar advantages under which they have committed their productions to the world. The three first of these poems we must dismiss with the observation, that no poetical description of a battle, can be rendered susceptible of permanent interest, as an independant whole: it is necessary, to its full and lasting effect, that it should introduce into action, and have some influence on the fate, of persons, in whose fortune we have been previously interested, and of whose characters we have a vivid and accurate conception. We do not suppose that Messrs. Croker and Co. suppose their powers of description to be superior to those of Homer, Virgil, Dryden and Scott; yet it will be found that the combats of these great poets, excite no comparative interest, but as they are connected with the progress of the story, or as they develope the characters, and suspend or determine the fate of the heroes of the narrative. Nor is it sufficient that of the life and character of the heroes of a combat, there are other memorials: to become the agent in a poetical contest, the principal personage should be introduced to our notice in a poetical garb and attitude, divested of the vulgar or tawdry accompaniments of common life, and girded for battle.

Mr. Wharton is a gentleman of cultivated taste, embued with more than a usual portion of classical and literary knowledge, and capable of applying the stores that he has accumulated with peculiar felicity, to the subject before him. He does not pretend, we believe, to the minute research of the verbal critic; but whenever an apt quotation or allusion from ancient or modern languages, can embellish or elucidate his theme of composition, his memory calls it to his use, and his taste directs him to its skilful and appropriate application. It has perhaps contributed to the excellence, both of his prose and his poetry, that he has chiefly studied the more early models of English composition. He is a submissive disciple of the old school; he regards Dryden as the model of English versification, and Johnson as the Seneca of English literature. In his prose style, therefore, he is more remarkable for chaste but easy volubility than for eloquence; and his poetical productions, while they are characterized by an equable flow of nervous versification, are seldom distinguished by grace of expression, or enthusiasm of sentiment. His compositions, in their general outline, remind the reader of Dryden's Versification of Palemon and Arcite; and it is no mean praise to say of Mr. Wharton, that, his versifications of Chaucer are scarcely inferior in elegance or spirit to those of Dryden.

That the poem of Roncesvalles will obtain any share of popularity, we shall not flatter Mr. Wharton by supposing. The scenery, the characters and the incidents, are so familiar to the scholar, as to awaken no sentiment but regret that they should be taken out of the hands, in which they had hitherto remained, and brought before the English public in any other shape than a translation; while to the multitude of readers, the manners and allusions scattered through the work, must be equally strange and destitute of interest. A short poem founded on the Witcheries of Urganda, and the exploits of Orlando, might be received with some degree of curiosity; but a production in twelve books, extending through 350 quarto pages, will never command an extensive circulation, by the mere unconnected introduction of Lord Wellington and the Spaniards, into the beginning or the middle of a canto, some years after the other parts of the work have been completed. Nor does the fable consist of a series of dependent and connected incidents, all tending to one great end: the story is composed of incident and counter-incident: of spell versus spell; and of unconnected accidents that impede or accelerate the *denouement* at the pleasure of the author. Mr.

Wharton, however, though his expression is sometimes awkward, and his rhymes often incorrect, deserves in his more fortunate passages the praise of a versification regular without monotony, and vigorous without harshness; melodious in its cadence, yet various in its measure, and uniting energy with mellifluence, in a degree unusual to the numerous manufactures of the heroic couplet.

The subjoined extract though harsh and incorrect, affords a favourable example of his dexterity in the imitation of his Italian originals.

> But Ferrau now crazed with tenfold fears,
> Urganda's curses echoing in his ears,
> Discumbered from the steed his flight renewed,
> Deeming himself alone the man pursued:
> Orlando's menace rode on every gale,
> The hissing sabre and the rattling mail,
> And ever and anon his mind misgave
> Over his casqueless head that steel to wave,
> Fierce as the felon's heart had been before
> When trusting in his own resistless power,
> So once that fury quelled, convinced his pride
> That strength superior might in man reside,
> He trembled: to an abject fear resigned:
> For firmness dwells not in a savage mind.
>
> * * * *
>
> As the steed snorted o'er a deep ravine
> Stretching his fury and the foe between,
> Orlando sprung indignant from his seat,
> And like a famished tiger plied his feet,
> Bounding from rock to rock, from cleft to cleft;
> And at each spring less hope of safety left,
> To him who flying felt his sinews fail,
> And his speed droop, when speed might most avail.
> As o'er the unlevel surface of the deep,
> Two ships before the gale their progress keep,
> Pursuing and pursued; and now on high,
> The foremost strikes her eager follower's eye,
> Then sinks beneath the billows; now the one,
> Now on the waves aloft, the other, thrown;

The death of Ferrau.

So fared Anglante's knight and *Ferrau*;
The rocks and glens obstructed oft their view.
But onward still the Pagan urged his way,
The christian breathing death pursued his prey,
Two master streams there were whose channels wide,
Swallowing the rage of many a lesser tide,
The swains with homely skill and patient care,
Had bridged, ere Roncesvalles shook with war.
But at that hour when discord late befell,
O'er Etna, 'twixt the sovereigns of the spell,
Its influence with such force o'er nature came,
That the earth trembled to its inmost frame,
Then were those arches burst: again the tide,
Progress to all forbad from side to side,
Save to Lanfusa's son: the nearer shore,
Reaching by paths he oft had trod before.
He bounded o'er the chasm, at stretch 'tis true—
But touched the further bank, and onward flew,
Orlando came: he sprung across the surge,
And many a fathom pitched beyond its verge,
Gaining at every footfall on his foe,
And aiming in his thought the deadly blow:
Thus hurried they: and nearer now they sped,
Where the thick woods extend a friendly shade,
When in the second bridge the Iberian saw,
Riv'n in that shock of things a second flaw,
And underneath, the stream, that made its way,
Whirling with eddies deep, and rough with yellow spray.
Stupendous was the gap, no might of man,
(Not Brava's knight) could measure such a span,
Yet Ferrau had lept, by fear struck blind,
To every danger save the one behind,
But from that self-same flood, for there the ghost,
Had from the Iberian claimed his helmet lost,
The well known form of Argalia slain,
All pale and streaked with many a gory stain,
Uprising, wide its meagre arms displayed,
And sullen seemed to smile, and nodded thrice its head;
Back instant shrunk the Iberian; fixt he stood
The chillness of amazement froze his blood!
His eyeballs chained by terror to the shape
That reft at once his will and power to scape,

His lips half opened as in act to speak
An earthy paleness stampt upon his cheek :
He trembled heedless that the sounds of *death*,
Louder and louder gathered on his path.
Even yet on Argalia glar'd his eye,
When fate aloud pronounced his time to die,
And from the central cave was heard a dismal cry;
Then from Orlando's arm a splintered rock
Reached his bare head : he bent beneath the stroke,
Another and another fragment came,
(Flung with the force of subterraneous flame)
Loading his head, and neck, and arms, and trunk,
Till prostrate on the earth the warrior sunk,
Oppressed, but fixing still his eyeballs dim,
Upon the ghastly spectre of the stream :
Even, till entomb'd beneath the weight of stone,
Half crush'd, half smother'd by the ruins thrown,
His unrepenting soul indignant fled,—
That image on his visual film was spread.

Since the period when the composition of these verses beguiled the solitude of retirement in a distant county, the progress of Mr. Wharton in the paths of ministerial favor, has been equally beneficial to his own fortune, and creditable to the friendly attachment of Mr. Perceval. That he is a man of unexampled industry, is admitted even by his enemies; and that he is as honest as it is possible for a modern servant of the Treasury to be under the present system, we can assert from our personal knowledge of his character. Yet we doubt, whether at the close of his public career he may not be reduced to confess that wealth and honor can be purchased at the expence of happiness : independence and singleness of heart, are the qualities of which we once supposed him to be one of the favored possessors ; whether these qualities can exist within the contagion of the Treasury atmosphere, we are more than doubtful : and comparing what he was, with what he may be, we would willingly forget the secretary of the Treasury, to retain, in the possessor of Old Park, the scholar, the gentleman, and the *friend.* H. C.

THE WHIPS, No. IV.

AN EXALTED INVALID.

Though the individual whose character it is our present duty to hold up to the indignation of the British public, disclaims the title of sportsman as a professional appellation, yet even his enemies must admit that in all the characteristics of a true member of the whips, he may bid defiance to the competition of a Buxton or a Hawke. Descended from a family of which the virtues are remembered only to the dishonour of so worthless a member; in the possession of a *princely* income, which only yields the means of debauchery to an extensive circle of lascivious minions; profligate without elegance, licentious without spirit, and profuse without generosity; what further qualifications are required to secure his preeminence in all the distinctions of whippism? Though he is in the regular receipt of twelve thousand pounds per annum, he has not discharged one solitary debt for the last ten years: yet the money of which he has defrauded his creditors, has not been converted to the liquidation of his honorary promises, or contributed to the happiness of the meanest instruments of his voluptuous indulgencies. Afflicted with alternate fits of avarice and profusion, his occasional extravagance is intermingled with the lowest arts of pecuniary meanness: the sums, therefore, that he lavishes are received without gratitude, and squandered without enjoyment. It is not many months since he became attached to Madam L―――― a ci-devant performer at the opera; who yielded without resistance to his solicitations, and obtained in addition to the use of his name at the usual resorts of fashionable extravagance, the greater portion of the first payment from the privy purse, of his annual income. The lady, grateful for his liberality, and willing to demonstrate that it was not thrown away on a thankless and mercenary woman, received him in a style of courtly elegance, and consumed the sums designed for her personal gratification in administering to his taste for the pleasures of the table and the bottle. Having spent the full amount of her finances, she acquainted her protector with the necessity of a further advance. He told her not to be alarmed, informed her that on making use of his name, she might obtain to any amount all the luxuries of life, and assured her that the next payment he received, should be devoted to the liquidation of whatever debts she might contract. Confiding in his promises, she ventured to obtain of his tradesman, wines and other requisites of good living to the amount of 600l. At the end of the year she applied to her protector for pecuniary aid; but in the mean time, his ——— had become attached to another frail one, and refused to assist her: the creditors had some hope that rather than suffer her to languish in a prison, he would come forward to discharge her debts, and therefore arrested her; but their hopes were disappointed, the ——— received the intelligence of her misfortune with perfect unconcern, and she now lingers in all the miseries of confinement and destitution.

To one female, well known in the musical world, he has indeed returned after every temporary indulgence in casual and meretricious love. A *chere amie* who at once contributes to the gratification of the passions, and the replenishment of the purse, is a rare and valuable commodity. How frequently she may have relieved her exalted lover from vulgar importunities, or embarrassing predicaments, those only who have had occasion to witness the manners and habits of a certain family, can conjecture. It is certain, however, that the sums drawn by his ——— on Mrs. ———'s banker, have seldom amounted to less than 3000l. *per annum :* nor is the lady destined to receive any other return for her generosity than the honour of an occasional visit from the pride of S———, and the ornament of I———. At an early period of life, he became the husband of a beautiful and amiable woman; the possession of whose person was the only object of his wishes, and whom he willingly resigned at no very distant period to the tyranny of law. They were divorced on the ground of legal informality, and the son was drawn from the protection of the mother, to be educated beneath the immediate auspices of the family. It is almost needless to add, because it is too well known, that with the title he has relinquished the affection of a husband; that his conduct towards the woman who in a moral point of view must still be regarded as his wife, has been distinguished by selfishness, and his correspondence by cruel and deliberate insult; and that into the mind of his son he has instilled those lofty impressions of self consequence, that would only become an acknowledged and legitimate descendant of the family.

He has long and arduously aspired to the reputation of a universal genius, and moderate as his talents confessedly are, he is certainly the *cleverest* of the family. He can speak for a few minutes in the senate, without talking nonsense, or betraying any symptoms of confusion: he writes very pretty verses; has indited one or two political pamphlets, sings a *so so* song, and plays the Battle of Prague on the piano. Above all things, however, he wishes to be regarded as a hearty whip and a sturdy bacchanalian: his driving talents have lately been eclipsed by the influence of disease, but his indisposition neither prevents nor restrains his devotions at the shrine of Bacchus.

He has long been the prey of the lowest of the multitude: conscious that to reveal the truth respecting his conduct and pursuits would be to render him the object of general abhorrence, he has been condemned to purchase the silence of discarded servants, and their employers, by sums nearly equal in amount to all the rest of his expences. The threats of a person to whom his private vices are well known, are supposed to have occasioned his late illness, which the newspapers stated at one time to be *severe,* and now declare to be *relieved.* The truth is, that all the relief which could be obtained has already been administered, and that the confinement of his ——— to his bed, is occasioned by the united operation of lascivious languor, bacchanial frenzy, and *remorse!*

ON PROSECUTION for LIBELS, and the PRINCE REGENT.

If any thing could have contributed to sooth the disappointment of the public, at the unequivocal determination of the Prince to support the present system of government, or appease the clamour, excited by the general persuasion of his personal irregularities; it would have been a magnanimous forbearance towards those writers, whose duty or enthusiasm might lead them, in the expression of their feelings, beyond the rigid boundaries of legal observation. The delusion, however, that had been excited by the assurances of his confidential friends, that he would leave the press to its free and regular operation, have been dissipated by the filing of an ex-officio information, against the editor of the Examiner; and unwilling as we are to anticipate the verdict of a jury, it is too plain that Mr. Hunt is now at the mercy of the Attorney General. The paragraph quoted in the declaration on the part of the king, is, acccording to the present construction of the law, a " *gross and infamous libel;*" which no man could write, without being conscious of his indiscretion, or without expectation of some advantage, more than commensurate to imprisonment in a distant gaol. For our own parts, we firmly believe that Mr. Hunt was influenced in his publication of the libellous paragraph, by the hopes of a handsome subscription. He himself declares that he can eat and write in a prison, and should regard it as no punishment to be restrained from walking; and he may probably suppose that two or three thousand pounds from the public purse, would alleviate the hardships of confinement, and give new charms to the prospect of his return to society. It will be easy for him to make an appeal to the British people, on the liberty of the press, to represent himself as a martyr to the tyranny of law, and the persecution of the Attorney General; and to institute a comparison between Mr. Drakard and himself, which may prove the comparative importance of his claims on the gratitude and generosity of a British public.

To the labours of disinterested and prudent patriotism, no honors can be too high, no reward too liberal. But there is some distinction between spirit and rashness. The Examiner's opinion of the Prince, might have been expressed in a form less tangible, yet equally expressive: he who will " run a muck, and tilt at all he meets," deserves not to be branded as a coward; but must resign his claim to the rewards that await the brave yet cautious soldier, who guards his own person from assault while he carries death and dismay into the ranks of his enemies.

We do not say, that if the side of *Pittism* and corruption were the most profitable, Mr. Hunt would embrace it; but we may be permitted to suspect that the vehemence and perseverance of his attacks on the Prince Regent, may be occasioned by other motives than pure and genuine patriotism; that to say pointed things of the chief magistrate may be to as great a degree a matter of trade, as of principle or feeling; and that he might have been a very lukewarm writer, but for his waking visions of a trebled circulation, the applause of the lovers of *rich* articles, and *a subscription*. Mr. Hunt is a thick and thin man: a conscientious observer would find some relief from the deep shade of folly or iniquity, that clouds the coup d'œil of the royal portrait: he would find occasional opportunities of coinciding with his opponents, and differing from his friends; he would not be the slave of political bigotry, or be content to obtain the character of a satirist without discrimination, and of a partizan whose most obvious qualification is *equability of violence.*

But the indiscretion of Mr. Hunt may be outvied by the injustice or the folly of those against whom his attacks have been directed, or to whom the task of legal vengeance is committed. It is vain to endeavour to persecute in the opinions of one man, the sentiments of a whole empire. Neither the terrors of Sir Vicary, nor the eloquence of a Stuart, can dissipate the settled conviction of the people, or restrain by the arbitrary exercise of an invidious office, that general indignation which legal violence can only exasperate into action, or restrain within the artificial limits prescribed by power, till by the impulse of internal agitation, it bursts its opposing boundaries, and overwhelms the great and the mean, the noble and the vulgar, every monument of ancient wisdom, and every trophy of profligate despotism, in one undistinguished and melancholy ruin.

Whatever may be thought or asserted by the parasites, who surround a court, the free expression of public opinion is the best security for the happiness of the Prince, and the safety of the throne. Discontent, when restrained from publishing its opinions, seeks refuge in private communication, and directs its powers to intrigues and conspiracies. The Prince, who never hears the sentiments of his people, walks on hidden fires with all the confidence of deceitful security. The animadversions of the literary public on the conduct of a mighty prince, can do no injury, but in proportion as they are just; and if while he admits their justice, he neither amends his life, nor reforms his political conduct, any misfortunes that may afflict him, are the result of his own fatuity. The persons who assume the title of antijacobins, ascribe the fall of Louis to the writings of the French philosophers; but their attacks were directed against a system which was confessedly oppressive; they loved the monarch, and if notwithstanding the character of Louis, he fell a victim to the triumph of just principles, in all their violence of operation, how strong an argument does the fate of that unfortunate sovereign afford for the correction of abuses, while there is yet time to make a voluntary sacrifice to justice? Had the writings of the philosophers been attended to, that reform would have been silently effected by the prince and the nobles, which became at length the pretext and the instrument of murder and rapine. Nor is the history of the French revolution less striking in another point of view. Had the queen been virtuous, the royal family might have obtained the suffrages of the multitude, if they had not gained the mercy, or overawed the resolution of their judges. One profligate member of a family, may become the involuntary cause of its destruction; and the history of Louis affords a striking lesson to all who violate or despise the laws of conjugal fidelity.

When the parasites of the Prince Regent, (for all Princes have parasites,) suppose the writings of the Examiner to be merely the expression of individual feeling, they become the most dangerous of his enemies. Falsehood excited by malignity, may gain the momentary notice of the people; but the language of truth alone can deserve or obtain their permanent confidence. If the people regard even the trivial errors of the Prince Regent, with unpleasing fastidiousness, they are justified in their alarm even at the approaches to evil, by the instruction of former ages, and the observation of foreign courts. The history of Europe, and the present state of the continental empires, sufficiently testify the dangers that await the progress of princely frailty; and jealousy is the more becoming towards those exalted individuals in proportion to their advance in life. The follies of a prince are often the follies of indolence and incautiousness; in him who ascends the throne at an early age, habits of business may supersede the frivolities of youth: the performance of his duties as a monarch will call for the full exertion of his mental and corporeal powers; he will not be compelled to fly from the lassitude of princely inaction to the arms of courtly lasciviousness, or to supply the absence of external stimuli, by perpetual recourse to the goblet of intemperance. But with an *elderly* prince, the danger is greater; it too often happens that as old age steals on, the habits of middle life obtain an omnipotent control over every faculty of the soul; voluptuous forty degenerates into impotent and profligate fifty: the vices of the Prince (whether the Dey of Algiers, or the Lord of Siam,) extend their baleful influence, from the palace to the villa, and from the villa to the cottage; beneath the reign of fashion, virtue, modesty, and temperance, sink into everlasting night: religion forakes the habitations of men;

" And unaware's mortality expires."

CUMBERLAND VICARS.

Sir,

Having admitted into the late numbers of your work a satirical history of the dissenting teachers to whom the people of Cumberland have committed, at various times, the guardianship of their spiritual welfare, I expect of your candor and demand of your justice, that the subjoined portraits of the regular clergymen, with whom the itinerant ministers were drawn into comparison, and from whose lectures their hearers fled to the "*tabernacles*," as you are pleased to call them, of the "*fanatics*," should meet with your immediate attention. It is in your power to verify my statement, and admitting its truth, you may ascribe the conduct of the multitude to other causes than the operation of curiosity acted upon by cunning.

The first vicar of the parish, who comes within the remembrance of your present correspondent, had been a tutor of St. John's College, Cambridge, and at the age of fifty was presented by the master and fellows to the living of Ashwell. Accustomed to frown authority on the university freshmen, he treated his parishioners like so many school-boys, was precise and formal in his demeanor, haughty to his tenants and uncourtly to his neighbours. When he first arrived in the village the rents of the glebe land were moderate, and the mode of payment liberal, the tithes were received with forbearance and paid with willingness, and the respectable inhabitants of the neighbouring country on every holiday and every festival, found a hearty welcome at the vicarage. But old Grumble Thorpe, resided in solitary state, and seldom appeared to his parishioners except in the form of a rigid landlord; or disguised in a cocked hat, and with a wig that might have vied in exuberance with that of Dr. Parr, he stalked along in all the majesty of clerical leanness, to the grief and dismay of the miserable gleaners. For the twenty years during which he resided at the parsonage-house, not a session or an assize elapsed that did not publish to the world his own litigious temper, and the oppression of his parishioners. He was well acquainted with all the laws respecting right of common, *delictus in ecclesiam*, and other questions pertaining to the increase of his revenues. His hatred towards vagrants and bastards was inveterate: in his situation as justice of the peace, he became the terror not only of every neighbouring poacher, but of the baker and the applewoman: shaving and cooking on the Sunday were banished from the village, and the unfortunate peasant who ventured to catch a few gudgeons in forbidden streams, were the objects of exemplary vengeance. In his deportment as a clergyman, and in the performance of his duty at the altar or the tomb, he was cold, formal, and supercilious, neither rejoicing with those that rejoiced, nor weeping with those that wept. His sermons were learned theses on abstruse points of theology, and he read the prayers and the lessons with the same tone of authoritative fastidiousness that marked his exposition of the game laws. The only human being to whom he evinced any marks of attachment was his housekeeper, who after having nursed and humoured him for the last thirty years of his life, was rewarded for her services by the bequest of his accumulated thousands.

On his death the presentation devolved to the squire, who selected his old friend Mr. Goodfellow as the fittest person to fulfil the situation of a minister of religion. He had obtained ordination from the bishop of —— in return for taking an active part in the election for the county. Whether he could construe the first chapter of St. John may be doubted; it is certain that he had received what is called an English education, remembered some part of Fanny Hill, and could repeat from the Apocrypha the history of Bel and the Dragon. He was now about forty years of age, short but portly, with a countenance expressing a mingled character of good humour and vulgarity: the acquiescence with which he engaged in any pursuit of the squire's, and the temper with which he listened to his jokes, were great recommendations at Ashwell hall, and of the " company" at the King's Arms he was the idol and the oracle. In the chair by the fire place surrounded by the exciseman, the landlord, and the barber, he cracked his jokes, drank his ale, and pegged his game at cribbage. How often Bill Hopkins and he had stolen when young into Teddy Fig's warehouse and eat or destroyed his comfits; by what stratagem he got to bed to Dolly Blossom without awaking her sister; how many bowls of punch he and the squire had drank at one sitting; what devilish lucky hits he had won at the last Carlisle races, when his old favourite Mrs. W—— of the Carlisle Arms, gave him a sly wink;

what jolly things had been said to him by Jack Curwen, just before he was made member for Carlisle, which he was sure happened only a year or two after that tremendous affair, the revolution, took place, in which as his company well knew, the French king was murdered,---and other subjects equally important, and equally indicative of his clerical qualifications, were the constant theme of his discourse. For a while the contrast between Mr. Goodfellow and his predecessor, was far from unfavourable: their parishioners were glad to have for a teacher a good-humoured man, who did not disdain to inquire after their families, or chat familiarly with their children. But folly soon degenerates into vice; he became so attached to the King's Arms as to be found no where else; children died in a state of reprobation, because Mr. Goodfellow had taken a walk to dine with the squire; many a happy couple were obliged to lament the miseries of "hope deferred" because their spiritual pastor had taken an overpowering quantity of spirituous liquors, and funerals were postponed, and bodies lodged in the church till a nap restored him to sobriety. At length the landlord of the King's Arms began to suspect his lady's fidelity; the squire's cook maid was pregnant, and " *laid the blame*" on the parson; an attorney of Cockermouth fell over the bridge and was drowned, and report asserted that he had been tippling to a late hour with Mr. Goodfellow. The clamour at length became so great that it came to the ears of the bishop of the diocese, who caused the requisite inquiries to be made, and finding that his conduct was a scandal to the church, and insulting to his parishioners, deprived him of his gown.

Our next incumbent was a person who had lived some time in the family of Lord P—— and had accompanied his son on the *grand tour*: for at that time the British isles were not in a state of blockade. On his return to England the morals of the son excited Lord P.'s despair, and the manners of the tutor aroused his indignation. He paid him the arrears of his salary, and then dismissed him. For several years the reverend gentleman subsisted by descending to the servilities of a hackney parson: fond of mixed society, the slave of intemperance, restrained by the necessities of a narrow income, and professing the character of a man of the town, he figured away at the club-houses and taverns, as long as the patronage of his pupil would atone for the imperfections of his wardrobe, or his sanction obtain him credit among the purveyors to gluttony and intemperance. When these resources failed him, he descended from the tavern to the pot-house, and from the societies formed by men of character and education, to the smoking rooms. His acquaintance with the low scandal of the outcasts of fashion, recommended him to the favorable notice of the frequenters of these receptacles: no man was more conversant in the history of intrigue: he could trace the progress of the Wyndhams of that period, from the tap to the drawing-room; knew the history and pedigree of every female who shone in the annals of crim. con.; remembered the quarrels between Lord D. and Mr. M. respecting the natural daughter of the Duchess of Izzard, and was perfectly acquainted with the circumstances that attended the introduction of a fair quaker to an exalted personage. By degrees he degenerated into a pot-house wag, could pour a glass of punch with more than usual dexterity into his neighbour's pocket, and displayed uncommon address in setting fire to the lawyer's wig, and then assuring him that he threw new light on every subject before him. As he had been driven to these societies by necessity, he was not ashamed to barter buffoonery for hospitality, and to become the jolly companion of any individual who would pay his *reckoning*. In this career of vulgar profligacy and voluntary degradation, he remained till the death of Lord P.'s father, enabled his *ci-devant* pupil to testify his gratitude for his early initiation into vice, by presenting him with the vicarage of Ashwell.

No sooner had he been properly settled at the parsonage-house, than he converted the parlor into a billiard-room, and invited all the young bucks of the parish to contend with him, in that edifying and profitable game. The claret, for now that he had become a vicar he attempted to resume his early habits, circulated with due celerity; and after spending the morning in drinking and gambling, he and his companions sallied out, either to reconnoitre the dwelling houses of the neighbouring farmers, in search of their daughters, or to scale the dairy of the squire, and bore holes in the bottoms of his milk pails. " Fun" and " intrigue" were the great objects of his pursuit: he repeated in the highways of Cumberland the profligacies he had committed in the nooks and corners of London, and edified the profligates of Ashwell, by retailing the scandalous memoirs of Suffolk-street.

From this person we were relieved by an action of bastardy, and an execution in the parsonage house. His place was supplied by a political parson, a dependant of Mr. Curwen, and a furious declaimer about reform and the constitution. He paid more attention to Magna Charta than the Bible, and talked more frequently of ministerial imbecillity than of faith, or grace, or good works. For three or four days in each week, he left the parish to take care of itself, while he harangued the populace of Carlisle, and carried addresses to his majesty on the grievances of the times. He broke a blood-vessel, as he was declaiming with unusual warmth, to a select assemblage of his parishioners, on pittism and corruption, and was led to the grave, by the persons to whom his eloquence was addressed.

To him succeeded our present vicar, a young gentleman of twenty-eight, a great favorite of the young maids and old misses of Ashwell, the writer of some very pretty effusions, sentimental and serious, in prose and verse. His first effort at celebrity, was a sonnet on the lap-dog of Miss Amelia Younghusband, which I have no doubt will be read with sympathetic pleasure, by every feeling and sensitive reader of the Scourge.*

---

* We think otherwise, and have therefore omitted it.—Ed.

Nor are his effusions as a novelist less charming, delightful and affecting. "The moon" (says he) in one of his novels, published by Mr. Newman—" the moon had just risen in lunar majesty, and tipped with silver glow the horizon sparkling with radiant beams, when Alphonso slowly treading over the fatal ground, observed a dark and gloomy figure stalk before him. Thrice did he start, and thrice resume his progress: at length the portal of the eastern-gate flew open, and presented to his astonished eyes the image of his long lost Almeida, ascending the grand stair-case." Again," with a heart beaming with sensibility, and eyes teeming the most transcendant desire, she received his heart-entrancing—soul-melting assurances. And oh! Almeida! he exclaimed, is such bliss extatic reserved for thy Alphonso; and wilt thou deign to seal with bonds of angelic rapture, purest vows of bright ethereal love? Yes, my Almeida, I see it in thy lips! Happiness celestial! oh, joy unutterable! Almeida regarded him not: with steady hand, and undisturbed countenance, she was in the act of conveying to her mouth a slice of the best plum-pudding, when suddenly the voice, &c. &c."

You will have observed, that to his other qualifications our vicar unites the talents of a punster; and the brilliance of his wit is acknowledged at the squire's. At some future time, I may perhaps send you a catalogue of his good things; but at present the following are the only ones that occur to my remembrance. " I am sorry to say, that this *mist*-erious affair is still involved in a *cloud* of difficulties." " It is as *plane* as my *ebony* walking-stick." "He has lost is *arm*, and is now a very *harmless* fellow;" " the Kent merchants have commenced a *hop*-ful season," &c. &c.

But you will naturally ask me, if while he thus amuses the idle and flatters the affected, he fulfils his more important duties as a clergyman? Oh! no, Sir—that would be too great a sacrifice of fame and pleasure to utility in such a poet and novelist as Mr. T. His sermons are stolen from Blair and Tillotson, except when on extraordinary occasions he applies the language of his sentimental productions to the spiritual instruction of his audience, and talks of heaven and hell in the superfine diction of a circulating library. His attention while in the pulpit is divided between his sermon and the fair admirers of his amatory productions: and the lisp and the look askance, inform even the most unintelligent of his congregation, that his thoughts are occupied on other things than religion and eternity. The time that ought to be devoted to the visitation of the sick, and the comfort of the afflicted, is employed in the reciprocation of acrostics with his female parishioners, or in the composition of sentimental tales for the Leadenhall-street repository.

After this short sketch of the various characters to whom for the last thirty years our spiritual welfare has been committed, your friend the Cumberland magistrate may cease to be astonished at the progress of methodism, or to blame the people for their desertion of the church. That every parish should be so unfortunate as Ashwell, cannot be supposed—the living is valuable, the occasional presentation in the hands of improper persons, and the conduct of the incumbent far removed from episcopal observation. To these causes *our* peculiar misfortunes may be ascribed; nor am I without hopes that they will be in some measure alleviated by this public exposition.

ONE IN RETIREMENT.

Dovenby, Cumberland.

EPIGRAMS.

ON THE MANCHESTER RIOTS.

The Court's in confusion, because it is found,
    An event for which H—— forgot to prepare,
That the wrong-headed people all MANCHESTER
    round,
    Oppose what is counselled in MANCHESTER
    square.

MATHEMATICUS.

ON SEEING PASQUIN, ALIAS DR. WILLIAMS, IN A VERY SHABBY COAT, PARADING THE PARK WITH HIS PATRON ROMEO.

How little Pasquin heeds our jeers,
    We all may understand,
Since out at elbows he appears,
    With *Coates* at his command!

Y. Z.

ON THE SAME.

When Jackey from his master's cloaths
    The clouds of dust would force,
'Twas once a common sight to see
    The *coat* upon the *horse*:
But valets spruce of modern days,
    Far wiser are than Jack,
For Craven Street and Hyde Park shew,
    Great COATES support the *hack!*

Y. Z.

THE WIDOW FAIRBUR'S BENEFIT.

Of kindred souls, indulgent fame
Vouchsafes to grant a kindred name;
Great COATES in buskin'd splendor shines,
And to his Juliet sweetly whines,
While Pasquin fired by rival thoughts,
Comes forth to view, in *Petty* COATES.

Y. Z.

A TART REPLY.

Says the squire to the parson " if you were to lie
In this dish we could make a substantial goose-pie:"
Quoth the parson, " if you in your grave were extended,
Which I hope won't take place till your morals are mended,
And I read the prayers, by a much better rule,
The parish might call me a *goose*-BURY *fool*."

RUSTICUS.

EPIGRAM.

Friend Tom* declares to his connections
That he retains no predilections:
And they who mark his conduct well,
That he declares the truth, will tell;
First to his wines in order placed,
He shews an equal warmth of taste:
And next lest any ——e should pall
Upon the sense, he tries them all:
And lastly, no one to offend,
In *every* rogue he finds an equal friend!

---

*   " A rose
By any other name would smell as sweet,"

A CATALOGUE OF QUACKS.

Sir,

Perusing your instructive and amusing publication of last month, an article caught my eye, upon a subject rather *new* to periodical reviews; but which convinced me of the great utility of such a work as " the Scourge" standing before the public, as the *palladium* of our property, by the just exposure of quackery, fraud, and imposition.

I have now lived about seventy years in the world, and mingled much in the active scenes of life; in which a man of tolerable discernment must have observed the human character in all the varied forms incident to our frail and imperfect nature;—it will therefore, Sir, not appear very surprising to you, to hear, that I have unfortunately run my head against a great number and variety of *quacks*, and that such persons have run their *hands into my pockets*!

But after reading your review of a certain architectural *catch-penny* publication, I meditated much upon the most dangerous of those characters, who obtain an existence upon the follies and credulity of society; and who would not be suffered to breath in an Utopian government, where useless persons are not allowed to annoy the humble inhabitants of such a happy region. But though the British constitution is better organised than any other, it has not the power of protecting the subject from plunder, or of reducing Utopian principles to the practical advantage of the body-politic; consequently we are obliged to elbow rogues, at noon day, who while smiling in your face, will *draw your high-tooth*, so that you may never have the advantage of *cutting it* even at the respectable *age* of seventy!

Among these polite *receivers* of your property, I do not know more dangerous *quacks*, than those of whom you speak:—and I beg to assure you, that my knowledge arises from dearly-bought experience in the practice of building! It is true the physician can write you a *line* or two of Latin, that will produce as much poison as will remove you and your whole family into the grave for *one guinea*, without your knowing what offence you have committed, that you should pay to become *immortal:* while the doctor returns home, and expends that money upon the most delicate viands of the season, which every one can analyse, and all persons know something about!---In this, however, you only lose two things, namely, your life, and a paltry fee; but if you consult an architectural physician, he prescribes apparently upon more liberal principles; and though he does not leave your house with a *guinea*, he takes your *order* and instructions for a " dose of building," which when complete, draws from your pocket ten hundred, or perhaps ten thousand guineas, *instead of one*, which is as bad as taking your life; according to the sentiment of Shakspeare, who says,

> " You take my house, when you do take the prop
> That doth sustain my house; you take my life
> When you do take the means whereby I live."

and therefore, I would from the conviction of long experience in these matters rather give *up the ghost*, through the medium of a guinea sleeping draught, than be allowed to terminate a painful existence in a building, which most likely would stand as a monument of disgrace to the abilities and honesty of the quack architect, and a tomb to my fortune and happiness!

Sir, we have quack patriots, who affect to administer to the diseases of the state; and though they profess to cure, without a motive of interest, they *never get* employed without " bleeding copiously" before their ignorance and deception are discovered; and then retire from their *officious* duties like other quacks, laughing at those whom they have plundered!

To be sure, Sir, the taking of a few thousands a year for their pretended knowledge and services, is a *species* of bleeding not so much felt by the nation, as when an architectural *lancet* gets into the *reins* of an individual---the *resources* of the body-politic and the body-natural being quite different. The first soon renovates from the abundant gains that supply it, while the other is left as *dry* as the *builder's rod*, which measures all the corners, holes, and crevices, into which the poor victim's blood has been artfully drawn to support quackery and fraud!

I have met, Sir, with quack gardeners, who conduct you through all the mazes of horticulture, only to bewilder you in the still greater mazes of a *long bill*, and who in the end, only twist nature into a shameful disguise, and make one wish that the *artist* was suspended to one of our trees, in compliment to his bad taste in displaying a *hanging-wood;*---near to whom might, with great justice, be *gracefully* placed many of our quack builders, as appropriate personages to the scene, and quite necessary to *feel* and *know the strength* of the timber so *properly employed!*

The world abounds with so many quacks, besides those mentioned, that I fear I shall fatigue your readers, by enlarging this catalogue: yet, as I have seen much of these characters in the course of a long life, it may be expected I should enumerate one or two more professors of *empiricism*.

What do you think, Sir, of your patent undertaker?---He is another kind of *architect* or *builder;* but not so good as the grave-maker, whose houses (as Shakspeare says) last till doomsday! You see, Sir, I cannot do without the assistance of the great poet; but as he knew so much of human nature, it is fair I should introduce him as a contrast to my list of quacks, who only live to violate all her noble and sublime principles!

This sable architect and builder can shew you a *fine plan* of the cottages and houses that he makes, which he very *gravely* says can never be *broken open, and robbed,* though he does not venture to deny, but *might* may overcome *right*; and instead of his *well secured dwelling* being *broken open*, by a thief in the night, it may be easily carried off by way of *execution upon body and goods.* .

Forty years ago I never heard of quack blacking-makers; but, now Sir, it matters not *however black* a thing may be, if it is but *patent black*—of all the *black things* that pass current in society, and certainly some of which are very pleasing to the *eye,* and *agreeable to the touch*, the one in question is the least objectionable, and carries no disguise or danger with it except to leather, which is an advantage to our shoemakers, who like architects and builders very well know how to *pinch* a customer !

But, Sir, the most agreeable quacks I ever run my head against, is one of those divine creatures *commonly* called a woman, who will profess to love you, while she is casting her secret peeper upon another—My friend, now at my elbow, swears that these kind of quacks are full as bad as an architect, and can *tickle* you out of ten thousand pounds with the same ease of deception; but I do not agree with him upon this subject—It is certainly true that the fair deceiver can run you *very hard more ways* than one ;—that she can spend *two* or *three* thousand a year, and then talk of it as mere pin-money ;---can make love to another, and instantly return home to give you a lecture upon domestic infidelity ;---can chide you upon being out of temper with her follies and extravagance, while she is scratching your face for more money! But, Sir, who would not rather give ten thousand pounds for such a piece of lovely structure, with all her little imperfections, or expend that sum in the support of her pleasures, than be the dupe of an *Indian ink* builder, or a dirty fellow that consolidates cold bricks into an architectural money-trap ?

If some of these fair creatures be quacks in love, still it is better to be robbed by a lovely woman under any mask, than by a *sly methodical knave,* who in his journey through life's vicious path fastens upon your purse, and by *one dip* draws out your *whole fortune;* whereas the enchanting female imparts the most delectable pleasure as a return for her protection, and affords those delights that can only render life supportable!

If she *diddles* you (to use a parliamentary phrase of a late member*) there is generally some consolation to your feelings. You take a retrospect of all the endearing moments which have passed between you, and lulled the mind into a delicious repose, or animated it into something upon which reflection feeds with rapture; but to hope for a pleasing thought to be produced by the cold hand of a bricklayer, and the hard and icy heart of his artist, is as forlorn and unpromising as that they will become HONEST MEN!!!

I am, Sir,
Yours, &c.

BARON GERAMB; STROEHLING THE ARTIST,
AND
PROFESSOR VON FEINAGLE.

When we ventured to pronounce from our observation of the manners and habits of the Baron Geramb, that his motives for residing in this country were such as to demand the attention of ministers, we are afraid that there are few of our readers, who did not suspect us of resentment or uncharitableness. Yet, now that he has been sent out of the kingdom, the thinking part of

---

* I believe Mr. Robson, who when speaking of the inability of the Treasury to pay its own bills, said that " we were *all diddled, by God!*"

the nation are rather inclined to wonder, that he should have been permitted to remain in England so long, than to accuse the government of injustice or precipitancy. That we ourselves contributed, in a great measure, to the detection of his villanies, we confess with pleasure; but accident alone made us acquainted with the particulars of his civil depredations, and his political intrigues; and how many foreigners of a similar character, and with similar views, may now be resident in London, of whom a similar concurrence of circumstances would disclose an equal degree of criminal ingratitude!

He seems to have been well acquainted with the English character. Beneath the garb of eccentricity, he concealed the most artful purposes, and secured an admittance into the circles of fashion, which, in the form of a gentleman, he might vainly have endeavoured to obtain. He knew that in England, to be ridiculous is to become notorious; and that to become notorious, is to secure a welcome reception into the best society. His whiskers introduced him to court, and eclipsed, in the opinion of Bond-street, the singularities of Mr. Coates—his stories of his own exploits—his extracts from the Vienna Gazette, and his relations of a challenge on Mount Etna, and the extrication of a fellow creature from the waves of the Danube, excited the laughter of those who ought to have watched his conduct with suspicious seriousness; and after he had flattered the great, eclipsed the gay, and cajolled the possessors of office, he found little difficulty in his attempts at depredation on the subordinate instruments of fashionable luxury.

We wish not to become the instruments of unjust prejudice, or to efface any impression which may tend to humanize the European world, while it tends not to weaken our own security or to degrade the national character; but after endeavouring to correct the prejudices of education, by accurate observation, after long and frequent conversation with the best educated foreigners, and notwithstanding every disposition to view their conduct, as it respected our own political safety, in every point of view, we have been more and more impressed with the conviction, that their friendship is more dangerous than their hostility; and that our protection, where it extends beyond the strict limits of forbearance, only tends to give ability to ingratitude. Whether it arise from envy, from an unjust but involuntary ascription of the miseries of Europe to the councils of England, or from the disgust excited by the hauteur of our national character and habits; it is indisputably true, that our manners are viewed even by the most enlightened foreigners with inveterate prejudice; that even the cause of his own country becomes less dear to a foreign patriot, as soon as it becomes identified with that of England; and that the latent feeling of those whom temporary circumstances may have drawn into temporary residence among us, or a momentary coincidence in our politics, is the hope of emancipation from the weight of obligation to Britain. But if these be the prejudices of honorable men, what can be expected of subordinate persons, but that they should become the voluntary spies of any foreign court that will employ them; that they should regard us with mingled sentiments of envy and derision; and should hate us for the superiority of our moral character, while they laugh at our vanity and credulity?

To the introduction of Italian castratos, we should, in times of peace and tranquillity, be unwilling to object: it is better that such beings should be imported from Italy than *prepared* in England; but at the present moment we think that our nobility might dispense with their services: the singers themselves, and their wives, (for even these men have *superfluous* luxuries,) and the long train of their companions, retainers, and dependants, not only obtain a large proportion of the public money, but contribute to extend and confirm the dominion of immorality. Our virgins are frenchified and italianized, by a crowded succession of foreign music masters, teachers of the graces, and instructors in the continental tongues: alien artists convert the pencil into an instrument of seduction; and in the person of the youthful pupils of the Waltz, elegance and impurity become synonymous.

So forcibly indeed is the distinction between the moral character of the English, and of almost every foreign people impressed upon the minds of the middle classes, that productive as the great branch of medical quackery has always been to the adventures of our own countrymen, it has never succeeded in the hands of foreigners. They are not to be trusted in the bosom of a family; and the necessity of possessing in a medical practitioner, a domestic friend, is so obvious, as in this instance to have counteracted the usual bias of English credulity.

In the province of the arts their efforts to usurp the honors that ought to be the reward of native merit, have been hitherto more dangerous than successful: they have obtained at intervals a slight and momentary triumph; but the empire of art is at present in the undisturbed possession of our own countrymen. The true character of Dubost was discovered in sufficient time to counteract the effect of his intrigues: and but for the appointment of Stroehling as historical engraver to the Prince Regent, scarcely any foreigner would have found employment but in those subordinate departments of art, which an Englishman would be ashamed to execute, or would regard as too unprofitable for his attention. What pretensions that ostentatious dabbler in Greek may possibly possess to this honourable appointment, we are unable to conjecture; but the public would form a juster estimate of his professional talents from an examination of some of those excellent and classical produtions of the graver, which he has doubtless produced in the course of his progress as an artist, than from the obtrusive proof of ostentatious ignorance, that adorns the front of his house in Welbeck-street. There is in every thing about himself and his establishment an air of quackery, which degrades him if he possesses the slightest portion of ability, and if he be a mere pretender must ultimately lead to his public detection and disgrace.

The preceding reflections have been excited by the conduct of a professor Von Feinagle, a person who *professes* to have made the most wonderful discoveries in the science of memory, and has therefore kindly undertaken to deprive one half of the subscribers of the Surry Institution of their right of admission. We are informed that he has not only been introduced into the establishment to the exclusion and discountenance of English talent, but that one third of the institution is set apart for his lectures, and that to these lectures the subscribers can only gain admittance by the payment of money at the doors. Were not impudence the usual attendant on quackery, professor Von Feinagle might have condescended, before he thus came forward to insult and defraud the supporters of an establishment instituted for the promotion of scientific knowledge and literary taste, to shew in what his claims even to the privilege of lecturing at all consisted: his discourses contain no instruction of any kind; he talks a great deal of the science of mnemonics, and tells his audience when and where, and at what prices, he communicates instruction; but his quackery is an insult to the public, and his ignorance a disgrace to the institution. Of the discoveries that he professes to have made, he gives no evidence, except the expertness of two or three pupils in calculation; but real science is open and honorable: it does not descend to the tricks of Mr. Boaz; it communicates what it knows; it seeks to instruct rather than astonish; and its professors disdain to render their discourses the *media* of information respecting the *terms* on which at some other place and time, may be unfolded, that knowledge which it is their *present* duty to communicate.

Judging only from the mode in which the professor has chosen to announce his discoveries to the world, we should conceive ourselves guilty of no precipitate opinion were we to assert that the pretensions of the professor to the discovery of a new art of memory are destitute of any solid claim to the attention of the public. That he may drill a boy or a girl into the recollection of a multiplicity of figures that they have seen before, we shall not dispute; but that in six hours he can teach them without collusion, at the time of exhibition to perform *extempore* the most difficult problems, and remember the most intricate combinations, we positively disbelieve. If his mode of tuition be peculiar to himself, and can perform the wonders to which it pretends, his pupils would have disclosed the secret, and extended its utility: the truth is, we are persuaded, that there is no secret to disclose. All the improvement of which the art of memory is susceptible, was effected by the publication of Grey's *Memoria Technica*. Professor Porson, whom we have heard repeat two columns of the Courier, after once reading them, was indebted to nature and regular application, and not to any arcanum, for so wonderful a gift; and Seneca who could repeat two thousand words in any order, after once hearing them, makes no mention of any peculiar art or invention by which his memory was assisted. If Professor von Feinagle, who has so unkindly left the inhabitants of his native country to labour under all the imperfections of a natural memory, be really in possession of an important philosophical discovery, he can only avoid the reputation of quackery by disclosing it: so great a genius and philanthropist cannot surely be restrained from doing an important benefit to mankind, by the fear of losing those dirty *tokens* that he now receives for admission to his lectures; and it should not escape his recollection, that unaided by the communication of his " divine" art, the people of England may not only *forget* to pay him the honors that are due to his exalted merit, but may cease to remember, before the expiration of a thousand years, that such a personage existed.

THE HYPERCRITIC. No. VI.

THE GENERAL CHRONICLE, AND THE INQUISITION.

Of those periodical publications, which are too dry and insipid for the general reader, yet too superficial and imperfect for the scholar; which contain classical essays, that communicate no information to the learned, yet cannot be understood by the unlettered; and are adorned by engravings, that possess no interest with the usual purchasers of monthly works, yet are beneath the notice of a cultivator or admirer of the arts, the General Chronicle is an example: nor should we have devoted any portion of our time to so common-place a subject, had not our attention been attracted to an article, in which its editors endeavour to prove that the suppression of the inquisition in Spain is not a benefit. We do not intend, however, to examine the article at length; but to deduce from the origin* of the inquisition, its congeniality with the Roman Catholic religion, and to offer a few casual observations on the general tenor of their arguments.

Domingo de Guzman, better known as he stands in the Roman Calendar, by the name of St. Dominic, being employed against the Albigenses, invented the inquisition to accelerate the effect of his sermons. His invention was readily approved at Rome, and he himself nominated inquisitor general. In one day he beheaded four score persons, and four hundred were burnt alive, by his order and in his sight. The few traits of character, which can be gleaned from the volumes of St. Dominic's biographers are all of the darkest colours. He never looked a woman in the face, or spoke to one on his preaching expeditions; he usually slept in the churches, or upon a grave; he wore an iron chain round his body,

---

* See the Quarterly Review.

and his fastings and flagellations were excessive. But if his disciples have preserved few personal facts, concerning their master, they have made ample amends, by the catalogue of his miracles: for St. Dominic is the Orlando Furioso of saints errant---the Hercules Furens of the Romish demigods. The dream of his mother, during her pregnancy is well known, that she whelped a dog, holding a burning torch in his mouth, wherewith he fired the world. Earthquakes and miracles announced his nativity to the earth and air, and two or three suns and moons extraordinary, were hung out for an illumination in heaven. The Virgin Mary received him in her arms as he sprung to birth; when a sucking babe, he regularly observed fast days, and would get out of bed, and lie upon the ground as a penance. His manhood was as portentous as his infancy: he fed multitudes miraculously, and performed the miracle of Cana, with great success. Once when he fell in with a troop of pilgrims of different countries, the curse which had been inflicted at Babel, was suspended for him, and they all were enabled to speak one language. Travelling with a single companion, he entered a monastery in a lonely place to pass the night: he awoke at matins, and hearing yells and lamentations instead of prayers, went out, and discovered that he was among a brotherhood of devils. Dominic punished them upon the spot with a cruel sermon, and then returned to rest. At morning the convent had disappeared, and he and his comrade found themselves in a wilderness. He had one day an obstinate battle with the flesh: the quarrel took place in a wood, and finding it necessary to call in help, he stripped himself, and commanded the ants and the wasps to come to his assistance. Even against these auxiliaries the contest was continued for three hours, before the soul could win the victory. He used to be red-hot with divine love, sometimes blazing like a sun, sometimes glowing like a furnace. Once it sprung out in six wings, like a seraph; and once the fervor of his piety made him sweat blood:

So much for the miscellaneous miracles of St. Dominic: but they are not more curious than the two classes of the rosary, and those which refer to the Virgin Mary, which were invented to play off against the Franciscans. A knight to whom Dominic presented a rosary, arrived to such perfection of piety, that his eyes were opened, and he saw an angel take every bead as he dropped it, and carry it to the queen of heaven, who built with the whole string a palace upon a mountain in Paradise. A damsel, by name Alexandra, induced by Dominic's preaching, used the rosary; but her heart followed too much after the things of the world: two young men, who were rivals for her, fought, and both fell in the combat; and their relations in revenge cut off her head, and threw it into a well. The devil immediately seized her soul; but for the sake of the rosary, the Virgin interfered, rescued the soul out of his hands, and gave it permission to remain in the head at the bottom of the well, till it should have an opportunity of confessing, and being absolved. After some days, this was revealed to Dominic, who went to the well and told Alexandra in God's name to come up: the bloody head obeyed, perched on the well side, confessed its sins, received absolution, took the wafer, and continued to edify the people for two days, when the soul departed to pass a fortnight in purgatory on its way to heaven. But these were trifling miracles: the bells at Thoulouse rang of their own accord to welcome Dominic's arrival, and signs and wonders commanded the reverence of the inhabitants of that city. As the saint was reading one day, the devil annoyed him in the shape of a flea, skipping backward and forward upon the page, in order to divert his attention from the devout subject before him; but Dominic soon spoiled his sport, for he fixed him as a mark at the place where he left off, and used him in this manner through the whole volume. On another occasion the devil came to teize him in the form of a monkey: Dominic was too much used to such visits to be embarrassed by them: he called him to hold the candle, which he made him do, till it had burnt down to the snuff, to the sore annoyance of the paw which held it. A tolerable epigram on this legend may be found in Sautel's *Annus Sacer*.

> Dum tulit ardentem Phlegetontius histrio cercem,
> Tum certe aut nunquam, *Lucifer* ille fuit.

In one of his visits to heaven, Dominic was carried before the throne of Christ, where he beheld many religionists of both sexes, but none of his own order. This so afflicted him, that he began to lament aloud, and inquired why they did not appear in bliss. Christ laying his hand upon the Virgin's shoulder, said, I have committed your order to my mother's care; and she lifting up her robe, discovered an innumerable multitude of Dominican friars and nuns, nestled under it. Let not the reader suppose that this is a protestant invention. It stands as it is here represented in the prayer book of the order.

But though the Dominicans pride themselves upon the establishment of the inquisition by their sainted founder, they do not consider him as the inventor of that tribunal. At the close of the sixteenth century, Luis de Paramo, who was a canon of Leon, and an inquisitor in the kingdom of Sicily, published a work; " *De origine et progressu* officii sancta inquisitionis, ejusque dignitate et utilitate." God, according to this writer, was the first inquisitor, and the first *auto-da-fe* was held in the garden of Eden. God cited Adam, because the process would otherwise have been null, and upon the culprit's appearance he *inquired*, that is *made inquisition* into the crime. The man accused his wife, after which the judge questioned her also: the serpent he did not examine, because of his obstinacy, for *angeli post adhesionem, immobiliter rebus adhærent, inflexibile habent liberum arbitrium, nec discurrere possunt.* Both parties were separately examined, and in secret, to prevent collusion, and no witness were called, because confession and conscience are as good as a thousand witnesses, and then the judge had nothing to do but to pass sentence. Even the garment which penitent offenders are compelled to wear, is after the pattern of the cloaths which God made for Adam and Eve; and because Adam and Eve were expelled from Paradise, for that reason all the property of a heretic is to be confiscated.

Abraham was an inquisitor, and so was Sarah; which is thus clearly proved from the words of Scripture. She turned Ishmael out of doors for idolatry. He saw him playing with Isaac. Now what is intended by the word playing. *Ludere*, says St. Jerome, is *idololatrare*. Nicholas de Lyra commenting upon a certain passage expounds *udentem* to mean *idolola-trantem*, and therefore it is plain that Ishmael was turned out for idolatry. In this manner does Paramo proceed through the Pentateuch, and the books of Joshua and Judges.

The inquisition was suspended after its work of exterminating the Albigenses was completed: it was revived in Spain upon the Jews, who had enjoyed more intervals of prosperity in that country than in any other part of christendom. When Alphonso VI. won the city of Toledo, the Jews who dwelt there, waited upon him and assured him that they were descended from part of the ten tribes whom Nebuchadnezzar had transported into Spain, not from the Jews of Jerusalem who had crucified Christ. They produced letters from the synagogue to Caiaphas the high priest, remonstrating against the death of Jesus, in the original Hebrew, and in Arabic, as they had been translated by order of King Galifre. It was a bold stratagem, and for some time succeeded to their wish; but the evil days of the Jews were at hand: Ferdinand and Isabel obtained from Sextus IV. the privilege of creating inquisitors, and six years after the work of devastation began; an auto-da-fé was celebrated at Guadaloupe, where 52 persons of both sexes, convicted of judaizing, after compulsory conversion, were buried alive: the images of 25 who had escaped, and the bodies of 46 dug from their graves, were in like manner committed to the flames : 16 were condemned to perpetual imprisonment, and they who were sentenced to the galleys, or to do perpetual penance in the dress of infamy, are said to have been innumerable. All professed Jews were ordered to leave the town within a month, at the end of that term strict inquisition was made for them, and above 2000 were burnt in different parts of the country as an example. But even this was but a beginning. The inquisitors who held their sittings at Guadulupe in the immediate presence as it were of the great goddess of that celebrated temple, were earnest in their entreaties that she would favor them with some miraculous sign of her approbation. The goddess condescended to this request. One of the inquisitors, by name Francisco Sanchez de la Fuente, took upon himself the office of recording the prodigies which were manifested: sixty miracles he wrote down, and then gave up the task, because his pen could not keep pace with the wonders which were worked. The system, thus begun, soon extended itself over all Spain : and before 1520, 4000 persons had been burnt in Seville, and 30 condemned to wear the *san benito* and to lose all their property. In the single diocese of Seville 100,000 were destroyed, converted, or driven into exile; and (as the catholic historians boast) in the city 3000 houses were left without inhabitants. Its subsequent progress was equally cruel, and is better known.

II. The first bloody harvest of the inquisition was over in Spain before it began in Portugal. A swindler effected what Rome had once before in vain attempted. This man's name was Juan de Saavedra. Having long lived by his wits, and being especially dexterous in forging public grants, he conceived that it would be a good speculation to act as inquisitor in Portugal; he accordingly made a journey into that country, for the purpose of reconnoitering it. Returning towards Andalusia, he met with a member of a newly established order, probably a jesuit, coming from Rome with certain bulls relating to its establishment. He had not been named himself to any place of trust and honour in these bulls, and this had soured him. Saavedra offered to forge new ones for him, and insert his name in the manner he desired, which was done accordingly, and the forger retained the originals for his own purpose. Having now a prototype before him, he drew up such a bull as he wanted, and affixed to it the genuine seals. This was done at Tavira in Algarve. His next measure was to return to Ayamonte, where there was a provincial of the Franciscans, who had lately arrived from Rome. Saavedra made his appearance in the character of a simple man, saying that six well drest men travelling post, had dropped those parchments on the road, which he had found shortly afterwards, and knowing that the provincial understood such things, he had brought them to him, meaning if they were of any consequence, to lose no time in following the persons to whom they must have belonged. The Franciscan examined the parchment, and was delighted to find that it was a bull for the establishment of the holy office, sent as it appeared by a cardinal. The cardinal he supposed was going either to Seville or Badajos, there to remain till things were ready for his reception in Portugal, and he concluded that he must be a young man by the indecorous speed with which he travelled. He charged Saavedra therefore to lose no time, but make it a matter of conscience to follow him as fast as possible.

The imposter had two reasons for proceeding in this manner; he wished to satisfy himself that the forgery was well executed, and with all the customary forms, which the provincial was well able to ascertain; his other motive was to spread about the tidings which would facilitate his operations. The next business was by means of his accomplices, one of whom acted as his secretary, to establish a household at Seville. They engaged six score domestics, and the chapel was fitted up for the cardinal's reception. At a fit time they gave out that they were going to Badajos to wait for their master there: accordingly all the baggage was packed up and they departed, but when they had proceeded a few miles, Saavedra met them: they received him with the greatest expressions of joy and surprise, and returned to Seville, where he made his entrance amid the rejoicings of the whole people. Here he was lodged in the archbishop's palace, and remained twenty days, during which he produced a bond for 13,000 ducats on the Marquis of Tarifa for money lent at Rome: the date was accurate, the signature well executed, and he found no difficulty in obtaining them. Having done this he moved on to Badajos, and from thence dispatched his secretary to the King of Portugal with letters from the pope and from the emperor. The king was astonished, and expressed displeasure by the manner of his silence; the secretary was alarmed and hastily returning to Saavedra, entreated him to be content with what they had already gained, and to think only of enjoying it in security. The dauntless swindler, however, persisted in his project, sent his accomplice back to Lisbon, and directed him not to leave the palace till he had received an explicit answer from the king: he told him also not to forget to observe that the cardinal was a young man, and would immediately return to Rome with the answer, be what it might. After taking twenty days to consider of it, the king complied. The impostor was lodged three months in the palace, and spent three months more in travelling about the country, exercising his inquisitorial powers wherever he went, and amassing money to a degree which seems to have bigoted him, otherwise he would have decamped in time.

The trick was discovered in Spain, and the Marquis of Barca Rota, having made a priest at Moura invite the mock cardinal to a feast on St. Ildefonzo's day, seized him and sent him prisoner to Madrid. Cardinal Tavira who was at that time grand inquisitor and governor of Castile, during the emperor's absence, examined him, and sent an account of the whole proceedings to the pope. Saavedra had speculated well, and the very magnitude of the imposture contributed to save him. He had done that for the Romish church, which the pope himself had been unable to effect; and the holy father, concluding that it must be the especial favor of heaven to bring about a good work by such extraordinary means, recommended a merciful sentence, and hinted that he should like to see the man who acted so remarkable a part. The royal council demanded sentence of death, but the cardinal favored him: the inquisitor of Llerena was appointed judge, and he escaped with condemnation to the galleys for ten years. Light as this sentence was, it was not carried into effect. Charles V. admiring the audacity of the man, was curious to see him, and having heard his defence, admitted that so good an end might be admitted in justification of the means, and rewarded him with a pension.

Such was the origin of a tribunal, which in its progress has been productive of the most dreadful miseries, and of which the revival would be accompanied by a repetition of every ancient scene of murder and atrocity. Yet the authors of the General Chronicle contend that the suppression of the inquisition is not a benefit to the people of Spain, because it is at present nothing more than " a censorship of books," and the learned and the wise should not be allowed to trample upon what the poor, the languishing, the ignorant, the feeble minded, hold sacred, and dear, and supporting, and consoling. In other words, we ought never to dissipate any prejudice or delusion, because it may be dear to the weak and the ignorant: the reformation ought not to have been begun, because it aroused many millions of the catholic church from pleasing but deceitful dreams, and the reign of bigotry ought to be perpetual. These writers forget that the inquisition is only harmless, because it is no longer beneath the guidance of political power, that Bonaparte might still convert it into the instrument of political tyranny, and that the only means of preventing its future abuse is its present dissolution. We hope that the doctrines of the protestant religion are not so detestable in their nature or effects, as to diffuse unhappiness, wherever they are imbibed, and we cannot sympathize therefore in the attachment of the General Chroniclers towards the inquisition, as a means of excluding from the Spaniards the " heresies" of Locke, and Clarke, and Tillotson.

D-----L SEDUCTION;

OR,

CORRESPONDENCE EXTRAORDINARY.

Sir,

When the uncle of the present Colonel of the * * * reg. of Dragoons invaded the domestic rights, and destroyed the domestic happiness of a peer of the realm, the example was regarded by the loyal with alarm, and by the virtuous with abhorrence. Since that period so many instances of similar indiscretion have occurred in the family of the late ------ of ---------, that the vices of its junior branches cease to be any longer the object of fear or detestation: the matron is not ashamed to associate with the objects of their illicit attachments, and the patriot having witnessed the patience and indifference with which their deviations from the paths of virtue have been regarded by the people, laments their errors as productive of personal unhappiness, rather than as the causes or the forerunners of political commotion.

Yet it might have been supposed that the Colonel, himself after his miraculous escape from the fury of jealous revenge, would have been taught the danger and the folly of perseverance in pursuits so criminal, as those which provoked the revengeful passions of his servant. The profligate of forty, who after innumerable escapes from the just punishment of his iniquities, displays no signs of returning virtue, may deserve the pity of his friends but cannot claim the indulgence of the moralist. The conduct of an individual whose station in society enables him to influence the moral feelings of the community is a just subject of literary observation; and if the general tendency of his pursuits and manners be pernicious, he has no right to complain if the satirist have as little regard to his individual feelings, as he himself displays towards the virtue and happiness of the dependants who surround him.

I call upon you, therefore, as an honest and impartial censor, with whom there ought to be no respect of persons, to hold up to the execration of a British public, his late violation of every principle of honor, and of all the usual decencies of life, in seducing from the arms of her husband, and taking beneath his open and avowed protection, the wife of a man whom he once disgraced by the name of friend, and who had deserved by important services the gratitude of this unfeeling and shameless seducer. Forgetful of the common sentiments of manhood, he first gained access to the bosom of the family, as a man of sorrow seeking consolation in the bosom of friendship; and insensible to the responsibility of his station in society, and regardless of the opinions of the world, he openly laughs at the credulity of the man whom he has injured, and proclaims to the extensive circle of his dependants the conquest he has made. To *him*, therefore, all delicacy would be foolish; nor can any relation of the circumstances attending her seduction, lacerate the feelings of the object of his adulterous love in her present state of degradation.

It is probable that neither remorse for the crime that he had committed, nor vexation at the damages awarded in a court of justice, had so beneficial and salutary effect on his late uncle, as the publication of the correspondence between him and the object of his affections. That the appearance of the subjoined letters will be productive of equal benefit, after comparing the two characters, I dare not hope; but if it do not shame the Colonel into virtue, it may teach him the value of discretion, and repress his propensity to relate the particulars of his triumph, till he has destroyed the documents by which his falsehoods may be detected and exposed.

I.

Dear ——,   *Monday Evening.*

I think you will find the scheme is not so easy as you flatter yourself. He will not be absent longer than two, and Anne remains to dinner, so that you had better do nothing till I see you, which may be to-morrow. Pray do not come to breakfast.

I saw ——— yesterday, and though he looked as blythe as *May*, —— did not look pleased. I am sure that he is the person. I am in *earnest*.

II.

Dearest darling   *Monday Evening* 10 *o'clock*

How your lovely letter frightened me particularly about Anne as the thing is very unfortunate if you suffer her to spoil all the opportunities and o my dear dear love if you knew how impatient your true ——— is to see you in spite of that man who I declare is unworthy of so sweet a jewel though I am glad he suspects brother —— as it may save us some trouble O if you knew how often I dream of your little hand and fancy that I am folding your dear dear bozom in such ecstacy as you have no idea of we go to morrow my charmer to ——— where P——— is to be and sister in law so that you see we are not the only miserable parted lovers o when I come do not speak to me in that cruel way if I had ten thousand thousand crowns they should all lie at your pretty feet at 6 I call on ——— who is to speak about the nation and we are all to give our protestations which I have consented though I think it will all be the same thing in the end you should have had a ring from Phillips auction where I saw your husband but was afraid that he would ask you whose gift it was which might lead to discoveries o my dearest love how I do long to see you and the great Pope says love opens his white wings and in a moment flies o I wish I could do so to my dear lovely creature but cruel fate makes me say adieu.

III.

(No signature or date)

The conversation we had together makes me more uneasy the longer I think of it. Depend upon it you will be discovered, and if you be, think for a moment what you have done. You have subjected me to the punishment of guilt, though heaven knows my innocence. I am now at your mercy, if you love me you will cease your visits and destroy these letters. For God's sake remember that my fortune, character, and happiness are in your disposal, and that you may be the guardian or betrayer of my peace. I can say no more.

IV.

Thursday, 3 *o'clock.*

My love should not be alarmed for her husband who never dreams of any such thing o how can you be so foolish heavens guardian stars protect the lovely creation and you cannot think what daggers your last letter gave me you know that I am sincere in loving you and if you did remember me as you say you would not be thus hesitating sure you cannot refuse to meet me at the Opera to night you should not mind the low ones who may stare at you but it is all envy and your husband may look black but he knows nothing and suspicion wont do we were at O——— yesterday and had music and a large company there was huge F. there and he and old Paunchy cast ogling eyes at each other till we were almost suffocated with keeping in our laughter it was very curious particularly to see Dr——— the chaplain eat the turtle soup at such a pace o my dear you would have laughed and I longed all the while for you to be there the custards were charming and I took too much madeira which this morning has made me cursed sick so you will excuse this scribble though your own dear hand is rather difficult to be cyphered W——— promised to lend me a thousand but I thought your dear dear purse would not be empty and the more as mine come three weeks after this though I mortally hate receiving it not knowing much of those stupid accounts which makes me admire P. who they say is a very clever fellow at such things but there is some difference between us and such people who are obliged to them being nothing naturally nor of consequence which makes me conclude this letter for want of room o my dearest assure yourself I am your true friend Adieu

V.

Monday Morning.

The more I think on the transactions of Saturday night, the more I hate the present, and dread the future. Did you know how much remorse and anxiety has rent my bosom, since it was pressed to yours, you would pity me. Every time I look on my husband, I feel how ungratefully I have acted, and how degraded I have become. The mansion in which I live, is no longer the scene of domestic pleasure; every thing around me, reminds me of what I was, and what I might have been: life beneath the roof of the injured is insupportable, and if you possess either love or compassion, you will take me from hence. I would sooner confess my guilt, than be obliged to act continually the part of a hypocrite. I know too, from the looks and the whispers of the servants, that all is discovered. Under such circumstances, my only refuge is beneath your protection; your rank will secure me from open insult, and to be always near you, will be some compensation for all the miseries I have endured to your unhappy friend:

VI.

My dear lovey will see by the enclosed letter that it is all managed as it ought to be you will get it copied and put in.

VII.

To A—— ——.   *January 26th,* 1812.

Sir,

If beauty and kindness be not disagreeable to a gallant officer, come to St. James's-square, at five o'clock. A lady in a pink coloured turban, parting an orange, will return your salute.

Ophelia.

VIII.

February 26th.

Sir,

I am not to be trifled with: send me the sum I ask, and all the letters in your possession, or by all that is tremendous, I will expose you. Your wife shall know all, and then if you appear to the world in the light of a despicable wretch, you will have to blame nobody, but yourself. Yours, as you act,

M——— L———.

IX.

Madam, *March 11th.*

Your violence has restored me to myself; though I have become the dupe of an artful woman, I will never submit to be the slave of a mercenary virago: having convinced me that you are utterly destitute of principle and feminine feeling, you have saved me from an act of generous fondness, that would have completed your triumph and ruined the victim of your hypocrisy. I thank you for the haste with which you have unveiled your real character, and am with *due* respect;

Madam,

To Miss M——— L——— Your most obedient servant,

N.

X

Sir, *Thursday Morning.*

The detection of your correspondence with Miss M——— L——— has determined me to leave your house, and throw myself on the protection of one who knows how to appreciate female worth, and can distinguish between love and mercenary attachment. An answer to this letter will reach me at ——— house.

N.

XI.

March 13.

If you still retain any affection for a husband whose only fault has been too blind and enthusiastic a regard for your happiness, and who but for the singularity of your late conduct would have shrunk with abhorrence from the thought of causing you a moment's uneasiness, for his sake as well as your

own, return to his protection. After what has past we never can be happy, but the censures of the world, will not reach you in the bosom of your family, or may die away and be forgotten. Your afflicted father joins in this request with
Your unfortunate husband,
N.

XII.

Thursday, April 2d.

Your depredations on my fortune, under pretext of necessity, and in the form of a pretended friend, I could have easily forgiven; but no elevation of rank, shall place you beyond the reach of an injured husband: the gentleman who delivers this is my friend, and will convey to me your sentiments, and as nothing but your refusal to wave the privileges of your rank, can deprive me of the satisfaction of a man of honor, he is authorized to mention the time, place, and manner of our meeting.

I have the honor to be,

———'s   Your most obedient servant,
N.

XIII.

Dear N.   *Half past eight o'clock.*

I waited upon his ———, and was received with politeness bordering on impertinence. He assured me that nothing on earth shall induce him to wave his privilege, on so trifling an affair, and he is determined not to receive any further intimations from a man who understands, or regards so little the common observances due to his rank and station.

Yours, truly,
R. G———R.

From the preceding correspondence it will be seen that previous to the elopement of the lady, a plan was concerted between her and her noble lover, by which they might not only throw the blame on the admiral, but prevent the possibility of a divorce; for this purpose a cast off mistress of the ——— was selected as the instrument of their intrigue, and in her name No. 7 was transmitted. Her blandishments overcame the a———'s fortitude, and after she had succeeded sufficiently for every purpose of evidence, she wrote No. 8, and sent it at such a moment, and in such a manner, that it might be opened by Mrs. ———— in the presence of her husband, and thus afford a pretext of elopement, that in the eyes of the fashionable world might almost appear to justify her infidelity. On the cowardice of evading the a——'s resentment by crouching behind the shield of privilege, or on the meanness and insensibility that have characterized every part of his ————'s conduct in the progress of the intrigue, and subsequent to the elopement, it would be superfluous to comment.

If I am not grossly misinformed the ———— is indebted to the husband, whose domestic happiness he has destroyed, in no less a sum than 20,000*l.* lent him for the supply of his necessities. Elopements are always accompanied by expence, and it is probable that the messengers from his to the admiral's house were paid for out of his own money. What a glorious example does the conduct of the seducer afford to the nobility of the kingdom! With what gratitude must every domestic man look up to the junior branches of a family so expert and so notorious in every description of intrigue, and in all the arts that contribute to the destruction of domestic happiness!

BRUTUS.

THE POLITICAL OBSERVER. No. X.

TO THE EDITOR OF THE SCOURGE.

SIR, *Glasgow, April* 18*th*, 1811.

I PERUSED the last number of your Scourge, (as indeed all the preceding ones,) with much satisfaction; but while the general sentiments contained in it appear to me highly creditable to your independence and to the abilities of their writers, there is a particular passage in the Political Observer for April, which I consider deserving of marked reprobation. It is as follows, "at present much as the people detest Lord Castlereagh, and despise the puppets who have been selected to fill the vacancies that might have been occupied by an Erskine or a Grey, they would rather obey the worst and most venial of the present ministry, than witness the unconditional return of the whigs."

Now, Sir, should this be admitted, all expectations of any change, and consequently of any improvement must be abandoned; and if such sentiments should unhappily be general, we have nothing to expect but the continuance of Mr. Perceval in office, and of those measures that have brought this country to its present state, and will ultimately bring it to total ruin.

For my own part I must confess, I would rather submit to the worst and most venial of the present ministry, and there never was a ministry in which such characters did so predominate, than witness any other than the unconditional return of the whigs— because did they abandon their former principles, they abandon the very things for which I conceive them deserving of support; and because in doing it they would shew themselves to be as base and venial as these whom they should displace.

When I see persons speaking, like your Political Observer *in this instance*, who in place of descending to argument, content themselves with abuse (even though that abuse may extend to both parties,) I am apt to think them only Percevalites in disguise, who wisely consider that the best method of defending the present is by abusing the late ministry—as though their friends may suffer at the same time, nothing can render them more thoroughly despicable than they at present are, while by this means they may (which is all they want) reduce the opposition to a level with themselves.

I do not pretend, Sir, to defend the sudden change of tone on the part of the opposition towards the Prince Regent: they now treat him as I think they long ought to have done—and what I blame them for, is not unmerited abuse now, but unmerited praise before—the filial duty which induced the Prince during the restrictions, to retain Mr. Perceval and his associates in office, proved so new a feature in his character, that for my part, I could not help feeling some surprise and a little suspicion, and time has verified my fears.

The Prince's letter to the Duke of York, I have always considered as a mere trick unworthy of his R. H——. However respectable those in power, it could not be expected nor even desired, (since it could only be effected by a sacrifice of principle) that the opposition should coalesce with those they had so long opposed, and in doing so, abandon all there former professions;—and to say that a united and powerful administration could not be formed unless Mr. Perceval, and Lords Castlereagh and Sidmouth formed component parts, is what few I believe will be weak enough to assert.

Permit me to add, that it appears to me rather hard to hold the whig leaders responsible for every paragraph in the Morning Chronicle—and that it strikes me as rather demeaning them, to make them act as editors to a daily newspaper.

But, Sir, the reasons why I consider that Lords Grey and Grenville and their friends merit a preference, is not that I conceive them altogether pure and blameless, but because I think them greatly more so than their political opponents; because they are of the first rank, character, and ability, while the others are equally destitute of each; and because, infinite good may result from a change of men and measures, while I cannot think it possible for worse ministers to be in power, or worse measures to be pursued than at present.

To conclude, Sir, the opposition recommend the concession of the catholic claims. They recommend a more conciliating spirit towards America and other powers, and while they do not wish us to abandon the war or our allies, they recommend a little more attention to economy in the prosecution of it; and since their conduct has shewn that they would not, like some others, sacrifice every principle of honor or duty to a continuance in office, I conceive them for these reasons deserving of support.

I am, Sir,
Your humble servant,
D. L.

We have inserted the preceding communication, because it comprizes, within a reasonable compass, the substance of a multitude of letters, and because the greater part of the positions it contains, will best be answered by the reflections that have been naturally excited by the political discussions of the month. We must confess, however, at the outset, that we do not see the impossibility of a compromise between the opposing parties: to yield a little on both sides has been the usual practice of men, who regarded their personal aggrandisement as only secondary to the promotion of their country's welfare: to lay it down as a maxim of political virtue, that the leaders of the two great parties can never coalesce, is to subject the monarch to the necessity of unconditional compliance with all the wishes of his selected counsellors. He cannot, according to the reasoning of our correspondent, accept the services of Lord Grenville, because that nobleman supports the emancipation of the catholics, without acquiescing in every mistaken opinion, or sanctioning every hasty resolution that he may have once expressed. Suppose for a moment that the Prince is resolved to persevere in the Peninsula war and to support the orders in council, and is yet inclined to emancipate the catholics; his decision is probably as wise as that of either party, and is certainly accordant with the wishes of the people, yet according to the doctrines of those who contend for the impossibility of a coalition, he would be unable to form a ministry that should carry his system of policy into execution.

But the assertion that a coalition would be impossible, comes with peculiar effect from the admirers of Fox and the retainers of Grenville: from the eulogists of a man who united in the strictest coalition with an inveterate political enemy, on whom he had exhausted every epithet of abuse; and from the partizans of a nobleman, who now condescends to make a common cause with those " lower Foxites," whose principles at one time he affected to abhor, and whom just before the death of Mr. Fox, he declared to be a mean, selfish and intemperate crew, of whom the aristocracy ought to be ashamed!

We shall admit, for a moment, because we have not time to dispute its truth, that the members of opposition outshine their rivals in ability; but if their talents be great, they are not of that description which renders an administration useful at home, and formidable abroad. Of what use are the accomplishments of the scholar, and the wit, unaccompanied by practical wisdom, and by habits of official regularity? We have seen the opposition in place, and what did they do? Indolence and irresolution were the characteristics of their progress; nor did they retire from situations, of which they had not fulfilled the duties, without robbing the unhappy people, who are now persuaded to clamour for their return, of sinecures and pensions to a greater amount than all the grants and defalcations of any seven years of Mr. Pitt's administration.

We can see no reason why the Prince Regent, in the choice of his ministry, must necessarily select his servants from one party or the other; but so long as this necessity is admitted, we must prefer, on the whole, the friends of Mr. Perceval. The *ins* are intent upon robbery, but they commit their depredations openly: the *outs* have already stolen the most valuable articles within their reach, and look forward to the prospect of future booty;

yet continue from day to day, to *cant* about patriotism and honesty; to commiserate the distresses of the people, and to declaim on the necessity of reform and œconomy. For their personal claims on the support and admiration of the public, they have no claims to superiority, but in the qualifications that facilitate the commission of profligacy without fear or shame, and the pursuit of political intrigue. Regarding the two parties as the authors and originators of certain political measures, we think that the Perceval administration is more likely to benefit the country, and deserve its gratitude than any which could be formed by the leaders of the opposite party. To the public there is only a choice of difficulties.— The men in power oppose the emancipation of the catholics, but support the orders in council, and persevere in the war of the Peninsula: to the last two divisions of our policy, the opposition are decidedly hostile; while on their services in the catholic cause, they rest their claim to the support of the Irish members. Now we think that considering the urgency of the question respecting the Peninsular war, the known sentiments of the outs respecting it, would afford sufficient ground in the opinion of those who regard the Spanish cause as neither unjust nor hopeless, for their exclusion from the Regent's councils. The catholic question may be postponed to times of quietness and content; the orders in council might be modified or given up, and reissued after the experiment in their original force; but the war in the Peninsula must be supported with vigor, or immediately abandoned. It is one of the misfortunes, therefore, that the exclusion of the opposition from power, cannot, even supposing the admission of all their reasonings, be productive of any immediate danger: the continuance of our troops in Portugal, for a few months longer, even supposing the Peninsular war to be impolitic, our perseverance a little longer in the orders in council, or the temporary postponement of the catholic discussion, cannot be productive of an immediate or fatal effect on the interests of the empire: while the effect of their return to power, supposing them to act up to their former principles, would be instantaneous, and if pernicious irretrievable. Of the Peninsular war, we have always been the enthusiastic, but not the irrational supporters: it is some encouragement to look forward with hope, that our former prophecies—prophecies hazarded in defiance of the forebodings of our adversaries, have been fulfilled beyond the expectation of the most ardent patriots: our success has been so striking and so undeniable, that those who at first reprobated our expeditions because victory was impossible, are now reduced to ask in what the use of victory consists, or to deplore the inadequacy of our resources to extensive operations in foreign warfare. The question of economy we shall dismiss, by observing that reform at home would more than repay us for ten years of protracted warfare on the Peninsula; and that since the sinecures and pensions obtained by the opposition, from the public purse, more than equal in amount the whole of the expences incurred by Lord Wellington during the last year, they could not more effectually testify their attachment to their king and country than by resigning them. If our dangers and difficulties be so great as the opposition represent them to be, there is the greater necessity for keeping the enemy at a distance. If we be on the brink of ruin, let us fight our enemy on the last outwork, rather than suffer him to attack the citadel itself. If a mighty machine under the direction of a skilful engineer, be about to be directed against us, it is better to prevent its play, and retard its motion, by entangling the wheels, or deranging the machinery, than to await the shock of its collected force. When Spain is conquered, England only remains; while Spain is unsubdued, England is secure: if the struggle in the Peninsula be favorable to liberty, other nations and other countries will be aroused to the assertion of their independence; if, on the contrary, our efforts be fruitless, we have fulfilled our duty to Europe, and to ourselves; we have done all that honorable valour could perform: the conquest of our own country is as distant as at the beginning of the contest; and our officers and troops have learned in a foreign clime to defend their native shores, and protect their paternal dwellings.

The determination, therefore, of the Regent to persevere in our present system of foreign warfare, was understood by the people, with a satisfaction that overpowered for a while, every sentiment of sorrow or surprize. But acts of fatuity like the reinstatement of Lord Castlereagh and the appointment of Col. Macmahon, (both of which we presume must be regarded as the acts of the minister,) cannot be repeated without receiving their just reward; nor did we *dare* to express the feeling of the public, in language proportionate to its warmth, should the adviser of His Royal Highness venture by any measures of equal infamy to exasperate an injured and insulted people. We will venture to assert that there is not to be found in the annals of the English history, an act of such wilful and gratuitous iniquity, so openly and avowedly committed in opposition to the wishes of the people, and in defiance of the most unequivocal expressions of the popular indignation as the reinstatement of Lord Castlereagh. In other days the dependants and parasites of a weak or profligate minister have been loaded with honors, and entrusted with the most important interests of the empire; but it was reserved for the present momentous æra to witness the return to an important office of an individual, from the delineation of whose character we are only restrained by the recollection, that to his immaculate reputation more than one public writer have been already sacrificed.

On this and other subjects of complaint, we are glad that the corporation of London possesses and exercises the right of expressing its opinion, however much we disapprove of several propositions advanced in the speeches of Mr. Waithman and his friends, and expressed in the printed resolutions. Neither the Prince Regent nor his counsellors, examine the specific points, that have become the subject of civic discussion: popular petitions are chiefly useful, as expressing the general bias of public opinion, and as affording to the sovereign, or his parasites *tangible* proof of the existence of an independent spirit. The Prince and his courtiers are well aware to what part of their public conduct they may justly ascribe the formal expression of popular sentiment: if many injudicious topics, and many unconstitutional doctrines be introduced into a petition, they detract but little from its general effect. Reform and the Duke of York, may be injudiciously mentioned at the present crisis of affairs; but were not the general conduct of the Prince Regent the subject of popular dissatisfaction, they would not have formed the subordinate topics in a list of grievances.

That the nation labours indeed under great and accumulated burdens is too evident from the solemn and melancholy silence, with which the people have witnessed the accession of the Regent to supreme authority. The combined impulse of adulation and the love of novelty, has been insufficient to arouse the people to the expression of any feelings accordant with so joyful an event. It is in vain that the antijacobins endeavour to persuade the people that they are perfectly happy, and ought to be the most joyous of mankind. Taxes, bankruptcies, and the cessation of labour, present themselves to view in undisguised and tangible reality.

That the quantity of national wealth is greater than at any former period of our history, and that those of the common classes, who do obtain employment, are better fed, and more copiously supplied with all the comforts of life than their immediate predecessors, we are disposed to admit; but is it a necessary consequence of our paper credit and the extent of our commerce, that wealth should be unequally diffused, and that while many of the lower classes enjoy even the luxuries of life, their fellow men should only be able to obtain an uncertain and scanty subsistence. Where many are rich, the majority are uncomfortable; the gentry are dwindling away, and there is no alternative between want and speculation. A fortune or nothing, is now the general choice; the annuitants have become too poor to support many dependants; their servants and relatives seek for employment in the houses of the wealthy, or become a part of the manufacturing or commercial community. In either case the majority have no capital to begin business for themselves, and cannot always find employment as subordinates. The new outlets to labour and speculation that we have lately discovered, do not compensate for the cessation of several branches of European trade: a spirit of adventure has been excited, and just when it was about to ripen into active maturity, its operations have been circumscribed within the most narrow bounds ; nor can any remedy be found for the miseries of our situation, but a total revolution in the affairs of Europe.

In the popular clamour against the pernicious effects of our paper system, we have always been unwilling to acquiesce. That the paper currency of this country has of late enormously increased, and almost entirely supplanted the use of specie, is certainly true; but we see in this increase nothing but what is ultimately advantageous to the commercial interest. The credit of individuals will always sooner or later find its level, and although some, by speculating in the public confidence in banknotes and paper money of every description, are enabled to raise fortunes without capital, and to live merely by assisting to depreciate the circulating medium, without adding any thing to the stock of commodities, we will venture to assert that they could not exist very long in such a false warmth, did not the individuals whose labours actually produce commodities find it their interest to afford their support. Many country bankers may be considered as nothing more than the banking clerks of the opulent manufacturers, land-holders, and inland traders in their respective neighbourhoods. The wealth of which these notes may be the representative, is not their own; but they are agents for the value of that wealth, which is in the hands of their employers. In all this we are so far from perceiving any thing reprehensible, that we are ready to congratulate the country on the credit which enables it to export its specie to those markets, where it may again become the price and the payment of commodities, the produce of British labour and of British commerce.

What then is the evil to which our paper currency gives the greatest support? The prosperity of a commercial and manufacturing country, while it adds to the comforts and to the enjoyments of those whose pursuits are attached to the course of its opulence, necessarily, by the depreciation which it causes in the value of money, contracts the powers of those who possess invariable annuities: these as well as the stock-holder must certainly see and feel their property sink yearly in value, without the means of preventing it. Since the vast accumulation of national debt, the number of persons whose sole or chief property consists of stock in the public funds, must be very considerable, and if we add to them the number of those whose sole or chief property consists of annuities, mortgages, or other charges upon land, the amount will probably appear not very insignificant when compared with that of the land-holders themselves. The great bias of the nation is to the active increase of property, and those who cannot sustain the rush of the current, but are compelled to drift in the shallows on either side, must be contented with a fate for which it is impossible to point out a remedy. The evil is great, but we are afraid that it is necessary. The circulation of credit is necessary to a state of unrestrained and extended commerce, and to the retention of that portion of national prosperity that we actually possess; and though the resumption of cash payments, might render that credit more secure, it would not have any tendency to alleviate the distresses that arise from that extension of the funding system to which the utility of a paper medium is proportionate.

ENGLISH INQUISITORS.

Sir,

In an early number of your work, you presented the public with a report of the society for the persecution of the poor, so perfectly descriptive of its' nature and pursuits, that no one can hereafter apologize for the commission of obnoxious acts on the Lord's day, by pretending ignorance of the pains and penalties, with which he may be visited. It is to be feared, however, that many of those who well know what is criminal, may feel some difficulty in determining what is *not so;* and I crave permission, therefore, in order to relieve them from their present state of hesitation and uncertainty, to lay before you a list of the enormities, that do not come within the cognizance, or usually obtain the sanction and approval of the suppressors and reformers. As this object will be best effected in particular instances, by opposition and comparison, you will excuse the recapitulation of several acts of the society, that have already fallen within the sphere of your censorial observation.

That a labourer who has employed six days of the week in obtaining the means of innocent enjoyment for the seventh, should have the iniquitous presumption to make himself decent on the sabbath, is deeply to be lamented. Washing and shaving on the morning of holy rest, are, in the poor and industrious classes, acts of the most gross impiety, and the most profligate depravity: the wretch who administers to the latter of these crimes, by the exercise of his razor, deserves the reprobation of every friend to social order and our holy religion, and is a fit object of legal vengeance. Petty barbers, therefore, should be prosecuted with the utmost rigor of the law: Bridewell is too good for them; and it is hoped and trusted that no magistrate from a principle of mistaken leniency, will so far forget his own dignity, or his duty to his country, as to mitigate the penalties attaching to this mode of violating the sabbath.

But let it be observed, that if the tonsor be rich, or his customers above the " lower orders of society," he may shave and frizzify from morning till night, without subjecting himself to the notice or interference of the society. A barber of Liquorpond-street, who is glad to earn a scanty subsistence, by mowing the beards of his Sunday customers, is a sinful and impious wretch, deserving the most immediate and exemplary punishment; but Alexander Ross, or Mr. Vicary, or any other *respectable* hair-dresser, who has already acquired a fortune by his puffs, may send out his servants in every direction, and thus contribute to adorn the persons of all the afternoon risers from Portland-place to Finsbury-square, without exciting a spark of momentary indignation in the bosoms of the worthy suppressors. Nor let it be supposed, that they themselves conceive it to be in any degree inconsistent with their religious duties, to make themselves " comfortable and pleasant," before they set out on their Sunday Inquisitions; they sally out in search of *barbarous* offenders, with chins well shaved, and wigs well powdered.

It is a shocking act of impiety in the poor classes, to send the only joint of meat that they can obtain in the course of the week, to the public oven; and the baker who presumes to save himself from starving by the receipt of Sunday pence, should be regarded by every true christian as a rogue and vagabond. Not so in the

" more elevated circles of society." A regiment of servants may be employed during the whole of the sabbath, in frying, and baking, and stewing, and boiling, without receiving even a frown of indignation from the suppressors. I have even been told, Sir, though I can scarcely believe it, that they will condescend to eat of dinners so profanely provided. Certain I am, that they feel no compunctious visitings of conscience at keeping the waiters of the London Tavern, from afternoon prayers, by retiring from their inquisitorial labours, to boast of their success over a bottle of particular Madeira.

A game at skittles is a dreadful abomination. When half a dozen clowns seek for relaxation in manly and athletic exercise, all the patriotism of the magistrates is aroused. Surrounded by a posse of constables, he marches in form to seize the vagabonds who venture to suppose that some degree of personal liberty is the birthright of an Englishman, and commits them to Bridewell with all the formality of law. But let a marquis kill a dozen horses, by a match at horse racing, and the worthy gentleman is silent: the nobility demand our reverence, and to wink at their follies, is the duty of every friend to social order and our holy religion.

Licentious pictures or naked statues, when exhibited to the lower orders of the people, are the just objects of reprobation; but the Phallic representation of Mr. Knight, or the exposure of the living person at the west end of the town, is perfectly innocent. An unfortunate sculptor in Holborn, has been compelled to take out of his window the Belvidere Apollo and the Venus de Medicis, by a suppressor who gloats upon the statues deposited in the private rooms of the British Museum, and has no objection to attend the anatomical lectures of the Royal Academy.

In short, Sir, if vice be fashionable or wealthy it is innocent. Gaming houses are *above* the attention of the suppressors; drunkenness and lasciviousness are deprived of all their disgusting qualities by being cloathed in silk, or practised by the wealthy: the poor alone are the objects of virtuous indignation; to religious inquisitors, an exalted harlot is the object of adulation, while a common s———t is committed to Bridewell.

That these assertions are not the result of prejudice or injustice, your readers will be able to determine for themselves by comparing the subjoined list of what the society has done eastward of Temple-bar, with what remains to be done a mile or two westward.

Abstract of proceedings at the Auxiliary Suppression Society. 1811.

17 Convicted of shaving between the hours of ten and twelve on Sunday.

42 Butchers fined for selling meat to poor persons whose work was not finished early enough on Saturday night, to leave them time for *market making*.

26 Sunday ovens closed.

2 Pastry cooks shops closed.

14 Publicans deprived of their licences for permitting the game of skittles.

1 Sculptor *indicted* for a nuisance in exhibiting a Venus at his window, &c. &c. &c.

It is not a little singular that while this auxiliary society is so anxious for the purity of pot houses it should pass without remark or procedure the house of entertainment of which the following is an advertisement.

COLONIAL COFFEE-HOUSE.

No. 1, Skinner-Street, (adjoining the Coffee Mart, London.)

WILL OPEN TO-MORROW,

Handsomely fitted up, for the accommodation of the public, and also with the view of promoting the welfare of the British coffee and sugar plantations.

  Coffee, &c. for Breakfast, &c. 1s. each
  Single Cup, &c. - 6d. each.

Morning and Evening Papers will be provided. Tablets, in gilt Frames, descriptive of the various professions in the Fine Arts, Trades, Manufactures, &c. may be put up in the Coffee Room. Also Bills of Sales by Auctioneers, &c. &c.

A Subscription Room, on the First Floor, is fitted up in *an elegant Style, with Private Entrance*, for THE USE AND AMUSEMENT OF LADIES AND GENTLEMEN, and will be opened in a few days, liberally supplied with Magazines, Reviews, Gazette, Morning and Evening Papers, Lloyd's List, Price Current, *Shipping Intelligence, foreign and domestic*, &c.—Subscribers to be allowed to take coffee in this room.---*A sitting room for the use of Ladies (Subscribers) exclusively.*

*** As it is intended the number of Subscribers shall be limited, and as select as possible; it therefore is requested *that Ladies and Gentlemen* who may feel disposed to support this superior establishment, will leave their address with MRS. Allen, at the Bar of the Colonial Coffee-House.

It is not to be supposed indeed that the society of suppressors have any legal jurisdiction over the general amusements of ladies and gentlemen ; but when these amusements are facilitated, or accompanied by *private entrances*, it might be expected that they would become the objects of suspicion to gentlemen so expert in *smelling out* indecency, and so watchful over every possible mode of incourse between the sexes. The advertisement indeed informs us that the apartment is intended for use as well amusement : now utility divides itself into a variety of branches, and perhaps the suppressors are of opinion that to make the barren fruitful, and the childless happy ; to instruct the ignorant and cherish the languishing, are objects deserving of magisterial sanction and popular encouragement.

Nor is it impossible that the lovely Mrs. Allen may be the sister of an inquisitor who visits the private room without the payment of a preliminary subscription, and convinced by ocular demonstration of its multifarious conveniences, is unwilling by the terrors of visitation to obstruct the amusement of Mrs. Allen's guests, or diminish the utility of Mrs. Allen's sofas.

The friends too of social order, and our holy religion may possibly remember the disasters that have befallen their exalted patrons, and may wish that private entrances had been long ago transferred from Skinner Street to ——— Place and ——— Palace. Had private entrances been common to places of amusement, the throat of ——— would not have been cut, by whomsoever that operation was performed, nor would the delicate investigation have puzzled the wits of Mr. Perceval. A private entrance to a long career of iniquity would have saved certain renowned personages from charges of sporting fraud, and is certainly more to be desired than a public *exit*. It is unfortunately the predominating fault of a particular family, that they will make their entrance into certain premises with so much ostentation, as to make us doubt, whether their attempts to be useful, are not more productive of *amusement*, than of living testimonials to their prowess.

To strain at a gnat and swallow a camel is not uncommon with fanatical hypocrites: I do not wish that even the Colonial* Coffee-house should be visited with an inquisition; but for the sake of decency let those who pass it without observation, cease their persecution of bakers and hair-dressers.

     I remain, Sir,
      Your obedient servant,
        P. WILSON.

Finsbury Square.

---

* That the advertisement is perfectly innocent, does not diminish our astonishment that it should have escaped the ready suspicion of the suppressors.

CLERICAL ATHEISM.

" No atheist, as such, can be a true friend, an affectionate relation, or a loyal subject."

BENTLEY.

THIS is saying a great deal in a very little room, and, I admonish my readers to bear it in remembrance, this multum in parvo, was the production of an English divine of the last century; if I were to hear a like solemn asseveration, from the mouth of most of the present, I do seriously say, I should not in the least be surprised; but it must be owned the thing would be received as—*words of course.* Much more has been said and written, concerning atheists and atheism than, I conceive, has been in any tolerable degree understood. The number of offences constituting atheism, in its common acceptation, are infinite; and the task would be tedious indeed to enumerate each particular link in the graduated chain, from the profane sneer at a trencher cap, or black silk apron, to the robbing of a wren's nest; nevertheless it may not be entirely irrelevant to aim at the institution of an inquiry, unto what class or classes of men, the title of atheism is justly imputable; as it is more than probable, numbers have labored under that opprobrium, who did not deserve it, while, on the other hand, many more have escaped, who have but too well merited the appellation. One leading feature in the concern, ought never, for a moment, to be lost sight of, namely, that in all ages, the *clergy* have been the first to raise the mob, upon any man the least notional in points of religion; there is little or no analogy, to be sure, between the *cloth* and the *ladies;* otherwise it might be rather suspicious, as among the latter, it is not at all unfrequent for the greatest * * * * * to cry out * * * * * first. *An atheist* is said to be a person, who denies the existence of a God. *Lay atheists* exist but in few places, and have never been very numerous any where; even though all those be accounted such, upon whom atheism has ever been charged. But where they do exist, they seem to owe their rise principally to their indulging themselves in comparing the *actions* of priests, with their *duty* as such; and the more flagrant the lives of the clergy have been, the more numerous have been the back-slidings to atheism: nay, there are men, who rather more than suspect there is just cause to believe *priests are more liable to be infected with atheism than other men.* The great mass of mankind, when left to the exercise of their sober senses, always make up their opinion of a man from his *actions*—not his *words.* A man may laughingly say, what excellent diversion it is to turn cyphers into sixes and nines on a rainy day, and yet never wilfully defraud a customer of a single farthing in the whole course of a long life. A woman may not " mince virtue, nor shake the head to hear of pleasure's name," and yet fill the several stations of maid, wife, and mother in the most exemplary manner imaginable; but, if the tradesman is once found slippery in his accompts, or the woman " nothing loath," all the palaver of the one, or the demure cant of the other, will never pass current against *actions :*—wilful, premeditated actions, are like facts, stubborn things. A character may not be inaptly compared to a new coat, once dashed, the more you brush, the more you injure the nap, its pristine lustre is fled, irrecoverably vanished. Priests suspected of atheism? There is something terrific in the sound? Ministers of the gospel of Jesus, denying by their actions the existence of a God? The idea of such traitorous openly-avowed rebellion against heaven is truly abhorrent, and yet, I fear, the suspicion is far from being groundless. I do sincerely, from my soul, pity those devoted beings, who, to sooth the vanity of a doting aunt, or hen-pecked father are destined *from their caudles* to the taking of *holy orders,* those orders which they afterwards, on receiving, swear, call upon the Almighty Creator of the universe to witness they were moved unto by the *impulse of the holy spirit.* Charity points out these poor wretches to be ranked among the victims immolated on the altar of pride, nevertheless

> The *means for food*, should still be *honest means;*
> " Else were it well *to starve.*"

But what shall be said of those impious men, who voluntarily, at age of apparent discretion, break down all the barriers of moral rectitude, and rush upon oath after oath, subscription after subscription, depending on subterfuge, sophism, casuistry, and logic (that literary bed of Procrustes) to elude the vigilance of omniscience. Can such a man be a *true friend*, an *affectionate relation*, or a *loyal subject* ? No, no, he may be a *jolly fellow*, a *sound bottom;* and as to loyalty he may halloo three times three to the emptying of the fourth bottle; but is there any comparison between a man's *merely saying there is no God*, and the *doing* such things ?— If a man, in *holy orders* were to leave a card-table under a wager to perform a certain part of his clerical duty before a stated number of *deals* had gone round, and by jabbering over *divine service* in the most indecorous manner, be enabled to perform it, if, under the ear-gratifying plaudits of fools and gamblers, that man should happen to reflect in whose presence he has been officiating, and whether had his patron my lord the squire been present, he would have acted exactly in the same style, his feelings, I conceive, would not be over enviable. If the preacher in the most forcible latitude of pulpit declamation, adjudges fornication and adultery to the penalty of eternal damnation, and yet before the next morning that identical being is chased from his neighbour's house by an enraged husband, or has his favorite female conveyed snugly once a year to her *native air* for the benefit of her *health*, can it, for a moment be supposed he can impose on his hearers to imagine he *believes* what *he says?* Can such a man be a *true friend,* an *affectionate relation,* or a *loyal subject*? Or rather can such a man, himself, believe there is a God? Believe there is a God? and dare him to the teeth! believe there is a God? and solemnly call upon him to be witness to a lie! What blasphemous, what most impious mockery! A loyal subject? he may be *useful* at an *election,* &c. &c. but as to subscribing to the idea of his *loyalty,* gentle reader—please to excuse me. A pious magisterial divine in a neighbouring county, not seven years since, having had, rather early in the morning, most urgent and *pressing necessity* for the assistance of his upper female servant in the bed-room; the girl, unluckily, was met emerging from thence, rather too much in the fig-leaf costume, by his infant daughter: dear me, Jenny, says the child, have you been in pa's room—so? Oh yes, my love, replies the wench, *that does not signify any thing*—Pa is too much of *a gentleman* to take notice *how such a poor girl as Jenny is*! Yet this man no one dare to think is *an atheist*—no I'll warrant not—vastly able—abundantly potent—Oh yes, Jenny acknowledges the superlative ability of his prowess exactly fitted to her *capacity.* I personally knew a biped in *holy orders,* he was also a *magistrate and D. D.* who, it must be owned, did live in the same house with his wife; but as much separated in fact as though they occupied different circles of latitude, met not in months; but as " it is not meet for man to be alone," his doctorship had regularly and nightly the assiduous soothing assistance of a sympathetic female neighbour to lull him to repose: he too could squeak *eternal perdition* as the lot of *adulterers.* Oft has that wretch slabbered over the whole of the morning service, sermon included, in thirty-five minutes; yet no one presumed to stile him *an atheist.* No—truly—his convictions *on the bench* were all vastly judicious—he was cordially received into what was called the *best company,* mighty witty and full of anecdote with the *gemmen,* most captivatingly polite among the ladies. If these things are not *practical atheism*, I candidly confess I am not able to form any adequate idea of the *term*. Let no one tax me with an endeavour to bring the *clergy* into *disrepute*. Let none advance the trite, the hacknied cant of, "there may be found *some few* erring members in the clergy of the established church of England ---*here and there one* who does not act quite so correctly as he might; but, taking them as a body they are the most respectable class of men that can possibly be conceived." I do sincerely believe, nay I know for certain there are *some* truly respectable characters among the clergy---men, the tenor of whose lives confirm the doctrines they inculcate; men, whom their parishioners look up to with confidence, with honest heart-felt gratitude; but before such palliating conclusions as the above are drawn, I beg the *worthy*, the *disinterested* assertors, to number up into one grand total the pluralists, the clerical magistrates, the commissioners of taxes and highways, the shouters after dogs and vermin, the drunkards, the gamblers, and all those *erring few*, those *here and there one*, and if they are authorized, upon comparing that total with the remainder, to affix the negative sign thereto, I do hereby promise to ask public pardon of that (in such case) *most injured most respectable body.* The colloquy in Genesis, 18 chapter beginning at v. 23, is not exactly in point; but *as learned men* are so very apt at drawing inferences, I should not much wonder if the recital thereof did not, at times, *make the ears of the readers to tingle.*

No Atheist.

Bingham, 13th April, 1812.

O'KELLY THE FIRST.

Sir,

Your account of Mr. Dennis O'Kelly has excited some notice among the lovers of genealogy; but your account, though correct as far as it goes, is imperfect; and I beg leave, therefore, to transmit to you a few memoranda drawn up long before my acquaintance with the other branches of the family, and universally allowed to be correct.

He was born in the province of Connaught, where the descendants from the aborigines of the island, and those of the old Milesian race mostly reside. His parents were peasants of the lowest order, and though in the latter part of his life, he was able to assume the *sang froid* in his manners and conversation, he was perfectly illiterate: but being blest with a good memory and native drollery, he was seldom at a loss in conversation, and took part in every subject proposed—always pleasant, and never offensive, for though his voice was coarse, his address was complaisant.

He rose by flattery, the gradations of his adventures were through the medium of gambling, and at last having been ruined by play, he was arrested, and laid for a considerable time a prisoner in the Fleet, where after several months residence, he became tapster to the warden.

It was here, that his acquaintance with Charlotte Hayes originated: she had money, and he possessed those abilities of person and constitution, which she preferred to all others, and they formed a connection without the interference of Hymen, which lasted till death stept in and dissolved the *sentimental* union; a proof on his part, if not of love, at least of gratitude.

After three years confinement, O'Kelly and his fair one were liberated from prison, and they both immediately set down in pursuit of plans which they had laid while in duress.

Charlotte took a house in King's Place, or rather a temple for the celebration of the orgies of Venus, and O'Kelly who had been invested in the Fleet with the title of count, got acquainted with customers, who in return for their enjoyment of his porter, made him a complete master of horse-flesh, and let him into all the arts arising from a knowledge of the turf. One of them permitted him to become a purchaser of the half quarter of the celebrated horse Eclipse, bred by the Duke of Cumberland uncle to the present duke, of which, in a short time, he became sole proprietor, and on the turf as a racer, and in the stable as a stallion, this animal first raised for its proprietor, several thousand pounds, and obtained him an annuity from the Jockey Club, on condition of withdrawing him.

In 1760 Mr. Kelly accepted an ensigncy in the Westminster regiment of militia, and by degrees arose to the rank of lieutenant colonel: from the above date to 1777, he found many difficulties in supporting his stud; but Charlotte being successful in her avocation, purchased a small estate at Clay Hill, near Epsom, where she built a house of which she constituted the count ostensible master; and here he kept his stud, and here saw the best company; but here he would never permit any species of play to go forward, or even matches for the course to be made.

The anecdote of Kelly's mistaking his bed-chamber at an inn in York, must not escape notice: mistaking his chamber, he got into that of a lady—he got into her bed. The lady startled, screamed, and alarmed the house. The count would have retreated, but was prevented by a crowd who surrounded the door, and prevented it; and if it had not been for the entreaties of the lady, he would probably have fallen a sacrifice to rash and ill-founded resentment. The business did not end here, the lady's relations commenced an action against O'Kelly, and he was terrified into the disbursement of five hundred pounds.

Scarcely had he got free from this difficulty, before another presented itself. A party having dined at a coffee-house, under the Piazza in Covent-garden, of which Dick England made one, a gentleman of the company came into the public room, where Mr. O'Kelly and a Mr. Rochfort, afterwards shot in a duel at Warley Common, were then abusing Mr. England, in terms of the grossest kind, though Rochfort had been under very many obligations to him. The gentleman returning to his company, repeated what he had heard, upon which England privately departed, and entering the coffee-room, seized each of his calumniators by the heads, which he knocked together, and afterwards beat both till they took asylum under the tables. For this assault he was indicted, and pleading guilty, the court of King's Bench on hearing the affidavit in mitigation of punishment read, fined the defendant *one shilling*.

Kelly by his successes at the turf, having acquired a very considerable fortune, purchased the seat formerly belonging to the Duke of Chandos, called Cannons, situated in the county of Middlesex, near Stanmore: and here after a very short possession, he was seized by a violent fit of the gout, which Dr. Warren could not, with all his skill, expel from his stomach, and he died at about the sixty-seventh year of his age.

As to his disposition of mind, it wanted nothing but early cultivation; for though the habits of his life, being a professed gambler, cannot be commended, yet his intentions were good, and expanded as his fortune increased. He was charitable without ostentation, and prosperity did not elate him with pride; for as you well know he called his relations from obscurity and penury, supported them in ease and plenty, and at his death left them independent.

     I am, Sir,
      Yours, &c.
          R. M.

CARICATURES.

Sir,

I have always regarded the caricatures, accompanying your valuable publication, as trifles intended to contribute to the amusement of your readers, rather than as the productions of grave and serious study, designed to inculcate any particular opinions, or calling upon the Editor of the Scourge for any share of personal responsibility, except that which may attach to their original conception. The multitude of readers must be amused as well as instructed; and because you sometimes exhibit Sir Francis Burdett in a ridiculous attitude, and sometimes represent a certain personage in a whimsical point of view; you are not in the one case, an enemy to freedom, and in the other a disloyal subject, or an enemy to kingly government.

But the Editor of the Morning Post, always alert on the side of persecution, and quick beyond example in the detection of treason and disloyalty, has lately indulged in a series of paragraphs, respecting these harmless instruments of general amusement, that if they have any meaning at all, are intended to excite the government to the suppression of all caricatures, that do not satirise the opposition or the reformers. He is pleased to describe the representations of Mr. Perceval, that are so frequently seen in the windows of the print-shops, as infamous and deserving of magisterial interference; he virtually praises the loyalty of the Baron Geramb, in breaking the window of a bookseller, that contained a caricature of the Prince Regent; and even ventures to imply that the Attorney General would do no discredit to himself or his sovereign, by visiting the authors of humorous prints, with indictments and ex-officio informations.

Unfortunately for the Baron, the nature and motives

of his loyalty, have been since developed to the satisfaction of every one but himself;' and so striking a proof, that the cant of loyalty may sometimes be assumed for sinister purposes, should not be forgotten by the people. If Mr. B. had not been equally destitute of modesty and recollection, it would have occurred to him, that the most " infamous and obnoxious caricatures" have been exhibited by the party of which he is the advocate; that Gilray was paid by the Pittite administration, for representing its opponents in the characters of traitors, and rogues, and vagabonds; and that this system is continued, if not under the immediate direction, beneath the indirect auspices of the present ministers.

He might remember too, that our beloved and unfortunate monarch, was not less the object of undeserved and severe exhibition than his successor; that during a long reign, and with all the power on his side, that attachment could give to established authority, he was either unwilling or unable, to subject the authors of the most offensive caricatures of his person, to legal visitation, and that at many of the more playful compositions, he joined in the laughter of his subjects. By suggesting the possibility of a different line of conduct in the Regent, he is exposing him to be regarded, for a moment at least, in a point of view comparatively and positively unfavorable; as a Prince who no sooner assumes the reins of government, than he encroaches on our freedom of thought and action, and gratifies a spirit of personal vindictiveness, at the expence of liberty.

The liberty of the press has been nearly extinguished by silent encroachment. One step further, and no man can exhibit a picture or erect a statue, without being in danger of Newgate or the pillory. A painter will be excluded from depicting the death of Nero, because the face of the tyrant may have some inconvenient resemblance to that of some despotic *minister* of state; and to delineate the amours of Caligula and his sister, may subject the artist to imprisonment, because it recals to the public mind the *loves* of a noble but licentious *hero*.

I am, Sir,

Your obedient servant.

V. V.

London, April 28*th*, 1812.

THEATRICAL REVIEW.

Nullius addictus jurare in verba magistri;
Quo me cunque rapit tempestas deferor *hospes*.

Covent Garden.

Our attention has been called from the novelties at the Lyceum by the unexpected demonstration at the rival theatre of a spirit of independent and legitimate criticism, which if its future perseverance be equal to its immediate energy, may effect an important and salutary revolution in the state of our national drama. It behoves every man who has any regard for the taste of the present or the morals of a future generation, to prevent the conversion of the only *play-house* sanctioned by law, into a menagerie or a circus, at the mere caprice of an avaricious or profligate manager. It is possible that at no very distant period, some individual of less modesty than the present proprietors of our national theatres, may convert those spectacles into the means of licentiousness, that are now the instruments of avarice; and that a wretched individual may be fond of exhibiting the most splendid and ingenious equestrian entertainments, not because it gratifies the town, or replenishes his private purse, but because it facilitates the display of his mistress in lascivious attitudes. The fate of the Secret Mine, however, may preclude the necessity of looking into futurity for evils more lamentable, than those which have a present existence.

When the curtain draws up a triangular bridge is discovered, at the foot of which Zobeide (Miss Feron) and her father, discourse on the merit of Araxo, a youth who had deserved by his exploits the favor of the Persian governor. Their conversation is interrupted by the appearance of the governor and his attendants, and the subsequent entrance of Araxo himself. Though the bridge is apparently in the midst of a wilderness, this does not prevent the monarch from discoursing with the hero on affairs of state, and informing him that if he aspires to the honor of his daughter's hand, he must first deserve it by disclosing the *secret of the mine*. This mine is inhabited by a race of Hindoos, who know not the use of riches, and are secured from the necessity of warlike preparation by the secret which Ismael wishes to discover; yet strange to say they shew themselves in the progress of the story to be very expert in military tactics, and to be provided with a supply of ordnance consisting of one brass cannon and two musquets. Araxo shrinks with abhorrence from the idea of betraying his country's safeguard, but distracted at the thoughts of losing Zaphira (Mrs. H. Johnston) he dissembles, and obtains of Ismael a respite, for consideration, till the next morning.

Scene the second. Liston afflicted with love and hunger reveals his sorrows to his mistress, who instead of relieving his miseries joins him in a duet. Scene the third and fourth, represent the exterior and interior of the mine into which Araxo enters by a secret opening. He orders the Hindoos to convey the treasures of the mine, so useless to them, to an adjoining cavern. Scene the fifth, he returns to the palace, having sent before him specimens of the riches he had deposited in the earth; the governor receives him with joy, but the daughter " cannot think" of marrying a traitor to his country, and reproaches him with his perfidy. He finds it necessary to inform her by what artifice he had cheated her father, and this paragon of heroines, who had just expressed her abhorrence of his treachery to a host of barbarians, flies into the arms of a man who has imposed on the weakness and credulity of her parent. Scene the sixth—Araxo leads Zaphira to the altar, but just as the nuptials are about to be celebrated, a messenger arrives from a traitorous Hindoo which unfolds Araxo's artifice. The hero is sent to prison, and Zaphira conveyed to the interior of the palace.

Act the second, scene the first, exhibits a view of a castle with a moat and a drawbridge. Liston comes in with articles of Chinese workmanship. By the luckiest accident imaginable, his old sweetheart Zobeida meets him in her morning dress at a fortress in all probability a hundred miles from the scene of former dalliance. They are not all surprized at seeing each other so unexpectedly. Zobeida has found a letter: Liston amuses the guards by shewing them various toys of Chinese workmanship, and, taking out a kite, fastens the letter to its back. By the luckiest chance imaginable, it flies to the very grating of Araxo's prison; by a chance equally lucky, he happens to be amusing himself at the time of their arrival, by viewing the prospect before him; and by an accident not less fortunate, the letter is discovered to be from his dearest Zaphira, who promises to come to his deliverance. She informs him that by the touching of a secret spring, his grating may be opened, and at the requisite signal he may escape. At the time appointed she arrives; rows her boat beneath his window; and then lands on the edge of the moat. Here again the ingenious author is indebted to one of those lucky accidents which had contributed to the progress of the preceding scenes. While Zaphira is landing, all the sentinels are very conveniently out of the way: nor do they arrive till she has fairly concealed herself behind a buttress; but accidents are not less useful to retard the progress of a melodrama than to forward it: the boat drifts from that side of the moat to the other, and Zaphira and her lover are in despair. In the mean time a shower of rain comes on, and the centinels place their muskets out of its reach beneath a friendly arch-way: for the better carrying on of the plot, they are less careful of their persons than their arms, and sit cross-legged on the grass, while Zaphira sallies from her hiding place, and throws their musquets into the river. At this moment Araxo touches the spring and descends from his grating. He and the gentle Zaphira overpower the ferocious soldiers, and nothing remains but to gain the opposite side of the moat. But how is this to be accomplished? The noble youth is unable to swim, and the boat has drifted beyond his reach: he has no aptitude for drowning, and if he stays he will fall into the hands of the executioners. At the very crisis of his despair, a band of retainers arrive, who by throwing a tree across the moat afford him a safe passage to the opposite shore. Now the curious reader, who may have sympathized all this while in the miseries of these devoted lovers, will no doubt suppose that the moat was at least twenty lines deep, " broad and unfathomable." It is not usual for boats to drift in a puddle, and it might be supposed that where other men could walk a prince might wade. But that these are the conjectures of ignorance, may be proved by the evidence of the authors of the *Secret Mine*. The retainers who fell the tree very coolly walk into the "wide waste of waters," that had excited so much terror in the prince, without suffering the most trivial inconvenience. So great is the superiority of Covent Garden genius to all the laws of common sense and probability!

But now that the godlike prince has obtained a safe footing for his mistress and himself, he hears the footsteps of approaching enemies. He hurries her across the bridge, but just as she gains the middle, she is alarmed by the report of a musquet. It would have occurred to a common heroine, that to fly from her enemies was just as easy and as prudent, as to retreat in the direction from which the noise proceeded. But Zaphira is no common heroine; she runs into the arms of her pursuers, and the great and godlike Araxo, instead of fighting in her defence, or waiting to see the issue, makes a precipitate retreat at the other end of the bridge. To heighten the effect of this absurdity, he takes her by the hand as she is retreating, and since she runs as fast as him, there is no reason why even after her first alarm, they might not have escaped together.

Scene the 2d. Liston and Zobeide (Miss Feron) are brought before the governor. They are surrounded by guards, but so trivial a circumstance does not prevent them from talking aside. Scene the third. Zaphira, in the disguise she had assumed for the purpose of facilitating her lover's escape, is brought before her father. She discloses herself, and he orders her to be placed under a guard, with an Amazon for a companion. The captain of the guard is resolved to attempt Zaphira's virtue, and therefore is anxious to get the Amazon out of the way. Zaphira comes forth disguised in Camilla's dress; and he orders the guard to conduct her without the walls of the city. Shortly afterwards the Amazon herself appears. He breathes revenge for the trick put upon him, and fights her. She kills him; another flies to his assistance, and he also falls beneath her Amazonian prowess. Scene the fourth; A wood. Zaphira having fled from the capital, arrives on the borders of the mine. Her enemies pursue her: the entrance to the mine, (which entrance she is not supposed to know) is too high for a common escalade; a band of soldiers, from whence we know not, form a ladder of their shields, up which her courser bounds, into the secret mine: she is followed by her father's troops, and the next scene is equally surprizing and unintelligible. The clattering of hoofs the crash of rocks, and the explosion of musquetry, all denote a terrible combat. A wooden horse falls, from a precipice upon the stage, Zaphira after galloping in and out, is at length discovered on foot with dishevelled locks, and in tattered drapery. In the heat of the contest, a servant wheels a cannon with the most amiable civility to one side of the stage, which Zaphira aims and fires with due deliberation. We suppose that it decides the contest, for the basaltic pillars fall in, and several steeds ride into the scene, that they may ride off again. Noise and confusion take possession of the stage, and the curtain drops, amidst the groans and execrations of the audience. How the plot terminates, or what may be the meaning of the last scene, we confess ourselves unable to discover. That there is a fight, and that many of the combatants are equestrian is evident; but the meaning of their evolutions is known only to the inventor of the spectacle.

The wit of the piece is confined to a couple of puns in the mouth of Liston, who swears by the *head* of the great Long Chin, and declares to the governor that " he never knew that it was death to get one's living." The language of the dialogue is vulgar without plainness, and obscure without energy. The only attempt at character is in the introduction of Liston as a Chinese servant; but such has been the want of skill in the combination of the incidents, and such the paucity of talent in the composition of the dialogue, that in spite of the peculiarities of his features, and the effect communicated to their expression by the nakedness of his forehead, he excites no merriment but that which greets his entrance on the scene.

But its great defect is the want of discrimination in the selection and developement of the incidents. There is a great deal of trick, but it is wholly ineffective. Even the splendor of the scenery and the dresses, only adds to the mortification of the audience. It is impossible to witness such costly and mighty preparations, without contrasting their magnificence with the paltry nonsense that they are intended to aggrandise and embellish: nor does the speculative profusion of the managers, excite any other emotion than that, with which an observer would contemplate the death of a cat in a storm of thunder and lightning, or the descent of Jupiter to assist the manual dexterity of a shoe-black.

The splendor of the last scene, the sword dance between Mrs. Parker and her attendant Amazons, and the ascent of Mrs. Johnstone up the declivity formed by the shields of the soldiers, alone commanded the forbearance of the audience. But when the curtain dropped one universal hiss announced their opinion of its merits. It was decidedly and deservedly condemned; and though the managers, unwilling to sit down with a total and irretrievable loss, desperately persevere in its repetition, their obstinacy must be soon corrected by the necessary diminution of their receipts.

The truth is, that they anticipated the success of any piece in which the horses should appear: and the lesson they have just received may teach them the imprudence as well as the impropriety, of administering to the public taste for splendor and spectacle. If one piece out of three of this kind fail of success, the circumstance must do away with the profits of the two that have preceded it: and it becomes, therefore, a question of self-interest, whether the attraction of a legitimate entertainment, which if it succeeds, is moderately productive, and if it fails, subjects the managers to no comparative expence, would not "in the long run" be more beneficial to their purses, than the alternate success and failure of costly spectacles, which if they be sometimes enormously profitable, must be not less frequently the source of pecuniary involvement.

By their return from the error of their ways, the rational and the irrational part of the public would be equally gainers. Equestrian spectacles are only pleasing when in their proper sphere, and with a proscenium and accompaniments accordant with such exhibitions. No one can witness the awkward preparations for the Secret Mine, by nailing to the front of the stage a row of foot timbers for the horses, without resolving whenever he wishes to be amused by similar spectacles, to transport himself to Astley's as the proper scene of *Houynnhnhmic* excellence. Between the spectacles of the two places, as exhibiting, in a just and proper point of view, the sagacity and agility of the horse, there is no comparison.*

The length to which we have already extended our remarks, precludes the possibility of doing justice to the managers of the Pantheon, and the Opera-house. The proprietors of the former place have been compelled by the Lord Chamberlain to affix to their advertisements a declaration of five architects, all pronouncing the theatre, after the expence bestowed on its alteration, to be *unsafe*. Our readers will remember that Colonel Greville withdrew his licence on the ground of the insecurity of the building: we are now assured from authority that the danger has not been obviated, and yet the Colonel permits the managers to act beneath the sanction of the legal document.

---

* Since this article was written the piece has been considerably altered, and on the second night, with the aid of 500 orders, was forced upon the town.

W. N. Jones, Printer, Green Arbour-court, Old Bailey, London.

THE SCOURGE.

JUNE 1, 1812.

CONTENTS.

TO CORRESPONDENTS. see back.	A varment Marquis............ 466
THE FEAST OF LOYALTY... 431	His pugilistic exploits......... 467
The praise of venison........... 432	THE REVIEWER. NO. XII . ib.
Dignum's dignity................ 433	Quacking of artists............ 468
An odoriferous catastrophe. ... 434	Sir Joshua Reynolds........... 469
The address of the Independent Livery........................ 435	The British School............. 470
	Wilson the landscape painter.. 471
CLERICAL DECORUM....... 436	COLONIAL COFFEE-HOUSE and SUBSCRIPTION ROOM, Skinner Street, Snowhill..... ib.
Drunkenness personified....... 437	
THE INSOLENCE OF OFFICE 438	The Colonial Coffee-house..... 472
Impudence of clerks........... ib.	THE REFORMISTS.......... 473
Bank clerks.................... 439	Sir Francis Burdett............ ib.
Public offices 440	Abuse of the word reform...... 474
Ministerial Newspapers....... 441	General education............. 475
NOBLE PUGILISTS......... ib.	Representation and delegation.. 476
Utility of pugilism.............. 442	Elective franchise.............. 477
Gregson's hotel................. 443	EPIGRAMS.................... 478
Pugilistic harmony............ 444	The mystery unfolded.......... 479
Pugilistic poetry 445	A lamentable case.............. ib.
Pugilistic eloquence........... 446	Mr. R———'s drowning comparison....................... ib.
A morning scene................ 447	
MRS. CLARKE and MR. COMRIE, ATTORNEY and MONEY SCRIVENER......... ib.	The Prince and Tommy O——.. 480
	Posterior wit................... 481
	MODERN AMUSEMENTS, or SPORTING EXTRAORDINARY.. .... ib.
Comrie and Lord Folkstone..... 448	
Intrigue on intrigue 449	
Clerkenwell sessions.......... 450	Scenes at Newmarket.......... 482
THE SOCIETY OF ANTIQUARIES................. ib.	Political bets.................. 483
	Y———'s prayer............... 484
Antiquarian learning........... 451	DANIEL ISAAC EATON...... ib.
Pioneers of literature.......... 452	Sir Vicary's Christianity....... 485
Nicholas Carlisle............... 453	Infidels and dissenters......... 486
Grigyrrys and Mandingoes..... 454	Sir Vicary's zeal for the glory of God........................ 487
Lord Aberdeen and Sir Harry Inglefield..................... 455	
	Cambridge studies............. 488
THE EMPIRE OF THE NAIRS. Part II....................... 456	The Examiner's scepticism..... 489
	Vagueness of sceptical language 490
A royal fete.................... 457	Deism sometimes pardonable... 491
The M—— "fairest of the fair." 458	FEMALE SHOE-MAKERS.... 492
Aphrodisian orgies............. 459	A LOYAL HARANGUE........ ib.
Courtly scenes................. 460	A turtle politician.............. 493
Blessings of pregnancy........ 461	A palatable speech............. 494
PROGRESS OF BANKRUPTCY........................... ib.	THE POLITICAL OBSERVER. No. XI...................... 495
Tradesmanlike extravagance.... 462	Ministerial arrangements...... 496
Transition from the chaise to the carriage...................... 463	Cicero and Grenville........... 497
	A union of parties.............. 498
Ruin and poverty.............. 464	Lord Wellesley's talents........ 499
THE WHIPS, NO. V.—THE MODERN ALTAMONT.... 464	CAMBRIDGE POLITICS.... 500
Ingratitude of the whips........ 465	THEATRICAL REVIEW 502

NOTICE TO CORRESPONDENTS.

The Exhibition has given place to the Review of the Fine Arts.

The melancholy fate of Mr. Perceval, has rendered the insertion of the Pocket Book, and other articles of a similar description impossible. W.'s *Windsor memoranda* are left at the office.

Our readers will observe, that, in this number, we have been materially indebted to the assistance of correspondents, particularly so to the Author of the Empire of the Nairs.

We regret Veritas's disappointment: and beg the favor of the promised interview.

Lansdowne memoirs, are, to our certain knowledge, wholly fictitious.

The communication respecting the new system of writing, introduced by Mr. Carstairs, shall meet with attention when we recur to Mr. Lancaster. We have been pleased and surprized by the specimens we have seen, and think the system may be rendered of essential utility.

Lady A.'s request shall be attended to at an early opportunity.

We are obliged to our Albany correspondent for his entertaining observations, and should be doubly pleased, did we know to whom we are indebted for so much amusement.

The Pulpit, on Mr. Wellesley, is under consideration.

The Hypercritic, on the Edinburgh Review, arrived too late for notice in our present number.

THE SCOURGE.

THE FEAST OF LOYALTY.

'Twas at the solemn feast of loyal sinners
Who love their country dearly as their dinners,
    Aloft in awful state,
    Kit Smith the vintner sate,
Rais'd on a cushioned throne:
His brother aldermen were placed around,
Their brows with spreading antlers crown'd,
So city spouses should be found;
His lovely lady by his side,
Sat like a plump high German bride,
Not less for fat renown'd than pride;
Happy, happy, happy pair,
None but Kit Smith, none but Kit Smith,
None but Kit Smith, e'er kissed the bouncing pair.

Obsequious Dignum placed on high,
Surveys with mute desire
The tempting feast, beneath his eye,
Then licks his lips, and then proceeds to try,
Such notes as civic joys require.

The song began from Billy's toil,
Who boldly left his native soil,
Resolv'd to share in war's turmoil:
    A col'nel's uniform belied the man;

In his own yacht so loftily he sail'd,
The sea gods their degraded state bewailed,
Eclipsed by him, as o'er the vessel's prow,
He thro' his opera glass surveyed the waves below;
The listening crowd admire the lofty sound,
A present Nelson—loud they shout around,
A present Nelson,—loud the raftered halls rebound.
  With prick'd-up ears,
  Kit Smith the vintner hears;
  Assumes the warrior's frown,
  And shakes the room about his ears.

—The praise of venison next, the hir'd Apollo sung,
Of venison, whether old or young:
The jolly haunch in triumph comes,
Sound the trumpets, beat the drums!
Flushed with a purple grace,
It shews its currant-jelly face:
Now give each feeder breath---it comes---it comes;
Venison's beauties, old or young,
How can language e'er reveal
 Fat of venison is a treasure,
 Eating is the glutton's pleasure,
Sweet as stuffing is with veal.

Sooth'd with the sound, great Kit grew vain,
Eat all his custards o'er again,
And thrice he pick'd the bones of ducks, and thrice
  of turkies slain;
Dignum saw his stomach rise,
His yawning mouth, his longing eyes,
And while he necks and sides defied,
Changed his note and checked his pride:
He chose a Newgate muse,
Soft pity to infuse;
He sung the poacher's sad untimely fate,
By law severe, tho' good,

Dignum's dignity.

Swinging, swinging, swinging, swinging,
Swinging before the felon's gate,
For spilling sylvan blood.
Deserted at his utmost need
By those his former thefts had fed;
Exposed to all this rabble town,
Without a friend to cut him down;
With joyless visage, Kit dejected sat,
   Tho still revolving in his altered soul,
The various turns of spits below,
   And now and then a *backward* sigh he stole,
While streams Pactolian sought their vent, to flow.

The modern Orpheus smiled to see,
That sleep was in the next degree;
'Twas but a drowsy strain to keep,
For muses lull their babes to sleep.
Gently dull in hum-drum numbers,
Thus he soothed his soul to slumbers;
Picking bones is toil and trouble,
Syllabub an empty bubble;
   Never ending, still beginning,
Eating, still the substance missing,
   Think if fat be worth thy winning,
Thy wife is surely worth thy kissing.
Both wife and venison see beside thee,
Take what fate, thy cook, provides thee,
The many rend the skies with loud applause,
So sleep was crowned, but Dignum won the cause.

Poor Kit, scarce able to keep ope his eyes,
   Peep'd at the food
. That warm'd his blood,
And licked his lips, and lick'd his lips,
And lick'd his lips (to stir, in vain he tries;)
At length as sunk in sleep's soft arms he stretches,
The snorting alderman defiles his ———

An odoriferous catastrophe.

Now tune thy whistle, Dignum, once again,
A louder yet, and yet a louder strain,
Break the bands of sleep asunder,
With noise more frequent than his postern thunder,
Hark! hark! the horrid sound,
   Has raised up his head,
   Tho' as heavy as lead,
And he stares and ———'s around.
   Revenge, revenge, Apollo cries,
   See the minions of excise,
See the permits that flutter in the air,
See supervisors pair by pair,
   Each eager for his smuggled prize,
Behold the well known band,
Each with a *guaging* bamboo in his hand,
Run down thy cellar stairs, a dreadful train:
Their office done securely they remain,
In Round-court or in Drury-lane.

   Give the drubbing due,
   To the wretched crew.
Behold how they toss their noses on high,
   Bid them seek Cloacina's abodes,
   Congenial temples for such hostile gods,
The company pleased such expedient was hit on,
Kit Smith caught up the permits to ——
   His wife the door unbarr'd
   To light him to the yard,
A theme for Patty Pan to shew his wit on.

Let Curtis yield Kit Smith the prize,
   Or both divide the crown:
That raised a turtle to the skies,*
   Kit gorged a turtle down.

---

* On Sir William's expedition to Walcheren, he suspended a turtle at the prow of his yacht.

To testify our impartiality, we give the following production of a friend as a companion to the preceding.

We the mayor, the council and commons resplendent
Of London, on none but Bob Waithman dependant,
Beg leave to express to your Highness magnificent,
Our wish that with temper and purpose beneficent
Your council you'd purge of all profligate elves,
And be guided by none but our worshipful selves!

Oh! sad is the duty of *reiteration*,
To the citizen students of pure legislation,
But it ill would become the civic addressers,
Not to tell you the great and the multiplied pressures
Under which this afflicted community labours,
The contempt of its foes and the scorn of its neighbours,
Might all be redeemed by directly forsaking
Your own privy council, and graciously taking
For your trusty advisers, and lights of the nation,
The council so grave of this old corporation.

Most humbly we venture to tell you your treasures
Are squandered like *counters;* we hate all your *measures*,
And are sure that the people will make a great fuss,
If you don't condescend to take *pattern* by us,
But if, mighty prince, your *foreman* uncivil,
You will graciously deign to kick to the devil,
And consent for the future, as just and expedient,
To be guided by us, your slaves most obedient,
The shouts of applause shall reverberate daily,
From Whitechapel turnpike to the Old Bailey,
And we all shall confess that England ne'er knew,
So sweet and so gentle a monarch as you.

---

* See the British Neptune, May 11th.

CLERICAL DECORUM.

> " Then he open'd the book, as if on it he'd look ;
> " But o'er the page only, he squinted:
> " Lord—Moses—I'm vex'd—I can't find the text,
> " This book is so cursedly printed."
>
> OLD SONG.

WHAT is sauce for a goose, ought to be sauce for a gander. There is more solidity in most of these old saws, than the " learned in the art of reasoning," will easily be brought to confess. I fancy their antipathy to them, arises from the infusion of an over proportion of truth in their composition—'tis not much to be wondered at, on recollecting that the darling poet of these elucidators, logic, is the love-begotten babe of lying and dissimulation. If a porter, half seas over, rolls in a kennel, or a cobler three quarters drunk, bolts his head through a shop-window, do we not laugh at them? And do not the *parsons*, if present, join in that laugh? Why then should one of the body—cloth, &c. &c. &c. &c. under similar circumstances, be screened from derision;

> " Worth makes the *man*, and want of it the *fellow*;"

and if a clergyman will, in open defiance of decorum, persist in the commission of those acts, which cast odium even on a coal-heaver; let him be hoisted aloft, as a butt for public infamy—up let him go, even though he should wear a mitre.

In the immediate vicinity of this place, only a few weeks since, the body of a child was carried to the church-yard for interment, the cavalcade halted—no minister—the *gentleman*—I beg pardon, as he was only a curate, the *journeyman gentleman* in holy orders, was not to be found on the premises—messengers were dispatched various ways; and one more lucky than his fellows, had the honor of popping upon his reverence, and taking him in tow (like a bear to the stake) to the scene of action. His appearance beggared all description; after a superabundance of fumbling, he was arrayed; and the book ready opened tendered to him with the utmost humility by his clerk: but no, thank ye—this savoring rather too much of dictation; he whips over the leaves, and begins, " Dearly beloved, ye have brought the child here to be baptized," Sir, Sir, says the clerk, you are wrong—hum, aye, *by G-d, so I am*—O—here it is—" Secondly, it was ordained as a remedy against sin, and to avoid forni-fornication, that such---such---per-persons as had not the gift—the gift of con-conti-continence might, might, do what?— marry and"—Lord have mercy upon us, Sir, says Moses— Why, why, you are got into matrimony, Sir—*I'll be d—d if I am not*, says the parson. The humble attendant now strenuously endeavoured to fix his attention to the right page, but in vain—off he goes again—" Happy is the man, that has---that has his qui-quiver full of them." Loud murmurs of disapprobation mixed with the audible sobs of the afflicted parents, now assailed his ears: he started, stared as if just awaked---and exclaimed, *I'll be d—d to h-ll, if I can do it*, and away he staggered. Very few words, indeed, by way of comment are necessary on procedure like this---it speaks for itself, with most " miraculous organs;" one would scarcely suppose it possible for any thing to be offered as palliative in such a case: yet, such is the force of habitual wrong-headedness, that numerous excuses have been framed and set up—such as the day was intensely cold; on leaving a warm room, the air operated too potently on the very moderate quantity of *beverage*. Not liquor mind ye—not the stuff that makes folk drunk—but *the beverage* he had taken---that had the parents acted *properly*, when they perceived the gentleman a *little indisposed*, they should have adjourned the business, till the next day; that characters like his ought not to be viewed with too critical an eye, considering the complexion of the times, as his *loyalty* was beyond suspicion, he never suffering for a moment any sentiment, expressed in his presence, favouring the repeal of the *test and corporation acts,* to pass without his most severe and pointed reprehension; (perhaps it should have been added, whilst he was sober enough to articulate.)

To all which genteel—considerate—linsey woolsey, I reply—the same law which authorizes the sending to durance vile a *journeyman cobler* for drunkenness, and neglect of business—ought under like circumstances, to operate in like manner upon a *journeyman parson.*

OBSERVER.

Nottingham, *April* 12*th*, 1812.

THE INSOLENCE OF OFFICE.

SIR,

THE insolence of persons in office has been so long notorious that it is surprising our directors, commissioners, &c. do not find clerks who are more courteous and more attentive. Every master is accountable for the offences of his servant. If the driver of a hackney coach be insolent, the master of that coach becomes responsible to the insulted person. Why should not masters of a higher station make atonement for the indiscretions of *their* servants? Let every clerk be immediately discharged upon any complaint of negligence or incivility, and we shall then find in our public offices more attention and politeness. To the insolence of office may partly be attributed the murder of our late prime minister. The assassin declared at the bar of the House of Commons that he was told " he might do his worst." Enraged at this reply, like a second *Zanga*, he meditated revenge and exultingly exclaimed,

———————————'Twas I!
I hated! I despised! and I destroyed!

This ought to be a caveat to men in office; they should beware of insolent replies, which, for aught they know, may have a fatal tendency. But it may be asked what are they to do with troublesome people? Surely the laws of our country afford them remedies in this case. What is the use of our constables, &c.? It is not by irritating insolence that troublesome people can be appeased.

Has the deep adder venom? So has man
When trod upon!

In the Bank of England we meet with some very civil characters and some of a very opposite nature. What a pity that civility should not be universal! It has happened that a person from the country who had business at the bank, and was totally unacquainted with the place, applied to one of the clerks who was reading his newspaper. The clerk enraged at this intrusion, petulantly replied—" why do you ask me? Go on—enquire and you'll be told." Probably the poor stranger made many enquiries without being told; indeed if all the clerks were of the same disposition, his enquiries must have been both numerous and fruitless. Soon after a gentleman (who had witnessed the uncouth manner in which the stranger had been treated;) came to the clerk, who was still reading his newspaper, and said, " Sir, you have given me two warrants instead of one." " Two!" echoed the clerk--- Is it possible? I wonder how that could have happened." " I'll tell you how it happened," said the gentleman in a sarcastic tone. " You were reading your newspaper instead of attending to your business. Had you done your duty the two warrants could not have stuck together, and the stranger who asked you a civil question, would have received the information he wanted." This reproof had a proper effect, the clerk instantly laid down the newspaper, and went to his books.

In Somerset-house many instances of rudeness and neglect may be enumerated—" you must wait ;" " have patience"—" I cannot attend to you yet," are the common replies;—at the same time these *busy, attentive* clerks are perhaps standing by the fire, consulting where they shall dine the ensuing Sunday, or displaying their critical abilities on a new play or a new performer.

Every public office daily exhibits similar examples, some more and some less. And to what may this be attributed? The truth is, men of idle habits are employed instead of men of industry and talents. We may frequently see in the diurnal prints a handsome reward offered to any lady or gentleman who will procure the advertiser a situation *not* in one of the public offices! Thus interest obtains what merit is entitled to. Is it to be supposed that a person of abilities should be obliged in London—" the seat of arts and elegance" to purchase an employment? Employments, thus purchased, we must certainly understand to be situations where there is *little to do* and the purchaser must be gentlemen unaccustomed to toil, without either the inclination or ability for business—Whether they read the newspaper, indulge in idle conversation, or devote only two hours in the day to business, they receive a regular salary, while the hard-working mechanic is only paid according to his labour. We need not wonder then, that persons in office are insolent and indifferent. The author of Zorinski admirably censures this contumely. When asked why he did not return a bow, one of his characters replies

" I can't———I am in office."

The answer to this is also an excellent satire on the general mode by which those situations are obtained—

" And I suppose you stooped so low to get into office, that you have got a pain in the back ever since."

It has been asserted that the insolence of office has been highly advantageous to a certain ministerial paper, which derived all its consequence from the dignified air and theatrical struts of the clerk. Whoever brought an advertisement was obliged to wait the leisure of this gentleman, and the indifference with which it was taken, caused many to imagine that the newspaper, then in a consumption, was in a thriving state, and by this means it acquired that consequence which it stood so much in need of. The example has been followed by clerks in other newspaper offices, but perhaps not with the same success, as they do not *act their parts* so well.

In public offices, however, insolence can be attended with no advantage; on the contrary it must be injurious to the state; and, therefore, it behoves all directors, commissioners, &c. to employ only men who are civil and industrious. If a linen-draper or grocer keep a saucy journeyman he loses his custom; and certainly government must frequently sustain losses by the neglect, and rudeness of their servants. In all public offices a list of the names of the clerks, mentioning each department should be held up to public view, with an address for receiving complaints; and though I would not wish every frivolous complaint to be attended to, yet this would certainly be the means of insuring attention and politeness.

CASTIGATOR.

NOBLE PUGILISTS.

Sir,

THE art of boxing has been defended by its admirers and professors as contributing to banish from among the

English people those secret and murderous ways of revenge so prevalent on the continent of Europe. Pugilism, it is asserted, accustoms its practisers to a fair and manly mode of determining animosities; in which no opening is admitted, nor any indulgence allowed, to subterfuge and trickery. It affords a just and open trial of the manly endowments of the combatants, and is unaccompanied by those circumstances of sanguinary atrocity that distinguish the various modes of personal contention peculiar to the other nations of Europe.

That all this, when applied to the situation of the lower orders, has an air of plausibility, I shall not dispute. A game at fisticuffs may keep the visitors of Gregson out of greater mischief, and be a more innocent mode of deciding quarrels than the employment of the pistol or the stiletto. But in the name of common sense and decorum, in what way does the argument apply to our young nobility, to the sons of our naval heroes, and the brothers of our statesmen. It might be supposed that *with them* there would be found a *native* superiority to stratagem and meanness; that the laws of honor would be so deeply impressed upon their minds as to exempt them from the necessity of pugilistic drilling; and that their time would be so precious, and their pursuits so honourable, as to render their attendance at Jackson's a matter of serious regret to their country and their friends. It is nevertheless most certain, that among the frequent visitors of the C——e in Holborn, may be found the descendants and the relatives of our national worthies, conversing with the lowest of the populace, and attempting to outrival the *milling coves* of that temple of blackguardism, in all the varieties of slang, and all their peculiarities of manner.

Two of these individuals, men whom fortune has nursed in the lap of refinement ; whose rank entitles them to senatorial honours, and whose wealth might enable them to indulge in rational and elegant pleasures, not content with avowing their admiration of the art, or expressing by occasional familiarities their disposition to encourage its professors, absolutely *live* with them; luxuriating in the delights of purl, and indulging in the repeated orgies of mingled obscenity and blasphemy. Having occasion the other day to inquire after one of these *gentlemen* (an old schoolfellow,) I was informed by his servant that he might be found at Gregson's Hotel, in Holborn. "Gregson's Hotel," thought I, "it is a strange part of the town that my friend has chosen for his temporary residence;" however, I ordered my coachman to drive to the place thus designated, but no Gregson's Hotel was to be found. Wearied out with being driven from Drury-lane to Hatton Garden, and from Hatton Garden to Drury-lane, I at length arrived at a hair-dresser's, resolved to make my enquiries in person. No sooner had I mentioned the object of my search than the fellow exclaimed, "Odds bobs, Sir, I'll be moozled if he be not one of the *fancy lads* among the fighting gills. A dozen to a penny that you are quite deep in the *fancy lay*. Beardmore! Beardmore at Gregson's Hotel: Why Lord, Sir, he is one of the most flaming *millers* you can conceive. Gregson's Hotel! That's a good joke! Ha! ha! ha! Come, Sir, I'll take you to him; and if you be in fighting trim, why he'll give you your *bellyful* on't." So saying, he preceded us, till we came to the wished for place, which turned out to be nothing more than a pothouse. I was ushered into a room, in which about thirty people, enveloped in smoak, were testifying their good fellowship, by their uproriousness. As soon as my friend, (who was sitting in the very midst of them, with *dominos* before him, and a pipe in his mouth,) observed me, he started up, and approaching me in a boxing attitude, was about to give me a *hit* in the stomach, which I prevented mechanically, rather than scientifically, and which if it had taken place, would have given a mortal blow to our mutual friendship. Perceiving that he was about to renew the attack, and surprized at such a mode of salutation, I exclaimed, "Hold, hold! don't murder me: I came hither to testify my friendship, and not to quarrel."

My confusion, and the tone in which I spoke, excited a universal laugh in those who surrounded me. Oh! Oh! exclaimed one of them, I see you belong to the *shy cocks*, and are *afear'd* of a *fibbing*. My friend having recovered himself begged my pardon for his rudeness, and assured me " that nothing but a knack of doing things as *them there fellows*," should have made him behave in so eccentric a manner. " But never mind, he continued, it's all as well as it is : come and join our squad, and d——n my eyes if you be not as well entertained as ever you were in all your *born days.*" Surprized at such language from a friend, whom I knew to have received the education of a gentleman, I could not but lament the infatuation that appeared to have depraved his mind, and corrupted his manners. His friend, however, was a more deplorable picture of fatuity than himself. In the chair was seated the Hon. B. C. ; his duty was to repeat the toasts, and arrange the succession of the songs. The former were without exception either obscene or blasphemous, and the latter would have done no discredit to the purlieus of Drury-lane. Curiosity, as well as some degree of anxiety to remonstrate with my friend on our journey homewards, detained me, and I took my seat amidst the plaudits of the company.

Immediately after the toast of the monosyllable, Mr. *Emery* was called upon for a song. He complied without hesitation, and I presume, therefore, that the *gemman* was well paid for his condescension. Such a tissue of vulgarity and blasphemy was never before uttered by a respectable performer, or listened to by the heirs apparent of nobility. It was a favourite ditty, I understood, and had been written expressly for the occasion of Crib's triumphant feast immediately subsequent to his victory over Molineux. The first stanza, which is in the true style of *flash sing-song*, affords sufficient evidence of the piety of the auditors and of the singer.

I.

Come list ye all ye fighting *gills*,
    And *coves* of boxing note, Sirs,
Whilst I relate some bloody *mills*
    In our time have been fought, Sirs,
Whoe'er saw *Ben* and *Tom* display
    Could tell a pretty story,
The milling 'bout they got that day,
    Sent both *ding dong to glory*.

The third stanza is equally remarkable for elegance and decorum, and the fourth conspicuous for the classic felicity of its puns.

III.

All nations came to claim the prize,
    Amongst them many a don, Sirs,
And Billy Ward swore *blast* his eyes,
    He'd *mill* them every one, Sirs,
At Bexley-heath, it happed one day,
    He was beaten black and blue, Sirs,
By one deep in the fancy lay,
    'Twas little Dan, the Jew, Sirs,

IV.

The *Ruffian* young next on the list,
    Laid claim to boxing merits;
A mere pretender to the fist,
    Who dealt in wine and spirits.
His hits were *rum*, none can deny,
    His *black-strap* none could bear it,
But of his *hog's-head* he was shy,
    Lest they should tap his *claret*.

Stanza the tenth, contains a curious and happy example of the hyperbole.

X.

 Next rings the fame of gallant *Crib*,
  A cool and steady miller;
 Who late of Yorkshire went to fib,
  A first rate man of colour.
 No matter whether black or white,
  No tint of skin could save him,
 A *horse's kick was pure delight*,
  To the BELLY PUNCH he gave him.

Stanza the twelfth, and last, introduces with the utmost delicacy, a compliment to Captain Barclay—a complimentto which no one will deny the justice of that gentleman's pretensions, who knows that he paid for it.

 Now fill your glasses to the brim,
  And honor well my toast, Sirs,
  " May we be found in fighting trim,
   " When Boney treads our coast, Sirs,
  The gallant Barclay shall lead on,
 The fancy lads adore him:
 And devil or Napoleon,
  Leave us alone to floor him.

Scarcely had the tenth stanza been *encored*, before a general murmur pervaded the room, and several sturdy fellows, apparently of the milling tribe, began to square their elbows, and put themselves in various attitudes of defiance. These I understood were the friends of Molineux, whose resentment had been aroused by the contemptuous mention of the man of colour. The opposite party observing the indications of an approaching storm, were already on the alert. The Hon. B. C. always prepared for action, on occasions of so much importance, and willing to act as a moderator between the contending parties, having cleared the table of the red-herrings, the tobacco, and the geneva, " rose upon his legs, and with a tankard in one hand, and his watch in the other, exhorted the company to unanimity. " Oh, ye milling coves," he exclaimed " silence is worth a jew's eye at any time, b——t me if it ben't. Its all very well to be in fighting trim, when one wants to give the young ones a milling; but what's the signification of showing off to one another here. Why, lord! people will take us for a parcel of flats. Not that I care a farthing for myself— *my cut's meat*, G— be praised, is as sound as any cove's in England, and as for my bottom, and an't you all seen it, and an't I ready to shew it at any time? But I hate a *set-to* among fancy lads when they should be jolly, so I'd have you put your ponderosities under hatches and keep your pluck for another market." This speech was received with enthusiasm, and succeeded by a multitude of toasts and songs of which I shall not insult you, or degrade myself by the repetition. Suffice it to say, that the two honorables were taken home at three o'clock, in a state of intoxication, besmeared with blood, and, to use the language of their companions, in *a decent pickle, and with two black eyes in nubibus.*

I remain, Sir,
Yours, &c.
P. P.

MRS. CLARKE AND MR. COMRIE, ATTORNEY AND MONEY SCRIVENER.

Though the name of Mrs. Clarke has been long the theme of hackneyed anecdote and puerile observation, the history of herself and her subordinate agents has lost but little of its original interest. The intrigues of a clever woman, placed by a singular concurrence of circumstances in a situation that enabled her to determine the professional fate of a large proportion of the community, must equally attract the attention of the busy, and the idle, and the singularities of coincidence so observable in the gradual developement of the evidence, exhibit a useful subject, of study to the lawyer, and of speculation to the moralist.

It is in the highest degree creditable to her abilities that she alone has escaped from the ordeal of public observation, and the pursuit of exalted anger, or popular prejudice, in a more enviable situation than at the outset of the enquiry. With the resignation of the duke, we are all acquainted; Colonel Wardle overwhelmed with debt and disgrace, has retired from the observation of the multitude to enjoy in rural solitude the luxury of retrospection; the gasconades of Clavering, the explanations of Folkestone, and the journies of Sir Richard, have contributed to the amusement of the public, and to the establishment of her claims; and the issue of her late proceedings against Mr. Comrie, her solicitor, are equally indicative of her spirit and her good fortune.

It will be recollected that in the progress of the investigation, Lord Folkstone was in the habit of constantly visiting Mrs. Clarke, " running up and down stairs like a cat," and assisting her when he could obtain an interview with verbal advice. On one of his visits he was introduced to Mr. Comrie, and not being prepossessed in his favor by his address or conversation, he took the liberty in a note to express his opinion of him in this laconic form of admonition " BEWARE OF THAT COMRIE!" The result of Mrs. Clarke's experience does credit to his lordship's sagacity; and convinces us that his acuteness is less doubtful than his discretion.

About two years ago Mrs. Clarke having received the stipulated price of suppression, from the Duke of York, was desirous to invest some portion of it in annuities. She therefore drew 3000l. from the bank and vested it in the hands of Mr. Comrie; intimating at the same time that she would expect him to act the part of a banker, and as he would be in the regular receipt or possession of considerable sums on her account, she would expect that whenever she wanted fifty or a hundred pounds, he would accommodate her with it. To this he answered that if it would do her any service he would gladly acquiesce in the arrangement. Mrs. Clarke replied that she did not ask it as a favor; that it was rather a favor conferred on him, and was the result of a wish to serve him. He assented by complying with the terms of the agreement, and for some time his payments to Mrs. Clarke were as punctual and as expeditious as could be wished. But at length he began to return evasive answers to her solicitations for money. She, however, became urgent as he became ambiguous; and having written a letter to him, couched in strong and determined language, she received for answer that he had no money belonging to her in his hands, " for her account had been already balanced." Astonished at so unexpected a reply, she transmitted him a statement of her demands, and finding that her remonstrances were not attended to, she put her case into the hands of an attorney, who called upon Mr. Comrie, and was told by him that Mrs. Clarke was an infamous woman, that she would say any thing, that he had none of her money in his hands, that he had never been employed by her to purchase annuities, and that he should stake his character against her calumnies. The attorney either unacquainted with his profession, or afraid of the success of a *femme couverte* in a civil suit, declared his inability to proceed, and the case was then put into the hands of Harrison the attorney by whose exertions Jew King was convicted of perjury. Unfortunately for Mr. Comrie, he had forgotten that Mrs. Clarke was in the habit of filing the letters of her friends, and that he had frequently written to her on the subject of the annuities. On examining the correspondence, Harrison obtained the clue to a perfect developement of the affair. He compared the dates of the letters with those of the annuity bonds, and obtained from them sufficient evidence of their transmission through his hands. On looking at the bonds themselves, and enquiring after the parties in whose names they were drawn, there appeared to be sufficient ground for charging Mr. Comrie with the insertion of fictitious names for the purpose of fraud, and a bill of indictment being presented to the grand jury of Middlesex, they immediately found it *true*. Mr. Comrie who till this event took place, had maintained a tone of absolute defiance, now expressed his wish for a compromise. He made proposals to Mrs. Clarke for an accommodation, and as money and not revenge was her object, she consented to refer the matter to arbitration : the gentlemen on whom the office of arbitrators devolved awarded 2000l. to Mrs. Clarke, and on the day of trial Mr. Alley having declined to bring forward any evidence to the facts, the prisoner was acquitted.

THE SOCIETY OF ANTIQUARIES.

The true object of antiquarian research is not to rake together in one undistinguished heap the riches and the refuse of former ages, but to separate the materials that possess an intrinsic and immutable value from the ancient dross by which they may be surrounded. A key is not an object of value or interest merely because it is old and rusty ; nor should the honors that are due to learning and genius be ascribed to the pedant, or the versifier, because he happened to exist in the reign of Edward. Yet as connected with important events, and elucidative of general views of history and manners the most insignificant relique becomes an object of rational curiosity : and it might be expected therefore that the Antiquarian Society would require of its members a moderate regard to the abstract or relative importance of the subjects to which they direct their observations and enquiries: that they should not dwell with serious prolixity on an image or an inscription, unless the image itself were worthy of admiration for its intrinsic beauty, or the inscription had an obvious application to the general purposes of science; that they should occupy the society with such facts only as were valuable in themselves, or derived a claim to importance from some connection pointed out with other topics of investigation; and that they should be less eager to announce unimportant discoveries than to combine and apply the materials that their predecessors have collected.

But of system or philosophy, the members of the Antiquarian Society have no conception. Throughout the seventeen volume s of the Archæologia, there are not more than three essays written in the true spirit of antiquarian research, and combining instructive speculation with minuteness of detail. The very index to these ponderous volumes (for the compilation of which Mr. Carlisle received 300l.) exhibits a just picture of the minds and acquisitions of his colleagues. The following are conspicuous subjects under the letter B.

"Breasrign an Irish monarch.
"Brembro or Grenacre, Sir Richard, knt. his combat."
"Bridgeman the gardener.
"Bridgen. Edward F. A. S. the treasurer of the society in 1775."
"Bryer Robert, F. A. S. his exhibition of impressions from two brass seals, discovered in digging the foundation for the county gaol at Gloucester."
"Byset John, Barony of.
"Babewynis, Baboons."
"Bag, an account of one, of some very coarse vegetable stuff, containing bones discovered in a barrow, in the linkes of Skail in Orkney."
"*Barber*, the instruction to Henry the eighth's.
"Barnwood in the county of Gloucester, its ancient font.
"Barnakle or clerkis
"Base Leres, pieces of money.

" Brickernes, an ancient armourer's tool.
" Birdcage walk, in St. James's Park, etymology of the name.
" Bittern, or Bitter, the proper term in carving it in 1508.
———" 204 of them provided at the great enthronization feast of George Nevil, Archbishop of York, 6th of Edward IV."

The collection or discovery of insulated facts, like those enumerated in the preceding list, can only be excused when it is accompanied by a spirit of generalization that ennobles the mean, and adorns the unattractive. The society is not to be blamed for attending to minute particulars, but for doing nothing else; and the Archæologia bears less resemblance to the volumes that ought to be issued under the imprimatur of the society, than the notes and references of Gibbon, may be supposed to have possessed to his finished history.

Not that they deserve particular credit, even for their activity or perseverance, as the *pioneers* of literature. The productions of a few individuals, claiming only a nominal connection with the society, and deriving no assistance from their funds, far excel in patient enquiry and laborious research, all that they have collectively produced. If Mr. Nichols be willing to ascribe the glory of his labours to the Antiquarian Society, who is there to share, or dispute the antiquarian pre-eminence of a Whitaker?

That there are men of talent among them, cannot be disputed. We could mention the names of many individuals, whose learning and abilities would do honor to the proudest of our national institutions; but their efforts to extend and exalt the reputation of the society, are relaxed, or obstructed by the intrigues and the jealousies of men, who in their dread of comparisons, that they know would be unfavorable to themselves, do all they can to keep genius and erudition at a distance; who, conscious that to engage in legitimate contest would be to ensure their own defeat, descend to the most degrading artifices, that meanness stimulated by fear, is able to invent, and accomplish by the united force of calumny and malice the banishment or interdiction of the learned and the good.

The newly elected president, Lord Aberdeen, whose abilities are testified his by examination of *Dutens* on the antiquity of the arch, in the Edinburgh Review, was *dragged* into his present situation by the officious interference of impertinent friends, and the intrigues of an individual, who of himself alone, is a *tower* of strength to the aristocratic party. Cold, supercilious and hypocritical: suspicious of his equals, a model of servility to the great, and of insolence to the little: envious of rival talent to a degree, bordering on insanity: a persevering book-maker, yet affecting to despise the profession of letters; this dabbler of antiquities, throughout whose ponderous writings not a single paragraph occurs, that displays original research, or contains an original idea, assumes the importance of a Mæcenas, while he practices the servilities of a Rufellus, and brow-beats genuine talent into silence, while he barters flattery for the attention of greatness. Having a superficial acquaintance with drawing, he strenuously opposes the introduction of every individual, who may be suspected of outvying him in the exercise of the pencil; having some claim to the appellation of a topographer, he is anxious to exclude, or to banish from the meetings, with the imputation of book-making quackery, every individual engaged in similar pursuits.

The secretaryship of the society is committed to Nicholas Carlisle, Esquire; the dull compiler of dull topographical dictionaries, which contain neither definition nor etymology. He is a prosing inanimate retailer of dates and names: without the erudition of a scholar, or the correctness of a manufacturer of indices. His coadjutors and emulators are Samuel Lysons and —— Carter. The former of those persons is the author of Antiquities of Gloucestershire, consisting of slight etchings, accompanied by slighter descriptions; an expensive kind of pattern drawing-book, entitled, *Reliquæ Romanæ,* and is now engaged on a work called Magna Britannia, which arranges the counties of England, not according to their geographical situation, but their place in the alphabet, but which we suppose to be as correct as plodding industry, uninspired by genius or philosophy can make it. Mr. Carter is an indefatigable contributor to the Gentleman's Magazine. He draws with some degree of skill, and no man can be more accurately enthusiastic on the merits of a rusty pocket-piece, or the meaning of an obliterated inscription.

These gentlemen and other individuals of *equal* talent and equal learning, are extensive contributors to the Archæologia, of which the essays are greater curiosities than the antiquities they are intended to record or elucidate. Stephen Weston on rusty coins; unwieldy plates, drawn by Carter, and engraved, or rather manufactured, by James Basire; insipid dissertations by Nicholas Carlisle; and notes on the *Grigyrrys* and the *Mandingos,* by Samuel Lysons, constitute the prominent contents of a work which is and ought to be considered as the repository of the society's most interesting papers. That the communication of more valuable articles to the society, or their publication when transmitted, has only been prevented by the undue influence of literary gossips, and envious compilers of books, and copiers of records, will not be disputed by any individual who has visited the rooms of the institution.

Previous to admission the certificates of three members are required, declaring that the candidate is well versed in the antiquities of his country. Of the truth and honor of the proposers, the reader of the list will be able to form a proper estimate, when he finds the well known names of the Duke of Norfolk, Landseer, the engraver, Sheriff Birch, Mr. Adolphus, and (*mirabile dictu*) Lord Valentia.

The honor of admission is rated at so low a value, or its

offices fulfilled with such a mixture of negligence and folly, that for some time, the walls were adorned with a list of defaulters, on the account of their original admission, or their annual subscriptions, and the names of Blore, Sir Egerton Brydges, Landseer, Mr. Tighe, and several eminent individuals, were exhibited to the fellows and the visitors, with the amount of their respective debts in the opposite column.

On the intrigues that have lately distracted the society, and have led to the election of Lord Aberdeen, in the place of Sir Harry Englefield, we shall express our sentiments at another opportunity. A man of spirit might yet do much towards the reformation of the society: with funds so extensive, and patronage so powerful as it possesses, it ought to be the chief contributor to the information and amusement of the public. But this effect cannot be obtained, unless there shall be found some one individual whose enthusiasm in the pursuit of science, is equalled by his knowledge of the the world, and his personal intrepidity. Such men as those whom we have described, when properly opposed, sink into comparative non-existence: and we hope that even the present observations, hasty and imperfect as they are, will tend to arouse the respectable members of the institution from their lethargy, and excite them to resolve that the rooms of the Society of Antiquaries shall no longer be reserved as a temple to Morpheus, of which a Lysons and a Carter declare themselves the priests.

THE EMPIRE OF THE NAIRS, &c.

PART II.

" The Empire of the Nairs!" a countess cries,
" Utopian fields beneath our northern skies ?
Bless'd be the dame, the magic of whose glance
Shall e'er produce this country of romance.
Yes, I confess, my fancy wafts me far
To the gay scenes that smile in Malabar.
In waking vision and in nightly dream
I see the Indus pour his sacred stream;
The beaux and belles disporting on the banks,
Plunge in the wave, and play a thousand pranks.
I see their lovely countesses resort
In their green girdles to th' Imperial court;
This simple girdle is their only pride,
No whalebone citadel, no hoops of six feet wide.
Light is their dress, and lighter is their dance,
They waltz, and Honi soit qui mal y pense.
Though weak my charms, they captivate some Nair;
I wake, and find myself in Berkeley-square.
If any prospect tempt us to remain
To grace the lustre of the future reign,
We will not vegetate—the times are o'er
When monarchs rose at six, and dined at four.
Let pedants guide the dull machine of state,
But let this reign be one continued fete,
His sire might quit his matrass with the lark,
The son is rich enough to keep a clerk;
Tellers have deputies—may he not too?
The R—— writes enough who writes a billet-doux."

She said—when lo! the brazen trumpets sound,
And to the gaping populace around
North, south, east, west, the herald king declares,
The court adopts the system of the Nairs.

When great Semiramis in days of yore*
Founded her empire on the Indian shore,
Thro' the wide eastern world the princess saw
Her sex the victims of the partial law:
For legislator man had judged that she
Should be his slave, his private property.
And as the miser hides his ill-got pelf,
To keep his pounds and shillings to himself,
The husband, whom vile jealousy alarms,
Forces his vassal wife to veil her charms.
While modesty, the source of female woe,
Was the pretext that humbled her so low.
So the sagacious queen, to cut the root
Of evil, and prevent the noxious fruit,
Ordain'd in freedom's cause, an annual rite,
A noble dame should bathe in public sight.
By such an institute th' imperial dame
Banish'd from all her realms all sense of shame,
Form'd by such laws the Nairesses were free,
And nature triumph'd over decency.

To tempt the fair to give their project o'er,
And fix the truants on their native shore,
(And why to Calicut should beauty roam
When love prepares a Malabar at home?)
The P—— resolves each pleasure to advance,
The costly feast, the carol, and the dance,
Minstrels and music, poetry and play,
And balls by night, and dejeunes by day.
His scarlet pages bid the noble train
Repair to folly's fashionable fane;
But now no more a theatre it proves,
'Tis a pantheon for the sex he loves.†
No more the dome repeats the eunuch's squall,
Now female merit decorates the wall.

* Empire of the Nairs, vol. 1. page 101.
† Ibid. vol. 11—192.

Above, below, in marble and in stone,
Th' illustrious dames, of every age and zone,
Both they, whose gallantries acquired applause,
And they who fell the martyrs of the cause,
Appear, Aspasia, Lais, Messaline,
Ninon the sage, and catholic Christine.
Semiramis there pulls her husband's ear
Here Katherine beckons to a grenadier.
Nor less the busts of British heroines prove
That Britain might become the isle of love.
And many niches unpossest remain
For the fair worthies of the present reign.
The dames of Albion in the midst behold
Harlotta's statue wrought in solid gold,
The great Harlotta, William's dam divine,
And the first mother of the Norman line,
For give the heralds all their merit due,
They can't mount higher than a W.
Below the pedestal her statue graced
The golden bath in readiness is placed.

But hark! th' artillery roars, the turrets ring,
And thousand minstrels strike the quivering string.
The massy door unfolds in all its pride,
The R———— enters, girt on every side,
With all who charm, who counsel, or command,
The rank, the wit, the beauty of the land.
Warriors, who frown in military show,
Whiskers above, and sabres dash below;
Mitres and coronets; the gartered knee,
The steward's wand, and chamberlain's gold key.
But chief the fair attract the R——'s care,
And chief the M———— amid the fair;
Th' inferior beauties, ranged on either hand,
Shrink at her air of dignified command,
Yet while they see her fair without compeer,
Something will whisper in a female ear,
" Fair as she is, no-rival should despair,
The P———— is fickle as the dame is fair."

The phoenix knight, arrayed as king at arms,
Proclaims the empire, and extolls its charms,
Th' imperial bird, expiring on the nest,
Burns on his back and blazes on his breast,
The proclamation he both said and sung,
In French, in German, and in English tongue.
And had he been there, he had sure been able,
To found his empire at the fall of Babel*.

The R—— shines a meteor from afar,
Gay as his plume, and brilliant as his star,
For him the dames all other loves despise,
And daughters blush whene'er he meets their eyes,
With fluttering hearts they see him now advance,
And scan their beauties with a critic's glance,
And to the dame, whom all-excelling grace,
Distinguishes as goddess of the place
To her the conscious handkerchief he flings;
Forward the eager dame enraptured springs,
And catches it—her girdle is untied,
Down falls to earth her robes impurpled pride,
And she in naked majesty is seen,
Beneath the statue of the Norman quean:
Naked as Venus rising from the sea,
Or as Godiva rode thro' Coventry.
The while she bathes a voice in Lydian measure
Chants a delicious air in praise of pleasure,
Ladies! applaud the bard ye all adore,
The Irish nightingale, Anacreon M——

And who was the distinguish'd dame whose hand
Caught the imperial token of command?
Who was the fairest in the critic's view,
To whom the palm of excellence was due?
Who was the dame?—Historians can't agree,
'Twas such an honour to some family,

---

* Mr. Lawrence has already published his romance in three languages.

That every pious son and tender brother
Hints that it was his sister or his mother.

See the bold Baron prancing thro' the hall,
Fling down his glove, and fiercely challenge all,
His very steed has such a martial air,
Some take it for the charger of Lord Mayor,
" Tho' I arrive too late to see the dame
Nor have adored her charms, nor heard her name,
Yet I maintain whoe'er a prince approves
Must be the very mother of the loves."

He says, and waves his sabre quart and tierce,
None dare to combat with a knight so fierce,
Hear then, ye gods, he cries, a Baron swear,
" Hear, powers of Paphos and M———— square,*
Who the dame is I neither know nor care,
But she must be the fairest of the fair
He who denies it, is a captive Nair,
And these black whiskers of Hungarian hair,
Which none but Magnates should presume to wear,
And comb and razor have been taught to spare,
These will I sacrifice when any prove more fair."

This said, he spurs his charger from the hall,
Unhappy Baron! here thy laurels fall,
Thy creditors are waiting in the street;
And ah! what powers can save thee from the Fleet?
Fortune assists the bold—in antient Rome,
When any culprit march'd towards his doom,
Should but a vestal meet him on the way
Th' obedient lictors straight released their prey,
There superstition waged with reason war,
But reason legislates in Malabar,
And all the laws of an enlighten'd nation
Are wisely framed t' encourage population:

* See the verses of Sophia.

So when a princess of imperial blood
Conceives an infant for the public good,
When her proud pregnancy parades the streets,
Her presence pardons any rogue she meets,
Spendthrifts exult, and criminals escape,
And debtors worship her auspicious shape.*

And now in Britain, Indian laws prevail,
Thus fortune saved the Baron from a jail,
The court gazette and papers of the day,
Announced a princess in a hopeful way;
For this event the nation's vows were raised,
The goblet sparkled and the bonfire blazed,
Now as the tipstaffs led the youth along,
He spied her highness midst a loyal throng;
While she who felt her time so near at hand,
Was buying baby-linen in the Strand.
Forward he presses, and in suppliant strain,
Falls on his knee and catches at her train,
The princess turns and smiles—his terrors cease,
The bailiff bows, and must depart in peace,
The Baron trusts his whiskers to the wind,
And leaves his grumbling creditors behind.
They've seized his uniform, his Russian furs,
His Hessian boots and military spurs;
So he, that would be a Hussar complete,
May now equip himself in Monmouth Street.

PROGRESS OF BANKRUPTCY.

Sir,

I cannot help supposing, that if tradesmen in general were better œconomists than politicians, and would attend to their own conduct, rather than the affairs of the nation, the clamour against taxes and the orders in council, as well as the number of bankruptcies, to which the mea-

---

* Empire 4. 247.

sures of our statesmen are supposed to have given birth, would be considerably diminished.

The progress of a modern bankrupt is usually this. A young man of good character, sets up in business, with a moderate capital and credit, and soon after marries a young woman, with whom he gets a little ready money, and good expectations, from the death of her father or mother, uncle, or aunt. In two or three years, he finds that his business increases; but his own health, or his wife's, or his child's, makes it necessary for him, to take lodgings in the country. Lodgings are found to be inconvenient, and for a very small additional expence, he might have a snug little box of his own. A snug little box, therefore, is taken, repaired, new-modelled, and furnished! Here he always spends his Sundays, and commonly carries a friend or two with him, just to eat a bit of mutton, and to see how comfortably he is situated in the country. Visitors of this sort are not wanting. One is invited because he is a customer, another because he may assist him in his business; a third because he is a relation of his wife's, a fourth because he is an old acquaintance, and a fifth because he is very entertaining; besides many who look in accidentally, and are prevailed on to stay to dinner, although they have an engagement elsewhere.

He now keeps his horse for the sake of exercise; but this is a solitary kind of pleasure, which his wife cannot share, and as the expence of a one-horse chaise can be but trifling where a horse is already kept, a chaise is purchased in which he takes out his wife and his child as often as his time will permit. After all, driving a chaise is but indifferent amusement for sober people: his wife too is timorous, and ever since she heard of Patty Pan's accident by the stumbling of her horse, has not been able to bear the idea of such a vehicle: beside the expence of a horse and chaise, with what is spent in hot days on coach-hire, falls so little short of what their friend Mr. Soso asks for a coach, that it would be ridiculous not to accept of an offer that might be made him again. The job coach is agreed for, and the boy in a plain coat with a red cape, who used to clean knives, wait at table, and look after the horse, becomes a smart footman with a handsome livery.

The snug little cottage is now too small for so large a family. They take a trip to Margate, and on their return home, are shocked at the idea of being shut up in a band-box. There is a charming house, with a garden and two or three acres of land, rather further from London, but delightfully situated, the unexpired lease of which might be had a great bargain. It occurs to the husband indeed that the premises are a little more expensive than he should want; but the house is new, and for a moderate expense might be put into excellent repair. Hither he removes, hires a gardener, being fond of botany, and supplies his own table with every thing in season, for little more than double the money the articles would have cost him if he went to market for them. Every thing about him now seems comfortable; but his friend of the livery stable does not treat him so well as he expected; 'his horses are often ill-matched, and the coachman sometimes refuses to drive them a few miles extraordinary, because " he's answerable to master for the poor beasts." His expences, it is true, are as much as he can afford; but having coach-house and stables of his own, with two or three excellent acres of grass, he might certainly keep his own coach and horses for less money than he pays to his friend. A rich relative too of his wife's is dying, and has often promised to leave her something handsome. The job coach is discharged, he keeps his own carriage, and his wife is now able to pay and receive more visits than she could before : yet he finds by experience that an airing in a carriage is but a bad substitute for a ride on horseback. In the way of exercise he must have a saddle-horse, and subscribes to a neighbouring hunt for his own sake, and to the nearest assemblies for the sake of his wife.

During this progress his business had been neglected,

but his capital originally small has never been augmented. His wife's rich relations die one after another, and remember her only by trifling legacies: his expences are evidently greater than his income: and in a very few years, with the best intentions in the world, and wanting no good qualities, but foresight to avoid, and resolution to retrench expences, which his business cannot support, his country house and equipage, assisted by the many good friends who almost constantly dine with him, drive him fairly into the Gazette. His country house is let; the equipage is sold: his friends shrug up their shoulders; enquire for how much he has failed: wonder it was not for more; say that he was a good creature, an honest creature, and no one's enemy but his own,—but they always thought it would come to this—pity him from their souls—hope his creditors will be favorable to him—and go to find dinners elsewhere.

L.

THE WHIPS.---No. V.

THE MODERN ALTAMONT. (SEE YOUNG.)

The exploits of this *illustrious* nobleman have rendered him so justly dear to the aspirants after whippism, that we should deservedly lose that best reward of our labours, the friendship of the club, were we to suffer another month to pass away, without recording his great and numerous virtues. The friend of Webster, the pupil of Angelo, the protector of Randall, the rival of Cambridge Jack, and the object of envious astonishment to all the coachmen between London and Exeter, what is there wanting to the absolute perfection of his character as a whip? For learning, indeed, he never was remarkable; his talents are just equal to the comprehension of a *double entendre*, and his virtues are those of the stable, rather than the church. But all these circumstances are creditable to his pretensions as a whip. Did he possess either the knowledge, or the ability, that are requisite to the guidance of national affairs, selfish people might have just reason to complain of his devotion to the management of horses; and were he possessed of common and vulgar notions of morality, he might disdain to swear, or wench, or indulge in any of the other little eccentricities, by which the true brethren of the profession are distinguished.

It has not a little excited our surprize, that the attention we have hitherto devoted to the Whip Club, has been received by several of its members with other feelings than respect and gratitude. We knew that they gloried in f——n, and we therefore recorded their amorous exploits; we were conscious, that they affected the utmost familiarity with their grooms and jockies, and we published their condescension to the world; we were convinced, that to become a third bottle man was one great object of their ambition; and whenever an individual among them had succeeded in his endeavours, we communicated his triumph to the public. We gave them credit for the attainment of every object they pursue, and carefully abstained from attributing to them any of those vulgar qualities that are the professed objects of their neglect and derision. Yet strange to say, the persons who suppose themselves to have been alluded to, have displayed towards us the most flagrant indications of anger and ingratitude. But it belongs to the profession of whippism, to be eccentric; and it becomes the Editor of a work like this, to receive such testimonies of human frailty with the calmness of philosophy.

The Marquis, we are sure, is a man of different character from many of his friends, and will thank us for detailing his progress in the career of whippism. About six years ago, the jolly fellows of Cambridge having been tired with the monotonous routine of amusements that are usually within the reach of a select portion of academical society : such as *catting* in-chapel, driving to Bolshom, sitting at the half-way house in a hunting dress over a bottle of wine, while some good-natured friend obtains from a poacher a couple of bloody witnesses to your exploits, smuggling a wench into your rooms in a cap and gown, &c.—resolved to establish a society for the improvement of the art of driving. As it was one great object of the institution to promote the cultivation of the language and manners, as well as the scientific skill of *coachmen*, it was called *in limine* the *varment* (or *vermin*) society. Of its costume and general pursuits, we have given a correct description in our second number: it may be necessary to remind our readers, however, that its chief characteristics were wenching, drinking, and swearing; a perpetual employment of slang, and a continual indulgence in obscene conversation. His lordship was the life of the society: no man could tell a *funny* tale, or kick up a row, or manage his tits, or sport a piece with greater animation or more complete effect. He was the idol of the ostlers at the Rose and Crown, the constant companion of Hell-fire Dick, the envied lover of Nancy Smith, and the theme of wonder and admiration to the passengers in the Telegraph. During vacation time, he whiled away the melancholy hours in driving the coaches between London and Cambridge, treating the lower orders of the passengers with gin, and paying the proprietors of the horses a handsome premium of insurance. In term time, as he could not practice the art of driving so often or so securely, he devoted his mornings to Angelo and ———. From the former he received instructions in fencing, and by the latter he was initiated into the polite and elegant accomplishment of *boxing*. We do not remember to have witnessed a more ludicrous exhibition than that of this uncouth, *squabby* looking nobleman, endeavouring to assume the graceful attitudes of a practised fencer. In his pugilistic endeavours he has been tolerably successful: his visits at Gregson's testify his love of the art, and the " peepers" of his grooms and servants, afford " black and bloody" evidence of his prowess.

Since the death of his father he has bid adieu to the groves of Academus, and has divided his time between London and his paternal estate in the sister country. His metropolitan career has been chiefly distinguished by his turbulence at the Opera, and by his endeavours to rival his friend H. in the good graces of his darling N——a: nor should we have selected him as the subject of the present strictures, had not the public attention been lately called to his exploits by his match to ———. We leave it to our readers to estimate how much courage it requires to travel in a post-chaise, and the degree of skill that is exhibited by the individual who wins a wager through the dexterity of his servants. After being conveyed with unexampled rapidity from one part of the country to another, he no doubt regards himself with renewed complacency. That he is a devilish clever fellow in his way, we readily allow; and since his first object is to become notorious, we are confident that our present endeavour to gratify his wishes, will obtain, as it demands, his everlasting gratitude.

THE REVIEWER. No. XII.

The Fine Arts of the English School, illustrated by a Series of Engravings, from Paintings, Sculpture, and Architecture of eminent English Artists, with ample biographical, critical, and descriptive Essays; by various authors. Edited, and partly written by John Britton, F. S. A. Longman. 1812. 6l. 6s.

THE natural operation of quackery in every branch of exertion, is to impede the progress, and obstruct the rewards of honorable excellence. Where a Rumford, or a Von Feinagle has gone before, it is difficult for a Leslie or a Hatsell to obtain the humblest testimonies of popular confidence, without descending to the arts by which their predecessors imposed on the national credulity. A sincere lover of science or the arts will not stoop to the meanness of emblazoning his own merits, by the usual artifices of puffing; the vulgar, therefore, accustomed to admire the pretenders, with whom ostentation supplies the place of more valuable qualities, will treat the unassuming candidate for public favor with neglect or derision; and the more enlightened few, who have once been deceived by the professors of quackery, will suspect even the honest competitor for the fair rewards of honorable industry.

The public has been so often and so frequently deceived by the lofty professions and the ostentatious jargon of book-making artists, that we are afraid the success of the volume before us, may be impeded by the distrust so natural to the victims of literary depredation. "A burnt child dreads the fire;" and we took up the volume, expecting to find it, like many other expensive works, which we might easily enumerate, a gaudy picture-book, of which the subjects were selected without taste, and engraved with no other purpose, than to catch the eye: containing dissertations, of which the egotism was as disgusting, as the jargon was unintelligible; and exhibiting pedantry without learning, finery without elegance, and prolixity without copiousness.

It is not to be supposed, that on all occasions, the compilers of such works sat down with a cool and deliberate purpose of depredation. There are men who mistake enthusiasm for genius, who suppose that to be always in raptures, is a decided proof of sensibility, and who in the ardor of their professional zeal, and in the fervor of personal importance, outstrip the boundaries of moderation. But while they demand a price proportionate to the conception of their works, the subscriber is condemned to compare the sums he has expended with their powers of execution; and it too frequently happens that men of warm temperament, and irritable nerves, are only zealously in the wrong, and that having pursued their studies under the influence of constitutional bias, their application has only confirmed them in error. The bookseller quarrels with the editor, on finding the work so different from what he expected; but the demands of the subscribers must not be entirely disappointed: the work is got up in some way or other, the man of taste views it with indignation, and the *amateur* alderman finds that he is *bit*.

The work before us is of a very different character: the subjects are selected with judgment, the plates are executed with equal correctness and elegance, and the essays, as might be expected from the productions of Northcote, Prince Hoare, John Mason Good, &c. &c. are replete with entertaining anecdote and enlightened criticism. Throughout the volume nothing can be found that is merely intended to catch the eye, and betray the observer into an unwary purchase: the book will bear examination, and does equal credit to the editor, to his literary associates, and to the artists to whom the execution of the plates has been committed.

We cannot indeed coincide with all the opinions either of the editor or his coadjutors. Of Sir Joshua Reynolds's picture of Garrick between Tragedy and Comedy, Mr. Britton asserts, that in design, composition, colouring, *expression*, and above all *identity of personal features*, and felicitous adaptation of character and sentiment, it is a performance that amply justifies those elegant lines of " Shee's Rhymes on Art," which apply to Reynolds.

> " Whose genius rais'd his country's name,
> Refin'd her taste, and led her arts to fame:
> Whose powers unrivalled envy's self disarmed,
> Whose pen instructed, and whose pencil charm'd.
> Hail! star of art, by whose instructive ray
> Our boreal lights were kindled into day."

To the merits of this picture, as a composition, we must join our testimony to that of every preceding critic; but the bias of prepossession could alone, we think, induce Mr. Britton to praise it for *expression*. The head of Garrick, necessarily the first object of attention, is, in our opinion, expressive only of vulgarity. His smile is not the intelligent emotion of a man of genius, but the convulsion of a simple ignorant fellow at once puzzled and delighted. He seems to say with Elliston, Lord! Lord! which shall I go with? The head altogether is a very tolerable likeness both in features and expression of that actor, as Walter in the Babes of the Wood. The vulgarity of effect so observable about the mouth, is occasioned by the distinct and unshaded whiteness of the teeth, which give to his face an appearance approaching that of a grin. It may seem too hypercritical perhaps to say that the leer of Comedy is roguish rather than *sprightly*, a circumstance which probably led the French engraver to mistake her for Vice.

The volume contains five portraits, eight paintings, six specimens of sculpture, four architectural views, and a design by Gandy. The artists are Reynolds, Shee, Mengs, Flaxman, Westall, Romney, Nollekens, Howard, Northcote, Turner, West, Banks, Gainsborough, Gandy, and Elmes; the engravers are Le Keux, Bond, Cardon, Scriven, Godby, Pye, Scott, and Roffe: the authors, Britton, Adolphus, T. Phillips, J. M. Good, Northcote, R. Hunt, J. L. Bond, Anonymous, Prince Hoare, and E. Aikin. Among the most interesting articles are the memoirs of Reynolds and Wilson, by Northcote and Britton, and from the first of these we shall make an extract.

" When (says Mr. Northcote) we contemplate Sir Joshua as a painter, we are to recollect that after the death of Kneller, the arts in England fell to the lowest state of barbarism, and each professor either followed that painter's steps, or else wandered in utter darkness, till Reynolds like the sun dispelled the mists and threw an unprecedented splendour in the department of portraiture. To the grandeur, the truth, and the sublimity of Titian, and to the daring strength of Rembrandt, he has united the chasteness and delicacy of Vandyke. Delighted with the picturesque beauties of Rubens, he was the first that attempted a gay and bright back ground, and defying the dull and ignorant rules of his master at a very early period of life, emancipated his art from the shackles with which it had been encumbered in the school of Hudson. Indeed there is every reason to believe that he very rarely, if ever, copied a single picture of any master, though he certainly did imitate the excellent parts of many. His versatility in this respect was equalled only by the susceptibility of his feelings, the quickness of his comprehension, and the ardor which prompted his efforts. His principal aim, however, was *colour* and *effect*, and these he always varied as the subject required. Whatever deficiencies there may be in the designs of this great master, no painter of any period better understood the principles of colouring: nor can it be doubted that he carried that branch of his art to a very high degree of perfection. As for his portraits, those of a dignified character have a certain air of grandeur, and those of women and children possess a grace, a beauty, and simplicity which seldom have been equalled, and never surpassed. In his attempts to give character, where it did not exist, he sometimes lost likeness, but the deficiencies of the portrait were often compensated by the beauty of the picture."

" The attitudes of his figures are generally full of ease, grace, and variety. He could throw them into the boldest variations, and he often ventures at postures that would frighten inferior painters, or if attempted would inevitably destroy their credit. In light and shade, in colouring and expression, he stands without a rival. His lights display the knowledge he possessed, and with shade he conceals his defects. Whether we consider the power, the brilliancy, or the form of his lights, the transparency of his shadows with the just quantities of each, and the harmony, richness, and full effect of the whole, it is evident that he has not only far transcended every modern master, but that his excellencies in these captivating parts of painting, vie with the works of the great models he has emulated.

"The opinion he has given of Raffaelle may with equal justice be applied to himself, 'that his materials were generally borrowed, but the noble structure was his own.' No man ever appropriated the ideas of others to his own purpose with more skill than Sir Joshua. He possessed the alchemy of painting, by converting, as it were, whatever he touched into gold. Like the bee that extracts sweets from the most noxious flower, so his active observation could convert every thing into a means of improvement, from the puerile print on a common ballad to the highest graces of Parmegiano. In short, there is no painter that ever went before him, from whom he has not derived some advantage, and appropriated the same with judicious selection and consummate taste. Yet after all that can be *alleged to him* as a borrower of forms from other masters, it must be allowed that he engrafted on them excellencies peculiarly his own, simplicity, sentiment, feeling, grace, and taste; together with richness, harmony of colour, and general effect. The severest critics, indeed, must admit that his manner is truly original, bold, and free. Freedom is certainly his principal characteristic; for this he seems to have sacrificed every other consideration. He has, however, two manners; his early works are without that extreme freedom of his dashing pencil, being more minute and fearful; but the colouring is clear, natural, and good. In his later pictures the colouring though excellent is often more artificial than chaste.

"As an *historical painter*, he cannot be placed in the same rank, which he holds in the line of portraiture. The *composition* of his portraits *are* unquestionably excellent, whilst his historical pictures are in this respect often very defective. They frequently consist of borrowed parts, which are not always in harmony with each other. Though often inaccurate and deficient in style of drawing, they must, however, be allowed to possess consummate taste, and some of them great expression. His light poetical pieces much excelled those of a narrative or historical character."

The character of Sir Joshua as a man, is described with the same impartiality of sentiment, and acuteness of perception, as his qualifications as an artist.

The phisiognomy of Wilson, as exhibited in the likeness here engraved from a portrait by Raphael Mengs, would have awakened in the mind of Lavater, greater doubts than he ever appears to have entertained of the universality of his art. The eye is the only part of his countenance that is not expressive of vulgar stupidity: he looks like a sign-painter about to exercise his talents in the production of a Red Lion or a Black Bull, rather than a man of exquisite taste, and creative fancy, surveying nature with the eye of a poet, and describing its beauties with almost intuitive powers of embellishment. Of this artist Mr. Britton, has written a very satisfactory memoir. But we have already exceeded our limits, and must conclude by recommending the publication to all who can distinguish the expensive from the valuable, and who with a taste for the fine arts and literature, possess the means of indulging in their favourite pursuits.

COLONIAL COFFEE-HOUSE AND SUBSCRIPTION ROOM, *Skinner Street, Snowhill.*

MR. EDITOR,

IT is due to the public, to the real merits of the above

useful establishment, nor less to the respectable person there presiding, that something should be said in negative of those vile insinuations regarding the above establishment, which appeared in an article inserted in your last publication, and which went the unwarrantable length of endeavouring to impress on the public mind that the whole establishment had for its object, or was calculated in its effect, to promote vice and immorality!! The insignificancy of the person avowing himself the author of that article, would justify treating him with silent contempt, were it not certain that characters of worse complexion too often avail themselves of the names of such hirelings that they may feel themselves the more at liberty to give full vent and publicity to their avowed malicious designs, or diabolical purposes.

Generally noticing a few only of the printed rules and regulations of the above establishment, which have for months past conspicuously appeared over the fire-place in the public coffee-room of the above house, will suffice to shew how partial your correspondent has been in his statement, and also by what spirit he was actuated throughout the whole of his remarks. Those rules and regulations plainly point out that a gentleman cannot become a subscriber unless he first leaves his name and address at the bar of the coffee-house, that inquiry may be made as to the respectability of his character; if that is satisfactorily ascertained, then, and not until then, will he be informed he may subscribe to the subscription and reading-room. That being done, he then may, if he approves, and others also approve, introduce his wife or daughter, &c. as occasional visitors, or as subscribers: but on no consideration whatever can he introduce a lady unless " of the *same family*" with himself. Whether your correspondent, or any of his associates, has ventured to undergo that ordeal of character or not, the public must judge. Certain it is, there are who have not been successful in their applications, and it is equally certain the manager will continue, under the countenance and support of subscribers, to accept or negative applications, in strict conformity with the rules and designs of an establishment calculated to promote public benefit and accommodation, consistent with principles of strict morality.

A Subscriber.

May 27*th*, 1812.

THE REFORMISTS.

Sir,

The account of the speeches at the late meeting of the reformers (Sir Francis Burdett in the chair), has naturally led me to a review of the conduct and opinions of the advocates of reform; and though I am not unaware that in your general principles you coincide with the individuals to whom the following strictures most immediately apply, yet I hope that neither the mode in which they are expressed, nor the doctrines they contain, will preclude them from the candid attention of your readers. Truth is best elicited by discussion, and they who wish to hear only one side of a question, submit themselves to the chains of voluntary prejudice.

" Reform in parliament" is a phrase that any man can adapt and modify to his own particular opinion, without being conscious perhaps that nine out of ten of his neighbours who employ the same expression, have fixed to it a different meaning from his own. Another unfortunate circumstance attending the use of this expression is that being accustomed to talk ourselves, and hear others talk of a reform in parliament, we insensibly make the admission, that there is something bad in parliament, and when we enter upon this important question, we find ourselves hampered by this preconceived opinion, which we are as much at a loss to get rid of, as we are to say how we acquired it. The advocates for a reform in parliament are not only bound to shew that abuses exist in the practice of our government, but also that they are the consequences of some defect in our constitution, which the specific remedy they propose will eradicate. Now I do not pretend to deny that some abuses have crept in, and I contend that the instant these abuses are discovered to have a mischievous tendency, and to act like a *remora* on the vessel of the state, they should be instantly removed: it is therefore a reform of abuses and not a reform of parliament, that should be the rallying point for men of every description. Among the abuses which have arisen, it must be confessed that rotten boroughs form a part. But this may be remedied without doing violence to our constitution; the abuse has arisen out of the impolicy of making those privileges local, which ought to have been general; and where would be the injustice of adding the members for such places to the members for the county? I am aware that many of these boroughs are become private property, and that the members are liable to be nominated by one or two persons. But any injustice that might attach to the alteration proposed would be avoided by giving a fair price to the present proprietor of the right. The bargain to the public would be cheap at almost any price; for what would the money be to a nation that can spend eighty millions annually? As to the crown, who is there that would not joyfully add to its splendor and means of gratification, if we were allowed, in return, to abate the indirect influence of ministers? Who would be jealous of the executive power, if the utmost degree of independence were given to parliament? Who would not cheerfully pay their taxes, if simplicity and frugality were introduced among the several branches of public expenditure: *if every improper expence were reduced, if sinecures were abolished, if places of exorbitant profit were regulated, if that part of the public money, which must necessarily remain under discretionary trusts were properly secured, if peculation were duly punished,* and if a wise, vigorous, and prudent administration of affairs were unequivocally to take place? But there is another measure still more important: I mean the amelioration and improvement of the lower classes by education. What other religious principle is seriously inculcated with a religious view among the poor, except that of bigotry, or to speak more plainly, that of hating their neighbour? What other mode of carrying the political wishes into effect is ever taught them but by means of violence? If abuses are thus removed on one side, and if the manners of the populace are softened on the other by education, no factious declaimer, no seditious demagogue, would be able to disturb our peace, or compromise our tranquillity. Liberty would not seek her temple on the sands of democracy, nor ambition find supporters in the people whose interests it betrays.

When the poor, in consequence of being ill-educated, are ignorant and dissolute, they are easily deluded or corrupted; and it is, therefore, difficult to preserve good order and tranquillity amongst them, and this is still less likely to be effected, if they are given a share in the representation before their minds are prepared to enjoy the boon with advantage. In this country we find our representative system made up of partial representation and partial delegation; and I for one am really desirous of maintaining this scheme, being convinced that it only requires to be practised upon its own principles to make us happy. When we survey the countries that surround us, it must surely exalt and confirm our patriotism to reflect, that our constitution has survived the shocks by which every other has been destroyed, and that we are not enquiring what constitution is the best, but whether the one we possess shall be preserved for us and for our posterity. I am far from asserting that this constitution is incapable of improvement, or that we have no right to improve it: as little am I disposed on the other hand, to admit the fanciful dictum of the indefeasible and imprescriptable right of man, in a state of society, to assent or dissent from the laws by which he is to be bound, either by himself or his representative; the fact is that these right, as they are called, are compromised and affected by a thousand incidental circumstances. If I were disposed, for the sake of argument, to admit the existence of such rights, I should still maintain, first, that large and extensive concerns, in proportion to their importance, have a claim to be separated from general rules, and are rather to be considered and decided upon as such, according to their own bearing and operations: secondly, I should maintain that the first right of man is to be as happy as possible, consistently with a similar right in other men, every other right being subordinate to this leading right, and serving only as the means to this end. In the great system of society, therefore, if it should happen, as it necessarily does, that a large description of mankind should be found below that temperament, either of virtue or knowledge, which is necessary to enable them to assist, either by themselves or by their delegates, in judging of their general welfare; the happiness of the whole will require the exclusion of such portion from all interference in the business of politics and legislation: an exclusion which though it is much to be lamented, and as soon as possible to be terminated, yet is, in respect to all good purposes, only nominal: since the exercise of the faculty of judging is only denied to those who are really destitute of the faculty itself. Men may, therefore, so far as relates to politics, be divided into three classes: those who can judge for themselves, those who are able to select others to judge for them, and those who are not capable of doing either. Delegation unites the two first of these classes. Now, great as the advocates for general representation, which shall include the last class, represent this blessing to be, they cannot deny that it ought at first, like life and food to men who have been famished in dungeons, to be administered with caution, and by degrees, and that therefore education must always prepare the way for extending the representation, in every scheme which has for its object to include the lower orders of society. But delegates chosen by them would endanger other rights far more important to them than those of election. They would also endanger the happiness of other men than those by whom they were chosen, and would prevent that gradual improvement in all classes which ought to be one great object of government. Demagogues consider the ignorant and the poor merely as the means of power, considering themselves as the end, and will have no scruple to employ that very despotism which they deprecate in others, both to acquire power and to support themselves in the possession of it. It is not therefore because they are poor that they are provisionally suspended from the elective franchise, but because the want of property indicates a state of dependance, and a want of that knowledge, without which the exercise of that right might be rendered more mischievous than beneficial to themselves: and this provisional exclusion cannot in my opinion be removed with safety, until that happy period shall arrive, when the administration of public affairs shall offer less temptation for doing wrong, and individuals have a better disposition towards doing right than at present. It seems a strange sort of conduct to neglect the poor and then to plead their ignorance as a reason for denying them either trust or engagement. Let them be educated first, and they will be worthy of confidence. Is it not a general scandal that the chief consolation of the poor in most countries is liquor, and that nothing is thought so dreadful as to let them have any time at their own disposal, though when men are rendered tractable by education, and their manners softened by knowledge, of all indulgencies leisure is the cheapest and most obvious. But though reform ought first to take place in the habits and manners of the people, the neglect of duty in those who have the power to promote it, is no excuse for neglect on the part of those to whom it rests to reform the abuses that press upon the feelings of the people; let a eform of those things anticipate their wishes, that those who have to grant it may themselves adjust its manner and its measure; but if it is to be adjourned to seasons of disappointment or distress, of danger or of difficulty, and if the people themselves shall be goaded on, till they prescribe the sort of reform that shall take place, to yield will be as dangerous as ungracious.

There is an Italian proverb which says that the Italians are wise before they begin a thing, the Germans while they are about it, and the French when it is over. Let us then be a little wiser than the French, *before it is too late*; for when the state of public affairs, and the temper of the times are duly considered by the wise and the good, it is but too evident that to correct what is actually wrong, is now the only just and efficacious means by which we shall be able to preserve what is really-excellent in the practice of our constitution.

W. G——.

EPIGRAMS.

ON READING THE FIRST LINE OF AN EPITAPH.

Here *lies* Tom Williams, who untimely died,
Well—what of that?—the fellow always *lied!*

THE MYSTERY UNFOLDED.

While disappointment bows their heads with shame,
Oh *fickle* prince! the downcast *Outs* exclaim:
As with their shouts of joy they rend the sky,
Oh *mighty* prince! the exulting *Ins* reply:
Yet in one sentiment they both agree,
For *mi*-ty things are often *maggotty*.

EPITAPH ON ADMIRAL COTTON.

In this family vault, a philosopher lies,
Who puzzled of Paris the students so wise,
Till at last having tried all the universe round,
That *Cotton* could never be *worsted* they found.

A LAMENTABLE CASE.

Unhappy Peter, always mellow,
Seized at last with jaundice yellow;
At once forsakes his wine and liquor,
And for the doctor, leaves the vicar;
But, alas, drenched with prescriptions,
Of all prices and descriptions,
He finds himself of drops and pill sick,
No longer *bil*-ious but *bill-sick*.

EPIGRAM.

When R—e in the "*bucket*," first dipt his sleek ears,
His bosom retain'd what would calm all his fears,
   And soften his frowning;
But indifferent he felt, if he sunk or he floated,
For he very well knew, who's to "*hanging*"-devoted,
   Should never fear—"*drowning*."

AN OLD EPIGRAM REVIVED.

What can *Tommy Onfast* do?
Why drive a phaeton and two:
Can *Tommy Onfast* do no more?
Yes—drive a phaeton and four.

The above epigram was made many years ago, upon the now venerable son of a venerable peer, whose ancestor having been formerly a great *speaker* in a great house of *common* resort, the said Tommy is as desirous of the fame of a fast speaker, as of a rapid driver, and aims at the character of a wit.

He was once in high favor with a certain portly gentleman, of great personal beauty; and now of the age of fifty, who was then and is still the absolute *regent* of all fashion and frivolity; who governs all the shapes of the tailors, all the gaudy varieties of the fancy waistcoat manufacturers, with unrivalled genius, and undisputed sway; and whom, therefore, we shall designate by the title of the *pink of the mode,* or for shortness the *pink,* or the P——.

This gentleman and the P——, it is believed, are no longer on terms of intimate friendship, and the cause of their difference, is stated to have originated in a dirty, but as it must be admitted witty and princely joke, upon Tommy O——.

The fact is thus narrated by Tommy himself, to some of his friends after dinner.

The P—— invited him to a festive entertainment at *Carburton-house,* with G. H. and many other wits and practical jokers of the day. Charles Fox's well known trick of getting a porter to bedaub his breeches, and then laying a bet that he had not done it himself, was it is believed amongst the pleasant stories that served to exhilirate the hours of *modish* gaiety.

The P—— was determined to imitate the wit and statesman, after his own fashion. The company sat late after dinner, and a dead sett was made at *Tommy O——* to get him drunk; when *big Sam,* or some other porter of adequate capacity, was ordered to prepare a bed for *Tommy,* and to warm it, not with the usual warming-pan, but with the warm contents of an infant's easy chair.

When thus prepared *Tommy* was put to bed in a state of absolute intoxication as great as a king, insensible to his present state, and dreaming of future greatness from the favors of his all accomplished and elegant *prince,* the *Adonis* of his day, the delight of all his friends, the terror of all his enemies, and the more than tenth wonder of the world.

In the morning the P—— and his friends were at *Tommy's* bed-side to hail his recovery and witness his confusion.

It is needless to add that as Tommy is a gentleman, he could not endure to expose himself to such practical jokes, for he says with the French, *Jeu de main est jeu de vilain,* or in other words, *horse play is fit only for horse jockeys and not for princes.*

He, therefore, has long since absented himself from *Carburton House* and the society of the P——.

MODERN AMUSEMENTS,
OR,
SPORTING EXTRAORDINARY.

How absurd to suppose that those men of high fashion,
Who still in the vortex of pleasure would dash on,
Will attempt no new methods, their purses to drain,
But the same round of pleasures again and again;
No! their spirits are such, and the public must own it,
In fact the late " *bettings*" completely have shewn it,
That sooner than suffer their tastes to be sated,
By common " *amusements*" they long time have hated,
And fearing that " custom" in time would be "law,"
They thousands have lost on the length of a " *straw.*"

See F—l—y at White's, play from morning till night,
With K-nn-rd on his left, L-v-s-n G-w-r on his right;
" A thousand! I have it,"—" I'll take you," " done;"
    " done;"
He throws—" Ha, ha! Kinny you see that I've won,"
" I'll again," " make it double"-—" ay, or whoever choses;"
He throws—Kinny laughs—pray why? F-l-y loses.

See E-g-r-t-n, Sh-l-y, and C-v-d-sh, three
As eager for sporting, as e'er they can be,

On Newmarket's heath met, midst their horses and
 hounds,
And thus bet on the sport, as they ride o'er the grounds;
Cries Sir John—" little Dimity's sure to be in,"
" No!" says E–g–rt–n, " Quixote will certainly win,"
" Pugh! Nonsense!" bawls C–v–nd–h, " to cut the debate
" I'll give you the odds, that Quixotte's in late,
" And that long back'd Potoooooooo's comes in for the
 plate."

Soon crown'd with success, then he swaggers away,
'Till R-tl-nd, or R---d, chance to offer him play;
" Done," " done!" still to all cries this turf-beating block-
 head,
And when doubling his bets, 'tis his chance to be jockey'd.

See B-r-l-y a brawny, rough broth-eating Scot,
Who's for walking, or fighting,—billiards, what not?
Who's even desirous to keep in the " *stocks*,"
And is up to all tricks, from the " *pit*," to the " *box* :"
Good at driving, or where better hand at a " *milling* ?"
On the " *Champion*" he'll take you a pound to a shilling,
Win his bets," *clash the tits*," to the bank, till they foam,
There deposit his winnings, dismount, and walk home.

And so pregnant with wonders, so bright is this age,
Some shine at the "*bar*," and some on the *stage*,"
For as W—sh on new readings has thrown a new light,
And shone at the " *'ar*" as a " *rogue*" clearly bright;
So C-a-t-s on the " *stage*," who would Romeo rule,
When he set up as " *player*," got set down a " *fool*."

But in telling my story, I mean to delight ye,
And not by a " *humbugging*" tale to affright ye:
So I'll on without any more fuming or fretting,
To tell you of Y-r-m-th's new method of betting;
Yet you'll not be surpris'd, such was born in his head,
When his brain is so hot, that his hair is burnt red;

Yet so *high* was his pride, and so *low* was his purse,
That he scorn'd the old way, (thought 'twas nothing
    to us,)
If he mix'd, (but for once,) his purse to make fatter
The *slang* of the *turf* with *political matter.*

To D-n-h-m-re off with a smiling complexion,
He started, quite big with his mighty projection;
" I'll bet you a thousand," his L—p out-thunder'd,
" That to-night on your list, you'll not count two-hun-
    dred;
And I'll give any odds, and to take them here's plenty,
You won't have *that* number, even by twenty."
" Done!" D-n-h-m-re cried, " I'll engage to have more
Than what you have mention'd at least, by a score,
For G-tt-n full well knows the sense of the house,"
" As for that," replied Y——h, " I don't care a louse;
If I win but my bet, and can keep but my station,
I don't care a d—n what becomes of the nation;
And so certain am I of succeeding to day,
That even my " *whiskers*" I'd venture to lay;
But will any more bet? pray M—v-lle will you?
The Scotsman " *nae*" answer'd, but gave him a " *boo;*"
Which Y——h return'd, to the rest made a leg,
Then went off to the house, his friend's voices to beg;
But ah! when got there, his amazement how great,
To find T—y and W—tb—-d ad settled his fate;
And his " *friends*" had to fill up his measure of woe,
Each answer'd to " *aye*" when he wanted a " *no.*"

Then quickly he hied to his mother the " *Quean,*"
And cries " dearest mother, I cheated have been,
But hope in my cause, you will join pure and hearty,
And give me revenge on the whole of that party;
Though T—y should turn his coat over again,
And for place should he sue, let him sue, but in vain;
And I hope to fright W—tb—-d, and punish his fault,
You'll propose an additional " *tax*" upon " *malt.*"

To the world his late actions have render'd it plain,
And decidedly prov'd him a *—————— in " *grain*,"
So I'll now take my leave, dearest mother, and since
People well know the power you possess o'er the P———e;
So influence his mind, as to work their undoing,
And speedily bring the whole party to *ruin*."

L. L.

DANIEL ISAAC EATON.

On the 2d of this month Daniel Isaac Eaton, an old man nearly seventy years of age, who had been convicted of publishing the Third Part of Paine's Age of Reason, was sentenced to be imprisoned eighteen months in the gaol of Newgate, and to stand once in the first month of his confinement in the pillory. It will no doubt afford the attorney-general unmingled pleasure to be informed that on the execution of the latter part of the sentence he was received by the spectators with the most evident testimonies of applause; but for our own parts, feeling as we do the most anxious wish that the influence of christianity may be extended rather than diminished, we could not but regard the prosecution and punishment of this unfornate old man as tending to give new vigor to infidelity, and to weaken the religious impressions of the multitude. The severity of the sentence, even supposing the guilt of Mr. Eaton to have been attended with every possible aggravation, could not but strike the most indifferent observer: the actual infliction of punishment, as it must be the offspring of persecution or necessity, implied in the one case, the inefficiency of argument to support the interests of religion, and in the other, the convenient assumption of religious zeal as a pretext for the

---

* *Brewer*, we suppose.

exercise of arbitrary power. It must have occurred to the most unreflecting spectator, that christianity is the religion of peace and charity, and that a mode of faith, which requires the interference of the executioners of the law, to support its interests, and defend its doctrines, possesses in itself no inherent principle of stability. That the last of those conclusions is erroneous, does not justify the imprudence or vindictiveness of the civil power: the people are not accustomed to distinguish between the folly of the conduct of the magistrate, as directed by the pressure of circumstances, and as influenced by the omnipotence of his own intemperate passions. It is true, that religion stands in need of no auxiliary support from the constituted authorities; but the natural tendency of Sir Vicary's conduct has been to teach them that it does. Those also who believe the punishment to be disproportioned to the crime, will transfer their prepossessions against Eaton's prosecutors, to the motives by which they have been avowedly directed. In their minds, religious zeal will always bear the semblance of persecution; and should the cause of infidelity obtain, in *any quarter of the world*, a partial or momentary ascendancy, its votaries when they devote the resources of the civil power to the extirpation of christianity, may appeal for a justification of their cruelties, to the example set before them by the " lights of our church, and the guardians of our laws."

If it be just to punish an individual for writing against the Christian religion, because it is the religion of the state, or because it conduces in the opinion of the attorney-general to the happiness of mankind, then it is equally just to punish to the same degree the literary advocates of the Unitarians and the Catholics. In the opinion of a Lutheran officer of the crown, the doctrines of Calvin are injurious to the happiness of mankind, and their universal reception would contribute to the downfall of the national religion; and their professors ought therefore to be visited with imprisonment and the pillory. The legislature has indeed defined the limits of punishment, and virtually declared that infidelity is more criminal than dissent; but it has left to the attorney-general a discretionary power of prosecution, and to the judges the privilege of pronouncing a sentence proportionate to the crime; and according to the only principles on which Eaton has been brought to shame, the laws against infidels and dissenters ought to be in the one case so rigidly, and in the other so leniently, enforced, as nearly to coincide. According to the argument derived from expedience, the guilt in both cases is the same, and the degrees of punishment therefore should be equal.

But we are told that the infidel attacks the *fundamentals* of religion, the dissenter only denies his belief to a few subordinate particulars. But it is still on the ground that a national religion is necessary to the existence of the state, that the infidel is punished, and *that* religion must be composed of articles, all of which are disputed in rotation by the various sects, and the fundamental articles therefore must be disputed by some of them. If the divinity of Christ be a fundamental article of the Catholic religion, it is equally denied by the socinian and the infidel. Yet even Sir Vicary Gibbs would be startled at the idea of subjecting a Socinian to the discipline of the pillory: and were Paine and Priestley to rise from the dead, the former would share the dungeon of his publisher, while the latter would be suffered to pursue a new career of wealth and popularity.

The argument so ingeniously drawn by Mr. Prince Smith from the circulation of the classic authors appears to us to be extremely defective in its application to the point at issue. We laugh at the mythology of the ancients as at a dream long past: in the system of their belief there is little that is impressive or seductive; nor would there be any danger that an individual unshackled by the belief of any other religion would be converted to the worship of Jupiter and Juno. Unless he be an ideot or a madman, the christian will not go over to them;

and there is nothing in the writings of their worshippers, that is directly applicable to christianity. They could not bring forward arguments against a religion that they did not know: there may be scattered throughout their works, the embryo principles of general scepticism; but there is nothing peculiarly applicable to the christian, rather than any other system of belief; nothing that deduces from the history of the faith itself, or from the language of its teachers, the grounds of its rejection. But works like those of Volney and Paine, combine the general principles of scepticism, to be found in the writings of the ancient, with arguments peculiarly applicable to christianity. Whether, therefore, their reasonings be founded on correct principles, and be conducted according to the laws of genuine philosophy, or be the mere delusions of disingenuous sophistry, their application is obvious: they shock the piety of those who can understand nothing but their object, and afford materials of superficial declamation or wanton ridicule to the impious. By what mode of reasoning the seminal system of Lucretius, or the atomical hypotheses of Epicurus, may serve the purposes of the atheist, reflection and learning will alone be able to discover; but when one passage of scripture is brought to contradict another, the argument is easily understood. The impression on the mind of a superficial reader, is strong and immediate: and a degree of patient investigation, not usually to be found in the middle and the lower classes of life, may be necessary to trace or to understand the refutation of a trivial and futile objection.

If zeal for the glory of religion, were the stimulus to Sir Vicary's exertions, how will he be able to justify his forbearance towards those, who beneath the garb of sanctity, expose religion to the pity or the derision of the multitude? - Eaton is surely a monster of unequalled virtue, compared with him who employs the name of the Almighty for the purposes of fraud; and to deny the divinity of Christ is a more venial crime than to degrade him to the level of a tailor or a shoe-black. Surely Sir Vicary is not of opinion that blasphemous hypocrisy is more pardonable than open infidelity.

If infidels be punishable at all, why has Mr. Eaton been selected as the only object of unexampled severity? Hundreds of books more dangerous in their tendency than the Age of Reason, issue daily from the press, some by the modern inhabitants of Grub-street, and some by the philosophers of other times and other countries. A correspondent has recommended to the notice of the editor, Middleton on the early Fathers, Gibbon's History (as to the origin of christianity,) Mirabeau's *Ami d'Hommes*, Mirabaud's *Systeme de la Nature*, Volney's Ruins, Adam Smith's works, Condorcet's last work, and Godwin's Political Justice. These he supposes the editor has not had time to read; but he is not probably aware that, abroad they are smuggled into monasteries, and are found at home, either in the school room, or the circulating library. At Cambridge, Adam Smith must be read by any man who pretends to general information: and Gibbon's history is of course on the desk of every studious undergraduate. Yet, strange to say, the same attorney-general who feels so sensitively alive to the interests of religion, when attacked by an Eaton or a Paine, stands tamely by, while the minds of many hundred individuals destined in future life to become the ornaments of the church, the senate, or the bar, are perverted, or corrupted! It does not follow that because they have received a university education they are invulnerable to the assaults of infidelity. Indolence, a love of hypothesis, the secret impulse of vicious propensities, restrained only by the irksome fetters of early prepossession, and the inability to distinguish between truth and sophistry, necessarily incident to the majority even of well-educated men, all conspire to enfeeble the resistance of the young enquirer to the approaches of scepticism; and if force be more efficacious in the service of religion, than the literary efforts of its champions, it is the imperative duty of the government to suppress the writings of Hume, and Smith, and Middleton.

It is not our present purpose to enquire into the degree of moral criminality that attaches to the publication of attacks even on the useful prejudices of mankind; but we cannot help expressing our contempt and reprobation of that common and vulgar cant which distinguishes the sceptical essays of the Examiner. If a writer will publish his infidelity, we have a right to expect that he will communicate the reasons on which he grounds his claim to applause or indulgence. The Examiner, instead of employing any arguments in favor of his apostacy, is content with appealing to a well regulated conscience. But the idea of a well regulated conscience, presupposes a *regulator*; and the definition of the word *conscience* itself, is yet a desideratum in the language of infidelity. If the sceptic means by conscience an innate principle, that independently of education, and of times and circumstances, judges intuitively of right and wrong, then no man ever fell into error through ignorance of his duty, the suicides of Jagernaut, are as deserving of admiration as a Howard, or a Hawes; and Bellingham, because he was perfectly satisfied with himself, which he could not have been, had his conscience afflicted him, was as virtuous a character as Mr. Perceval. But if by conscience be meant a faculty of determining between right and wrong, conferred by education, it is natural to ask, from what source the principles impressed on our minds by our instructors were derived; and by what motives we are excited to obey them in the regulation of our conduct. If it even be admitted, that a knowledge of vice and virtue, could be derived from any other source than revelation, the latter part of the question exposes the sceptics to a dilemma, from which they have not yet endeavoured to escape. They assert, indeed, that they refrain from vice, and practice virtue, because they believe, that to do so is the surest mode of obtaining happiness. Now supposing contrary to all experience, that goodness was its own reward, and that vice entailed upon itself the just punishment of its errors, how few among mankind could be taught to regulate their conduct, by this conviction. Mankind are more forcibly influenced by immediate impressions than by abstract conclusions. They see the idle and the profligate in the full and undisturbed enjoyment of wealth and honors, while virtue is doomed to languish in indigence and obscurity: whatever philosophy may tell them, they believe that the possessor of rank and fortune is happier than the victim of poverty and neglect; with no other motive to guide their steps than the pursuit of their own individual happiness, they would rather be prosperous with the wicked, than unfortunate with the virtuous. Even those who believe, contrary to daily and repeated evidence, that in the affairs of life, *honesty is the best policy*, will not, even on the principle of self-interest, be restrained from the commission of vices not immediately inconsistent with their professional pursuits. The soldier may in the hope of preferment fulfil his duty to his monarch; but will his propensity to seduction be restrained by his desire of happiness?

Human nature, influenced solely by the consideration of temporal advantage, cannot be always on its guard. The prospect of a great but improper advantage to be obtained with little prospect of discovery, tempts the avarice or ambition of the merchant or the statesman. It is but a balance of probabilities; the future is at a distance, and present happiness is within view. Who can blame the sceptic if he hesitates, or if he snatches the present enjoyment, and trusts the rest to fortune and futurity?

The Jews alone, of all the nations with which we are acquainted, looked forward to no other rewards and punishments than such as were of a temporal nature; and their character the same and unchangeable from age to age, has been a compound of meanness and artifice. In every transaction of life, the present advantage is always before them, and honor and interest equally give way to the desire of immediate gratification. To render virtue firm, undeviating, and consistent, it is necessary that the rewards of virtue, and the punishment of vice, should be independent of contingencies; offering no promise of evasion to the artful, or of concealment to the timid. That final retribution from which even death affords no refuge, and from which neither artifice nor talent, assisted by good fortune, can escape, is the only punishment that influences the imagination of the wicked in its most secret purposes, and gives to futurity precedence over the present.

We firmly believe that from that religion of which they express their disbelief, the sceptics have derived all their notions of that sublime morality, on the beauties of which they dwell with such rapturous enthusiasm; that the best of them fulfil the various duties of life from the habitual influence of religious education, and from secret but unconscious impressions of the fate that await the virtuous and the wicked in a state of future retribution.

That there may be conscientious deists, no one but an uncharitable bigot would deny; but the duty of proselytism is not enforced by any law of reason or philosophy: and granting for a moment that the christian religion were a wild and extravagant system, originating in superstition, and upheld by interest, it may still become an object of serious inquiry with the conscientious deist, whether by extirpating what is intrinsically false, he is not likely to destroy much that is incidentally valuable; and whether in attempting the destruction of the tree itself, he may not be the cause of destruction to the beautiful and salutary plants that were supported by its trunk, and waved beneath its branches?

FEMALE SHOEMAKERS.

MR. EDITOR,

You will no doubt be astonished to hear that in the vicinity of Bloomsbury-square, and indeed in other respectable places, ladies whose external appearance betokens gentility and independence, are now become their own shoemakers. Yes, they absolutely manufacture all their summer and winter shoes, which must surely be a greater injury to the trade than employing journeymen who have not served their time. How any delicate lady can sit down to such laborious work, and spoil her tender hands, by drawing a wax-end, is to me surprising. It is an evident proof of the caprice of the female sex. Were any husband to enjoin his wife to undertake the task, she would become indignant on the occasion, and tell all her neighbours, that her good man, forsooth, wanted her to make her own pumps and boots. This I am wisely assured of, by the conduct of my own lady, who though not of a very tender delicate frame peremptorily refused, during the honey-moon, to cut out an upper leather for me. " I suppose," cried she, in a voice of thunder, " you will next desire me to cut out a *sole;* but no, Mr. Crispin, I will never do any thing that is derogatory to the *soft* sex."

In this improving age, it seems ladies are losing a major part of their *softness;* they are not only determined to hurt linendrapers, &c. by curtailing their dresses, but they are absolutely taking the bread out of shoemakers' mouths, and I should not wonder, if by and bye, they dispensed with all tradespeople. This industrious conduct can only be ascribed to an affectation of prudence and economy ; and since ladies can voluntarily work so hard, husbands may now exact from them a double portion of labor. But, in my opinion, they save nothing by manufacturing their own shoes; domestic business (which *men* cannot perform) must be neglected, and while they are affixing *heels* to their boots, they ought perhaps to be darning the heels of their stockings.

I have written these few lines, as hints to leather-*sellers*, hoping that they will put an additional price upon these materials, when selling them to any person not in the *trade*: ladies will then find themselves out of pocket, by making their own shoes, and they must be very industrious indeed, if they then continue the employment.

I am, Sir,
Your humble servant,
CRISPIN.

Holborn.

A LOYAL HARANGUE.

Sir William Curtis rose, and expressed himself in the strongest terms of enthusiasm. He assured the chairman and the company, that nothing could be more *palatable* to his taste, than the testimony of their approbation, just conferred upon him. He flattered himself, that he felt a peculiar *relish* for the society of the loyal and respectable members of the livery of London. He hoped that their resolutions would be thoroughly *digested*, and would convince the people, that the citizens of the metropolis of the world, disdained to *purvey* to the public *appetite*, for democratical insolence and abuse. He felt a *pie-house* awe, whenever the name of patriotism was employed, for the worst of purposes. People had accused him of *fishing* for popularity; but he defied any one to prove that he had ever *swallowed* a bribe, or drank so deep as the patriots themselves, at the fountain of corruption. He was convinced, that the proceedings of that day would place the rebellious and disaffected in a very aukward *pickle*—he begged pardon, he meant to say *predicament*. They had *floundered* terribly of late, and would soon be *dished*. He had never mounted the *roast-rump*—yes, *roast-rump* he repeated, for he had heard the word in Julius Cæsar, for the purpose of deluding the multitude. He had already witnessed many scenes of noise and turbulence, but hoped that the vessel of state would ultimately ride in safety, like a civic yacht in the *port* of London. There was plenty of *food* for observation in the remarks that had been already made by the gentleman who preceded him; but he would not trouble the company with *soup*-erfluous observations. He would, however, hold out the *olive*-branch of peace, to his political opponents; and though he *boiled* with indignation at the thoughts of compromise, he could find in his heart to eat at the same table with the bitterest of his foes. It was not his custom to *mince* matters, and if he thought that any individual in that room was inclined to a compromise, he would *spit* him. The opposite party were extremely *saucy*, and deserved to be well *peppered* by the Attorney General. He was surprized to see so few gentlemen of the *cloth:* he was aware that some persons might mistake his meaning, and he therefore thought it proper to declare that he did not allude to the table cloth. He was surprized, he repeated, to see so few clergymen in the assembly; since no three things accorded so well as religion, loyalty, and good-living. But he must now hasten to conclude: he was melted almost to a *jelly*, and would sit down perfectly *satisfied*, if he should be allowed the humble merit of having fulfilled all the duties of a good citizen: he certainly preferred solid pudding to empty praise; but syllabub, though unsubstantial in itself, was a very good accompaniment to turtle or venison. He thanked the company for the attention they had paid to him, and after thanking the chairman for the intellectual feast afforded them by his opening address, gave place to the next speaker.

POLITICAL OBSERVER. No. XI.

The formation of a vigorous ministry has already occupied a fortnight, and the arrangements have not yet approached to a conclusion. Lord Wellesley disdains to serve under the banners of a Liverpool; and Lord Liverpool declares that he will not truckle to a Wellesley. The Catholic question, on which these patriotic statesmen profess to differ, is only a secondary occasion of quarrel; personal precedency is the important subject of dispute, and to the selfish vanity of these individuals the interests of the country, and the dignity of the prince, have become an equal sacrifice. That the Marquis should indeed obtain the first place in whatever administration may be formed, is due to his services and his talents: as a politician, who is willing to serve his country when his services are likely to benefit himself, he may not deserve our reprehension; but as a patriot, the importance he attaches to his own precedency, degrades his character, and effaces his pretensions to public virtue. But what in him may in some measure be excused, as a just sense of his own importance, is in Lord Liverpool the downright fatuity of egotism: like wiser and better men, he has mistaken length of possession for original right; and fancies himself a great minister because fortune in one of her sportive moods deprived the counting-house of a useful servant, by opening to his view the honors and emoluments of office.

The same regard to etiquette is observable between the Marquis and Lord Grenville. Lord Moira was at one time to be made first lord of the Treasury, that Lords Wellesley and Grenville, who both aspired to the presidentship, might be placed on an equal footing. Last night, however, a *projet* was actually circulated, in which Lord Grenville's name was affixed to the presidentship of the council, that very office for his acceptance of which Lord

Sidmouth has repeatedly sustained the taunts and ridicule of the opposition. " How is thy greatness fallen," exclaimed the partizans of Lord Grenville, when the ci-devant Chancellor of the Exchequer sunk into the insignificance of of an unimportant office. " How is thy greatness fallen," we exclaimed, on reading the *projet* of last night, and learning, from unquestionable authority, that it was the production of Lord Moira, and had been received without humiliation by Lord Grenville. Yet it was not for any want of inclination to accede to the overtures of the Regent, that Lord Grenville has sustained so bitter a disappointment. Both he and his colleagues have displayed a pliability of principle, commensurate with their eagerness for the enjoyment of place and power. With regard to the war on the Peninsula, (which they at first opposed, *merely* because to oppose it would annoy the ministers,) they declare "that to give any decided opinion on its management, would be impossible without access to official documents:" intimating, in reality, that when they come in they will tell us more about it; and preparing the way for their conversion, without subjecting themselves to the charge of inconsistency. They had forgotten, when they so unwarily declined to offer an opinion on the management of the war, without access to official documents, that they had already expressed themselves, rep atedly and decidedly, in reprobation of the manner in which it had been conducted. According, therefore, to their own declaration, they censured the measures of the persons to whom the prosecution of the war was committed, without any materials before them from which to deduce an opinion, and excited by no other motive than the mere necessity of pertinacious opposition.

'If Lord Grey, the haughty " *propugnator*" of aristocracy, hot with the tuscan grape, and high in blood at the moment of expected possession, has found that as long as an English governor respects the popular opinion, so long Lord Grey must be content to amuse himself with distant speculations on the pride, pomp, and circumstance of the foreign office.' Lord Grenville, whose whole political life appears to have been expressly of that nature, which it would be most advantageous for a true statesmen to study (as navigators study a map of rocks and shoals) has passed sentence upon himself, and under no aspect of public affairs, can he hope to obtain the public confidence. What man can rely on his political honesty? What man will believe his political creed? What man will be attached by his popular professions? We believe, solemnly, not one. And is this all that can be done, by high rank, large fortune, and public opportunities? Is this the melancholy account, of all that is left to Lord Grenville, after a political life of thirty years. *Annon* (says Cicero), *Annon vindices fiunt Dei immortales ipsi? Annon æstuat cœli ira eos, qui capessant, tantum ut prodint rempublicam.*

But we have still some feeling for Lord Grenville. Cicero in the *De Senectute* talks of the incomparable delight of retirement, to a man who has no other task than to recapitulate his good deeds, and prepare for that state, to which the Greys and the Grenvilles, the weak and the wavering, the petulant and the proud, must go down like Pitt and Nelson. But we do not wish the faculties of those distinguished peers and accomplices to be altogether indolent. We will give Lord Grenville, in the first place, as matter of contemplation, the necessary odium which falls sooner on every man hardened and heartless by nature, tricking and shuffling by habit, using the popular cause to push himself within the reach of power, participating in the clamours of the multitude without a consideration of the mischiefs which they might extend; but only looking forward to the impulse which they might give to his own advancement. There are such men in society; but they are generally to be found among the low in fortune, the ruined in character. It was left for *us* to see one of the leviathans of the state raising the storm, exciting it by every means that great power and great influence gave to his use, careless of the evil which might be done by its tumult, and only looking on each successive burst of the great ocean of popular feeling, as a successive impulse to his progress. It gives us all the genuine delight of retributive justice, to see the leviathan, just as he had reached his object, deserted by the waves, the waters at once retiring from him, and leaving him a spectacle of helpless awkwardness on the shore; a mark for every petty weapon; a mass of lifeless blubber, without animation or vitality.

We do not say that it is impossible for the Grenvilles to obtain an ascendancy in the Prince's councils: the weakness of one party, and the uncompromising character of another, may render the conditional appeal to a third not only expedient but necessary. But whatever they may have hitherto declared, even a regard to their own characters will compel them to adopt the leading features of the foreign policy pursued by their predecessors. They know that to withdraw our troops from the Peninsula would expose them to the execration of their country and of Europe; that it would obliterate in the nations of the continent all remembrance of British honor, and excite throughout the empire a mingled feeling of indignation and despair. Even admitting the impolicy of beginning the contest in the Peninsula, we are pledged to its continuance; but to continue it without exertion would be to expose ourselves to the resentment of our allies, and the ridicule of our enemies. We can maintain a body of inactive troops at home at a less expence than in Portugal; and a lingering and defensive warfare may exhaust our resources as effectually as an enterprising system of offence, without affording even the possibility of a triumphant issue.

We take it for granted, therefore, that if they return to power, they will feel it necessary, even at the risk of subjecting themselves to the charge of inconsistency, of pursuing the line of policy already recommended by Lord Wellesley: and since that nobleman is an advocate for the Catholic claims, what advantage do the friends of Roscoe, and the opponents of foreign warfare, expect from the return of the opposition to power? If even an objectionable line of policy be pursued, it is desirable indeed that it should be conducted with consummate talent, and atoned for by the attention of the ministers to domestic economy. Now, even the admirers of Lord Grenville will scarcely endeavour to place him on a level of political talent with Lord Wellesley; and if any doubts remain as to the inclination of either party to mitigate the burthens of the people, they are in favor of the latter. The former has been tried at home, and his pretensions to the character of a disinterested economist are well understood: the profusion of the latter, in a country where profusion was necessary, and where power is absolute, is by no means decisive evidence of his unwillingness to comply with the wishes of the people at home, by husbanding our revenues, and diminishing the amount of an unnecessary and extravagant expenditure. We may say of *him*, at least, what we cannot say of the opposition, that he squandered his treasures to some purpose; and was not at once timid and extravagant. Inattention to the minor considerations of pecuniary prudence, may be forgiven to the statesman and the warrior: the appropriation of the spoils of warfare may be granted to the conqueror; but contempt and detestation, only, are reserved for him who squanders the property of others because it does not impoverish himself; who claims the reward of services that he does not perform, and while he exhausts the resources of the empire committed to his guidance, neither extends its sway, nor confirms its stability.

May 29*th.*

CAMBRIDGE POLITICS.

Sir,

In an early number of your valuable publication you gave a detailed account of the intrigues employed to exclude the Rev. Dr. Browne, the Master of Christ's College, from his succession to the office of Vice Chancellor. That these intrigues were partly occasioned by the dread of his fearless and independent spirit, you hinted at the time, and your supposition has since been confirmed by the conduct of his opponents. Having fulfilled his duty according to the dictates of his conscience, he is now accused of being lukewarm in his country's cause, by men who have no other pretext of complaint than that he has opposed their endeavours to monopolise all the power inherent in the university, and to render it the instrument of base subservience to the existing government.

Dr. Mansell, the bishop of Bristol, having drawn up an address, expressive of the condolence of the university on occasion of the death of Mr. Perceval, and having contrived amongst other matters appropriate to the subject, to introduce the expression of certain political sentiments; Dr. Browne, coinciding in the general tenor of the address, yet unwilling to sanction the irrelevant and disputable sentences, laid before Dr. Mansell an amended address; in which the bishop, however, refused to acquiesce; and the original being actually presented by him to the *caput*, Dr. Browne in the conscientious performance of his duty threw it out. The amended petition was now introduced by Dr. Browne, after having received the approbation of every individual to whom it had been previously submitted. It conveyed no political sentiments, it merely condoled with the Regent on the death of Mr. Perceval, and expressed the satisfaction of the university, that the hand of the assassin had not been directed by the rage of party, or his crime been accomplished in participation with any description of political malcontents.

Yet, strange to say, the address was rejected at the instance of those who had approved of it, in private, not because it was improperly expressed, or conveyed any sentiment in which the whole university did not coincide, but because, to reject it, would revenge the cause of Dr. Mansell, and be retaliatory upon Dr. Browne, for his opposition to the original address. Such is the splendor of university wisdom, and such the radiance of academical virtue!

That Dr. Mansell accustomed to lord it over this establishment, without being opposed by the shadow of resistance, should have expressed much irritation at the issue of his exertions was to be expected. But he has not endeavoured to repair his defeat by any new effort at political composition: the University is quiescent; and the deputation to Carlton House, is in all probability postponed to a more favourable opportunity.

In the mean time the progress of the friends to Catholic emancipation is unexpectedly rapid. The heads of colleges are the only individuals who actively oppose it; petitions against it may be presented by secret combination and *finesse,* but the general disposition of the University is favourable to their claims. No one can accuse *us* of being inattentive to our own security, or the interests of the church; and if *we* be satisfied, the community at large need no longer be startled by the cry of emancipation.

W. J.

Cambridge, May 29, 1812.

THEATRICAL REVIEW.

*Nullius addictus jurare in verba magistri ;
Quo me cunque rapit tempestas deferor hospes.*

To flatter the Irish, is as dangerous as it is unnecessary. In the general character of the natives of the sister kingdom, an assumption of precedence is one of the most obvious features. The *ingenuus puer, ingenuique pudoris* is a phenomenon that we have not witnessed in the course of an extensive intercourse, with the juvenile part of the Irish community : they are loth that either their virtues or their talents, should remain undiscovered by their associates, and generously proclaim the mental and moral endowments, of which they suppose themselves to be the possessors. If any one species of *clap-trap* has been within the last five years, more disgusting than another, it has been the introduction of common-place eulogy on the Irish character. Scarcely a play is represented, in which we are not told that "though the head of an Irishman may sometimes lead him astray, his heart is never in the wrong place;" and "that dear little Ireland is the land of generous souls, but hasty tempers." That these assertions are partly true, we admit; but why must we be disgusted with their frequent and fulsome repetition ? From the anxiety of our playwrights, to introduce them into their productions, it might be imagined that the virtues of the Irish were problematical: gratitude is most warmly felt by those who possess the fewest claims upon our favor, and with whom the demonstration of our kindness is most unexpected ; and they who best deserve to be eulogized for their virtues, least regard the language of flattery or exaggeration.

Mrs. Lefanu, however, conceiving that a general prejudice against the natives of Ireland was entertained by their English brethren, has written a comedy for the sole purpose of exhibiting upon the stage 'an *Irish gentleman*' such as he now exists in society; and this purpose she has endeavoured to accomplish in the portraiture of Fitz-Edward. But her hero, though intended for an Irish gentleman, might be with equal propriety regarded as a Frenchman, a German, or an Englishman. In the written play, and independent of any additional feature of manners or character, superadded by the performer, Fitz-Edward is a young man of education and address, of generous sentiments and amiable habits. Mrs. Lefanu well knows that such individuals may be met with in as great a number even in this profligate and dissipated town as in the capital of Ireland; they have trodden the English stage from time immemorial, without exciting a suspicion that they were the " Sons of Erin," or being recognized as their brethren by the natives of the sister country.

To detail the plot of a comedy, affords but little pleasure to those who have not witnessed its representation, and is superfluous to those who have. The story of the Sons of Erin, is sufficiently interesting to keep the attention alive, though it displays no unusual powers of contrivance. To develope the good qualities of Fitz-Edward is the first purpose of the authoress, and she has therefore, introduced him as an amanuensis into the family of his wife, who are all provoked by her running away with an Irishman, and with whom she has in vain implored a reconciliation. Under the name of Melville, he obtains the confidence of his father-in-law (Mr. Rivers), the *love* of his maiden sister, and the respect of the other members of the family, and when he has succeeded in removing their prejudices, he discloses himself. The chief characters are Fitz-Edward, (Mr. *De Camp*); a fluttering, but insinuating coxcomb, who endeavours by flattering her passion for poetry and sentiment, to gratify his vanity rather than his passions; Patrick, the Irish servant of Sir Edward, (Mr. Johnston); Lady Ann Lovel (Miss Duncan) an Irish widow, whose vivacity is chastened by good sense, and whose frankness of manner gives new grace to virtue ; and Miss Ruth Rivers, a chemist and a blue stocking. The chief merit of Mrs. Lefanu's portraitures is the natural and unobtrusive expression of character. The features of the individuals are distinctly marked, and their deportment characteristically expressed ; yet the most perfect repose, and the most charming facility of manner, pervade the composition. Mrs. Lefanu is the Reynolds of the drama. She gives to common characters a grace and an expression that they do not originally possess, and conscious to what purposes her talents may be most effectually devoted, resigns the vain ambition to create, for the conscious certainty of giving new charms to truth, and new animation to virtue.

The dialogue, though it does not sparkle with wit, exhibits occasional examples of genuine humor, and is written with taste, feeling and simplicity. The sentiments when they are original animate the language of the dialogue, and when they do not surprize or impress the audience by their novelty, deserve the praise that Pope regarded as peculiarly applicable to wit; as being " what oft was thought, but ne'er so well expressed." Lady Ann speaking of *Oddly*, an eccentric, exclaims, " not that I like these mannerists in general: for singularity as often springs from affectation and vanity, as from peculiarity of character ; and we are seldom recompensed for th absence of good breeding, by the qualities which displaced it." Sir Frederic Fileamour, speaking to Mr. Rivers in th presence of his wife, exclaims officiously. " I shoul think Mrs. Rivers's uniform propriety puts calumny t defiance," and the observation gives rise to this reply an rejoinder.

" Sir F—— (*aside.*) Jealous by all that's fortunate I am well convinced of that; but surely you have n objection to all the world's paying homage to it ?

Mr. R—— not in the least, provided it be a silen one: but *praise from a common acquaintance, for thos* qualities, that *intimacy alone can discover, is as offensive to sense as delicacy.*"

The following is well expressed, though concluded by a pun.

"*Oddly.*—I rather doubt that, Sir: **your nervous ladies** can't endure the address of blunt honesty. They can brave the midnight air, after a hot ball-room, and the cold they take is nervous; but they are too delicate to risk their nerves by going to church. Their ears are nervous, their eyes are nervous, every thing is nervous about 'em, except a good nervous understanding."

The language of Patrick, the Irish servant, is neither crowded with oaths nor blunders; yet there is a raciness in his phraseology, that at once delights by its singularity, and impresses by its conformity to nature. He is an odd mixture of gallantry, affection, and amusing vanity.

Of the dialogue it is difficult to convey a correct idea, by a detached extract. The following scene affords a fair specimen of the diction.

"*Lady A.* Stop, I guess what you are going to say. But tell me about this fair lady of yours; for as my intimacy with her family commenced since her marriage, I never saw her: describe her, that I may judge whether she is worthy of having supplanted me.

Fitz. It would be difficult to find any one who could.

Lady A. Handsome no doubt she is; but has she an air, a manner, an indescribable something which is more alluring than beauty, more captivating than wit, more attracting than sensibility? Is she, in short—

Fitz. Like your charming self, my sweet cousin? no, positively, she is not like you, yet she is lovely.

Lady A. But how does this extraordinary goodness accord with her marrying you in a clandestine way.

Fitz. The only fault she ever committed. I found her at Bath, with an old deaf card-playing relation. She was in no great delight at her father's marriage. We pitied each other, and it led us further than we intended, even to Scotland.

Lady A. And your father, I suppose, in a spirit of

christian forgiveness, disinherited you for marrying without money.

Fitz. Oh, no, no; he did much worse—he left me his whole estate, and my own discretion was my only guide. Not to weary you with a history of thoughtless extravagance, three years almost completed my ruin: my estate is mortgaged—I left Ireland, where Emily remains to collect our little wreck of fortune, and came here to try mine in the lottery of great men's promises.

Lady A. And have you succeeded?

Fitz. No: nor do I think I shall. I have a very troublesome inmate in my heart that *won't* leave me a moment's quiet, *were* I to fashion my principles to my necessities.

Lady A. Perfectly right. But my heroic cousin might induce to starve rather than bend: yet for the sake of your Emily, I think you ought to try to accommodate matters. Let me interfere, I will speak to your father-in-law.

Fitz. Enough of self. Tell me, my fair monitress, something of your affairs. Fame has given you many lovers.

Lady A. She is too courteous; I wish for none. I have not the least inclination to part with my dearly prized liberty; I hate control; and when that submissive animal, a lover, is changed into that lordly one, a husband, adieu to all the delights of life.

Fitz. Why no; honestly speaking, you who are formed to inspire love—

Lady A. Oh! your servant, Sir!

Fitz. Do you pretend to say you never felt it?

Lady A. No, I never have. A vagrant Cupid may, in fluttering round me have brushed me with his wing, but I have escaped his dart. My father chose to marry me at sixteen to a man whom I tried to esteem, but whom nobody could love; and when after six years bondage I recovered my freedom, I determined not to surrender in a hurry.

Fitz. And therefore you refused me?

Lady A. If my heart is not very susceptible of love, I feel that it is capable of friendship; and believe me, Fitz-Edward, I will not rest till I have done something to serve you.

Fitz. (*Takes her hand and kisses it.*) I cannot express my gratitude.

Lady A. You need not. I do not require such warm acknowledgments."

The performers, with the exception of De Camp, fulfilled their respective parts, to the satisfaction of the audience, and evinced, by the success of their exertions, the possibility of representing with due effect a modern play that has not been written *for the actors*. Every individual was at home except the representative of Fitz-Edward, whose *hardness* and aukwardness of manner prevent him, notwithstanding his natural qualifications for the stage, from personating with success the heroes of genteel comedy. Elliston is the only performer on the stage who is capable of giving its full effect to a character like Fitz-Edward. Jones is too spruce, and smart, and *dapper*; Wrench is deficient in energy and enthusiasm, and Melvin gives to all his gentlemen the manners of a player. Elliston alone is at once the ardent lover, and the easy gentleman: graceful without foppery, and spirited without extravagance.

We are by no means the ardent admirers of the manager of the LYCEUM, and it is possible that the regard he has hitherto displayed to the interests of the legitimate drama, may be owing to his consciousness that a theatre so circumscribed in its dimensions, as that of which he is the manager, can neither remunerate the expence, nor afford occasion to the effective display of equestrian exhibitions. But to whatever cause the distinction may be ascribed, it will at least be recorded, that during the sojourn of the Drury-lane company, at the circumscribed scene of their present efforts, nature and decency retained their predominance, and the exhibition of human passions, and human manners was more frequent than the display of animal agility. The House of Morville, and other productions of a similar character, have atoned for their intrinsic defects by their exclusion of dangerous, and less rational performances. The productions of Mrs. Lefanu, have not only this negative merit, but a positive tendency towards the cultivation of legitimate taste, and the promotion of correct and genuine morality. It gives us pleasure to bear testimony to the chastity of diction, purity of sentiment, and the elevation of character, which adorn and embellish her only effort as a dramatist: at an era when indelicacy is regarded as the most seductive accompaniment of wit, and *malignity* of expression is received as a compensation for every intellectual deficiency, a praise like this must be as grateful to him who ascribes, as to her who receives it.

END OF THE THIRD VOLUME.

W. N. Jones, Printer, No. 5, Newgate-street, London.

CPSIA information can be obtained
at www.ICGtesting.com
Printed in the USA
BVHW04*1352190818
524841BV00005BB/215/P